The Pregnant Majorette

To', Councilmember
Elveyo Davis.

TOM
H

The Pregnant Majorette

LIFE IN A TWISTED
FAMILY, VOLUME ONE

Tom Liggett

Cover art by Candace White

Back cover photograph by Eric Seymour

Direct inquiries to: tomliggett.net

ISBN-13: 9781543244373
ISBN-10: 1543244378

All my words are dedicated to Blanche Weber Liggett. Sweetheart, you mean everything to me.

A woman asked me what I'd do
If she let me love her.
I'd treat you right
And tell no tales
To you or about you.
You might find
When day is done
And all is added up
That I might find
My life within you
And I'd be true to you.

My thoughts seldom drift far from Edna Rose Brensing Liggett.

You saved my life—
(When I was a babe)
For that I must give thanks.

You tried again—
When I was three.
Cold hearts drove you away.

This book exists because Linda Reeves reminded me to keep writing. Thank you, Linda.

I want to offer special thanks to David "Buzz" Knapp. He is the finest attorney I have ever met. His peers seem to agree with me.

Finally, this book is dedicated to Fay Mariah Wolfe. She was the first person to love me unconditionally.

You were eighty when I met you
I was just past ten.
You took me in
And stole my heart
It's yours forevermore.

The Main Players

Cowboy Number One. Myron Thomas Liggett. Commonly known as M. T. Tom Liggett's biological father.

Cowboy Number Two. Glen H.

Cowboy Number Three. William Frank McMillan Jr. Commonly known as Frank.

Edna Rose Brensing Liggett. Tom Liggett's paternal grandmother.

Frank. See "Cowboy Number Three."

Cleve Snow. Tom Liggett's maternal grandfather.

Gladys Pierce. Ruby's sister.

Granny Mac. Nickname for Gladys McMillan, Frank McMillan's mother.

Lita. Loeta Bernice Fay Snow Liggett McMillan. Tom Liggett's mother.

Momma. Ruby Lois Stewart Snow Holden Tomlinson. Tom Liggett's maternal grandmother.

M. T. See "Cowboy Number One."

Ruby. See "Momma."

Tom Liggett. Myron Thomas Liggett Jr. The author of this book. Also known as Tommy, Tutor or Tooter.

Tommy. See "Tom Liggett."

Tommy Tomlinson. Royal "Tommy" Tomlinson. Ruby Tomlinson's third husband.

The Minor Players

Arthur McMillan. Frank McMillan's uncle.

Betty Snow Kirkley. Tom Liggett's maternal aunt.

Bill W. One of Lita's lovers.

Byron Liggett. M. T. Liggett's twin brother.

Gary McMillan. Frank McMillan's brother.

Heine. Albert Brensing. Tom Liggett's paternal great-grandfather.

Indian Preacher. Tom Liggett's earliest known Indian relative. Given name unknown.

Jack Stewart. Tom Liggett's great-uncle.

James Liggett. Tom Liggett's ancestor.

James Rumpee. Tom Liggett's hypothetical friend.

Janita Hayes. Frank McMillan's sister.

Jerry Silvers. Also known as Uncle Jerry. The husband of Frank McMillan's aunt Ona.

Jimmy McMillan. Frank McMillan's brother.

Jody Liggett. Byron Liggett's wife.

Joe. Pseudonym for Byron Liggett.

Larry McMillan. Frank McMillan's brother.

Nita Hayes. Frank McMillan's niece.

Velma Lizenby. Frank McMillan's sister.

Wilbur Earl Liggett. Tom Liggett's paternal grandfather. Also known as Pop.

The Stories

Hang on, children.

—Stringbean Akeman

CHAPTER 1

Cowboy Number One

cow·boy (kao-boy) *noun*

1. A man who works with cows. 2. A man who works with
cattle in the tradition of the western portion of North
America. 3. A man who seeks adventure. 4. A risk taker.
5. The stereotypical caricature of a man among men.

—TOM LIGGETT'S PERSONAL GLOSSARY OF TERMS

MY MAMA WAS IN THE habit of marrying cowboys. Things went downhill from there. It's not that cowboys are bad people. But some of them are a lot like politicians, movie stars, and Russian mobsters. They try to live down to the popularized images the world has made of them.

In the case of cowboys, that image tends to revolve around a couple of inescapable facts. Many of them truly aspire to leave a place in better shape than it was when they entered. But they also like to ride into the sunset at the end of the last reel.

From the female perspective, the ending of this Western soap opera can turn into a horror flick, right quick-like. This is especially true if a little "trailer" is left behind. A baby. Many women have been disappointed by this surprise ending. It is the frequent consequence of buying into the animalistic side of a culture that is very physical in nature.

Look at this from the male perspective. For a real cowboy or a "wan-nabe," the raw power and pure sexual energy that is embodied by that classically American ideal is addictive stuff. Just imagine how the cowboy of legend or the poser of today feels as he rides into a new town. There he is, sitting tall in his metaphorical saddle. Think of the expectant faces staring up at him as he rides by. Each one of them seems to be asking his or her own question.

But it is to and from the race of women that the most pertinent questions seem to be addressed. Cowboys have a freakishly visceral effect on them. Some women are quite willing to remove their panties and wave them in surrender when they are in the presence of real cowboys. This is especially true with women of the citified type. I wrote "of the citified type" because cowboys are a contagion to which they might not have been exposed.

The opposite is true with country girls. They have been inoculated with cowboy charms since they were babies. Country girls have seen the effect that tight jeans and athletic bodies have on the women in their vicinity. Country girls know they should be wary of the cowboys who ride through their lives.

Looking back on my life, I seem to have absorbed that particular skill set from my cowboy mentors. I am grateful I wasn't made aware I possessed such terrible knowledge until I was a much older man. Had I known sooner, I might have emulated my male ancestors by leaving a trail of broken hearts and dirty diapers in my wake.

I look at cowboy sex from a knowing perspective. I am the product of my mother's union with one cowboy. I suffered for decades from the effects of her liaison with another. From that point of view, I can state with some surety that many cowboy traditions are sociopathic in nature. In popular lore, that concept is best typified by the movie *Shane*. He was a new-kid cowboy who rode into town and killed off a bunch of bad guys. True to form, he rode out of town immediately thereafter. The story ends with a little boy pleading for Shane to come back.

But that trite little movie left out an important subplot to real western life. By the end of the last reel, everybody in town liked Shane. Many of those adoring people would have been female. A *real* cowboy would have found a way to return some adoration to a few of them before he left.

Taking that knowledge into consideration, I have written a likely postscript to the story line. Shane was gone, but his legacy lived on in town. No, not the bad-guy-killing story. Everybody knows *that* one. I meant his *other* legacy. A real-life Shane would undoubtedly have left a few babies in the bellies of assorted wives and daughters. Because of the circumstances of their conception, these children would have been of the bastard and cuckoo-bird types.

If Shane had defied a stereotypical story line by returning to town, the movie might well have had a different ending. This new climax would have manifested itself in the form of an anonymously delivered spray of buckshot for our hero's posterior. That was a typical form of revenge for those who were unwillingly given the task of raising a Shane bastard. Men on the western frontier were not shy in their use of firearms.

You've got the drift. The great American West is the theater in which my life was staged. It's time to get on with introducing the players.

Myron Thomas Liggett is the cowboy who rode through my mother's life just long enough to create me. That's a lot of name to say in one mouthful. I ought to know, because I am Myron Thomas Liggett Junior. Both of us sought to lessen the effort of having to regularly voice such a monster name. My father and I chose simpler names. He calls himself M. T. I chose plain ol' Tom.

M. T. Liggett was a perfect model for the stereotypical American cowboy. He seemed to personify the best and worst attributes of that type of man.

M. T. was raised on the high plains of southwest Kansas. That area is defined by a concept that has been called the "buffalo grass controversy." The proponents of that idea state that the combination of hideous weather, poor soil, and the lack of reliable quantities of water render the area unsuitable for permanent human settlement. As such, there are some who say that Kiowa County, Kansas, should have been left in its natural, undeveloped state. Some area residents argue strenuously to the contrary. They say that the place is just fine.

Cowboy number one, M. T. Liggett. Campbell, California. July 21, 1949.

Sex on a stick: M. T. Liggett and Lita Fay Snow.
Campbell, California. July 21, 1949.

M. T. Liggett and Lita Fay Snow. Campbell, California. July 21, 1949.

My readers are welcome to evaluate the fine points of the buffalo grass controversy for themselves. You might want to take a side trip through southwest Kansas. Allow the facts to speak for themselves. Most of that area is a treeless, rolling prairie. From a distance, the grassland appears to be as smooth as velvet. The hills and undulations look like the swells of a mighty ocean. The land passes away in rolls and dips, right on to the endless horizon.

If you drive down almost any road in southwest Kansas, you will probably note an unusual thing. Every mile or so, there is a clump of scraggily trees standing alone in the middle of the bald expanse. Most of these were once home sites. They now stand empty, excepting the trees that were planted as windbreaks. Each of those tree islands marks decades of toil, lost money, and grief. They represent the death of a dream and the probable diaspora for the family who once lived there.

In many places, a homesteader's 360 acres might have been large enough for subsistence farming. It was a tougher proposition in many parts of southwest Kansas. It was almost impossible to eke out a living on just 360 acres. Many, including my grandparents, managed to do so by the sheer force of will and thrifty living.

I have been to southwest Kansas three times in my adult life. The memories of those visits stand firm in my mind. I recall shriveled towns with huge graveyards. The area reminds me of the scenes in *The Lord of the Rings*. I felt like I was wandering through an abandoned ruin. The withered trees of former homesteads offer mute testimony to the difficulty of life in southwest Kansas.

It's ironic to think that my father's white ancestors killed my mother's Indian ancestors to steal their land. In southwest Kansas, most of the white settlers couldn't make a go of it on the stolen land. They quickly moved away. I never cease to be amazed by the childlike nature of mankind. We cry for a toy and then cast it aside when it no longer draws our attention.

A crucible is a pot-like device that is used to liquefy metals and create alloys. When the metal is in a liquid state, it can be poured into a mold. When the metal cools and solidifies, it retains the shape of the mold.

Kiowa County is the crucible that was used to melt the rare stuff of which my father was made. The fire that melted his being was sparked by his upbringing. M. T. was raised in difficult conditions, even by the harsh standards of southwest Kansas. That was sad. Why? It didn't have to be that way. There were several avenues by which M. T. could have had a better youth. Sadly, they were all squandered long before he was born.

It all began with M.T.'s great-grandfather James Liggett. James was just thirteen when he left the family farm in Missouri to seek his fortune in the California gold rush. Some folks in my family believe that young James Liggett walked halfway across the continent in his quest. Others doubt that fact. I am firmly in the camp that believes he covered the distance on foot. I base that assumption on a simple fact: James Liggett made his journey west alone. No friends, companions, or family members journeyed with him. Many of you are thinking, "How terrible. How lonely. How sad." But that was not the case.

Let's take a moment to compare James's probable solo trek with his pioneer contemporaries. When a prosperous farmer got the "pioneer bug," he didn't go out West alone. Oh no. That poor soul took his wife and family with him. Such expeditions generally had a lot of members. Wives, babies, children, married children, their children, in-laws, outlaws, and assorted hangers-on all wanted to get in on the fun. It was the CliffsNotes version of the Israelite exodus from Egypt.

Prosperous people like their toys. Things were no different in 1848. Many pioneers took a lot of stuff with them on their migrations. Essential things like parlor organs, silver cutlery, fine furniture, and leather-bound collections of English literature. Thus was born the necessity for the fabled "prairie schooner" freight wagon of lore and legend.

Huge wagons require lots of large animals to pull them. Thousands of pioneers bought teams of fine horses to pull their wagons. Four horses, six horses. Whatever it took. The pioneers looked smart as they rolled away from their neighbors.

When the travelers got to Saint Joseph, Missouri, experienced eyes took a jaundiced view of their animals. Outfitters told outraged pioneer patriarchs that their thoroughbred horses would not make it halfway across the wastes that lay before them. The work of pulling huge wagons over the roadless wastes would kill the horses. Then there was the tricky part: horses that work hard require grain and high-quality forage. The pioneers weren't going to find those commodities out on the trail.

The pioneers needed draft animals that were tough and expendable. Animals that could survive on scant rations. Enter a man leading teams of oxen. Cows. Steers. Mostly of the large, strong, stupid, and slow variety. Picture some of the lumbering creatures that you saw in *The Hobbit* movie, but on a smaller scale. Still in large numbers, though.

What a shock it was to the pioneer patriarch and his family. The same man who'd led in their new oxen was now leading away their fine horses. Papa patriarch didn't look very smart anymore. At this point, papa patriarch's family was beginning to have doubts about his leadership skills. Some of them thought, *maybe this guy isn't invincible after all.* History proved their fears to be correct. The roads out West were littered with parlor organs, fine furniture, leather-bound sets of English literature—and unmarked graves.

The formerly prosperous patriarch was moving a whole world with him. My ancestor James Liggett, on the other hand, had a fifty-dollar gold piece and whatever would fit in a rucksack. This enabled him to walk to California. When I tell people that my ancestor walked from Missouri to California when he was barely a teenager, they are surprised. They think it was an unusual thing. That's not true. More American pioneers walked to their destinations than rode in wagons or on horseback.

"Shank's mare" served our ancestors well. Our species evolved to walk. *Homo sapiens* was created by the act of walking. Here's a little-known fact: an adult human can walk farther in a single day than a horse can. That same person can hike through places that are too rough for the most vigorous burro. But there's a trick to this concept: humans can't carry much when they walk long distances. James Liggett avoided the problems of transporting tons of animals, wagons, possessions, and family across the frontier. I'd say that he was brilliant.

James apparently didn't like California, though, because he didn't stay very long. In the late 1860s, he decided to return to Missouri and his family. James didn't have to walk back across the continent a second time. He rode the newly completed transcontinental railroad. Partway back to his family's home in Missouri, he got off the train in Dodge City, Kansas. James fell in love with the area.

James got back on the train and continued on to Missouri. When he arrived there, he told his family about the great place that he had found. He somehow managed to talk them into returning to southwest Kansas as settlers.

Any of you who have toured both regions know that Missouri is infinitely better suited to agricultural life than southwest Kansas. The soil and climate are more favorable in Missouri.

My readers might be asking themselves a question: How is it that someone would leave an excellent place that is settled for one that is less suitable and unsettled? The answer is restlessness, the power of popular lore, and the news media. From the first moment that white people settled on the North American continent, they were surrounded with a compelling concept: better land and wide-open spaces were waiting just over the horizon. Read the histories of American pioneers. You will find reference after reference to folks who left wonderful places so that they could cast the loaves of their ambitions onto unknown waters. Many of those people ended up on homesteads in regions that have wretched climates and soils.

By the time my white ancestors moved to southwest Kansas, a crucial obstacle had already been overcome. The Indians had been removed or killed. The human slate of Kansas was wiped clean with a lily-white cloth. None of the Liggett clan killed any Indians in Kansas. Someone else had already accomplished that deed for people like them. White people of the time acted as if exterminating the Indians was a sound agricultural practice. Every farmer knows that you must get rid of the "vermin" before you can plant a crop. That was sad and wrong.

Once the greater Liggett clan settled in Kansas, the usual pioneer struggles ensued. There were sod houses to build and land to till. Beyond that, I know little about the life of the first James Liggett or the family he produced. That makes it easy for me to keep his story short. He stayed in southwest Kansas for the rest of his life. Four generations later, I inherited his last name.

My paternal grandmother, Edna Rose Brensing Liggett, had a more unusual entry into southwest Kansas. She told me how she came to be in that place. Even though I took I took no notes of that or any other conversation we shared, I remember Edna's story quite well. She was an honorable woman. I trust Edna's words. From what I have seen of human behavior in my own lifetime, I'm certain her story is true.

Please have patience with the words I've used to write about Edna's past. I have had *very* little interaction with my father's family. That is especially true of the Brensing side. I might be a little off on some of the fine details of Edna's story, but the punch line is right on target.

Edna Brensing Liggett and her daughter Jean.
Southern California. Date unknown.

Edna's grandfather was born in Germany. He was part of a great wave of immigrants who fled the turmoil that was caused by the unification of Germany. Edna's mother came from Switzerland.

Edna's forbearers settled in Madison County, Illinois. That place was populated by people who sought to build a "Little Germany" in America.

Subsequent German immigrants came to get a piece of the American dream, but they still had to buy into German culture. Why? Because that was the only type of culture to be had in western Illinois. Parochial schools were taught in German. Newspapers and books were published in German. Church services were in German. German was the language of community and commerce.

The immigrants applied the legendary Swiss/German industry to their new homes, and the community thrived beyond their wildest dreams. They had fine homes and farms. This is the world to which Edna Rose Brensing was born on December 31, 1899, at 11:59 p.m. Yes, that's right; my grandmother lived through one minute of the nineteenth century. She was quite proud of that small statistic.

The Brensing family believed that the old world and its inequality were things of distant memory. They were wrong in that assumption. Edna told me that English-speaking people in their area grew increasingly resentful of the Germans. They thought that it was downright un-American for those "Krauts" to be speaking German.

That wasn't an unusual language choice at that time, though. There were a lot of Americans who spoke German at home and in their communities. Edna told me that the real problem with their neighbors was much more cynical in nature: the English-speaking folks were jealous of Germans' industry and success.

Tensions escalated. A tide of anger rose against the vastly outnumbered German families. Edna said that threats were made against her family. She spoke of buildings that were burned. Edna's family was told that they had to get out immediately, or worse things would happen to them.

The Brensing family knew they had to move. But they didn't know where to go. Two generations had passed since they settled in Illinois. In that time, most of the good land on the American frontier had been taken. Southwest Kansas seemed to be the only affordable place that was available to them. It would ultimately turn out to be a wildly flawed consolation prize.

The family hurriedly made plans to move everything they owned all the way across the state of Kansas. It was decided that the family members would travel by train. But they didn't have the money to ship their belongings by rail. It was far too expensive. The family's clothing, furniture, and tools would travel by wagon. The Brensing family used a type of wagon that was called a grain bin. The sides and bottom were tight, almost like a boat. This prevented grain from leaking through the cracks.

The family was ready to go. But a last-minute complication raised its ugly head: Edna was sick. She was suffering from a lingering case of scarlet fever. That dreaded disease killed Britain's Prince Albert and millions of other people of that era.

It was well known that scarlet fever was spread through casual human contact. Due to fears of contagion, people who had active cases of scarlet fever were placed in quarantine. Infected people weren't allowed on trains or other modes of public transport.

Edna was refused passage on the train. She had to ride in the grain bin along with the family belongings. Edna was deathly ill, but she traveled across all of Missouri, most of Kansas, and some of Illinois. That was a distance of over six hundred miles. She rode in the back of an open wagon. This did nothing to help her recover from scarlet fever. The rigors of the trip caused Edna to develop a heart murmur. She lived with that condition for the rest of her life.

Edna had been raised in a fine home in Illinois. She'd lived in a beautiful area. Her new home was far removed from what she was accustomed to. Edna said that their new home was rough and ugly. She said that the landscape in southwest Kansas was harsh and ugly. Edna felt that it was a horrible place to live. She never outgrew that sentiment.

Edna's family brought fine horses with them to their new farm. They didn't have a barn, so they stabled the horses in a tent. The Brensings soon discovered that their fancy horses couldn't survive harsh local winters. Edna cried when she saw the ugly mules that replaced their pretty horses. Edna cried a lot in southwest Kansas.

Despite the hardships of their new life, the Brensing family thrived. They built a better house and bought more land. Once again, their frugal, hardworking Swiss-German temperament enabled them to prosper.

But the Brensings learned from their experiences in Illinois. They did not want to be a family of German speakers who lived amid English neighbors. They did not want to stand out as being different. Edna's family chose the wise route: they blended in with their neighbors. The Brensings became an integral part of their new community. That was a timely thing to do. War with Germany was just around the corner.

Edna was an excellent student. She graduated from high school with high marks. She then attended what was called a normal school. The purpose of those schools was to train new teachers. Edna was emphatic in recalling her reasons for attending a normal school. The first of these was quite basic: it was the only local venue that provided a source of higher education.

The second reason why Edna chose to educate herself was far more poignant: she believed that she would have to earn her own income. Edna harbored serious doubt that any man would take her for his wife. She had ample reason to believe in the validity of that concept. The average height for an American man of that time was about five feet seven inches. By the time she was eighteen, Edna measured in at an even six feet. Making matters worse, Edna was no beauty. Her facial features mirrored those of another remarkable woman, Eleanor Roosevelt. God bless the plain women of the world. They will be forever damned. Short-sighted cultures always demand that women possess a finite set of characteristics that define them as being every man's universal sex object.

Edna was an incredible person. She was cultured, accomplished, and wealthy. She was also smart enough to know that she was damned to be a marital consolation prize. Edna was spot on with her projections. She gratefully married the one man who would have her. Edna told me that my grandfather, Wilbur Earl Liggett, was the only boyfriend she ever had. The pool of available young men in her area was shallow.

From what I can tell from the distance of years and separation, Wilbur Liggett was nobody's jackpot suitor. Much of that aspect derives from a simple fact: the Liggetts bore the whiff of scandal. One of my male Liggett antecedents sequentially abandoned two sets of wives and families in his goal to end up with a third. The fruits of his loins are liberally salted across Kansas and beyond.

I suppose that this explains why Wilbur Liggett was born into very poor circumstances. You would expect more from a family who had been one of the very first to settle in southwest Kansas. But when men put their personal goals above that of their families, women and children are forced to pay a price that continues into successive generations.

In all ways, the Liggetts were polar opposites of Edna's prosperous, educated family. The few accounts I have heard of Wilbur's family offer nothing to counter that assertion. His family's reputation aside, Wilbur brought very little to his marriage with Edna. True to form for the times, he stood just five feet seven. He was a hardworking, hard-drinking, profane man. Wilbur was intelligent but not an intellectual.

The combination of a plain woman and a vaguely unsavory man is the sort of recipe that often makes for a thin marital soup. But don't discount the power of duty and obligation as marital glue. Edna's society demanded that she marry and make a good job of the deed. Who knows? Maybe there was more to their marriage than was obvious to outsiders. Perhaps Edna's hormones pushed her to reproduce. Maybe the poor woman just wanted to be held by a man.

Had she not felt obligated by her social connections or betrayed by her feminine biology, Edna might have allowed the bitter dregs that she was offered as a marital cup to pass her by. Alas, it was not to be so. Edna married out of duty and social expectation. Thus was paired the racehorse to the plow. Feminism was invented to save women from fates such as the one Edna Rose Brensing Liggett was forced to bear.

She went into her marriage with Wilbur Earl Liggett with little more than the hope that her adult life would be better than her childhood. Her optimism turned out to be entirely unfounded. Edna was supposed to inherit a huge parcel of prime farmland from her father. That didn't happen. Edna was emphatic on *that* subject. She said, "I was robbed." Edna refused to say how that eventuality had occurred. Each time that she told me about her lost inheritance, she burst into tears. Edna cried because she and her children bore the brunt of that loss. It forced them to depend on Wilbur's particularly poor section of land for home and sustenance.

The local historical society later wrote that it was supposedly impossible to support a family on that small, poor farm. But Edna and Wilbur did that very thing. They bore and raised eight children together. One of them was my father, MT.

Under such harsh and impoverished conditions, everyone had to pull their weight. MT indicated that by today's standards, the details of such cooperation would be called child abuse. Wilbur hired out his sons to work as laborers on other folks' ranches. He kept their earnings for his own use. He was a drunkard. Wilbur was cranky and autocratic. He was brutal when he thought that his children needed to be disciplined.

Wilbur had very little to do with raising his children. He believed that his main job was to provide food and shelter for his family. He did this in large part by farming wheat. Some of the time, that vocation demanded hard work and long hours in the field. Other times, there was little to do save sit around the house or go to town to get drunk. This was especially true in the winter.

Wilbur was typical of the men of his times. He believed that his job stopped at the front door of his home. Whatever work was needed in and around the house was Edna's job. Cooking, cleaning, teaching, and mentoring. Edna did that and more. When Wilbur came home, he expected his house to be tidy. He wanted to see a hot meal on the table. Like most men of that time, he was a perpetual guest in his home.

Edna took care of the Liggett household with few resources and fewer complaints. She was a magnificent cook who used dry cow turds as fuel for her stove.

Edna insisted that she'd lost a tooth for each of the eight children she bore. Those lost teeth were just the symptoms she could see. There were undoubtedly worse ones she could not.

Edna bore one set of twins—my father and his brother, Byron. Many people think that Myron and Byron make a funny-sounding pair of names. But that fine detail marks my grandmother's intelligence. Each of those names means "twin" in Greek. I mention Edna's twins because of a remarkable detail: they *each* weighed over twelve pounds at birth. I saw their birth certificates. More than twenty-five pounds of baby came out of Edna's body in one day.

During the end stage of that pregnancy, Edna couldn't lift herself out of a sitting position. She was too heavy. Edna was forced to stand on her feet all day. When Wilbur came home at lunch, she could finally sit down. When she was done sitting, he helped her stand.

Damn any man on earth who wants to take women back to the Dark Age in which my grandmothers lived.

In later years, I went to visit Edna. I remember the disconsolate look on her face as she stared out the window and beheld the flat, brown prairie that surrounded her home. When she spoke about what she had left behind in northwest Kansas seventy-odd years before, Edna broke into tears. She hated *everything* about southwest Kansas. I suppose a lot of that sentiment arose from her loss of the promised inheritance. That bequest would have saved Edna and her children from the crushing deprivation they endured.

I believe Edna was disinherited because she lowered herself to marry a coarse man from an undesirable family. That is not a far-fetched notion. A few years down the line, another Kiowa County father reacted in similar fashion when his daughter married one of Wilbur Liggett's sons.

Edna paid a horrible price to keep a home and raise eight children under wretched conditions. But something magical took place on that farm. She produced an incredible bunch of kids. All of them were full-blown, world-class, off-the-scale geniuses. I don't blame you if you are skeptical about that assertion. In this hyperbolic, self-aggrandizing age, half the people in the world seem to be running around telling the other half that they are geniuses. Because of that conceit, the term genius has been diluted to the point that it no longer means very much. But in the case of Edna's children, it wasn't hyperbole. *All* of them were geniuses.

Let the facts speak for themselves. M. T. had a brother who was a pioneer surgeon. His sister provided the startup capital for the Wham-O Corporation. That company introduced three of the seminal icons of the baby-boomer era: the skateboard, the Hula-Hoop, and the Frisbee. One of Edna's children was instrumental in the development of modern saw blade technology. M. T.'s oldest brother, Earl, stayed home in Kiowa County. He successfully managed a ranch that was larger than some eighteenth-century German principalities. I'm certain that Edna's other children accomplished great things too.

By all accounts, M.T.'s intellect overshadowed that of his brilliant siblings. He had a memory and knowledge that was best described as being encyclopedic. He could be charming, knowledgeable, and witty. Sadly, M. T. squandered his incredible intelligence and work ethic. He chose the easier road of being the black sheep of his profoundly accomplished family.

M. T. was an alarmist. He took great pride in knocking people off balance with his overtly stated opinions. I believe that he was *the* greatest contrarian I have ever known. It is almost as if he would say "blue" just because someone else said "red." M. T. was hard to pin down on any subject. He enjoyed keeping people in the dark. Getting the punch line of any story out from him was damn near impossible. This seemed to be especially true if he knew that you wanted to hear something.

In most cases, men with M. T.'s temperament would have trouble getting laid. But you don't if you look like a god. Through late middle age, M. T. redefined the concept of a chick magnet. Simply stated, M. T. was one of the most incredibly good-looking men, *ever*.

I have repeatedly heard women say that he looked a lot like Robert Mitchum. Those women chased that sentiment with a harsh truth: Robert Mitchum resembled an inferior version of M. T.

M. T. had charm, intelligence, wit, and looks. It was all packaged into a tall cowboy body that was hardened by a lifetime of work. It made a combination that was irresistible to women and girls of all ages.

When you look back on any person's life, you can see that they have left behind them a body of work. Be it the houses they built, the dishes they washed, or the students they taught—everybody did *something*. M.T. did women. He left behind a body of bodies. I heard M. T. say that he had sex with "thousands of women." M. T. told me he fathered approximately twenty-seven children by as many women. History has always called such progeny bastards. M. T. prefers to call them his "love children." That small conceit reveals a pivotal fact: he didn't know what it was like to be raised as an unwanted bastard.

But I am getting ahead of myself. I am the first of M.T.'s children and the only one who is named after him.

My mother, Loeta ("Lita") Fay Snow, was no more immune to cowboy charms in 1949 than her many successors. She was just sixteen years old and living in a personalized Campbell, California, version of hell when M. T. first appeared on her doorstep in the early summer of 1949.

The Disneyfied, late-1940s American dream version of M. T.'s sudden arrival would require that he meet her at the corner drugstore or at a dance. In that type of fiction, he would have asked her to go out for a glass of Coca-Cola and a walk around the block. The truth of the situation was far grittier in its details.

Immediately after M. T. graduated from high school, Wilbur forced him to move out of the family home. M. T. joined the navy. M. T. was just out of basic training when he was sent to Moffett Field Naval Air Station in Sunnyvale, California.

That facility is in the middle of the Santa Clara Valley. After the white conquest, some folks took to calling that place the Valley of Heart's Delight. Now, as accurate as that name once was, I always thought that it was a bit wordy and contrived. But it was more graceful than what folks call the place now: Silicon Valley. For M. T.'s purposes, it didn't qualify for either of those terms.

M. T. was eighteen years old when he arrived at Moffett Field. He was away from home for the first time. He had the overactive hormones of most young men of that age. And M. T. was surrounded by fellows of like mind. M. T. received an emphatic answer from a sailor named Tommy Tomlinson. Tommy's sister-in-law, Gladys Pierce, was a "grass widow." Just for the record, that type of widow is created by a divorce decree, not by the death of a husband.

Tommy told M. T. that Gladys would be willing to spread her legs. But there was a catch to the deal: M. T. would need to part with some of his navy-given two-dollar bills to speed the courtship's progress. That detail was not a hindrance to M. T. He wasted no time in finding his way over unpaved back roads to get to the address his buddies provided.

When M. T. knocked on the door of the de facto bordello, he expected that it would be answered by an older prostitute. That didn't happen. The door was opened by the most beautiful girl M. T. had ever seen. She was Lita Snow, the niece of the hooker M. T. expected to meet. The surprise of that moment gave the involved parties a pause. By all accounts, it could not have lasted very long. I appeared on the scene a year later. Lita was a shock to M.T.'s senses. She was the perfect object of every heterosexual man's wildest fantasy. Lita and two of her sisters were beautiful. They went *far* beyond the normal definitions of that term. No trio of siblings was ever born who were more spectacular. It's not humanly possible.

My mother was the prettiest girl in that bunch. But it was her younger sister, Betty, who capitalized most on their similar beauty. Among her credits, she was Elizabeth Taylor's body double in three movies. That detail caused me some problems in middle school. No one believed me when I told them that my aunt Betty was the babe who was famously rolled out of the carpet for Richard Burton's benefit in the movie *Cleopatra*.

My aunt Betty eventually became one of the highest-paid strippers in history. Family lore has it that she was paid an insanely high amount for a six-week tour of Vietnam in 1968. My aunt was paid a high figure so that servicemen could look at *her* figure. It was a family tradition, folks; Betty just got paid a higher wage than the other women in my family.

Looks aside, there was another aspect to this: Betty was batshit crazy, a stone alcoholic, and mean as a snake. Betty's pièce de résistance topped those horrible traits: she hated men. That set of behaviors was a recurring theme among some of the women in my mother's family. It continually wove its variations through my life.

But I'm getting ahead of myself again. There is a question here: Why was my future mother answering the door at a whorehouse? The explanation for her predicament is as old as the European conquest of the Americas.

CHAPTER 2

Who's an Indian?

MY MOTHER IDENTIFIED HERSELF AS an Indian. Not "Native American." Not "original people." She said, "I'm an Indian." My maternal grandmother lived to be ninety-four years old. Her brain was sharp right to the end. She called herself an Indian too. Come to think of it, my maternal grandfather also said he was an Indian.

Folks have occasionally criticized me because I say that I am an Indian. Until I was almost sixty years old, I had a ready solution on hand to deal with that brand of idiot. I would dial a telephone number, hand the person the handset, and say, "Here, speak to my grandmother. Tell her that I'm not an Indian. I want to hear her to tell you what a fool you are."

When it comes down to blood percentages, I don't think either of my mother's parents was more than about 25 percent Indian. At least my mother looked the part. My grandmother was pasty white. Just for the record, I'm fairly white too. My son is very light. But my daughter looks like Pocahontas. Funny how that stuff skips around.

The percentage of Indian blood that flows through my veins is irrelevant. My family's Indian background sets the beat for my story. Indian ancestors provided the foundational culture of my childhood.

The older folks in my mother's family liked to say they came from the great state of Oklahoma. That statement is entirely factual in its premise. Sadly, it is also very short sighted in its scope. I can't blame my relatives for giving that explanation. Oklahoma is where they and the six or seven generations that preceded them lived before they moved to California. Oklahoma was what they knew as home. It was the place that they remembered.

"Remembered" is the operative word in the last sentence. Memory is the vehicle that carries traditions from one generation to the next. Traditions are passed on as stories. Sadly, very few stories about our Indian ancestors have survived. It's not that no one cared enough to pass them down. There was simply no one left to tell the stories. My ancestors were wiped out.

Here's how that happened. The conquest of the Americas didn't happen in a year or a decade. It took a couple of hundred years for Europeans to nibble away at Indian lands. They took a bite of land here and another one there. Bit by bit, Europe was transplanted into the Americas.

It took many explorers to accomplish that piecemeal conquest. They left written accounts of their journeys. The first European explorers who passed through an area always noted they were heavily populated with Indians. Sometimes they saw cities, fields, and villages. They saw bands of hunters. Everywhere that those first explorers went, they saw people. Recent evidence suggests that more than two hundred million people lived in North and South America before the European conquest. I believe that is a low estimate.

The second set of Europeans to pass through a given area wrote a different story. They told of empty villages and untended fields. The Indians the white men found were a tiny remnant of the former multitude. Everybody else was dead. The survivors were a stunned and dispirited group.

How did this happen? People and diseases develop together. Microscopic organisms and their human hosts do a dance of mutation and resistance. In this way, Europeans developed resistance to European diseases.

Indians had no resistance to foreign microorganisms. Some European diseases killed 90 percent of the Indians who contracted them. The Indians who weren't killed outright were sometimes weakened and disfigured.

Whole cultures were wiped out. In about two hundred years, the indigenous population of the Americas was reduced by over 90 percent.

In what was to become the United States of America, this was seen by most white people as being a part of Manifest Destiny. More importantly, it was viewed as an indication that God was on the white man's side.

Christians and their God had great experience with that concept. When Moses looked down upon the Promised Land, it was heavily populated with Canaanites. The Israelites smote an entire country's population dead so that "God's chosen people" could safely live there. As you recall that trite little story, try to remember that the Bible says, "God is love." Tell that to the Canaanites. Or my ancestors.

In the portions of the Americas that were conquered by the Spanish and Portuguese, the surviving Indians were put to good use: they were enslaved. Under Spanish and Portuguese rule, every region had its own form of Indian slavery.

On the western edge of the future United States, the Spanish forced the Indians into concentration camps. But the Spanish didn't use that term. It took the English another five hundred years to give places of similar nature their proper name. The Spanish called them missions. Such institutions arose from the deep religiosity of Columbus's benefactor, Queen Isabella I of Castile.

In some parts of the New World, Indians have not yet escaped from slavery. An old saying still holds true: "South America is carried on the backs of Indians."

In what has become the United States, Native Americans weren't commonly used as slaves by white men. Americans had a deep well of African slaves and indentured Irish to draw upon. Both of those latter groups had a long history of being oppressed. They were more malleable. That's the European side.

Here's the Indian side. North American Indians were different from many of their brethren in the south. Many of them lived as wild creatures. Some Indians withered away when they were put into shackles. This further reduced their population.

European water was sometimes unsafe to drink. They purified water by converting it to alcohol. European bodies were adapted to alcohol consumption.

Before the conquest, relatively few people in the Americas consumed alcohol. Because of this, their bodies did not develop a tolerance for alcohol. This would have a deadly effect on Indians. When Indians consumed alcohol, they generally became much drunker than Europeans. Part of that was due to a lower alcohol tolerance.

Another part was pure human nature—some Indians don't know when to stop drinking. They drink until they pass out cold. That is unhealthy for an Indian's body. For everybody else, the worst part generally comes *before* the Indian passes out.

The veneer of civilization isn't very deep on any human being. Right underneath, we're all creatures who are driven by hunger, thirst, sex, and emotion.

The veneer of civilization ran even thinner on my Indian ancestors. When they got drunk, it was readily stripped away. They acted like savages when they got drunk.

Some Indian activists will undoubtedly flinch when I call our people savages. I have a wonderful retort for *that* sentiment: I was raised in a world of people who were part Indian. They became unhinged when they were drunk or angry. When my relatives got drunk, they were destructive forces of nature. Fists and weapons sometimes finished what words alone couldn't. In my mind, their behavior marked them as being savages.

Thus was visited upon Indians another tune from the great suite of European maladies. The first malady killed most of their people. The second one made them dangerous and unreliable. This deadly combination enabled the conquest of the Americas. Religion, gunpowder, iron, and horses sealed the deal.

It is important that we not view the white conquest as an event but as a process. Each area saw a different type of white-versus-Indian struggle. On the eastern coast of North America, Indians were willing to let Europeans settle in their lands. They thought that there was plenty of room for everybody. That generosity was wrought from a simple concept: most Indians didn't believe they owned the land. They saw themselves as caretakers, not landowners.

That key factor made it possible for a few white men to gain two small footholds on the eastern shore of North America. That was all they needed. As an old adage warns, "If you allow a camel to get its nose under the tent, the rest of the camel will surely follow."

By the time the Indians figured out the white concept of property ownership, it was too late. The conquests of New England and coastal Virginia were over before the Indians knew they had begun.

Farther south, things were different. The Indians there were organized and prosperous. They heard what had happened to the Indians in the north. This caused the southern tribes to take note and to stiffen their resolve. Southern Indians were prepared to fight like hell for their land.

The US government didn't want to fight a war with a bunch of well-organized Indians. Government leaders concluded that it was best to leave the southern tribes alone. The Indians breathed a sigh of relief. Maybe they wouldn't suffer the fate of their northern brethren.

Ah, but they were innocent babes. They didn't know that power abhors a vacuum. This is especially true if that vacuum consists of a continent that is nearly devoid of white people.

By the early 1800s, the handwriting was on the wall. Large numbers of white people were moving into the traditional lands of the southern tribes. This angered the Indians. White people were not happy with the results of Indian anger. The US government had to do something to prevent wholesale war. The government came up with an idea they thought would keep everybody happy. Europeans would be allowed to settle in certain areas. Some of the Indians who lived east of the Mississippi River would be allowed to keep their traditional lands. In return, the government demanded that the Indians become "civilized." In modern terms, I suppose that would translate as "manageable."

The southern tribes accomplished that task admirably. As American settlers began moving into the Southeast, they encountered members of the Cherokee, Choctaw, Chickasaw, Creek, and Seminole tribes. They were different from the warlike, dispirited, and drunken Indians the settlers encountered farther north. The southern Indians were settled agriculturalists.

Many of them had European-style homes and farms. Others owned slaves. Whites and black freedmen became fully integrated parts of their tribes. They used modern technology such as iron and gunpowder.

The US government allowed southern tribes a higher level of humanity than they did other Indians. They were officially labeled "the Five Civilized Tribes." They inhabited the regions that white people eventually named Alabama, Florida, Georgia, North Carolina, and Tennessee.

The southern Indians were incredible agriculturalists. Early explorers who passed through areas that they inhabited were stunned by verdant fields and orchards. English gentlemen wrote that the forests the Indians maintained were more park-like than those that grew back home. The English believed that these forests grew naturally. Europeans had no concept that the forests were not wild things but carefully managed constructs.

East Coast Indians were magnificent foresters. They encouraged tree species that bore fruit and nuts. This strategy produced food for man and animals alike. Trash trees were used for firewood and construction timber.

Indians understood what trees needed to thrive. They saw fire as being the chief friend of forest and meadow. Indians knew that unburned grasslands quickly became weedy with scrub. This meant that there would be less grass for the deer to eat. Fewer deer would provide less meat for the people.

Indians also knew that when underbrush grew tall, it burned long and hot. When that happened, the larger trees would be damaged too.

Indians burned their forests, fields, and meadows every year. Many Indians carried hot coals with them when they traveled. This was especially true in the autumn. Here, there, and everywhere, they started fires. The Indians would take coals from one fire and start another, miles away. Because of this sound management, forest fires weren't the problem they are now. Modern foresters should note the methods of my Indian ancestors.

The forest provided food and other necessities for all Indians, even the settled types. It was the ultimate big-box store. Best of all, the forest system operated in a sustainable manner. The southern Indian tribes were the best forest managers in history.

When whites journeyed south of New England, they saw huge groves of wild peaches. The trees grew for miles in every direction. White people assumed that peach trees were native to the region. But they were actually new arrivals to the North American continent. The Spanish brought peaches to the New World in the 1500s.

Indians in the Southeast quickly adapted their fields and palates to this incredible new wonder food. Peaches added starch, sugar, vitamin C, and flavor to their diets. The fruit was eaten fresh in the summer and preserved for winter eating. Peaches and peach trees came to be revered objects by the Indians who grew them.

You might be wondering at this point why I am using space in this book to write about peaches. It is because Indian Blood peaches are the sole Indian cultural icon that has survived in my family. My maternal grandmother grew misty-eyed when she spoke of "them little red peaches." It appears that our familial love for peaches will stop with me. That's why I am writing this book. I want someone to remember other times and other stories.

European societies are strongly patriarchal. This means they are dominated by men. To varying degrees, the Five Civilized Tribes were matriarchal. This means they were dominated by women. Some of the southern tribes had female chiefs. In many cases, men were not allowed in the family home except by invitation from the women. Men sometimes slept in a common house with other men.

Women grew the gardens and fields. The knowledge of gardening was passed down from mother to daughter. Lacking a daughter, my mother passed that love down to me. I am grateful that my Indian grandmothers imparted this wondrous gift to me. Bless you, grandmothers.

For the most part, the women of my ancestors' tribes were much shorter than their husbands. When it came to intergender negotiations, however, that disparity didn't create much of a disadvantage. Few sane men were willing to face the small, fast, bony fists of those women more than once. This too is one of the traditions that has been passed down through my family. Women were the main domestic abusers in my mother's family. They were hell on wheels.

That was a shock for European men. They had never seen men being dominated by women. That was one of the cultural differences that made white men hate Indians.

More and more white people poured into eastern North America. Those who were already settled had large families. They wanted land for themselves. White men pushed farther west and south to find space. This brought the settlers into close proximity with members of the Five Civilized Tribes. Earlier in our nation's history, when the white man chose to expand into new areas, it meant going to war with Indians.

The US government knew this. So did the members of the Five Civilized Tribes. No one wanted war. For a time, white men were happy to live around Indians. The Indians were good neighbors. They had bought into the nascent American dream. Many Indians thought they were a part of that fantasy.

But the white settlers were not happy. They could not fail to notice that their own fields declined in productivity after a few years, while Indian fields never seemed to do so. White people thought the Indians had long-lasting garden plots because they owned superior land. Whites failed to recognize that Indian women knew how to care for the land. Those women were garden goddesses.

There was another cultural problem. Whites were angry that their neighbors were heathen "savages." Preachers raved from the pulpit about the "depravity" of societies that allowed their women dominance and free will.

White people put their anger into action. They raided and burned Indian fields. The law did not stop them. White people squatted on Indian lands. They were prepared to defend their stolen holdings with guns. The Indians were quiet. They lost more land. For the most part, Indians were acquiescent in the face of white aggression and invasion. Why? Because most Indians were living well.

Things might have progressed in this manner for a long while. Alas, that did not happen. A precipitating thing occurred. The lives of my ancestors were ruined by a white fiber: cotton.

Europeans had known about cotton for centuries. They knew that it has a much wider range of uses than flax, silk, or wool. But cotton is much more difficult to spin into thread than other fibers. This and other considerations kept it from being affordable or popular in Europe.

In the last half of the 1700s, however, everything changed for cotton. Improved spinning and weaving methods made it easier to produce cotton cloth. Smart people in the early 1800s realized that cotton was the coming thing. New mills sprang up, first in England and then in the United States. There seemed to be an insatiable demand for this "new" miracle fiber. Over the course of a single human generation, a whole new class of industrial barons arose from the huge profits that were created by the production of cotton cloth. For the first time in Western history, commoners became wealthier than their noble counterparts.

By the late 1700s, lots of people knew how to spin thread and make cotton cloth. The technology got better and better. The main problem for cotton barons shifted away from cloth production. They were more concerned about their future supply of raw cotton. The cotton barons had good reason for worry. Cotton is a tropical plant. It will thrive only in places that have the perfect combination of climate, soil, and water.

At the beginning of the cotton boom, those places were a long way from cotton mills in England and America. Some of those places had unpredictable weather patterns. Others had political or labor problems. This made them unreliable and expensive sources for the new miracle fiber. Cotton barons didn't like the phrase "unreliable and expensive" as it applied to the base material that kept their mills running.

By the late 1700s, people were beginning to realize that the finest cotton-growing lands yet discovered were only about a thousand miles south of America's growing industrial heartland. These were in what was called the "cotton kingdom" of Alabama, Florida, Georgia, North Carolina, and Tennessee. These were the same areas that were already occupied by Indians of the Five Civilized Tribes. White men wanted the land that grew the cotton. Indians stood in the way. The stage was set for the destruction of five successful nations of people.

In the first decades of the nineteenth century, the US government revealed its true intentions for the southern tribes. Earlier promises to the Indians were revealed as being little more than well-intentioned delay tactics. That strategy worked. America was now stronger and more populous. It had gained the strength it needed to fight the southern Indians. The Indians didn't stand a chance against a new and mighty America.

The US government prevailed. It seized Indian land. But what should be done with the Indians? Whites decided it would be inhumane to kill the red people. It would be uncivilized.

Someone looked farther west. They decided there was plenty of land out there for the Indians. Just move them on. That's exactly what happened.

Between about 1830 and 1840, more than fifty thousand southern Indians were forcibly removed by the US government from land they had legally possessed for countless generations. Many of the Indians were taken from their homes in the middle of the night. They stood shivering as they watched white neighbors loot their belongings. It was repeatedly noted that the Indians were passive when they witnessed the destruction of their lives.

But the cruelest part was yet to come. The Indians were marched west to what is now Oklahoma. Many of them didn't take many possessions. Some were forced to walk through winter weather without shoes, warm clothing, or blankets. Many were forced to make the journey in chains. Tens of thousands died along the way. In many cases, their bodies were left unburied along the side of the road. Oh, but those were good times for coyotes and other scavengers!

Tribes that had been decimated by white man's diseases a few decades previously took another big hit. I suppose that having one such death march would be a horrific blight on America's soul. But they went on for about a decade. The tribes called their journey west the Trail of Tears. That name is quite apt.

My ancestors were surprised by the region to which they had been moved. They left a verdant country of mountain and forest, river and field. Oklahoma had scant portions of those useful places. It was flat and prone to being dry—except, of course, when rain fell in hellish proportions. In places, Oklahoma was sparsely wooded. Its climate seasonally varied between hell hot and subarctic cold. Those extremes sometimes occurred within the course of a single day. Most of the Indians were not psychologically prepared for their new home. Societal malaise spread through the battered survivors of the white man's oppression.

Over the years, all kinds of Indian tribes were sent to Oklahoma. It was like the central collection point for the crap that a city's residents don't want anymore. Oklahoma became a massive Indian junk heap.

Fast-forward a few more decades. White people figured out that Oklahoma was America's last frontier. Whites eyed the place enviously. There were so many settlers and so little land.

But there was a major obstacle that prevented whites from settling in Oklahoma: the place was already infested with Indians. Like flies at the dump, Indians always seemed to be in the way of progress. Someone in government eventually decided that they needed to clean up the Indian dumping ground. You know, get Oklahoma ready for white people to inhabit.

But how could the Indians be removed from land that was legally theirs? The government used law. Law is a system of rules that are made and enforced by local and national leaders. The purpose of law is to keep civilization moving along at a well-regulated pace. White people have lots of laws. When they don't have enough, they dream more into existence. That's the Caucasian side of the Oklahoma deal.

Indians were different. They didn't have very many laws that were enacted before 1492. Indian life was regulated by season and locality. That's the Indian side.

White people hated Indians for not having laws. This marked Indians as being savages. Uncivilized. Laws were forced upon the Indians when they were moved to Oklahoma. Whites provided more laws after the Indians arrived. This gave whites the tools they needed to evict the Indians from Oklahoma. It was brilliant. Whites gave law to the Indians and then used the law against them.

At this point in the game, just one question remained for the US government: "How do we get rid of the Indians in an efficient manner?" Most of the tribes in Oklahoma had already been moved once. Some had been moved twice. Moving Indians is expensive. But wait, there's more! After you move the Indians, you must deal with subsequent generations in the new place. There weren't many people in the US government who wanted to move Indians a third time.

In the case of one of my mother's tribes, someone figured out how to avoid moving Indians.

Every ending has a beginning. My mother's family stopped being Indians because of a statistic. Centuries of white man's diseases, alcohol, bullets, and law wiped out my Indian ancestors. In the eyes of the government, there weren't enough Indians living on the tribe's reservation to justify its existence.

The government decided to sell the reservation and give the proceeds to the remaining Indians. It would be treated as a normal transfer of real property. Any obligations that the government had to the Indians would be satisfied.

Well, that's exactly how it went, folks. Papers were signed. It was a done deal. What happened next was typical of white-versus-Indian transactions. The government's Indian agent and the lawyer who handled the sale took off with the money. They left the Indians bereft of both land and money. For the Indians, there was no recourse. In the eyes of our celebrated system of law, they had been paid off.

The chaos the white man visited upon my Indian ancestors moved into another dimension.

CHAPTER 3

From Indians to White Trash

White trash: A term for poor people that is widely used in the
southern United States of America. It typically denotes white
people who live in a socially degraded manner because of their bad
behavior. In the current era, the term white trash is worn by many
as a badge of honor. Many other people (but especially African
Americans) use the term as the vilest form of personal epithet.

—Tom Liggett's personal glossary of terms

THE TRIBES THAT WERE NOT removed from their reservations have a vested
interest in retaining their Indian culture. No matter how many times reservation Indians interbreed with white people, they still get help from
the government. Come what may, if they live on the reservation, they are
considered to be Indian. This is a very pragmatic viewpoint. Reservation
Indians saw what happened to other tribes. They know they must retain
their Indian identity to maintain the status quo.

It was different for my mother's family. Their reservation was gone. The
children and grandchildren of those who had been moved, removed, and
wiped out by the white man's priorities saw little tangible value in retaining the cultural identity of their Indian forbearers. Getting kicked off the
reservation was only one part of the problem. When they were around white
people, they were called dirty Indians, heathens, and drunken savages.

Remember, this was right after the great American frontier was conquered. Custer's death at the Little Bighorn was at the forefront of American consciousness. "Those damned Indians killed our hero" was a common refrain. "The only good Indian is a dead Indian" was on the lips of a many white person. This type of sentiment was especially strong for those who lived in former Indian lands. The children and grandchildren of people who fought Indians remembered the old days. They added another name to the long list of anti-Indian epithets: killers.

By the time my relatives got kicked off the reservation, they probably had a fair percentage of white blood in them. To the eyes of contemporary Americans, many didn't look like Indians. My ancestors looked like dark-haired white people. In many cases, that was the guise they assumed. Lots of folks in the 1900s wanted to forget that some of the blood flowing in their veins was derived from Indians. They wanted to avoid the low-class stigma that was commonly associated with native ancestry. Mixed-bloods didn't advertise their derivation in post frontier America.

Some of my Indian ancestors looked like dark-haired, dark-eyed white people. Lita Snow, age five. Cache Bottom, Oklahoma.

This concept is not limited to Indians. I have known lots of Mexicans and Indians who claimed they were "Spanish." Considering how I have seen Indian-looking folks treated during my lifetime, I am certain that still happens. Possessing Indian genes has only become fashionable in the past fifty years or so. Before that, it was a social stigma.

I know folks of even the common sort who can trace their ancestors back for many generations. But that's just not the case with my mother's family. The chaos of being repeatedly wrenched away from everything they knew erased my family's memory of its own collective past. By the time of my grandmother's birth, very few family stories remained. Few stories escaped the filter of the lazy passivity that governed her life. Few memories of Indian culture or ancestry remained for me to hear as I was growing up.

My grandmother told us about the Trail of Tears. She provided no specific details about what happened to our family during that period. She just said, "The trip was horrible. The weather was cold. Most of the people died." That was it.

Sadly, those faint echoes of familial horror had little relevance to me or the others of my generation. The age into which I was born in 1950 was rife with death. Our parents and grandparents were reeling. Well over one hundred million people were killed in World War II. Mao was killing his people by the tens of millions in China. A few thousand Indians who'd been wiped out more than a hundred years previous didn't resonate with the cultural psyche of the 1950s. The Trail of Tears became just another vague story that became lost in the blender of US history.

A lot of American history was taught to my parents and me via novels and movies. In the America of my youth, the murdering Indian always died in the last scene. Who wanted to be that guy?

Writing this book changed my life. It enabled me to put a lot of separate things that were wandering around in my head into order. Before I wrote this book, I didn't number the individual pieces from the Indian cultural puzzle that were passed down to me. When I finally put them together, they were pitifully few. I wanted to cry.

Just three cultural artifacts were passed down to me from my Indian ancestors. These tiny hints reveal a vibrant and inclusive culture. It will take me only a handful of paragraphs to tell you all that I know of my Indian heritage. How sad. Nonetheless, it is my pleasure and honor to share these small gems with you. I am doing this so that someone in the future will recall those who have been forgotten.

Almost everyone has an ancestor they can point out as being their earliest one of memory. Growing up, I never heard anyone in my grandmother's family ponder who that ancestor might be on our Indian side. When I was in my twenties, one of my uncles contacted someone from a remote branch of our family. People on that side cared about their history. My uncle told me that somewhere back in an undefined time, we had a remote ancestor who was called the Indian Preacher. Aside from that, neither I nor anyone else in the family knows any more about him or his legacy.

But there is something telling about that old Indian's moniker. In the minds of the whites who recorded his existence, he wasn't granted the use of his given name. He was memorialized because he wore the mantle of his conqueror's religion. That is a very small amount of data to give you about the man whose blood flows through my veins. But, like the cartoon character Porky Pig said, "That's all, folks."

I got the love of gardening and the sense of how plants grow from my Indian grandmothers. One of my very earliest memories was of my mother telling me, "Push the bean into the soil half the length of your index finger. Now gently close the hole." How many hundreds of her Indian grandmothers did the same with that seminally Indian food?

My grandmother took almost nothing from Oklahoma when she migrated to California. She knew that her new life was going to be better than the one she left behind. My grandmother said she missed just one thing that was in Oklahoma: "them little red peaches." Those fruits were holy things to her. My grandmother implanted that same love into me. Indian Blood peaches are the one tangible object I can point to and say, "These came from my Indian ancestors."

A final shard of Indian culture was passed down to me. It came as a story. It is just one sentence long. When my elders recited the story, they always used the same words: "Your Indian relatives stole white women, and your white relatives stole Indian women." In its length, that anecdote is quite small. It is nonetheless prescient in what it reveals about the succeeding generations of my mother's family.

CHAPTER 4

The Rape of the Indian Maidens

LEGEND HAS IT THAT ANCIENT Rome was founded by a bunch of outlaws and rejects from neighboring tribes. Those boys were pretty good at hammering out a new city-state. But their dating skills were *not* up to par. Women from neighboring tribes were not allowed to marry into the outlaw band.

The proto-Romans were smart enough to realize that if they were going to become founding fathers, they needed to find founding mothers. Match. com, eHarmony, and Craigslist weren't around for the proto-Romans. Rather than taking time to brush up on their manners, the Romans took matters into their own hands: they kidnapped a bunch of women from the Sabine tribe. Rome was saved for the next twelve hundred years or so.

The rape of the Sabine women is remembered today mainly because of the salacious paintings that were done by later European artists. That type of picture was about the only form of pornography that was publicly available in those days. If we believe what those paintings depict, all women of the period were young, beautiful, and had large breasts. In my opinion, that is the main reason why men want to invent a time machine.

Pioneers in North America went into places with thin or nonexistent populations. Such places were entirely lacking in the amenities that women find to be appealing. You know, things like houses, food, and the security of not being killed by competing pioneers.

For these reasons, it's not surprising that there was an acute shortage of women out on the American frontier. This led to a curious state wherein my white relatives stole Indian women and my Indian relatives stole white women. Sadly, this one-sided bargain always favored the men.

I'm not going to tell you about the plight of white women who were kidnapped by Indians. That story has been told and retold in a thousand dime novels and movies. Most of them indicate that the white women were plunged into ungodly, heathen barbarism. Sometimes they were. Sometimes they weren't. There are exceptions to every rule.

It was far worse for Indian women who were kidnapped by white men. When white people came to the Americas, they found that Indians lived better lives than most contemporary Europeans. That truth was confirmed by many writers of the time. The Indians who met the Europeans at Plymouth were sturdy. They were taller and fitter than contemporary Europeans. This concept does not fit the popularized notion of civilized whites versus savage Indians.

But there is abundant proof to support it nonetheless. Over a period of centuries, untold thousands of white children were abducted by Indians. Many of these were later repatriated to the white world. Repatriated whites frequently escaped and returned to live with Indians. They saw that life with Indians was better than it was with whites.

In many Indian cultures, women had power. Men were taught to respect women. Indian women could be counted on to use knives on men who did not. Indian women lived in tough cultures, but they generally received their due.

European women of the day were little more than chattel.

Think about the typical white man an Indian girl was apt to meet out on the frontier. There was a good chance that he was much older. The man had probably failed somewhere else. Successful men don't leave their families as frequently as unsuccessful ones. A white abductor had probably left at least one wife and family behind. He might have been running from something or someone. Many men fled west to escape from the law, creditors, or jealous husbands.

Most white men of that era drank alcohol. Many frontiersmen were alcoholics. While they were out in the bush, they would go long periods without drinking. When frontiersmen obtained alcohol, they would make up for lost time and get crazy with drink.

Few contemporary white frontiersmen shaved. It was well known that beards were excellent protection against the elements.

There were other reasons for not shaving. Most people don't know that shaving has not always been the benign operation that it is today. Shaving with a straight razor inevitably opened nicks and cuts. It was easy for these to become infected. Untold tens of thousands of men suffered and died from shaving-related infections. That's why nineteenth-century men kept their own razors, shaving mugs, and brushes at the local barber shop. They knew that shared shaving implements spread disease. There weren't a whole lot of barber shops out on the open frontier.

The beards of frontiersmen generally bore traces of the last thousand meals they had eaten. Many men of that era chewed tobacco. The remains of that disgusting goo hardened into a smelly plaque. White men's beards smelled rotten when they were pressed against an Indian girl's face.

Most lone frontiersmen never took their clothes off long enough to wash them. Can you imagine how a leather shirt smells after it has been on a man's back for a year? Why didn't they take of their shirts? Because white frontiersmen seldom bathed. If they did bathe, they didn't repeat the experience more than a few times a year. That part about bathing is crucial to this discussion. There was no toilet paper on the American frontier.

All in all, that package of contemporary Caucasian masculine traits doesn't sound very appealing. Unknowing modern folks have a ready reply to my assertions about foul-smelling white frontiersmen. Some might say that Indians weren't any cleaner or attractive. To them, it would appear to be an equal match between dirty people.

But that was just not the case. Yes, it is true that by today's hyper sanitary standards, an Indian girl of that period might appear to be dirty. I counter that most Indians regularly bathed or went swimming. Indians cleaned their teeth with willow twigs. They also ate better and wore cleaner, better-made clothes. Any way you cut it, most contemporary Indian girls looked and smelled a heck of a lot better than most white men they met.

A white abductor probably looked like a wild animal. He undoubtedly smelled like rotten shit, sweat, and the animals that he killed or rode.

Imagine what it was like to be an Indian woman who was abducted by a white man. He would usually seek out the youngest Indian woman that he could find. An older one might be able to pack, cook, and clean for him, but she wouldn't be as much fun in bed. An older woman might not provide sons for the abductor.

At best, sex with a white abductor would be rape. I seriously doubt that such a man cared if his new woman was ready for the act. Chances are that he gave her a dry, rough fuck.

There is a high probability that the white abductor frequented bordellos. Such institutions were much more common than they are now. Most nineteenth-century prostitutes ended up with one or more venereal diseases. Indian women had no resistance to white man's diseases, especially gonorrhea.

It was the perfect recipe for a short, unhappy life. Many Indian women who were abducted by white men lived just long enough to produce one or two children. In the case of my female ancestors, that was long enough to pass down their remarkable genes to subsequent generations of their daughters.

I have seen five generations of my mother's female relatives. It is easy to see why their ancestors were such ready targets for white abductors. There is a distinct look that skips around the children in my mother's family. It is like one flower that stands apart from its sister seedlings.

Those who have the full set of Indian characteristics have high cheekbones and large, liquid-brown eyes. Some have profuse, fine, reddish-brown hair that never turns fully gray. Many of my relatives have short legs. I do too. This precludes us from being fast runners. But our trunk-like lower members gift us with amazing endurance.

Our skin is not the red or brown that one generally associates with American Indians. It is yellowish in color. My mother received several letters from people who worked in the schools I attended. Each said approximately the same thing: "Tommy has jaundice; you should take him to the doctor." My mother always explained to them that my skin faded to its natural yellow color in the winter.

For the men of my family, the Indian gene set makes for decent but not exceptional looks. It is quite different for many of the women, though. Indian genes created spectacular beauty in the women of my family. Many of them have the faces of angels and the bodies of goddesses. That look is inevitably paired with an intelligent, insightful mind. Cleverness and beauty combined.

But there is a downside to that genetic combination. Many of the spectacular women in my family inherited tempers that were instantaneous in their progression and incandescent in their force. That temperament was generally coupled with a compact, work-hardened body. It was a combination that created incredible potential for trouble. One of the cowboys my mother married described her perfectly: "Dynamite comes in small packages."

Alcohol was the coup de grace for many members of my mother's family. They had an affinity for alcohol but very little resistance to the stuff. Its effect on the stronger-minded of my kin is a sight that few people care to behold more than once. This was especially true in regard to alcohol's effect on those gorgeous women.

When one of the women in my family "went off," she instantly cast off the trappings of civilization. Those episodes were inevitably preceded by a woman screaming at somebody. Most of the time, that poor soul was a man. But other women were not immune to such attentions.

The magnitude and duration of a woman's tirade were variable things. They depended generally on the depth of her resentment and the quantity of alcohol she had consumed. If the target instantly expressed sufficient quantities of abject contrition, it might all be over in a few minutes.

As often as not, however, that's not the way it ended. Generally speaking, no amount of reasoning could stop an avalanche of anger from crashing down on the moment. It didn't usually take much time for those women to go from words to action. Any available object could instantly become a weapon. When my mother threw an ashtray, she seldom missed her target. She came by that trait naturally. Indian children mastered the art of throwing stones to kill tasty birds.

But the yelling and the throwing were just a warm-up. The women in my family seemed to prefer a direct frontal attack. They would throw themselves at their chosen victims with a force that I have only seen duplicated in Siamese dams protecting their kittens. My female relatives landed fists, teeth, elbows, knees, and feet on their chosen victims in a buzz-saw blur of movement.

The real assault stars in my family got style points for their pièce de résistance. They would jump on a man's back and wrap their legs around his waist. That left their arms, fists, and teeth free to wreak havoc on the intended victim. I never saw any man, woman, or child who could respond to a direct attack by one of the women in my family. Most of their victims just hunkered down and took a beating. It might take four or five strong men to get her off the victim's back.

You might think that the women would confine their abuse to private settings. That's not the way it worked out. When my female relatives thought that someone needed chewing out or a serious correction, they got it right then and there. When one of those women exploded, it didn't matter where they were or who they were with. No care was given if they were in a car, restaurant, bar, or even the dining room of the largest cruise ship in the world.

It might be easy to lay this havoc at the feet of the white man's alcohol. When my aunt Betty got drunk, she got angry. Then again, she was a beautiful loon when she was sober. Where am I going with this? Some of my female relatives didn't need alcohol in order to explode. It's as if they were pissed off when they emerged from their mothers' wombs. It was a genetic thing. They came from a long line of strong Indian women. Their talent for ferociousness had been tuned by eons of natural selection, like a hunting dog's nose for game.

What generally happened after one of my female relatives calmed down makes for strange telling. In a normal family, she would have been subjected to the righteous condemnation of those around her. Some people would have called the police to haul her mean ass off to jail. Not in my family. Some of the worst public tirades I witnessed ended in cheers for the female victor. Part of this came from the view of the Christian religion—someone receiving their just deserts. But it ultimately came down to gender studies. It was usually the women who were praising one another for raining hell on some poor soul.

Then there is the male side: the men in my family didn't want to stay angry, because their women looked like goddesses. I saw cowboys look at women and say, "I'd drink a gallon of her piss just to see where it came from." Well, guess what? In a metaphorical sense, they accomplished that task. Males are always betrayed by their testicles.

The female side of this dynamic played out in a different way. The women in my mother's family had a deep hatred and resentment for men. They left no room for speculation. I have heard many of my female relatives express their antimale sentiments with great abundance and precision.

The combination of fawning men and hating women created a toxic stew that spanned the generations in my family. It was perpetuated by gorgeous young women who got away with far more than should have been allowed. From puberty onward, people cut those girls a lot of slack.

San Francisco, California. 1953.My maternal grandmother's last child has a different father than the rest of her siblings, so she only received half the dose of Indian blood that her siblings did. That woman has blond hair and blue eyes. She escaped having the Indian look and much of the temperament. It saved her family a lot of grief.

I want for my readers to pause for a moment. Consider what I have just written about my female relatives. You should never discount the benefit

Lita Liggett and Betty Snow. The combination of fawning men and hating women created a toxic stew that spanned the generations in my family. It was perpetuated by gorgeous young women who got away with far more than should have been allowed. From puberty onward, people cut those girls a lot of slack.

of feminine beauty and sex appeal as social lubricants. The old saying that "all the world loves a pretty girl" has great power. Mighty kings have been brought to their knees by teenaged peasant girls.

All of us who experienced familial tirades developed coping skills. The best of those was to take cover. Try to become invisible. If you were the recipient of their anger, that was difficult to accomplish. Most people just hunkered down and took the abuse.

Thinking back on those occasions, it is amazing to me how quickly things got back to normal once the yelling stopped. Folks went back to drinking, smoking, and chatting. I guess that's because abuse of one type or another was the norm for our family.

Later in my life, people tried to excuse my mother's behavior to me and her last husband. They said that my mother should get a pass because she went crazy at the end of her life. I was never shy in calling bullshit on *that* one. You see, they seem to forget that my mother was frequently compared with two of her aunts. Those comparisons were generally made after my mother had gone off in public. It is interesting to note that one of those aunts probably got away with murder. Her husband simply disappeared. The other women in the family said, "He was a son of a bitch who was better off gone." I rest my case.

If they are uncorrected, single incidents can become bad habits. In turn, such things become the new normal. Over the years, the hellish behaviors of some of my female relatives became the de facto law of our family.

I firmly believe that my aggrieved Indian grandmothers got the last laugh on their white abductors. The latter-day behaviors of many of the women in my family created waking nightmares for their husbands, brothers, and children.

White men had no idea the Indian women they abducted possessed a hellish set of heritable traits. That knowledge might have guided them away from what turned out to be a genetic powder keg.

But I have lived long and seen much. I know about the ways of a man with a maid. No matter what, for the knowledge they possessed, my white ancestors would still have succumbed to the smoldering beauty of my female ancestors. Our family would have been better off if those men had taken the safer course by becoming celibate or that age's version of homosexuals.

CHAPTER 5

Out of the Dust Bowl

The Dust Bowl is one of the common names given to a period
of extreme drought in parts of the North American Great Plains.
Modern mechanical farming methods destroyed the native,
deep-rooted grasses that had previously anchored the virgin
soil. Drought turned the soil into something resembling talcum
powder. Normal area winds caused the soil to blow away. The
resultant dust storms formed dense, choking clouds. Agriculture of
all kinds in the affected region was totally devastated. Hundreds
of thousands of people were forced to move to unaffected areas.
The Dust Bowl was the largest diaspora in American history.

—Tom Liggett's personal glossary of terms

MY MATERNAL GRANDMOTHER WAS NAMED Ruby Lois Stewart. She met my
grandfather, Cleve Snow, while she was walking down a Central Oklahoma
trail. He was coming out of the forest with a gunnysack full of animal traps
on his back. Ruby said that Cleve scared her. She must not have remained
frightened for very long. The two of them were married when she was
thirteen.

Ruby liked to say that while their first home as a married couple was a
barn, it was OK, "because it was a new barn." She was adamant in her belief
that the barn was better than their next home. That was a tent. Ruby said

that they lived in the tent "until the weather got real cold. Then we found us somewhere else to live."

Ruby bore her first child when she was thirteen. That baby died. Ruby was always vague about the reasons for that child's early demise. At best, she provided hints about how hard life was for her little family at that time. Life in a cold tent probably had a lot to do with Lola Mae Snow's death.

Ruby had a second child when she was fifteen. That one lived. Ruby cooled her reproductive jets for a while before she bore her third child at twenty-one. That baby eventually became my mother.

Some relatives dropped by to see my mother on the day that she was born. One of them had somehow become enraptured by the name Lolita. Ruby was a suggestable sort. She agreed that was fine name for her new baby girl.

The clerk at the County Records Office had never seen such a name. Somehow Lolita got changed into Loeta in the official record. Ruby lacked the gumption to get her lazy ass down to the county seat and change my mother's name back to its intended spelling. Ruby allowed Loeta to stick as my mother's name. In typical country fashion, the family contracted the name to Lita.

Just for the record, the county clerk got my mother's middle name wrong too. To the family, her middle name was Fay. On the record, it was Bernice. Loeta Bernice Snow. What a horrid mouthful. When my mother was in her sixties, she officially changed her middle name to Fay.

My mother was born in Cache Bottom, Oklahoma, in 1933. That place doesn't exist anymore. The Arkansas River washed it away. Oklahoma was at the epicenter of the Dust Bowl and the Great Depression. It was ground zero for hardship of all kinds.

My grandfather Cleve Snow was a sharecropper and farmhand. In those hard times, theirs was the worst plight of all workers on the Great Plains. No rain meant little work in the fields. Life was terrible for Cleve and his rapidly growing family. Anyone who knows about that era will not be surprised by this revelation. They were rough times for many Americans.

Even factoring in the Dust Bowl, it is surprising that my grandmother's family was in such dire straits. Ruby's grandfather was a prosperous physician in Spiro, Oklahoma. You would expect a learned and successful man to pass some ambition to his descendants. Sadly, none of his children or grandchildren aspired to do anything more than the bare minimum with their lives. Neither my great-grandmother nor my grandmother was a bad person. But they didn't do anything but rear children and retire. Blind passivity drove them to a lackluster existence.

My great-grandmother spent a lot of time reading the Bible and waiting for the better life that was promised in the great beyond. My grandmother sat around doing nothing but housework. She patiently waited for whatever crumbs life threw at her feet. Playing her part to the max, Ruby then made a quiet show of being happy with crumbs.

My grandfather Cleve was raised in the all-enveloping, primordial bottomlands of the Arkansas River. For anyone who wanted a backwoodsman's life, it was like being in Disneyland. The bottomlands were a self-contained world. They possessed almost everything that was needed for life and pleasure. As seen from the perspective of Cleve Snow, it was heaven on earth, Dust Bowl or no Dust Bowl. Conditions in that place were little changed from when Indians of a purer sort lived there a few decades in the past. Men like Cleve hunted and fished. If they found a patch of ripe blackberries, they loaded up their hats for pie filling.

In the winter, men and boys trapped animals for their fur. That is a vocation that is foreign to modern sensibilities. But in that era, there weren't many avenues for earning spot cash out in the sticks. This was especially true for young boys. Local jobs were few and far between in those times, and they were sometimes reserved for men who had families to feed.

Running a line of traps was appealing to and popular with rural Americans. A large percentage of them depended upon the ready cash that the penny fur trade brought to them. The back of many magazines carried ads for companies that wanted to buy furs.

It was a win-win situation for someone like Cleve. He got an excuse to play in the woods all day. Cleve would process, cure, and mail the resultant animal pelts to fur buyers. The money for the pelts was paid by mail. Start to finish in that process, Cleve didn't have to leave his beloved Arkansas River bottomlands. The animals and the money were delivered right to his doorstep.

In the summer, men like Cleve worked for the local farmers. Sometimes they were paid a straight day rate for their labor. If it was available, such work was a guaranteed way to make money. But a lot of men in Cleve's position worked as sharecroppers. That type of farming made laborers partners with a landlord. The landlord provided the land, tools, seed, and supplies. The laborer grew the crop and received a fixed portion of the profits.

Laborers could potentially make a lot of money by sharecropping. But it was a far riskier proposition than working for wages. Things don't always go as planned. The fields that Cleve worked were dry-farmed. This meant they didn't receive human-assisted irrigation. Farmers depended upon water that fell from the sky. Too little rain would prevent plant growth. Too much at the wrong time could ruin a perfect crop. When either of those conditions occurred, an entire year's production would be lost. In those cases, the sharecropper was paid nothing. During the Dust Bowl, crops failed over a huge swath of middle America.

But Cleve Snow had seen crop failures of another kind. Those failures were wrought by failed government agricultural policies. During the First World War, the government encouraged farmers to plant every square inch of land because soldiers needed the food. But that war ended much sooner than anyone had anticipated. The government didn't want the crops they told farmers to plant. American farmers ended up with huge quantities of surplus agricultural commodities. Prices for those commodities fell. Recession hit the American heartland before the Dust Bowl occurred. This was the world into which Cleve Snow was born. It made him depend ever more on the produce of the Arkansas River bottomlands.

Most of Cleve's jobs were part-time in nature. He practiced them with varying degrees of success. This was dependent upon on the weather and his current level of ambition. But there was one occupation that the men in Cleve's family pursued full-time: making moonshine whiskey. They always had a still hidden somewhere.

Producing illegal whiskey in those days was not as foreign, dangerous, or glamorous as it might sound. It was a common thing. People wanted alcohol. Other people made the stuff. I am no great fan of booze in general, but I have a wonderful view of this matter. This is because people in both of my parents' families made moonshine whiskey.

Viewed through the lens of our modern-day perspective, such a view might seem to be a little unusual. That's because the modern view of moonshiners has been delivered through sensationalized movies and television shows about the failed experiment of America's prohibition of alcohol.

The fanatics who banned strong drink were overlooking a fundamental fact about human beings: throughout recorded history, mankind has diligently sought mind-altering substances. In most cases, ethyl alcohol offered the safest and most cost-effective way to "cop a buzz." I have read that almost every culture on earth fermented something to convert it into alcohol.

In practical terms, this means that throughout our history as civilized beings, somebody's grandfather was making alcohol. The pioneers who kidnapped my grandmothers were no exception. Those dudes liked to get drunk. They also liked to make money. Hard alcohol was a universal commodity on the US frontier. Almost everybody wanted the stuff. Thus was born the first cash crop of America's frontline pioneers. Ambitious sorts could turn grain or fruit into booze. A cask of high-proof alcohol doesn't weigh much. It is easy to transport over rough backwoods trails.

When America became more settled, the taxation of alcohol became an important revenue steam for the government. Home alcohol-distilling operations were a threat to this revenue because they produced less-expensive, tax-free products. The suppression of home stills became an early priority for the US government. Lots of people still produced homemade hard alcohol, but they kept their operations small and secret. Moonshiners were always afraid of the law.

That changed when alcohol was banned in America. When prohibition shut down the corner liquor store, the moonshiners stepped in. They were filling a need that was artificially created by the government. Prohibition enabled the resurgence of large-scale home alcohol production. It also led to its end through increased enforcement of revenue laws. My relatives were the beginning of the end of a tradition that stretched back thousands of years.

Some folks made money on their moonshining operations. Not my grandfather Cleve. He personally consumed the bulk of his own whiskey. Cleve told me, "I sold just enough whiskey to buy sugar to make the next batch."

Since he was part Indian, Cleve didn't have a high tolerance for alcohol. Like many in my family, he got very drunk, very fast. He also found alcohol to be irresistible. Cleve became the worst kind of incorrigible drunk.

You would expect that of a man from Cleve's family. His father was a moonshiner too. That man provided Cleve with hard alcohol while he was still a young child. My grandfather cheerfully admitted that he was an alcoholic before he was ten years old.

During prohibition, huge fortunes were made by the producers and procurers of alcohol. Some of the notables who profited from such ventures were Al Capone and Joseph Kennedy (the father of future president John F. Kennedy Jr.).

My paternal great-grandfather Albert "Heine" Brensing made that kind of fortune. He bought tons of nearly worthless corn and made huge quantities of moonshine whiskey. Heine put the proceeds of his illegal alcohol production to good use. He bought square miles of devalued Kansas farmland for pennies on the dollar.

Heine's whiskey-making activities stand in harsh contrast to those of my maternal grandfather, Cleve Snow. Stories about Cleve Snow's whiskey-related foibles were commonly told by members of my mother's family. They made for interesting conversation. For many years, I pondered the destruction my grandfather visited upon our family as the result of his singular entrepreneurial endeavor. These thoughts inevitably centered on one topic: Cleve couldn't support his family because he was always drunk or in jail. Beyond that, I never gave the subject too much thought.

I met Heine Brensing's daughter when I was thirty-two. She helped me look at moonshine whiskey from a different perspective. "Cleve didn't sell much whiskey," she said. "He drank it all. Because of that saving grace, he ruined just his own life and that of his immediate family. My father didn't drink much, but he sold lots of whiskey and ruined the lives of everybody in the county." Wow! Heine's daughter believed Cleve Snow was the better man. How about *that* for a turnaround?

Platitudes aside, I find the views of Heine Brensing's daughter to be quite revealing. In my opinion, they are a load of self-righteous bullshit. Why? It's easy to be noble when you have plenty to eat, a stable home life, and adequate preparation for adulthood. Kids living on the ragged edge of survival can't be so picky. They grasp at straws.

In the overall scheme of things, it's not supposed to matter what your grandpa did way back then. I take a slightly different view of that concept. If what Grandpa did still pays for your groceries, it's worth talking about. Considering how I was raised, I wouldn't have minded if fortunes had been reversed between Cleve Snow and Heine Brensing.

Let's fast-forward our story for just a moment. Forty years after prohibition ended, Cleve finally drank himself to death. He was sixty-seven years old. Cleve's family members took up a collection to pay for the funeral.

It is a different case entirely with my father's family. Some of them still own prosperous farms that are measured in square miles, not acres. Heck, I hear they found natural gas on Heine Brensing's land.

The Dust Bowl ended Cleve Snow's long idyll in the beloved Arkansas River bottomlands. He had a growing family to feed. Cleve got his first view of the outside world when he worked in an Oklahoma coal mine. That was the only job that was available to him.

Cleve's brief stint as a miner caused him to develop black lung disease. Cleve was just in his thirties, but he was crippled with bad lungs. Endless packs of cigarettes didn't help that problem. Coal mining skewed Cleve's perspective. He never wanted to be anything more than a backwoodsman. Why would he want to be anything else? Cleve believed that the rich bottomlands of the Arkansas River contained the necessities of a good life.

Cleve didn't want to leave Oklahoma. But nearly everyone that he knew was leaving. They were forced to escape the ravages of the Dust Bowl. Still Cleve dithered. He didn't want to leave. His wife and children had already gone to California. Many of his relatives were there too. If Cleve stayed in Oklahoma, he would be alone.

Cleve joined the great western migration of Okies, Arkies, and Texans in 1936. My grandfather was typical in his feelings about that move. Most people planned to stay in California only "until things got better back home." They believed that they could ride out the rough patch and return to their old lives sometime in the future.

Okie farm laborers were a dime a dozen in 1930s California. They huddled in groups at farm gates, waiting for work. Many were not successful in their aspirations.

On the other hand, heavy-equipment operators, or "cat skinners," were rare. Cleve was one of the best cat skinners in Oklahoma. Because of this skill, he was immediately met with lucrative job offers in California.

By today's standards, driving a tractor might not appear to be much of an accomplishment. Viewed from the perspective of his times, though, a heavy-equipment operator was the equivalent of a jumbo-jet pilot.

Heavy earth movers were new inventions. In less than twenty years, the process of plowing and earthmoving changed. One man with a tractor could do work that once required hundreds of men and mules. In just a few years, the cost of moving dirt was reduced by 90 percent.

But those huge tractors required an incredible amount of skill to operate. Huge fields must be leveled to a fine grade to facilitate the flow of irrigation water. That task is accomplished by a massive piece of equipment called a terraplane. There were no laser beams to guide those beasts across mile-wide plots of land. It took a skilled man with a sharp eye. Cleve Snow was one of the best.

Cleve Snow with Caterpillar tractor. These machines required an incredible amount of skill to operate. Cleve was one of the best.

Many other contemporary Okies in California were living in improvised shantytowns called Hoovervilles. As soon as he arrived, though, Cleve had a job with perks: he was given a house and a milk cow as a condition of his employment. My grandmother and her children loved their new life in sunny California.

In a very short time, farmers up and down the great Central Valley knew of Cleve's skill. He helped to transform untold thousands of acres of alkali waste into some of the richest farmland in the world.

But that was not enough for my grandfather. California offered him limitless opportunity, but his heart was back in Oklahoma. Homesickness exaggerated Cleve's need to find the bottom of a whiskey bottle.

By that time, my grandfather had been an alcoholic for over twenty years. In Oklahoma, such behavior was not a big deal. Cleve could be half drunk all the time and still wander through his various occupations with some measure of success.

Then there was the social aspect. When Cleve got drunk in Oklahoma, he was annoying, but he was surrounded by people of long acquaintance. They would cover for him when he fell off the wagon. But California was not like rural Oklahoma. It was part of a much larger world. In that new place, he was surrounded by strangers. They had no ties of kith and kin to moderate their responses to Cleve's drunken behavior.

Farmers didn't want a drunk man piloting a ten-thousand-pound tractor around their fields. Those early tractors were expensive to buy, easy to break, and difficult to repair. Times were tough for California farmers. They didn't want a drunken idiot costing them time and money.

Cleve got drunk and unruly in public. He got into fights. He began to spend a lot of time in jail on charges of public drunkenness. That was the beginning of the end for Cleve Snow, both as a man and as a father. You can't show up for an important day's work when you're in jail. You can't be a father when you're not around.

Cleve gained a bad reputation with farmers. They told each other that he was unreliable. That old Indian bugaboo remained alive in my family three hundred years after the white man introduced it to the New World.

Jailers knew about Cleve's legendary reputation as a heavy-equipment operator. This inevitably meant that he was sent to the county jail farm. When most people hear the term jail farm, they think of Paul Newman in *Cool Hand Luke*. But California's county jail farms weren't institutions of that sort. They were places where trusted prisoners were sent to work off their sentences. Jail farms were profit centers for the county, not jails of extreme punishment.

Yes, most of the people who were sent to the jail farm spent their days hoeing weeds in the fields. But they weren't brutalized by men with whips. Inmates who did well at the farm got time off their sentences.

Cleve didn't hoe weeds at the jail farm. As soon as he got there, he was put on a tractor. For Cleve, that wasn't a bad thing. He got to operate heavy farm machinery, and he dried out from alcohol. The jail farm was my grandfather's spa.

Cleve spent a lot of time at the jail farm in Porterville, California. That institution abutted the vast wilderness lands of the Sierra Nevada ranges. In his walks around the farm, Cleve noted that it was teeming with the same animals he'd trapped in Oklahoma. Cleve somehow persuaded his jailers to allow him to trap fur-bearing and nuisance animals in the area. If an animal's skin had value, Cleve would cure and prepare it for sale. Any proceeds went to the county. For his portion of the deal, Cleve got to be in his beloved outdoors.

Cleve's jailers outfitted him with traps and tools. Among these was a .22-caliber rifle and ammunition. That last tool was crucial to being a good trapper. The fur would be ruined if the animal wasn't killed in a quick and humane fashion. The guards cheerfully sent my grandfather out of the jail with a rifle and bag of traps. Cleve was always given a friendly admonition: "Be back in time for bed check." In today's tightly controlled world, such behavior would be enough to give news anchors days of lead stories. In those times, it gave Cleve Snow the opportunity to trap and skin the largest bobcat ever recorded in the state of California.

I knew my grandfather had trapped a record-breaking animal. Writing this book made me see it another way: Cleve Snow skinned two kinds of cats. I believe that God sends us irony so she can smile.

CHAPTER 6

Earlimart, California

Earlimart is a small town in California's Central Valley, north
of Bakersfield. The town's singular historic moment occurred
when the Dalton gang robbed a train there in the 1890s.

—Tom Liggett's personal glossary of terms

SOME FOLKS WANT TO BE heroes, if only in their own minds. Ruby wasn't
the heroic type. This was not due to a character flaw on her part. It came
from generations of cultural training and reinforcement.

A lot of people seem to have an idealized view of Depression-era women.
In most cases, that vaunted reputation is well deserved. The hardships
Depression-era women endured and the sacrifices they made kept their
families going. They made all futures possible for their families. Most of
them grew backbones of iron.

Women of that era had very little power. Any they did have was generally confined to their homes. But most of them didn't have the material
resources they needed to adequately manage those homes. That circumstance reduced their power even more.

Depression-era women payed an incredible physical toll for their productivity. They did a lot of work. They generally survived on short rations.
Many of them lost a tooth for the children they bore every year or two.

Life was hard for their children too. Many of them died before they were a year old. This strengthened the women's resolve. When you had a gang of hungry children to feed, the past had to be ignored.

In most cases, women from that period went from Daddy's house to their husband's house. They had their physical needs met from cradle to grave. Even though they faced daunting trials, some of those women never quite grew up. Someone else always made the hard decisions for them. Many of those women were quite weak. They never developed a true sense of individuality. They were kept women. Since before we all came down from the trees, that's how a lot of men have wanted their women: compliant and uncomplaining.

Get a group of heterosexual men alone together for more than thirty seconds and the topic will inevitably land on women. With the cowboys I knew, lots of those conversations culminated with the same one-liner: "Women are best kept barefoot and pregnant." Now, since the males in the group laughed, that statement was generally taken as a joke. But it was not a joke. That sentiment was an important part of the suite of oppressive behaviors that were ingrained in their cultural DNA.

Men made sexist jokes in the presence of their male children. This reveals the true nature of their methods. Those old cowboys were depending upon the known value of oft-repeated phrases as tools for indoctrination.

I have been around many families in cowboy country. Each of them usually had at least one weak woman of that generation in its midst. If someone else paid the freight and protected them from the big bad world, such women generally stayed their courses for a lifetime. I call that type of women "cowboy concubines." Their husbands and fathers were their imperial keepers.

There's a masculine side to that concept. Every weak woman I ever met had a glowering buffoon who kept her under his thumb. But it's curious to note that those men were made eunuchs by their insecurities. They were hobbled by the effort of being macho all the time.

Even in a world of powerless women, my poor grandmother was counted as an exceptional weakling. Her indoctrination made her docile and uncomplaining. Ruby's passivity and laziness allowed her to willingly accept what came her way. Perhaps that was her only viable course of action. In that place and time, she had no possible futures beyond the childbed, cook stove, and laundry kettle. She did her job with efficiency but little cheer.

Ruby Stewart Snow Holder Tomlinson. Even in a world of powerless women, my poor grandmother was counted as an exceptional weakling.

Ruby's babies arrived about every two years. In practical terms, this meant that a four-year-old could change diapers for subsequent arrivals.

The family lived on beans, potatoes, biscuits, gravy, and corn bread. Some of you might note that the first three items on that list were developed by Native Americans. Many people in my family still love those foods. But Ruby's children complain that she served them twice a day, every day without variation.

It was not lost on my mother that other families lived in similar conditions. Drunken men were commonplace in 1930s California. My mother used her observation of how other families lived to come to some harsh conclusions about her own. She saw that other impoverished women cooked a variety of foods.

That's not as tough as it might appear. The meanest labor-camp hovel generally had a patch of dirt out back. These were provided by the ranch manager as garden spots for farm workers. Many contemporary women grew a garden to provide what they couldn't afford to buy. Many of them canned produce for their families to eat in the winter. Not Ruby. She set a bare-minimum standard for her home. Ruby ran her home with mechanical efficiency. Any variation from her fixed routine or menu usually indicated that somebody had screwed up. Woe be one of Ruby's kids who did that. She was instant with her invective and free with her switch.

My mother told me that before the family went out as a group, Ruby lined her children in a row. She checked their clothes, shoes, and fingernails. Ruby then explained to her children what was expected of them where they were going.

That type of inspection was common in that time and place. But Ruby departed from convention at that point. She sometimes gave each child a spanking. This was for "what you are going to do when we get there." Two of my grandmother's children told me that story, word for word. It must be true.

Ruby took the safe path, but her children paid for that lack of industry. Some might well say that it was because she lived with her mother, Mary Elizabeth Stewart, for much of her life. Those keen students of history among you might recognize that she shares a name with Mary, Queen of Scots. That legendary sister of Queen Elizabeth I had nothing on my great-grandmother in terms of being formidable. It is apparent to me that Mary Stewart was the last real Indian woman in my mother's family.

I truly believe Ruby wilted under her mother's eternal, piercing stare. But I can't entirely attribute my grandmother's behavior to Mary's influence. That is too easy. I think that my maternal grandmother was lazy by nature and overwhelmed by her life.

Lazy or not, who wouldn't be overwhelmed by her circumstances? After Ruby came to California, she moved from place to place with Cleve's jobs. In a relatively short time, the family lived in a tent, a railroad boxcar, and too many old houses to mention. The boxcar was the best of their homes. It was insulated to carry cold freight.

As usual, Ruby made light of her situation. She said, "At least in California, there were no winter storms to blow the newsprint wallpaper off."

In 1946, Ruby was thirty-four. She was the mother of six minor children. Ruby was in a real pickle. It was nearly impossible to raise a large family on the unreliable wages of a drunk.

Cleve continued to bounce in and out of jail with predictable regularity. Finally, the Earlimart justice of the peace called my grandmother into his office. He wasted no words when he spoke his mind: "Ruby, Cleve is getting out of jail. Take those kids and get out of town before he gets home."

The stage was set. My grandmother was on the cusp of accomplishing the one great heroic act of her lifetime.

CHAPTER 7

Pacheco Pass

RUBY KNEW THAT CLEVE WAS getting out of jail. He loved his children. Cleve would have raised high holy hell if he found Ruby preparing to move. She needed to quickly get a lot of distance between her and Earlimart, California.

My grandmother had relatives in Campbell, California. They said that they would help if she could get there. Ruby had five minor children to transport. Mary Stewart was coming too. They each had things they would need in their new home. That's a lot of people and a lot of things.

No one offered to transport Ruby and her family to Campbell. Times were tough for everyone in their circle.

Ruby decided that she would drive her old Chevrolet to Campbell. I don't know the year or model of that car, but those details are irrelevant to this story. What did matter was that Ruby's car had no brakes. Oh, it had a brake pedal. But that device did nothing. It just sat there on the floorboard. Neither the main or emergency braking system on Ruby's Chevrolet functioned. There was no money to repair them.

Most people would not consider driving a car that had no brakes. Not Ruby. She spent her entire life doing without things other people thought were essential. In Ruby's mind, brakeless cars and poor food came out of the same trick bag.

Ruby borrowed a utility trailer to haul the family's belongings. She loaded everything and everybody up into their pitifully small set of conveyances. Trailer and car alike were packed solid. It was time to go.

Ruby didn't spend much time looking in the rearview mirror as she drove away. That was a snapshot of her past. Ruby had 250 miles of problems ahead of her. By American standards, that distance doesn't sound like much. But by California standards, it is one of the most dangerous journeys. That's saying a lot.

California is covered with mountains and hills. Trips of any length are measured by the number of mountain passes that must be traversed. Ruby only had to cross one pass in her overloaded, brakeless, trailer-towing car: Pacheco Pass.

Pacheco Pass measures in at just 1,368 feet. That's not very high. But the grades are long and steep. They tangle around the curves of the aptly named Diablo ("devil") range. The winds that blow on the eastern side of Pacheco Pass are hellish in their proportions.

Pacheco Pass Road is still narrow and dangerous. In my grandmother's day, it wasn't much more than a wagon road. It carried a huge amount of car and truck traffic. Pacheco Pass is the main route between the San Joaquin and Santa Clara Valleys. It is still one of the most dangerous highways in America. It was far worse in 1946.

I loved to hear my grandmother tell of her epic drive over Pacheco Pass. For me, it was like hearing a favorite song. I never grew tired of hearing the tale. In typical fashion, Ruby made light of her journey. By her reasoning, it was akin to eating nothing but potatoes. It was just something that she had to do.

When I pressed Ruby, she grudgingly provided me with more details of the drive. She said, "I kept it in low gear all the way down. When I got to goin' too fast, I brushed up against the mountains on the side of the road." Wow! Put yourself in Ruby's seat for a moment. Imagine what it was like to initiate a long series of controlled crashes into native mountain rock to slow down a car and trailer. Imagine doing it with a car full of terrified, screaming children. Could you accomplish that? Ruby did.

Ruby and all hands made it safely to Campbell. Her life with Cleve was buried in the dust of the San Joaquin Valley. He would not live with Ruby or his children again.

CHAPTER 8

29 Gilman Avenue

THE FINE DETAILS CONCERNING WHAT happened next to Ruby and her family are a little fuzzy. Part of this is because the events transpired before I was born. In a larger sense, the mystery derives from a simple concept: folks who lived through those times didn't subsequently care to speak about them. Their overriding sentiment was a good one. They had good reason to forget they'd lived through a shocking, tawdry, and shameful series of events.

Ruby's sister was named Gladys Pierce. She bore a bunch of kids with her husband. They divorced. Gladys received a decrepit house in Campbell, California, in the resultant property settlement. It was located on the corner of Gilman and Campbell Avenues. A few years later, MT journeyed to that house to buy sex. Gladys was the prostitute he expected to meet.

A few years before that pivotal event occurred, Ruby and her children moved in with Gladys. My great-grandmother Mary Stewart was there too.

Ruby divorced Cleve. She was a single woman for the first time in her adult life. Ruby was in her mid thirties. She wanted to have some fun. Ruby found an able companion with Gladys. I have heard they went to bars and night clubs as frequently as possible. Partying was the medium by which Gladys secured most of her tricks.

Ruby sometimes provided me with small hints about what went on during her wild times with Gladys. My grandmother was a very earthy person. She repeatedly mentioned the antics of one of her more ardent suitors. Ruby

Gladys Pierce and her friend Mae Benzler at Stevens
Creek Reservoir. Date unknown.

said that the man "fell in love with me the first time he ever seen me. Before I knew it, he was a-drinkin' champagne out of my shoe."

Wild But in 1940s America, it was a rare thing. The birth control pill hadn't been invented. A fair percentage of women got pregnant when they had sex. That dynamic generally held relations between the sexes on a respectable level.

Gladys escaped the fate of having an undesired, post divorce child. Ruby wasn't so lucky. At the age of thirty-six, she had a brief relationship with a no-account man. She became pregnant. A temporary marriage avoided bastardy for my grandmother's last child.

Ruby quickly divorced the last child's father. He was never seen again. He paid no child support to Ruby. Things went from bad to worse for my grandmother. In that age, divorces were exceedingly rare and shameful. Ruby had two of them under her belt by the time she was thirty-seven.

In 1948, Ruby and her family were still living in Gladys's house. As far as I can determine, about eighteen people lived in the place. Several more of my relatives lived in a ratty camp trailer that was parked in the backyard.

Ruby didn't work. Her mother, Mary, didn't work. Gladys didn't work. Well, on the face of it, that last part is technically wrong. Gladys did get money from her clients. But she immediately spent those earnings with Ruby in nightclubs. Gladys probably thought that she was plowing money back into the family business.

Great. Ruby and Gladys got plastered on alcohol in bars. They then got plowed by the strange men they picked up. I guess that the women in my family were a real bunch of farmers. But there was a problem in the deal: they were on the wrong end of the plow.

Ruby and Gladys were having a good old time. But their chosen lifestyle was rough on their families. Between them, the two sisters had about ten or twelve minor children. They ranged from infants to teenagers. That nightmare of a home had more kids than it did shoes, socks, or underwear. Fistfights determined which boy would wear underwear or socks to school on a given day.

It was bad for the boys but worse for the girls. Women sometimes synchronize their menstrual periods with other women with whom they closely associate. That is precisely what happened with the girls in Ruby and Gladys's extended family. That caused a lot of problems for the girls.

None of the adults who were living in Gladys's house was willing to buy underwear, shoes, or socks. They damned sure weren't going to buy anything as frivolous as sanitary napkins. This meant four or five high-strung, combative white trash/Indian girls were contending for any textile scraps they could find. The girls settled matters in similar fashion to the boys: with fistfights.

Sleeping arrangements for the children of that family were no better than their wardrobes. Sleeping four to a bed was the norm. Two people slept on one end of the bed and two slept on the other. Someone's feet were always in someone else's face. It didn't make for a peaceful night's sleep. The children who endured those times never got accustomed to the experience.

Three adults lived in Gladys's house. None of them worked for wages. My great-grandmother prayed, read the Bible, and listened to gospel radio. Ruby and her slut of a sister lazed in the house during the day and partied at night. None of the adults in that household was willing to step up and do the right thing.

In cowboy culture, the eldest female child was usually called upon to fill the gaps for overburdened or lazy adults. But that wasn't a viable option in this case. Ruby's eldest surviving child, Marilyn, was sullen and petulant. Worse yet, Marilyn took after her own mother; she was insufferably lazy. That set of attributes made Marilyn worthless as a candidate to be Ruby's fervently desired house slave and diaper nurse.

When Ruby moved to Campbell, that option had already been removed anyhow. Marilyn was just thirteen when she married a much older and decidedly strange man. She got the hell away from Ruby and her brood of needy children.

That left my future mother, Lita, as the de facto eldest child. If you are keeping score, you might note Lita was Ruby's third child. This indicates that the order of birth for caretaker children is not that important. To qualify for that role, such people just need to have their wits and be female.

My lazy grandmother displayed cynical, prescient forethought when she selected and trained Lita to be her personal slave. My mother frequently advised me about the fine details of that indoctrination. When Lita was six, Ruby taught her how to wash dishes. Lita was too short to reach the sink, so Ruby put the dishpan on the seat of a kitchen chair.

On the face of it, my grandmother's reasoning was simple. She needed someone to wash the family's never-ending cycle of dirty dishes. But the larger component of the job was much more cynical. Ruby was training Lita to be her personal house slave and drudge. "As the twig is bent, so grows the tree" is a saying that has inspired millennia of Christian parents, both good and bad.

When Lita began her dishwashing career at six, she had three younger siblings. At that age, she was already an old hand at changing diapers and caring for babies. But that wasn't enough for Ruby. She kept adding jobs to my future mother's repertoire of hard labor. Before Lita ever saw the inside of a schoolroom, she was stacking firewood, hauling water, washing clothes with a scrub board, and caring for floors. At six, Lita was already an accomplished kitchen helper. She knew that pots of beans needed to be stirred every few minutes. Mess up that operation just once and you'd learn that the beans would scorch. If that happened, Ruby's family would have eaten fried potatoes and corn bread for supper. Lita would have eaten that repast standing up, her ass having been thoroughly blistered by Ruby's switch and too sore to sit on.

At six, Lita was also learning the fine art of biscuit making. To a lot of modern folks, biscuits are quaint little treats that are served on special occasions. But for much of the world's population, they are the staff of life.

Biscuits are a type of quick bread. Quick breads don't require yeast. They are cooked flat (like flour tortillas) or risen with chemicals (like biscuits).

Yeast-risen breads are widely recognized as being the most desirable kind. They are softer, fluffier, and have a better crumb than other types of bread. But yeast-risen breads are much more difficult to produce than flatbreads. Yeast is difficult to grow, use, and save. Yeast-risen breads require much more time, skill, and technology to produce than flatbreads.

That last set of requirements reaches beyond the capabilities of most of the people who prepare food on our harsh planet. Many cooks lack the technology, fuel, or knowledge required to produce yeast-risen bread.

But that lack doesn't change an essential dynamic: cooks must quickly convert raw flour into food for hungry people. Many baseline cooks make flatbread. Wheat flour, salt, and water make a tasty, nutritious flatbread. Corn or barley flour can be substituted for wheat.

Flatbread can be mixed on any flat surface. It can be cooked in an open fire or on a hot rock. That's a big plus if you don't possess baking tools.

If cooks have an oven of some sort, they can move their breads up a notch on the gastronomic scale. They can make biscuits. Wheat flour, salt, fat, water, and baking soda are the universal biscuit recipe. Mix it up in a cast-iron Dutch oven. Knead the dough. Shape the biscuits. Arrange them neatly around the bottom of the Dutch oven. Place it under a bed of hot coals for baking. Julia Child would cry tears of joy.

The white men who kidnapped my Indian ancestors knew how to make biscuits. I can guarantee those men made biscuits whenever they could. They carried the extras around with them until they were eaten. A man on the move loved to have a pocketful of biscuits. They could keep him and his dog going for days.

It would have been natural for my white ancestors to teach their new Indian concubines how to make biscuits. Those guys didn't kidnap Indian women just so they could rape them. They were pragmatic sorts of men. They also needed slaves to do their scut work—like making biscuits. Enter the family biscuit tradition. It carried us into the modern era.

There were better than a dozen mouths to feed in Gladys's house. Biscuits were one of the main foods that went into those mouths. That's a lot of biscuits. Someone had to make them. It damn sure wasn't going to be one of the three lazy women who lived in that place, and no one else was old enough to do the job. That left my future mother to fill the gap. By the age of eleven, Lita was making huge pans of biscuits each day.

My family once possessed two different biscuit recipes. Lita used the one that was taught to her by her grandmother Mary Stewart. It was an ancient method. The Indian way. All of the dry ingredients were placed on a flat surface. A small crater was made in the center of the dry ingredients. Everything was mixed and shaped on the flat surface. The biscuits were baked on a cookie sheet.

The other biscuit recipe was more traditional. The ingredients were mixed in a bowl, then shaped on a flat surface. Mary Stewart believed this method was "frivolous and wasteful." Why? Because it took soap, water, and time to wash the mixing bowl. In her mind, it was thriftier to make biscuits the Indian way.

Mary Stewart also threw in another consideration. She said, "Get used to mixin' your biscuits on a board. Ya don't know when ya ain't a-gonna have yourself no mixin' bowl." Hard times had made her a cautious person.

Lita freely admitted that the appearance of her biscuits was entirely dependent on one factor: time. If she was in a hurry, the biscuits would be large and rough. Lita said, "Big biscuits take less time to make." If a guest was eating with the family, Lita made sure that each biscuit was equal in size and shape. No matter how my mother's biscuits looked, they always tasted like sunshine.

Lita began to do an adult's job when she was about six. Just a few years later, she was working harder than most people of any age. The work that Lita did at home was crushing. But it didn't bring any money to Ruby's perpetually needy family. No one else had the age or gumption to work outside of the home. That left the only hardworking member of the family to fill the gap: my future mother.

Field labor was the only money-making venue that was available to Lita. She looked to the ground for sustenance. Lita knew that Mother Earth provides.

For most of human history, crop weeding was accomplished by one of two methods: bending at the waist or standing on the knees. Both of those activities are extremely debilitating.

The development of lightweight tool steel changed the world of weeding. This was because of that material's use in the common hoe. The hoe is one of the greatest yet most hated inventions. One person with a hoe can quickly weed a large area. Hoes can also be used to accurately thin a whole field of seedlings.

The common hoe has another attribute: it is light enough to be swung by a young child. Children don't work as fast as adults, but there is a ready solution to that problem: bear more children and give them hoes.

Lita was taken into the fields when she was still a baby. There were no day-care centers for poor people in those days. Babies went with their mothers. My female relatives knew that fruit crates made dandy cribs. Lita grew up watching people do farm work. In her eyes, it was a natural thing. As soon as Lita could swing a hoe, she worked in the fields.

Farmers need ways to assure that individual hoers are doing their part. They do this by assigning each worker a row. The farmer can easily determine how long it takes a given worker to complete their row. This is very important if the farmer is paying workers by the hour. They want to get good value for the wage.

But smart farmers know there is a more economical way to accomplish hoeing: pay by the row, not the hour. The workers get paid a fixed wage for each row they complete. For both the farmer and the worker, it's simple concept: hoe more rows and you will receive more money. Hoe fewer rows and you will receive less money.

When workers are hired to work in the fields, they are immediately advised about several things. The first of these is the quantity and quality of the work that is expected for the day. To the worker, the most important part will be how much they will be paid for the job.

Workers on farms and ranches are called hands. Each person is measured as a statistical unit called a single hand. Most people work as single hands. They do the quantity of work that the boss expects from an experienced adult.

When Lita was about twelve, she figured out that she could finish her row twice as fast as most of the adults. Workers and bosses were amazed by the dark-haired little girl with the flashing hoe. Ruby saw dollar signs in the blur of Lita's hoe. My grandmother was never shy about deriving benefit from other people's hard work. Ruby told Lita, "Since you finish your rows twice as fast as anyone else, why not hoe *two* rows at the same time?" Ruby made it seem like a game. Lita wouldn't forge ahead of the work crew. She could stay with the slower hoers and chat while she worked. But by hoeing two rows at once, Lita would get paid twice the usual adult wage for a day's work. Ruby made it sound easy. Lita just had to work twice as hard as a typical adult male farm laborer.

Aside from Lita's age, there was nothing unusual about that concept. Farmers even had a term for that class of chronic overachievers. They are called double hands. Lita took on the mantle and role of that job title with gusto. Cutting apricots or hoeing weeds, she was the wonder of the fields. When she was fifteen, Lita was earning more money than everyone in Gladys's house.

Lita's heroics sustained Ruby and Gladys's families. Her cooking skills and housework made the house a home. Her pay augmented the county assistance that kept the lights on for Ruby's family. Welfare in those days was less generous than it is now. Those were rough times for my mother's family.

The hell house on Gilman Avenue in Campbell was the theater in which the first act of my life would be staged. But it would take a couple of years to assemble the remaining players for our sad melodrama.

CHAPTER 9

Enter Sergeant Bilko

RUBY WAS SICK OF "LIVING in shit." When people get to that point in their lives, they know they must do something different or be trapped forever.

I have seen many people attempt to drag themselves up out of the stink of their messed-up lives. Those who succeeded accomplished the task with consistency and hard work. Some of them joined addiction support groups. Many worked two jobs to pay off accumulated debts. Others decided to make better choices in terms of how they selected their friends and lovers.

Ruby had no problem with the knowledge that something had to be done to solve her problems. The "do" part was the sticking point. Ruby was well trained in her role as a cowboy concubine. The seedbed of her passivity grew a fine crop of indifference. Her unrepentant laziness provided the practice she needed to perfect her sloth.

Ruby was absolutely unwilling to get a job, even though that simple move would have been enough to nudge her family into a better life. But Ruby had other plans. In her mind, there was only one logical solution to her problems: Ruby needed to find another meal ticket. At this point my grandmother became a pioneer. She forged a wide path for her daughters to follow. Ruby dipped her bucket into the well of horny military men.

During World War II, the greater San Francisco Bay area was the main West Coast hub of military activity. Bases, shipyards, and manufacturing facilities were scattered all over the region. One of the largest of these was Moffett Field Naval Air Station in Sunnyvale, California.

In those days, most sailors who were on shore leave didn't have access to cars. They sought their fun in places that were close to their military bases. The cities of the Santa Clara Valley were invaded by sailors and marines. Mountain View, Sunnyvale, San Jose, and Campbell were swarming with horny young men. Those guys had money to burn. Sailors and marines found that the women of the Santa Clara Valley were their willing collaborators. It was one of the most successful friendly fire incidents in history.

Good hunters know that watering holes are the best place to find prey. Sailors and marines gravitated to dance halls and bars. Those places had the three essential elements of every sailor's dream: booze, women, and music. Every cab driver knew where the men wanted to go. Ruby and Gladys frequented the same places. They had a lot of laughs with sailors.

After the birth of her last child, Ruby's partying focus changed. She came up with a whole new plan for her life. Gone were the days of hit-and-run fun. Ruby wanted to find a sailor who would support her and her seven minor children.

Ruby somehow managed to defy the odds. She caught a fairly good man. Royal "Tommy" Tomlinson was the prince and savior of Ruby's family. Yes, readers: Tommy Tomlinson was the man who pimped his sister-in-law to M. T.

Ruby married Tommy Tomlinson in 1948 or 1949. I'd like for my readers to ponder the statistical side of that marriage. It occurred in a time during which divorce was rare. Getting two divorces was unheard of. Ruby got married for a third time, transcending the normal possibilities of late-1940s fiction. But Ruby needed a sugar daddy. She even needed a father figure for her children. Note the order in which I put those two requirements. It is not an accident. Ruby needed someone to take care of her. The needs of her children came last (if at all).

Tommy Tomlinson was a blond, blue-eyed, six-foot sailor from Virginia. He was a very good-looking man. He was also more than ten years younger than Ruby. This is yet another area in which my grandmother was a trendsetter. She was decades ahead of the modern fad that lionizes older women who find succor in the arms of boy toys.

Tommy Tomlinson brought sex, money, and discipline to Ruby's life. Those three things were very important to him. He was apparently free with the sex. Ruby liked that aspect of his personality. Tommy sometimes provided hints about their sex life. Right up to the end of his life, Tommy would hold up his middle finger and say, "This is my hole finger." Ruby would blush. That always seemed strange to me. But then, my family always was open in sexual matters. Any way you cut it, there was no doubt that Tommy Tomlinson floated Ruby's boat.

Tommy Tomlinson wasn't so free with his money. Low-ranking sailors in 1949 didn't get paid very much. The sex organ that Tommy Tomlinson loved brought him eight additional mouths to feed. In that regard, he had a lot of help. The navy paid Tommy Tomlinson an allotment for Ruby and each of her children. He thought that was wonderful. Tommy Tomlinson loved money more than anything. He never really had much of it, but his every action demonstrated his affinity for the stuff.

Tommy Tomlinson rescued my mother's family. He brought more than a few wonderful moments to those who knew him. But through it all, Tommy always seemed to find ways to use money as a torture device. He began that program the day he married Ruby. Lita was the first person in the in the family to feel the sharp end of his avarice.

Lita was still the de facto eldest child in Ruby's family. For people who were raised in old-time cowboy and Indian cultures, that was a big deal. Between puberty and marriage, elder children were expected to take on a full set of adult responsibilities. That course of action had a purpose that transcended helping the family. It was the finishing school that facilitated a young person's transition into adult life.

Lita had been making adult wages since she was about twelve. When Tommy Tomlinson rolled into her life, she began working more and more. On one level, there was nothing wrong with her actions. Heroic people do what needs to be done. Our family needed the help.

But Tommy Tomlinson found a way to turn the kindness of Lita's hard work into a cynical thing. He took 100 percent of her wages. He didn't allow her to keep a single penny. But it was never enough for him. After Lita gave him her pay, he interrogated her about the fine details of the work she had done. Those sessions inevitably ended with accusations that Lita was holding back some of "Tommy's money." No, Lita did not hold back any of her money. She was dedicated to her family.

Sure, she would have liked to keep a portion of her earnings for her own use. But that wasn't going to happen. Not with Tommy Tomlinson. If Lita wanted to buy something, she had to ask Tommy for the money. Nine times out of ten, he automatically said no.

Lita told me of a time when she started her menstrual period early. She went to her secret stash of sanitary pads and found that it was gone. One of the other girls had stolen the pads. She asked Tommy for money to go to the store. Straight up, Tommy refused. She had to explain in detail what she wanted to buy. When Lita told Tommy that she needed to buy some sanitary pads, he started leering at her. He was getting turned on by hearing about her menstrual period.

Lita told me that she pleaded with Tommy for several minutes. She begged him for money to buy sanitary pads. She was playing right into that twisted bastard's hands. He loved to have people groveling at his feet. Why would Tommy do that? Because he was a low-ranking sailor. He had no power in the navy. At home, things were different. Ruby's family depended on Tommy's money for their very existence. Tommy knew that they were helpless. He enjoyed seeing Lita's embarrassment. Lita finally got money for her sanitary pads. But at what price? She paid for them with a part of her soul.

Put yourself in Lita's shoes. Imagine what it was like to be a fifteen-year-old girl who was forced to advise her new stepfather about the fine details of her menstrual period. Worse yet, imagine him leering at you while you explain yourself. Tommy Tomlinson adds definition to the word creepy.

Tommy Tomlinson derived great pleasure from humiliating the weak. But that was what he did for fun. Deep inside, he was a more pragmatic sort. You can bet that somewhere in that little interaction with Lita, Tommy got something in return. You can bet that she ended up doing a scut job no one else around the house would accomplish.

Tommy never gave anything away. He always got something in return. If you asked Tommy for something, he saw it as the opening move of a larger negotiation. When Tommy Tomlinson began his twisted bartering sessions, he sought to gain advantage over his opponent. Since he was generally negotiating with minor children, he almost always got the better part of the deal.

Lita told me that Tommy's negotiations soon took on a more sinister tone. She said that he offered her money or relief from chores if she "did special things for him." I didn't press her on the issue. It was clearly an uncomfortable topic. But she provided me with enough detail to make one thing certain: at the age of fifteen, Lita was providing Tommy Tomlinson with sexual favors of one sort or another.

In later years, Phil Silvers was featured in a popular television show. The main character was called Sergeant Bilko. That man continuously scammed the men in his unit. He took their money and tried to find ways to make other people do his job. When that show came out, Ruby's children couldn't fail to miss the similarities between Bilko and Tommy Tomlinson. Truth be told, they were raised by someone who made Bilko look like an amateur.

Tommy Tomlinson was a Virginia backwoodsman. He grew up dirt poor. He had to work as soon as he could walk. He received little in the way of formal education. He barely managed to learn how to read and do basic arithmetic.

Tommy Tomlinson was among millions of half-starved boys who joined the US military during World War II. He emerged from that conflict scarred but able. Most of the men who served in that war got out of the military as soon as they could. They saw better futures at home. Tommy Tomlinson looked at postwar life from a different perspective. He damned sure didn't want to go back to Virginia. The US Navy was Tommy Tomlinson's ticket to a better life. He decided to make it a career.

The main goal for a man like Tommy Tomlinson was to become a chief petty officer. They are the sergeants that run the navy. Tommy Tomlinson repeatedly took the chief petty officer test. He failed each time. Tommy Tomlinson was not intelligent enough to pass the tests.

He was far more successful at home. Tommy Tomlinson exercised the harsh regimen of a ship's captain upon all who dwelled in his home. He did weekly inspections of the house and yard. He could be counted on to wipe a clean white glove across surfaces to test them for grime. He looked into every outside nook for weeds and litter. If he found a gum wrapper on the ground, someone was in trouble.

Lita bore the brunt of the new standard of cleanliness that Tommy Tomlinson imposed upon Ruby's household. He took full advantage of Lita. He was already eating the food she cooked. He was enjoying the money she earned. But still he ramped up the pressure on Lita. He made her his main servant and house drudge.

But Lita went along with that and all of Tommy Tomlinson's other abusive behaviors. She had better things going, away from home.

Royal "Tommy" Tomlinson. Card cheat, small-time con man, small-time pimp, child molester, tightwad, pervert, bully, all-purpose son of a bitch—and main savior of my mother's family.

CHAPTER 10

Wild Times at Campbell High School

LITA WAS A MAGNIFICENT ATHLETE. She earned two sports letters in the eighth grade. One was for field hockey and the other was for basketball. She said, "I was the shortest girl on the team. I ran right between the taller girls' legs. No one could block me when I went in for the score."

Lita didn't do quite as well in her studies. She was a poor student. She said, "I didn't have time to study. When I wasn't at school, I was working." Well, that statement was partially true. But Lita was also playing. She went on outings with the family.

Lita went on outings by herself. She loved to walk down San Jose-Los Gatos Road to the San Jose Municipal Rose Garden. Lita enjoyed the vibrant beauty of the place. Most of all, she liked to sit on the massive urns that lined the central fountain. The rose garden was Lita's most hallowed place. It remained so for her entire life. She imbued that love in me.

Lita attended gatherings and dances. She was quite popular at parties. Even at an early age, she was the star in a family of great dancers. She spun, leapt, and soared like a ballerina. Every move was right on cue. She could give any dance partner new confidence. She made them look *good*.

Lita played the guitar a little, but she sang like an angel. Others were content to accompany Lita while she sang old-time songs. The room stilled when Lita sang a sad duet with her sister Betty.

Lita always grew quiet when she spoke about the loss of her singing voice. She underwent a botched appendectomy when she was fifteen. The anesthesiologist damaged Lita's vocal cords during the operation. She said, "I ain't nearly as good a singer as I used to be." Ah, Lita, I never thought that you sounded anything less than perfect when you sang.

Lita also swore like a sailor. You might expect she came by that tendency because she was raised around sailors. But that wasn't the case. Lita's father, Cleve Snow, wasn't a sailor, but he had the foulest mouth of anyone I ever met. Swear words quickly became part of young Lita's lexicon.

Early on, that got her into trouble. When she was three years old, she wanted some salt for her food. She asked for the salt shaker, but she used Cleve's words. Lita said, "Hand me that cocksucker, will ya, Ruby?" Ruby beat high holy hell out of Lita for that indiscretion. But it didn't stop Lita from swearing. Especially when she was angry or excited. And Lita got angry a lot.

When she was about fourteen, Lita changed from a lovely child to a voluptuous woman. She developed hourglass curves. Hard work sculpted Lita's perfect little body better than any gym.

At school, home, and parties, men gave Lita a lot of attention. Lita lost her virginity to her cousin when she was about fourteen. She said, "It was a lot of fun. He's a fun guy. I still like him."

Lita's cousin acted as the training wheels on her sexual bicycle. That experience lit Lita's fire. She began to get even more male attention. Some of it came from the men who were attracted to Gladys's de facto brothel. Most of them were soldiers, sailors and marines.

One serviceman fell hard for Lita. On December 12, 1948, he gave her an eight-by-ten-inch photo of himself. The inscription reads, "To Lita with all my love." She was fifteen years, ten months of age. That man was the vanguard of the fawning legions of male admirers who would regularly arrive on Lita's doorstep for the next half century.

Lita reciprocated the attentions of her male admirers. She liked the way they walked. She liked the sound of their voices and the things they said. She liked the way they looked. She liked the way they looked with their clothes off.

I'm going to cut right to the main point about Lita and men: she liked to fuck. That verbiage might come off as being a bit strong for some of my readers. But I don't know a more delicate way to honestly deliver the facts. I won't candy coat the truth. Lita was hot on the street and hotter in the sack.

Yes, Lita was a romantic. She liked to be held, caressed, and cherished. She liked to be courted. But most of all, Lita just wanted to get laid. And not just any ol' fuck, either. Lita was a sexual connoisseur. She liked to have sex with well-endowed men. She wasn't shy in stating that preference. It was a personal characteristic that was to follow her throughout her life, and it caused an unholy shitload of problems.

Lita graduated from the eighth grade in June of 1948. She worked all summer in the fields. Her favorite job was cutting apricots. She said, "I could cut two trays of fruit for any other girl's one." I know she wasn't exaggerating. I saw her accomplish that feat many times.

Lita made a lot of money that summer. But it all disappeared into the greedy hands of Tommy Tomlinson. He refused to give Lita money to buy school clothes. He said, "You ain't grown much since last year. Them clothes still fit. You can wear 'em this year too."

Yes, Lita's clothes did fit. But she didn't own a pair of shoes. She'd worn out her last pairs over the summer. Lita persisted in her assertion that she needed a new pair of shoes. Ruby made light of that fact. She laughed and said, "Gladys has shoes a-comin' out of her ears. You can borrow a pair of hers."

Lita couldn't walk into school barefoot. Her own standards and those of the school wouldn't allow that. Lita borrowed the shoes. But there was a problem: Lita was barely five feet tall. She wore size 4½ or 5 shoes. Gladys was a large woman. She wore size 9 shoes.

Lita wore Gladys's worst pair of worn-out, stretched-out ballerina slippers on her first day at Campbell High School. There was an inch of space between Lita's heel and the rear of the shoes. If she raised her foot off the ground, the shoes fell off her feet. Lita shuffled her way through the doors and down the high school hallways. Lita said, "The other girls sniggered and laughed as I passed by."

The other girls didn't laugh for long. Lita tore them up on the hockey field and basketball court. She was the best player on every team. Years of practice with mops and hoes fine-tuned her coordination and speed.

The folks at Campbell High School rewarded Lita for her athletic prowess. They gave her B team and varsity letters for her efforts on the courts. That's quite a feat for a freshman.

Lita's varsity letter joined its predecessors in her dresser. I have them. They are like new. They were never sewn on a garment. Tommy Tomlinson told her, "You don't need no damned letter sweater."

Lita carried out her war on the laughing girls in another way: she stole their boyfriends. If Lita set her hat for a man or boy of any age, he inevitably succumbed to her charms.

That caused problems with the other girls. One of them wrote an interesting inscription Lita's yearbook: "And I don't hold anything against you about Albert 'cause he's just a happy-go-lucky guy and just went with them all." That same girl went on to gush, "I have had problems about boys and you have helped me in every way you could and I don't know what would have happened otherwise. So let's keep our friendship like it is for always." Wow, Lita. That's a good trick. You stole a girl's boyfriend, and she pledged her eternal friendship to you.

Lita's high school yearbook was filled with notations. Most were of like kind. They read: "Sweetheart of CUHS [Campbell Union High School]. Eyes turn. Heads follow. I get a lump that's hard to swallow??" "Bright eyes. To the prettiest eyes in school." "Here's to that cute little dimple in your left cheek." "To the best-looking girl in school." "I still have a dancing date with you."

Many people wrote about Lita's hot little body. "Dear Loeta I love you in school shorts." Another boy inscribed the photo of a donkey's rump: "When I see one of these [an ass] I think of you."

But I also saw other types of notations. These came from jealous classmates. Three boys signed one inscription, "I don't wish you good luck." Another wrote, "Don't rob anyone's castle." A girl wrote, "Be good to the boys and save some for me."

When I took a closer look at Lita's yearbook, I was able to plot the progress of her convoluted love life. The senior prophecy page was particularly revealing. The listing for one senior said, "Eddie M. will still be dating a cute sophomore." Lita's copy of the yearbook had twenty-two penciled affirmative hashmarks on its margins. That sophomore was obviously Lita.

High school yearbooks take a lot of work to write and publish. It takes the printer a long time to produce the finished books. The printer sets a hard deadline for yearbook submissions. That deadline is usually in March or April for publication in June. That meant Lita and Eddie were a hot item when the yearbook staff sent the copy to the printer.

When Lita's friends, enemies, and admirers signed her yearbook on June 16, things had changed. Yes, at least twenty-two people believed she would end up with the just-graduated senior hotshot. But Lita's yearbook is peppered with inscriptions that tell another story. They read, "Lita, how's the sailor? Keep real good care of him." "To Lita, the sailor's gal." "To Lita, the sailor's special." "Love the sailor?" "To a swell girl. Come back next year." "I'd rather not lose you." "Dear Loeta. I hope to see you again next year." "Come back."

When Lita's yearbook was inscribed in June of 1949, she was obviously thinking of dropping out of school. Everybody on campus must have known. M. T. had arrived. Lita wanted to play wife and lover, not point guard on the basketball team.

But Lita defied the odds and returned to school in September of 1949. She immediately bested all of the accomplishments of her freshman year. A photo in the 1950 yearbook shows a group of girls in action underneath the basketball hoop. The shortest girl has her hands on the ball. That was Lita. The taller girls had a foot in height on Lita. That didn't matter. She jumped up through the other girls and grabbed the ball. You can bet that she scored a goal with that rebound.

Lita surprised everybody in 1949. She decided to become a majorette. She had never done that type of thing before. She said, "That looks easy."

Somebody said, "I'll call bullshit on *that*" and handed Lita a majorette's baton. Folks say it took Lita about ten minutes to master the baton. It took her about a month to become more accomplished than the girls who had been twirling the baton for years.

Lita became the lead majorette for Campbell High School early in her sophomore year. That was quite an accomplishment. Competition for that job was keen. All of the other contenders were older. They had more practice.

But they had no chance against Lita. Generations of ancestral selection had tuned Lita's dancing skills. Those skills were revealed whenever she had a baton in her hand. Lita stunned everyone when she stuffed her perfect little body into her skimpy majorette uniform. She was the prettiest girl in school.

Lita was still living in a tiny, condemned house with about twenty people. She was still working like a dog. But things were getting better. Two more years of public education and she would be ready for a bright future away from the hell house on Gilman Avenue.

CHAPTER 11

Forty Thousand Kodak Moments

RUBY WAS AN AVID PHOTOGRAPHER. She documented family events, when she had money for film.

Lita took Ruby's photographic tendencies to a much higher level. She took lots and lots of photographs. About forty thousand of them still exist. Lita's photographs plot and display the progress of her life. That life revolved around men. There are many, many men in Lita's photographs.

M. T. first appeared in Lita's photographic archives on July 20, 1949. He is depicted with Lita and two other men in a photo set that was taken in Alum Rock Park in San Jose, California.

The July 20 photographs demonstrate a tendency that would follow Lita for most of her life: she always had a potential replacement waiting in the wings. How do I know that? One of the other men who is depicted in that set was besotted with Lita in 1948.

For several years, Lita took that concept a step further. She went on group outings with several men she was simultaneously dating. Some of my readers might find that improbable, but photographic and written evidence proves otherwise. Men would do anything to get next to Lita, even if it meant hanging out with several other men who were currently having sex with her.

Don't ever underestimate the power of a mega beautiful woman, folks. As often as not, she'll be calling the shots. Men can do her bidding—or walk away.

Immediately after that first set of photographs was shot, Lita's other suitor disappeared from the archives. M. T. obviously didn't want the guy hanging around.

Lita definitely didn't want the other guy. M. T. was Lita's sexual equivalent. Every woman of every age who met M. T. instantly wanted to cuddle, chat up, or fuck him where he stood. No joke, folks. The guy was a serious chick magnet.

CHAPTER 12

Beneath a Scented Bower of Apricot Trees

M. T. Liggett's sex-seeking knock on Gladys's front door occurred in July of 1949. At that time, I don't believe M. T. had heard of Helmuth von Moltke. That man sagely wrote, "No battle plan survives contact with the enemy." But the truth of Moltke's words was revealed in what happened when Lita answered the door. M. T. forgot that Gladys existed. Lita became the main objective of his life.

I never asked M. T. or Lita about the specifics of what happened next. I didn't believe that it was any of my business. But I know that on that night or one shortly thereafter, M. T. and Lita took a walk. They wandered through the apricot trees that grew near Gladys's house. The couple eventually ended up along the banks of the Los Gatos Creek. It was the only spot where they could be away from the crush of people in Gladys's house. Somewhere down among the trees, M. T. and Lita had sex. They couldn't have chosen a more romantic spot in which to consummate their relationship. It is a wonderland of water, willow, mountains, and sky. It is redolent with the fragrance of the wild licorice that grows thereabouts.

Lita was on top of the world. Things were going better at home. Her success at school exceeded her fondest expectations. Now she had the topper of all toppers: the most handsome man she had ever seen was on her arm and in her body.

I believe that the problems we face define us as individuals. Gandhi, Lincoln, U. S. Grant, and Flavius the Younger were made great by the troubles of their times.

The next big occurrence in Lita's life defined all of her future problems: she got pregnant. In the way that she solved that problem, Lita was more like Flavius the Younger than U. S. Grant. Flavius destroyed every living thing in a wide swath of Italy. He did this to save Rome. To this day, such actions are called Flavian tactics. Flavius won what is sometimes called a pyrrhic victory. In those cases, the victor is ruined by the circumstances of the victory.

I doubt if Lita ever heard of Marcus Flavius. But I can state with absolute certainty that his methods were not unfamiliar to her. Lita's Indian grandmothers taught her to destroy everything to win a point.

Lita was an unmarried, pregnant, gravely impoverished, sixteen-year-old white trash/Indian girl who was living in a de facto bordello. She knew that Gladys's house did not provide much of a support structure.

In Lita's mind, it got worse from there. M. T. had only been in her life for a couple of months. She barely knew the man. What knowledge she did have about him was not entirely favorable. Lita knew that MT looked like a god. When she first met him, that had been very appealing. But that aspect didn't hold much weight when she was doubled over with morning sickness. Lita also knew that MT had a horrible temper. He was verbally abusive. There were hints that he was unfaithful.

Then there was the bad part. By that time, Lita had been around sailors for years. When they came into her family's life, they made a big noise. Everybody, especially the women, had a rip-roaring good time. Then one inevitable day, the sailor would show up at the house, twisting his cute little white hat in his hands. He would say, "I'm sorry. I'm being transferred. I have to get back to the base by morning."

There would be a last wild party to celebrate the fun and money that he brought. The sailor would eventually get the woman off by herself. In those days, women were less free with their sexual favors than they are now. There was a darned good chance that she had not yet spread her legs for the sailor. But this was his last night in town. He would make promises. She would want to set the hook. The seaman would leave her with his semen.

They would party until the last wild moment. A father or brother would rapidly drive the couple across the valley. Everyone would laugh with delight as the sailor barely made it into the main gate before curfew. The group would exclaim, "We fooled them ol' navy policemen, didn't we?" Ha! Ha! Laughs all round! The girl would get back into the car with her relative. She would blubber all the way home. Her empty room became a cavern as soon as she closed the door.

Lita had seen variations of that story played out with the women she knew. Sailors were good at soothing a woman's loneliness. But they always seemed to leave you alone. Sometimes the guy came back, sometimes he didn't. Sailors made big promises. They also tended to find another woman in the next port.

Lita was in a terrible fix. She had just begun to learn that life could be sweet and fun. She knew the growing mass of cells in her uterus was going to sweep her happiness away. Lita knew that a time bomb was ticking in her body. She had to do *something*.

Lita didn't get much of a chance to decide what she was going to do next. Others decided for her. Tommy Tomlinson made Lita's first decision. He knew about sailors and the "next port syndrome." Tommy told M. T. that he was going to marry Lita *now*. Campbell City Hall was only a couple of blocks away from Gladys's house. Ruby, Tommy, Lita, and MT walked there. My parents got married on November 8, 1949. The ceremony took about three minutes. A somber, abbreviated party finished off MT and Lita's wedding day. All who were involved in the procedure quickly went on with their lives. Everyone had to get up early for work the next day.

Lita and MT moved into a decrepit old camping trailer. It was parked in the backyard of the whorehouse/hellhole where they met. The new couple paid a steep rent for the trailer. The money went to Tommy Tomlinson. "Nobody gets a free ride in *my* house" was one of his favorite refrains.

The trailer was old, cramped, and run down. Life there was rough for the new couple. But the trailer provided them with separation from the main house. It gave them a little privacy.

Lita's next decision was made by others too. She got kicked out of Campbell High School. The official transcript indicates that Lita withdrew from school on November 27, 1949. The official reason states she was going "to Kansas." That was bullshit. Lita didn't go to Kansas until much later. Everybody at school and everybody at home knew the truth: Lita got kicked out of Campbell High School because she was pregnant and married.

That's the way school administrators handled pregnant students in those days. You couldn't have a pregnant Indian running around showing "fertile Myrtle" Croatian girls how to make babies. That shit might be contagious.

One day, Lita was a basketball star and lead majorette in the marching band. The next day, she was called to the principal's office. Lita became the girl who never came back.

Five months after MT and Lita got married, a bizarre event occurred. It was a cynical footnote to my mother's expulsion from Campbell High School. The school band was scheduled to march in the local Founder's Day parade. That was a big deal in those innocent times. The new lead majorette got sick and couldn't participate. The band director contacted Lita. He asked her to fill in as lead majorette.

Ever the worker, ever the pleaser, Lita accepted the offer. My soon-to-be mother was six months pregnant when she stuffed herself into her skimpy majorette's uniform one last time. Lita said, "You couldn't even tell that I was pregnant." She looked like a movie star. I have no doubt that she was the prettiest girl in the parade.

Lita told me that she gave her best performance ever that day. All accounts indicate that she moved liked a ballerina. But no ballerina ever threw a baton like Lita. Looping, twirling, and spinning. The thing looked like a demented airplane propeller in her hand. People said that she could throw the baton twenty feet in the air and catch it behind her back.

Lita told me that story many times. She was quite proud of her accomplishments at the 1950 Campbell, California, Founder's Day parade. It was the pinnacle of her high school experience. But my poor mother was too close to the problem to get the gist of the thing. She didn't see the hook in the worm. When the sons of bitches at Campbell High School expelled Lita, they damned her to a life of second-class jobs. But they had no problem asking her to do one last job for *them*.

There was no operational reason for Lita to be out in front of the band. She didn't lead the players. Somebody else did that. Bands march every day without majorettes or drum majors. Those people are just window dressing. They make bands look classy. Lita added a level of sex appeal to what would otherwise have been a bland occasion. The public display of female flesh was a rare commodity in those days. Any way you cut it, the result was the same: the people at Campbell High School wanted to get one more look at Lita's magnificent little body.

Lita didn't know it, but she was living out an old family tradition. The white men at Campbell High School used the little Indian girl for quasi sexual purposes and then threw her away. Hypocrites will always be with us.

CHAPTER 13

The Lucky Pin

WHEN FATE CALLS YOUR NUMBER, you are obligated to respond. Lita was born in hell. Every day of her life had been lived there. The circumstances of my birth added new chambers to that place.

Military men make lots of babies. Those guys need places where their women can birth those babies. Enter the US military hospital. Those institutions provide top-notch patient care. This is especially true in terms of their obstetrical departments.

Moffett Field Naval Air Station didn't have a hospital. The base had a tiny branch infirmary. The physicians at Moffett Field looked at M. T. and Lita. They got scared. Lita was a tiny Indian girl who was carrying the fetus of a Swiss giant. Remember, M. T. and his twin brother had a combined birth weight of more than twenty-five pounds.

Ever content to play the egotist, M. T. was proud that he had produced a huge baby. He told the doctor, "If you want a big calf, you've got to use a big bull." Well, guess what, asshole? Your supposition *definitely* proved true with me.

But there was a problem with Lita's big calf of a baby: M. T.'s mother was a Swiss giant. She stood six feet tall. She was a mature woman. She had successfully delivered several children before her phenomenal set of twins. But Lita was just sixteen years old. Her body was still growing. Lita barely measured five feet when she was pregnant with me. She was a child who was bearing a child.

By the eighth month, it was apparent that Lita's baby was not going to disappoint M.T. It was going to be large. Lita's obstetrician emphatically asserted that her pelvis was too narrow to deliver such a large baby. She would require a cesarean delivery.

The Moffett Field physician wanted Lita to give birth at Letterman Army Hospital in San Francisco. At that time, it was one of the best hospitals in the world. But there was a problem: Letterman was better than fifty miles away via two-lane surface roads. And no one in my family was willing to drive Lita to San Francisco to give birth. Lita did all for her family but got little in return.

Lita's family convinced her not to have the baby at Letterman Hospital. They said that it was silly to go all the way to San Francisco. Tommy Tomlinson said, "There is a great hospital just about a mile away." Part of that statement was correct. The Santa Clara County Hospital was just down the street. Whether it was great was debatable. No, it wasn't a bad hospital. But was the place of last resort for a wide range of people. Because of this, it was always flooded with patients. In such cases, it is easy for any given patient to get lost in the shuffle. When that happens, the patient receives substandard care.

That's precisely what happened with poor Lita. Her assigned obstetrician at the county hospital was competent—you would expect that at a hospital that hosts a lot of births. The county hospital physician agreed with those at Moffett Field: Lita needed a cesarean section. The county physician told Lita to come back for regular examinations and let nature take its course.

That's not the way it worked out. Lita went into labor a couple of weeks early. Maybe Lita's tiny Indian body knew that it needed to expel the giant baby before it grew any larger. Maybe everyone miscalculated the date that Lita became pregnant.

I believe it was something else. Lita told me that it had been a normal day. She was hanging laundry on a clothesline when the first labor pains hit. There's your clue: Lita was working her ass off. She was taking care of other people. It should have been the other way around. She should have been resting.

Tommy, Ruby, and Lita went to the county hospital. For some reason, Tommy had to park the car a long distance from the hospital. They walked across a plowed field. How fitting for an Indian mother-to-be.

While they were walking, Lita found a diaper pin lying on the ground. To Ruby and Lita, this was an omen of deep consequence. They were both raised with the words "See a pin, pick it up. If it's pointed toward you, you'll have good luck." Ruby looked at Lita and said, "You're going to have a lucky child."

When Lita got to the hospital, she discovered that her obstetrician was on vacation. She was assigned to a physician who had never given her an examination. Lita told the doctor that she was supposed to have a cesarean section. He laughed at her. "You are only in your thirty-fourth week. The baby couldn't possibly be that big. It would be a waste of taxpayer money to provide you with a cesarean section. Be a big girl. Shut up and have your baby."

Lita didn't argue with the physician. She was in too much pain. MT's "giant calf" of a baby was using its head as a battering ram against Lita's girl-sized pelvis. My poor mother went berserk with pain. They left her lying alone on a gurney. Lita screamed her lungs out. She screamed her way through multiple staff shift changes. Lita lost several pints of blood. She was bleeding to death.

After eighteen hours, I emerged. Truth be told, I was ripped from my mother's womb. One physician or the other finally grew tired of Lita's screams. He yanked me out with forceps. They were not shy in the way they used such tools in those days. Every woman from that era grew up hearing tales of babies who were damaged by forceps. I was more fortunate. The county hospital physician was competent with forceps.

M. T. was at work when I was born. He came by later in the day. M. T. said his first sight of me shocked him to his core. My head was not round; it was long and cylindrical. Lita's tiny pelvis had molded my head. M. T.

told me, "I've seen a lot of babies in my life. I never saw one that looked like *that*."

This is how I arrived on the scene. And baby made three.

Myron Thomas Liggett Jr. Daddy's little cowboy. And baby made three. Campbell, California. 1950.

CHAPTER 14

Diaper versus Paycheck

M.T. AND LITA CONTINUED TO live in the backyard trailer for a few weeks after I was born. In an ideal world, a seventeen-year-old new mother who lives at home could expect help from her family. That's not the way it worked out for Lita. Three lazy women and a huge bunch of minor children were still living in Gladys's house. They needed someone to care for *them*. No one wanted to lose my mother's biscuits, housework, or paychecks. After I was born, Lita continued to assume the lioness's role as it pertained to providing support for Ruby's family.

Most mothers don't want to be away from their newborn babies. That kind of separation goes against millions of years of primate conditioning. But Lita wasn't like most mothers. In her brief seventeen years on earth, she had already seen Ruby give birth to six new babies. The last one of them was just two when I was born.

Each of Ruby's babies was immediately given over to Lita's care. By the time of my birth, Lita had been dealing with needy children for fifteen years. In her mind, she had already done enough. She would rather work outside of the home and let somebody else change my shitty diapers.

Lita's mind-set turned out to be an economic boon for Ruby's family. Anybody could change diapers or feed a squalling infant. In that crowd, people who were willing to bend their back to earn a paycheck were a rare breed. The adults in Ruby's family thought it was best to let another family member, rather than Lita, care for the newest brat. This would free Lita to get a full-time job.

All in all, my birth played right into Tommy Tomlinson's hands. Ever the opportunist, he saw it as a way to enhance a proven profit center. Lita could now work longer hours, both at home and away. That greedy miser ramped up his efforts to squeeze every penny that he could.

Tommy Tomlinson made sure that the new couple continued to pay him an exorbitant rental fee for the ratty old backyard trailer. He disregarded the fact that his renters were his struggling seventeen-year-old stepchild and her infant. In theory, Tommy wasn't far off course. I believe that family members should pitch in for the common cause when they live together. But Tommy Tomlinson was a greedy bastard. Lita's work, Lita's money, and the rent from the trailer weren't enough. He found creative ways to get his hand into M. T.'s nearly empty pockets.

Tommy Tomlinson loved to play poker. I have known many sailors who like to play cards. Sailors spend a lot of time in cramped, remote spaces. The men play cards to relieve the boredom. Some men lose lots of money in navy poker games. Some make a lot. The players get a lot of practice.

M.T. was not a gambler. He certainly wasn't a skilled poker player. Tommy Tomlinson knew that. He pressed M. T.'s lack of skill into a personal advantage. On payday, Tommy Tomlinson would approach M. T. He asked M. T. to play "a few friendly hands of poker." M. T. always deferred. He didn't like poker. He knew Tommy Tomlinson was the better player. M. T. didn't want to lose his money.

Tommy Tomlinson wheedled, pestered, and teased M. T. Lita heard Tommy Tomlinson say, "Come on. What are you afraid of? Don't be such a pussy." M. T. resisted Tommy's Tomlinson. But the older, more experienced man pressed on with his poker-seeking entreaties. M. T. inevitably gave in. He played along with the sick little game. Tommy Tomlinson always won. He sometimes took 100 percent of the younger man's pay. M. T. got angry. He knew that he had been duped by a pro.

M. T.'s anger inspired Tommy Tomlinson even more. He laughed in M. T.'s face. Tommy Tomlinson was lucky M. T. wasn't the fighting sort. Lots of men would have punched the cruel bastard in the mouth.

Some of my readers might be thinking, "You were a newborn baby when Tommy Tomlinson did that to M. T. How could you know that those stories are true?" I don't doubt their veracity because Tommy Tomlinson did the same thing to me. Except I wasn't an adult. I was a child when it first happened. It began while I was in elementary school. Tommy badgered me into playing poker. He regularly cheated me out of my lunch money. Lita said that Tommy Tomlinson used the same words on both me and M. T. Uncounted years of missed lunches drove Tommy Tomlinson's life lessons home to me.

Ruby saw what Tommy Tomlinson was doing to M. T. At most, she said, "Tommy, you know that you shouldn't be doing that." But she never made him return M. T.'s money. Hey, Ruby, at what point does weakness become something far more sinister? When does a weak woman become an enabler?

One way or the other, a good portion of my parents' income was going into Tommy Tomlinson's pocket. That made it tough for Lita. She had to work more to make up the difference. But Lita did that very thing. And she did it with remarkable good cheer.

Lita was born a worker. She was relentlessly trained to be one from a very young age. She learned almost any task quickly and did it well. Her compact Indian body was hardened by a decade of manual labor. Lita had incredible stamina. She could work harder and longer than anyone I have met.

Lita was just a toddler when she learned an important lesson: when she did a task well, she received a dollop of appreciation from her family. But on rare occasions when she did not perform to standard, she received instantaneous condemnation from one or more members of her family. Some of this would have been demonstrated by Ruby in the form of corporal punishment.

My mother went back to work a few days after I was born. Most women would find that horrific. Not Lita. From her perspective, it was a good thing. In the workplace, there were no diapers to change.

But what about me, Lita's days-old newborn? I wasn't neglected during that period. I was in good hands. Lita said, "You were like a new doll to the women and girls of the family." I received love and care from everyone.

But in that hyper regimented family, even infants had rules to follow. Babies didn't cry a lot or else. Weeks-old, uncomprehending infants were loudly told, "Stop crying or I'll give you something to *really* cry about."

In later years, I watched some of Ruby's children spank babies on their diaper-clad bottoms. This made me realize they had learned their lessons well. I am quite pleased to report that trait has died out in the subsequent generations of my family.

Toilet training in my grandmother's family commenced at a ridiculously young age. Lazy, overwhelmed mothers didn't want to change shitty diapers for a longer period of time than was necessary. My toilet training began when I was seven months old.

I raised two children. Judging from that experience, I find it to be almost unbelievable that anyone attempted to toilet train a seven-month-old baby. But whole legions of women in my family were willing to speak eloquently on this topic. My grandmother's sister-in-law ("Sis") enjoyed recounting that I was "three months late."

Does insanely early toilet training rate as a new benchmark for familial dysfunctionality? Hardly. It is just another sad indicator of the incredible corporate sickness that once existed in my mother's family.

CHAPTER 15

Follow the Bouncing Ball

IN THE YEARS AFTER WORLD War II, low-ranking enlisted men were transferred quite frequently. Lita followed M. T. to a couple of his navy posts. In between, she lived with Ruby and her family. Moving from place to place is hard on anyone. This was especially true for a couple of unprepared teenagers.

Under the best of conditions, the union between a seventeen-year-old girl and a twenty-year-old sailor/cowboy would be difficult to hold together. M. T.'s antics made it impossible. Lita seldom spoke of the brief time she spent with M. T. She spoke even less of his faults. Lita always said, "You'll figure it out for yourself."

M. T. wasn't around my mother's family long enough for anyone to know him well. Ruby knew him best. But she only said, "The more you stir shit, the more it stinks."

I received a few hints from other relatives. They said that M. T.'s temper was more incandescent than Lita's. It was fueled by raging jealousy. I have always been amazed by men who marry beautiful women and then drown them in a tide of jealousy. Some things never change.

Lita and M. T. lived together for a just few months. That was time enough for my mother to lay the foundation for two hideous trends that would follow me around for the rest of my childhood. The first of these was easy to understand. Lita moved from apartment to apartment with amazing rapidity. Since she was married to a sailor, that was explainable.

But Lita looked at her moves from a more pragmatic standpoint. When my mother lived with Tommy Tomlinson, she was forced to give him 100 percent of her pay. She had to beg for the return of a portion of her own money for the things she wished to buy. That gave Tommy Tomlinson a lot of power over Lita.

When my mother lived on her own, she didn't have to pay Tommy Tomlinson. He lost his power over her.

When Lita was home, she did a long list of domestic chores. She accomplished these under the unerring gaze and harsh invective of two generations of angry women and a power-hungry sailor.

When Lita worked outside of the home, she found a partial escape from domestic labor and criticism. When she lived elsewhere, she was free of her mother's endless list of chores. Those considerations were enough to make Lita want to live on her own. This was especially true when M. T. was stationed elsewhere. This is one of the reasons Lita moved around so much. From apartment to apartment, in and out of Ruby's house. Back and forth she went. It was the ol' Lita two-step.

Rents in the Santa Clara Valley were much lower in 1950 than they are now. This allowed Lita to find affordable housing. She had plenty of money to live a decent but Spartan life. Lita knew that she would be all right. She knew how to stretch her money.

Lita received her financial training from Tommy Tomlinson and Ruby. She knew what was important. Before I was born, Lita had already learned an important concept: money that was spent on rent, food, and babysitters was money that could have been spent on clothes, parties, and cigarettes. She applied that lesson with chilling efficiency.

Lita died when I was sixty-three. A few days before her death, she told me a story that brought the circumstances of my childhood into sharp focus. The story began innocently enough. Lita told me how she learned to bake cakes while working in a bakery in Mountain View, California.

Lita spoke briefly about the fine details of cake baking. She then got to the main point of her story: Lita liked the people who ran the bakery. They loved her. Everybody loved Lita. Lita said that the bakery job was perfect for her because it was "just a few blocks from home." Why was that important? Because Lita could go home at lunch to visit me.

Lita's last story to me was quite revelatory. Before I heard its fine details, I never quite grasped an important aspect of my childhood. I was just a few months old when Lita began her job at the bakery. I always knew that I spent most of my childhood alone. It was an inescapable fact. Lita's bakery story made me realize that sick trend began much earlier than I previously thought. It is the harbinger of the lifelong neglect my mother visited upon me. Thus was wrought the second hideous trend of my childhood.

Over the years, I repeatedly heard Lita tell others about her job at the bakery. To Ruby's family, it is just one of many tales in the epic saga of the heroic Lita, the woman who sacrificed all for her undeserving, semester child.

No one in my family ever realized what it was like to be in on *my* part of the deal. Imagine being an infant who spent uncounted hours in an unheated apartment. I lacked food, water, or affection. I spent at least four hours in a dirty, festering diaper.

I have no direct memory of that time. But Lita regularly reminded me about what had transpired. She wanted me to know how fortunate I was to have her as a mother. Year in, year out, Lita persisted in her narrative. Too bad she waited sixty-three years to deliver a semi honest punch line.

Lita told me that she and M. T. agreed on very little during that period. But they found common cause about me; they said that I cried incessantly. M. T. said, "You cried more than any baby I ever saw."

Considering the circumstances, who wouldn't cry? Most of the time, I was locked away in a quiet room, all alone. That was the good part. At irregular intervals, my solitude was punctuated by Lita and/or M. T. Lita told me they yelled at each other all the time. This inevitably caused me to start crying.

My screams gave M. T. an excuse to complete his anger. Lita said he screamed the same phrase at me over and again: "Shut up, shut up, shut up!"

That course inevitably failed. This angered M. T. even more. Lita said that he would swing his clenched fist down at my face, then pull his punches at the last moment. Lita said, "I never saw him actually hit you. I wouldn't have allowed *that*."

Lita always added that last detail to make herself look good. When I was young, it offered consolation to what would have otherwise been a sad story. The experience of years has allowed me to finally ask a rhetorical question: What did M. T. do to me when you weren't around, Lita?

I cannot remember anything about the early imprinting that I received from M. T. and Lita. But I'm certain that it made an impact upon my developing psyche. Any way you cut it, those times introduced the prime concept of my childhood: I learned to depend upon my own resources to provide what I needed. Some of those needs were pretty basic. Like maternal love.

I'd like for my readers to think back on their own early years. In everyone's mind there is a word or phrase that can be identified as being one's earliest recollection. Let's take that concept a step further. What are the first words you remember your mother saying to you? I can clearly remember Lita's words. They were spoken when I was about two. Some folks believe that is too early to remember anything. I counter that it's hard to forget a raging force that is screaming, "You ruined my life by being born!"

That's a heck of a revelation for anyone to absorb. I don't remember the words themselves as being terribly distressing. I must have heard them many times before. Everyone around me made it clear that my arrival added an unwanted complication to Lita's life. In my mind, it was just another operational detail. I knew that I had messed up by being born.

From my perspective, this sad situation wasn't as bad as it might seem. That is because I didn't really understand the concept that Lita was my mother. I knew that she was my birth mother, but that detail didn't mean very much.

When I was very young, Lita provided the rhythm for my life. You know, the drumbeat that sets the pace for a song. But the melody was being carried elsewhere. By Ruby.

During my first four years, Lita and I lived with Ruby and her family about 75 percent of the time. I lived with six of Ruby's minor children. I am just a couple of years younger than her last child. My aunts and uncles were like siblings to me. They called Ruby Momma. So did I. That wasn't much of a stretch. Ruby provided more of a mothering influence than Lita. I was told ten thousand times over the course of my life that I was "Momma's last child."

Ruby's family called my mother Loeta or Lita. I emulated them in that behavior too. Lita blended in with her siblings. She got lost in their crowd. It was a great crowd.

Many factors were involved in the devaluation of Lita's status as a mother. Hunger was one factor. My grandmother's family had lots of mouths to feed. There was a shortage of people living in our home who would or could bring home the bacon. Lita continued to work long hours away from home.

Housework was another factor that prevented Lita from taking an active role in my early life. When Lita lived in Ruby's house, she spent her time cooking, baking, or cleaning. The same people who couldn't or wouldn't be motivated into working didn't wander much in the direction of housework, either.

Lita and I shared a narrow cot for sleeping. It was a comfortable arrangement. Lita didn't need an alarm clock to get her out of bed. She had her grandmother Mary to do that. I grew accustomed to being awakened at an obscenely early hour by Mary's voice. That woman could be counted on to loudly bark out the same one-liner each morning: "Lita, get up and make the bread!"

Mary didn't have to yell at Lita more than once. Lita also didn't have to respond. Mary knew that Lita was fully trained in her role as house slave and all-around drudge. It was a given that Lita would speedily carry out her assigned tasks. There would be no complaint. Therein lies the value of early imprinting and an apt student.

My poor mother quickly got dressed in the dark. If she turned on a light, it might awaken someone else in the overcrowded house. Lita went into the kitchen to make biscuits for at least ten people. After the biscuits were in the oven, Lita would steal a few moments to fix her hair and apply makeup.

When the biscuits were done, Lita would put them on the table and call the family to eat. If she was running late, Lita wouldn't have the time to eat with the family. She would grab a biscuit, put it in her pocket, and head out to work. Biscuits—the traveling food of my ancestors. Lita was the last in her line to carry that long tradition.

From the moment I was born, the die of all my possible childhood futures was cast. My life revolved around Lita's jobs, housework, partying, and men. I was quite young when I came to an inescapable conclusion: anything I requested from Lita would take her away from her other activities. I knew that any care I received from her would be brusquely and reluctantly given.

CHAPTER 16

Thank You, Edna, Part One

WHEN I WAS A FEW months old, Lita and I stayed with my paternal grand-parents, Wilbur and Edna Liggett, in Kansas. All accounts indicate that they were entranced with my mother.

While we were staying in Kansas, I contracted whooping cough. At that same time, a huge blizzard descended upon the family farm. It was obvious that we would be snowed in for days. There was no way anyone could drive a vehicle through miles of drifted snow to take me to the nearest hospital thirty-odd miles away.

I was almost dead, but Edna Liggett wasn't willing to let me go eas-ily. That brave woman pulled together every bit of her determination and knowledge to save me. Edna placed my crib next to the kitchen stove. She used blankets to enclose my crib. The crib became a tent. She piped steam from a teakettle into my crib. Edna stayed by my side for days. She stoked the cow-turd fire to keep the kettle steaming.

Physicians later told Lita that under those primitive circumstances, it was the very best thing that could have been done for me. Edna's knowledge and heroism saved my life.

CHAPTER 17

Nobody's Right If Everybody's Wrong

Nobody's right if everybody's wrong.

—*Buffalo Springfield*

LITA WAS AN AVID COLLECTOR of romantic mementos. She saved the cards and letters she received from her lovers. There was also a very surprising set of letters from another source. Some of the material is mind blowing.

Between June and December of 1951, M. T. wrote a series of letters. He was aboard the USS *Bon Homme Richard* in the Asian Pacific.

Three of letters are addressed to Lita. One is to me. In the letters, M. T. repeatedly calls himself "your honeyman." He uses the terms "darling" and "dearest darling" an average of five times per very short letter. It was the same with his use of the word "love." Taken at face value, there is no substance to the letters M. T. sent to Lita and I. It was pure fluff. The type of sentiment that can be found in a dime-store greeting card. Polite, brief, and banal. Nothing in those letters deserves direct repetition here.

But M. T. revealed something important in one of his letters to Lita. He was broke. M. T. wrote, "Darling, I have to borrow stamps to mail this with." Why was M. T. so broke he didn't have six cents to mail a letter? He certainly wasn't spending his money on Lita. Ruby and Lita agreed that when M. T. was away on ship, he didn't send any more money than the navy required. M. T.'s other letters provided the answer to *that* question.

M. T. had a twin brother named Byron. From what I can determine from old photographs, Byron was the more handsome. Anyone who ever saw M. T. in his youth might disagree—until he or she met Byron Liggett.

Byron Liggett, M. T.'s twin brother, with an unknown woman. Was Byron better looking than M. T.? Note the enraptured look on the woman's face. The caption reads, "Outside of Children's Hospital, San Francisco. Visiting Jody." Date unknown. Byron was also a sailor. He somehow managed to court and marry a very wealthy young heiress named Jody. Jody and Lita quickly became best friends. Everybody loved Lita.

M. T. wrote a letter to Jody Liggett, and Jody forwarded it to Lita. From my biased perspective, it appears as if M. T.'s letter was a feeble attempt to explain his way out of a series of problems. Read on to see if you agree.

Dec 5, 1951
Yokosuka Japan
Hi Jody
I just borrowed a couple of sheets of paper from a buddy & decided to write a few lines. I do like that you guys are not mad at me for

kinda upsetting the plans of you meeting me in San Diego. I am sure it will be a lot better to work it this way. The ship won't get in till the afternoon of the 16th & my leave will not start until the next morning. I can be at your house that evening. I know it would be a lot of trouble for everyone. The ship might arrive late since we are not leaving until tomorrow. Please try to explain to Loeta. I know she will feel kinda bad over it. I am so anxious to see her. I am almost counting the hours now. I guess I am really crazy over her.

About the date with the red head (Mary J.). I don't know rather I answered your questions in my last letter to you. The only woman I will ever be interested in is Loeta. She seems to be everything I have ever dreamed of. Sounds crazy doesn't it, but that is the way it is.

From the way Lita talks to you guys you must really be friends. I am glad you like her. She is a real good kid. You guys do so darn much gabbing she never gets time to write me long letters (just kidding). Your old man says that you & Loeta like to gossip.

Loeta will never have to worry about me being mean to her anymore. I can see I was wrong.

I am so darned anxious to get home all I do is sit & smoke & think. I don't know what I would do if I had another month over here.

Jody, I really feel bad when I have to tell you not to meet me in San Diego.

Lita must have felt like a bomb went off in her head when she read M. T.'s letter to Jody. The asshole admitted that he'd gone out on a date with another woman. He subsequently stood Lita up in San Diego. Chances are good he wanted to spend a day or two alone in town. M. T. also admitted that he'd been abusive to Lita. He was broke too—had to bum paper from another sailor to write the letter. What a guy.

Sadly, M.T.'s behavior gets worse from here. He sent at least three letters to Byron Liggett during this period. Actually, he addressed the letters to someone named Joe. But the letters were addressed to Byron at the Monterey Naval Air Station. Joe was obviously a pseudonym for Byron.

Jody somehow obtained M. T.'s letters and forwarded them to Lita. M. T.'s letters to Byron reveal the true man. They stand in stark contrast to the pithy letters he was sending to Lita and me during that period.

The October 28, 1951, letter below is the best of the bunch. I have included all the text. Don't worry, gentle reader, you won't be bored. In fact, I'm certain you will be amazed.

Oct. 28, 1951.

Hi Joe

The ship leaves the whole tomorrow & I am sure glad. I am in debt and all I got is the shakes. Sure put on a couple of good bounces [bouts with prostitutes or other willing women]. The whiskey here sure was good but God I sure feel rough.

I swore off the stuff this morning. I am going to quit for good after I & Lita get back together. I think that she [Lita] is all right. Maybe she has fucked up [screwed other men]. But who cares. I goddamn sure ain't an angel. I'll bet I have fucked 50 women since we got married. I ain't got no pick coming. I still don't think Lita has fucked off. She doesn't seem like the type. Joe you know something and won't tell me!!!!!

When you come to San Diego I want you to bring Loeta. I am anxious as hell to see her. I have got 8" of hard cock & I will need some place to cool it.

Joe, I think Loeta is a goddamn good kid. If I am wrong it still will not make me divorce her. I want to see her so goddamn bad. If she isn't in San Diego I will go nuts.

Will close for now

Your brother the future civilian Street Sweeper.

Shore duty pooge

Yuk-Yuk.

A page from MT Liggett's letter to Joe (Byron Liggett). Highlighted
text: "I'll bet I have fucked 50 women since we got married." Written
aboard the USS *Bon Homme Richard*. Asian Pacific. 1951.

Wow! Imagine how Lita felt when she read that and the other letters
M. T. sent to Byron. They were all of like kind. The other letters speak of
whoring, drinking, and riotous bar fights. Taken in aggregate, they paint
a fine mental picture of M. T. as a Jekyll-and-Hyde character. It was pretty
shocking stuff.

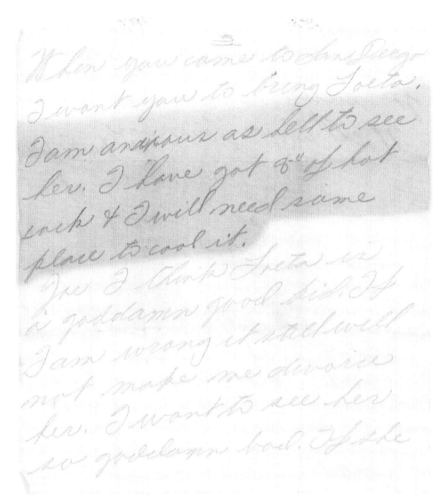

A page from MT Liggett's letter to Joe (Byron Liggett). Highlighted text: "I am anxious as hell to see her. I have got 8" of hard cock & I will need some place to cool it." Written aboard the USS *Bon Homme Richard*. Asian Pacific. 1951.

But look beyond the shock value. Look at it from a pragmatic stand-point. Lita discovered why M. T. wasn't sending more money home. He was spending it on booze and women.

From M. T.'s perspective, the letters to Byron were all fun and games. But two of them also project a sinister tone. M. T. knew that it was over with Lita. M. T. wrote, "She cannot divorce me until I get home." But MT wasn't grieving over the loss of my mother's love and companionship. M. T. had shifted his attentions to me. He wanted to gain sole custody.

M. T. indicated he wanted Byron to hire a private investigator. M. T. wrote, "I need so darn much evidence to get my son. You know how those California courts are." M. T. finished this thread by writing, "I wrote to pop [Wilbur Liggett] and I imagine he will send you some money." Wow! Lita must have felt as if half the people in the state of Kansas were gunning for her.

But M. T.'s letters to Byron introduced another character to our story. His name was Glen H. M. T. also provided Byron with the address of a mysterious house that was associated with Lita and Glen. M. T. wrote, "If you go around there be sure to stay clear of there. Lita and Glen hang out at The Old Corral. "

The name of that tavern set alarm bells off in my mind. I knew a man who spoke fondly of the place. He said it was "rough, but square." It was well known as being a hangout for hookers. Bingo. Was Lita dabbling in the old family trade? Was she selling her hot little ass? That question will never be fully answered. But later hints add tantalizing fuel for speculation.

Lita's archives reveal the answer to another question that was contained in M. T.'s letters: Was Lita hanging out with Glen H.? Yes, she was. More intensely and earlier than M. T. could have ever imagined. Better than a dozen photos of Lita and Glen show a happy, playful, relaxed couple.

One series of photographs from that period is a real doozy. They were taken in April of 1951. The photo series depicts Lita and Glen on a romantic trip to Washington state. The stated purpose of that trip was for Lita to visit MT. But she traveled in the car (and arms) of another man.

One of the photo captions from that series reads, "This is the view from the window of our room at the Anchorage Hotel—Bremerton, Wash. April 18, 1951." That photo is a well-framed shot of trees and water. It was obviously a lovely, romantic view. Another photo shows Lita wrapped up in Glen's arms. That man clearly knew how to hug a woman the right way. You can tell Lita was enthralled.

Glen H., cowboy number two, posing with Lita Liggett. Lita was on her way to Washington state to visit MT. She traveled in the car (and arms) of another man. The caption reads, "Somewhere in Oregon." 1951.

Glen H. didn't last long. He was a blip on Lita's radar. But he marked a milestone in our story: Glen H. was Lita's second cowboy boyfriend. He was cowboy number two.

Glen's letters reveal that he liked to work with cows and horses. You can tell that he loved children. Especially me.

I'm not certain why Glen and Lita broke up. Glen's letters suggest he might have gone home to care for his ailing father.

When Lita told me about this period of her life, she used sad, grave tones. She always mentioned how poor she was. She said, "I had to work all the time just to keep a roof over our heads."

But Lita's photographs tell a different tale. They depict a lovely young woman who is all dolled up. She is wearing trendy clothes and smart shoes.

Silk underwear, 1951 style. Don't be fooled by Lita's shy smile.
She draped herself over the chair like a Siamese cat in heat.

In two photo sets of a similar vintage, Lita is never wearing the same outfit. There are lots of dressy party photos in Lita's archives.

Many photos from that period depict Lita in sexy poses and sexier clothes. Grass skirts. Bathing suits. Silk underwear. Even a nightgown. She uses every person, every object in the photos as a prop or backdrop. She drapes her fine little body on and around everything in sight. She looks like a Siamese cat in heat.

The captions on Lita's photos and her own words belie any claims of dire poverty. She flitted between Washington state, San Diego, Carmel, Earlimart, and the Santa Clara Valley. She was having the time of her life.

Ah, Lita; your lies ran deep. But that statement begs another question: Were you lying to me, yourself, or the world?

Something is missing from most of Lita's glamour photographs: me. In photos from that period, I appear alone or with other family members. By and large, I only appear in photographs with Lita when she is wearing work clothes. That aspect is very revealing about my place in her life. I wasn't a member of Lita's party crew when I was young. Alas, she never altered as I progressed through the various stages of my life. I was doomed to be a perpetual outsider. I orbited Lita's world of fun, family, and friends. But she never allowed me to become an acceptable part of her existence.

M. T.'s purloined letters gave Lita a powerful tool. They allowed her to thwart his attempt to gain custody of me. M. T. finished off that venture in typical fashion: he dropped out of sight. He doesn't appear in Lita's archives for ten months. In October of 1952, he sent Lita a telegram. It read, "Sorry I haven't written explanation follows=Myron=."

That's it. No explanation followed. The man vanished. His money vanished from Lita's pockets too. Why? M. T. got out of the navy when his enlistment was up. No one in authority was standing over M. T.'s shoulder. No one was demanding that he support the mother of his namesake child.

Lita did not miss M. T. She didn't care if M. T. didn't visit me. It bothered Lita that M. T. refused to pay child support. It bothered her that M. T. wouldn't give her a divorce. Beyond that, my mother was pleased the angry, womanizing asshole was gone.

Lita was nineteen years old. She was still the prettiest girl in every grocery store, apricot-drying shed, and dance hall in Santa Clara County. What am I saying? Her beauty hadn't begun to reach its peak. She was getting prettier every day.

Lita was ready for action. When she wasn't working, she wanted to party. Tommy Tomlinson came to the rescue. He brought servicemen from Moffett Field Naval Air Station to Ruby's home. They were his drinking buddies. Those guys brought their buddies too. Life was a big party for Ruby, Tommy, and Lita.

Men sometimes paid Tommy Tomlinson to introduce them to Lita. Her beauty and hot-blooded reputation were well known by the men at Moffett Field. Everyone seemed to be looking a way to get next to luscious Lita (and her equally luscious sisters!).

Lita told me about Tommy's bribed introductions. She mentioned them with pride. Maybe even a nostalgic tear or two. Lita didn't seem to mind that Tommy Tomlinson was pimping her out on one level or another.

Tommy Tomlinson's minor-league pandering played right into Lita's hands. Lita always needed to have a throng of willing admirers waiting in the wings. When Lita's main actor took a dive, one of the understudies stepped into the big role. He became Lita's main guy. Wow! That was heady stuff for any heterosexual man.

Lita's next boy toy lasted longer than his predecessor. He was in her life for over a year. His name was Bill W. More photos of Bill exist than any of Lita's early lovers combined. Bill and Lita at the beach. Bill and Lita at Stevens Creek Dam. Bill and Lita in a smokin' hot studio pose. Bill with Lita's family at Christmas dinner.

The look on Bill's face in Lita's photographs makes one thing clear: he thought he had the deal locked up. The man thought that he and Lita were a forever thing. Sadly, Bill W.'s photographs also reveal another fact: he was short. Lita didn't like short men. She liked tall, wiry cowboys.

But something else finished the man: Lita told me, "Bill had a little bitty winkie." When Lita delivered that last line, she held up her hand, wiggled her little finger, and laughed. Ah, Lita. You damned more than one good man because of *that* conceit. You always went for the sizzle more than the steak. Big mistake, girlie. Big dicks will thrill you, but they seldom buy the groceries.

Lita's other photographs and letters reveal that she never stopped cowboy shopping while she was dating clueless Bill. Men came and went from her circle, but Bill remained—for a time. Meanwhile, Lita needed him to

Bill W. was a lot of fun, but he was short. Lita liked 'em
long and lean. Santa Cruz, California. 1953.

pay the tab for her parties. She needed a good dancing partner. She played
Bill for a sucker.

Lita's social activities were like a drug. She was chasing an endless high
of emotion and orgasm. But every drug has side effects. Even those of the
romantic kind.

Lita cycled through six beaux before the end of her freshman year in
high school. She told me that was true. Her archives reveal that she was
seriously involved with at least six men between 1951 and 1954. All of them

were infatuated with Lita. All of them wrote spicy anecdotes on the letters and photographs they sent to her. Some of the guys were still writing to Lita years later. After she had left them in the dust.

Where am I going with that last thought? Each of those men went to Lita's home when they were dating. None of the men were happy when Lita cast them aside in favor of a new arrival. I know how guys think. Some of them undoubtedly wanted a second chance with Lita. You know that some of Lita's cast-off lovers went to her home to beg for reconciliation. Men knocked on her door at inconvenient times. Just for the record, *any* time is inconvenient to receive an unannounced visit from an ex-lover.

But Lita created a vicious cycle. Lita didn't have a car. Each new paramour picked her up at home. As soon as Lita didn't want to see his face at her door, she moved again.

Lita had a lot of lovers. She moved at least thirteen times between 1950 and 1955. She undoubtedly didn't initiate all of those moves to escape her lovers, but most involved men in one way or another.

Lita's ex-lovers acknowledged her frequent moves in their letters. One of them wrote:

Dear Loetta
I really don't know how to start this letter. I hope you won't get mad at me but I got your address from someone on Sunday night. You said you would keep in touch with me. I don't know if you really meant it or not but I can't wait to hear from you. I meant every word I said to you that night.

He goes on to state, "I am crazy about you and always have been." That man finished his letter in stunning fashion: "Oh I hope I spell your name right and I'm using your maiden name because I don't know what name your going by."

The rest of the guy's letters indicate that he and Lita "had a real good time." Lita hauled his ashes before he knew her name. She then dumped the guy and moved to another residence.

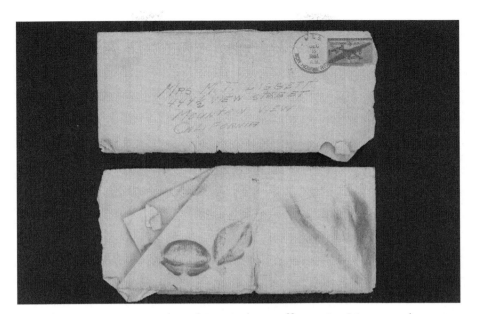

MT was in a war zone, launching airplanes off a carrier. Lita was at home using his letter to blot her lips so she could kiss another man's lips— or something else. USS *Bon Homme Richard*. December 30, 1951.

A good while later, the dumped guy's letter appeared at Lita's new apartment. Odds are he appeared soon after. Lita couldn't afford a telephone. He couldn't call ahead. The guy might have just shown up at her home. That might have precipitated another change of residence for Lita and me. What a vicious, heartbreaking cycle for everyone—excepting Lita, of course.

I always wondered why Lita moved so frequently between 1950 and 1954. Now I know. The truth was contained in Lita's romantic archives. She was running away from her ex-lovers.

My mother's archives contain a lot of momentous revelations. Each new item I examined seemed to be more mind blowing than the last. But her archives also contain a lot of small, revealing tidbits. I carefully examined each photograph, letter, or other artifact from Lita's past. I didn't want to miss anything.

For example, I found a commemorative token. It reads, "LOETA SNOW LOVES MYRON LIGGETT."

That's no big deal, right? Love struck couples do that sort of thing all the time. But Lita carried that concept a step further. Her archives contained another token. It reads, "LOETA LIGGETT AND BILL W(XXXXXXX)."

Both tokens came from similar machines. Lita visited the same places with different guys over and over again. Those men didn't realize they were sequential loads traveling down the ol' Lita pipeline.

Lita's archives reveal her approach to romance. For example, she obviously knew men are attracted to red lips. It took the Mary Kay company until 1963 to begin marketing that concept. Lita was ahead of her time.

My mother applied lipstick heavily. She wanted to have good coverage. But she also didn't want it to look like wallpaper paste. Lita removed excess lipstick by blotting.

Many women blot their lips after they use lipstick. Most of them use tissue paper of one sort or another. Not Lita. She liked other kinds of blotter paper. Bags from the grocery store. Old receipts. Envelopes.

Some of you might be wondering where I'm going with this. Well, Lita also blotted her lips on the envelopes of letters from her lovers. Never on the front, though. That would have obscured her name. She always blotted her lips on the back. Lita was careful to leave a full-color, picture-perfect outline of her lips.

That might sound like a thoroughly romantic thing to do. It was, but in a twisted sort of way. The men were writing Lita from far away. They weren't around. Lita blotted her lips one man's envelope before she walked out the door to see another. The woman was *cold*.

I always knew MT was a piece of shit. Lita's archives reveal she was too. My own experiences with the woman cemented that assertion. Lita was feckless. As soon as one man's taillights were out of sight, she lined up another to give her a ride.

CHAPTER 18

Dear Eleanor

LITA VISITED M. T. AT least twice while he was in Washington state. I mentioned one of those visits in the previous chapter. One of Lita's lovers drove her up and back.

The other trip was much more prosaic. Ruby drove Lita and me to see M. T. I was about a year old. But that trip took an unexpected turn.

Ruby stopped at a roadside diner. It was in the middle of the afternoon. The place was almost deserted. Ruby and Lita selected a large booth. We all sat on the same side.

Ruby and Lita placed their order. They chatted while they were waiting for the food to arrive. The two women were soon wrapped up in an animated conversation. They forgot about me. A couple of minutes later, Lita noticed that I was having a conversation of my own. I was standing up in the seat of the booth, leaning against the back and playing with someone in the next booth. Lita said, "You were laughing and carrying on."

Ruby and Lita didn't allow their children to make noise in public. They believed such behavior reflected poorly on their parenting skills. Lita barked, "You shush now. You stop bothering other people."

Lita turned around in her seat as she spoke. She came face to face with Eleanor Roosevelt, the former first lady of the United States. Lita was flabbergasted. It made her cease her ongoing harangue. That pause gave Eleanor the chance to say, "Oh, that's all right, dear. I was encouraging him. He is a delightful child."

Lita said that she had a brief conversation with Eleanor. They stopped talking when the food arrived.

I wish that I was grown when I met Eleanor Roosevelt. She was a charming and accomplished person. I believe that we would have enjoyed a fine conversation.

Alas, I was just a baby. The conversation was one sided. But I'm happy that I was able to bring a measure of happiness into Eleanor Roosevelt's lonely existence.

CHAPTER 19

Red Rubber Ball

A LOT OF PRETTY YOUNG girls lived in Ruby's house, and they liked pretty clothes. In those days, pretty clothes needed to be ironed. My aunt Betty was ironing a dress one day and walked away from the ironing board.

I was an infant. I didn't know how to walk, but I was good at crawling around on the floor. I pulled myself upright on the legs of the ironing board. The hot iron dropped to the floor. The hot side was facing down. My hand was pinned between the iron and the floorboards.

My aunt Betty returned a few minutes later. She said that I was frozen in place. I was gape mouthed but not emitting any sound. The searing pain of the hot iron caused me to go into shock. I didn't cry.

Betty was horrified. She removed the iron and grabbed me up; *that's* when I began to cry. Lita got a ride to the county hospital. The attending physician was grim. He said, "There's nothing I can do. The muscles and tendons are cooked. They are going to contract. This child is going to be crippled for life. His left hand is going to be a claw."

Lita took me home. She was horrified. I was a big, beautiful, perfect baby. Now I was going to have a claw instead of a hand.

Lita's grandmother Mary Stewart heard the commotion that surrounded our return from the hospital. She asked, "What's going on?" Lita told her what the doctor said about my hand. Mary said, "Hogwash. My daddy was a country doctor. He knew how to deal with things like this. I'm gonna tell you how to fix that child up good as new." She told Lita exactly how that miracle would be accomplished.

Mary Stewart began her tutorial by saying, "Lita, you get yourself a jack ball."

Now, my younger readers might not know about the game of jacks. That's sad. Countless generations of little girls played jacks. The game was simple: it had small pieces ("jacks") and a red rubber ball. Since Ruby's house was well populated with girls, someone quickly found a jack ball.

Mary Stewart said, "Lita, you change that child's bandages four times a day. Don't you let them bandages stick to that wound. Every time you change them bandages, you place that jack ball in that child's bare hand. Then you're gonna put his hand inside of yours. You're gonna squeeze that child's hand round that jack ball. You're a-gonna squeeze an' relax, squeeze an' relax that ball. That way, you're gonna make that poor child's hand flex. You ain't a-gonna let it freeze up into a claw."

Lita tearfully accepted Mary's advice. But my great-grandmother added a caveat. She said, "Now, you're gonna have to warn the neighbors what's gonna be happenin' round here. They're gonna hear that child's screams from two blocks away."

Lita cared for me with every ounce of her determination. She followed Mary's advice to a T. Lita said that it wasn't easy; you *could* hear my screams from far away. She said, "It's a wonder someone didn't call the cops."

Well, guess what, folks? Mary Stewart's sound advice paid off for me. My left hand is terribly scarred, but it functions normally. Bless you, wise old woman. You knew how to heal people in unconventional ways. You saved me from a cripple's life.

CHAPTER 20

Mozart in the Garden

ENGLISH IS A RICH LANGUAGE. Its words possess great power and subtlety. But many words are used far too frequently. When this happens, their meaning becomes diluted. The words lose their value. That is what happened with the term Renaissance man. The modern world tolerates far too many claimants for that honor. Their legacies do not match the value of the term.

A Renaissance man is a polymath. Wikipedia says that a polymath is a person "whose expertise spans a significant number of subject areas." That's a darned good definition of that term—and me. I have excelled at most of the things I have attempted. I'm not saying that it was easy for me to accomplish the tasks that life put before me. It was far more difficult for me to learn some of them than it was for others. But there was a trick to my success: I worked a hundred times harder perfecting my skills than most other people did.

But some people have talents that are innate, not learned. Those talents transcend human comprehension. It seems that God has given a small piece of herself so that the world will have useful and interesting things. I have that kind of gift. I was born with a certain talent. It resides in my earliest memories. I have a genius for gardening. Oh my! I've used a word to describe myself that's not modest. Too bad. I heard about a hundred great cowboys say, "It ain't braggin' if'n you can do it." They were right with their assertion, if not their English.

My entire cultural identity was formed by a prime aspect: when I was a child, I was surrounded by walls. The high mountains that surround the Santa Clara Valley are the most obvious of these. But my identity was formed in the shadow of another kind of wall: endless rows of fruit trees. Fruit trees grew in the Santa Clara Valley like nowhere else on earth.

At one time, the yearly rhythms of the Santa Clara Valley were measured by the progress of fruit tree bloom, leaf, harvest, and dormancy. Locals who had no direct ties to orcharding noted when the trees were in bloom. Someone in the family always seemed to know when the Blenheim apricots were ripe. Ah, that most versatile kind of fruit.

Apricots have a very short season. They all seem to get ripe at the same time. Many hands were required to prepare the fruit for drying. Legions of imported Mexican laborers couldn't keep up with uncounted tons of dead-ripe apricots. A high percentage of local teenagers made extra money cutting apricots. That task cut across all social strata. Twelve-year-old girls from Mexicali stood shoulder to shoulder with stockbrokers' children.

My grandmother moved to the Santa Clara Valley to escape a drunken husband. It could be argued that there was an instinctual component in her chosen refuge. Fruit trees were in her cultural DNA. As soon as Ruby's family arrived in California, they reverted to their default position. My family worked in orchards and vineyards in the San Joaquin Valley. They continued to do so when they moved to the Santa Clara Valley.

I was conceived in a creek bed at the edge of an apricot orchard. My mother worked in the orchards when she was pregnant. When I was a few days old, my photograph was taken in an orchard. When I was a few weeks old, Lita took me along when she worked in the orchards.

When the next year rolled around, I demanded to be with Lita, out in the trees. My family said that I would cry if I was left behind. So it was that I learned to toddle my way between tractors, trucks, fruit boxes, farm workers, and trees.

My first sentences contained phrases about trees and fruit. When I was three, I could identify the various types of fruit trees that grew around the

Santa Clara Valley. Leaves on, leaves off. Summer, winter, driving down the road, I could name 'em all.

Part of this knowledge had been imparted because I had spent my young life in and around orchards. I constantly heard people talking about fruit and trees. I remember someone saying, "Those damned Royal Anne cherries bruise too much!" I remember someone else saying, "Moorpark makes the best dried-slab apricots, but it bears in alternate years. Can't make no money on 'em. Blenheim can be relied on for your steady crop."

Those long-gone orchardists were a lot like some physicians I have known: they complained incessantly about their professions. It's very telling that both groups persist in the trades about which they complain.

In March of 1954, I was three years, eight months old. Lita and I were riding together in a car on the road that led to Ruby's house. We passed by the orchard where my family worked. I asked Lita to stop the car so that I could see the cherry blossoms. Cherries and wild almonds are my favorite flowering trees.

It wasn't difficult for me to convince Lita to stop. We shared a love of fruit blossoms. Lita parked the car on the side of the road and walked out into the orchard. Farther on, the rows of cherry trees stopped. A planting of young apricot trees stood on the other side. We saw the owner of the orchard, Pete, standing in the row that ran between the young apricot trees. Pete was speaking with another orchardist. Lita walked over toward the two men. I wandered off to look at the young apricot trees. They were just my size.

The apricot trees had almost completed their bloom cycle. I saw few whole blooms on the trees. But I was not long deterred in my quest for beauty. I pulled a supple branch down to eye level. I found very few un faded blooms. But I soon made an amazing discovery: many of the spent blossoms had tiny but recognizable apricots in their centers.

By that tender age, I had already witnessed three cycles of apricot bloom, fruit, and dormancy. I was just a little kid, but I remembered how apricots looked and tasted. I knew with absolute certainty that the pointy little doodads in the middle of the spent blossoms were baby apricots.

In a flash, the life cycle of fruit trees was revealed to me. Each bit of my small repertoire of knowledge about fruit trees coalesced into a firm understanding of them as individuals. It was the defining moment of my entire life. If I were a religious sort, I would say that I received a vision. Whatever happened, the sight of the baby apricots exploded in my mind. It was as if the clouds split open and choirs of angels descended to impart me with their knowledge.

I remember what happened next as if it were yesterday. I knew that Pete was the "top dog" of fruit people in our area. I rushed over to tell him what I had seen. I tugged on his jacket sleeve and said excitedly, "Pete, Pete, come here!" I was taught not to interrupt adults. But the excitement of my discovery caused me to momentarily lose my reason. Lita was mortified. I could tell from her body language that she was getting ready to unload on me.

But Pete was a very sweet man. He asked me why I was so excited. I asked him to walk over to the young apricot trees. I said that I wanted to show him something. In my small mind, I wanted to surprise him with my discovery. Pete decided to humor the young child who had grown up in the orchard. I took Pete's hand and led him over to the little apricot tree. I said, "Pete, Pete, there are going to be a lot of apricots this year!" He laughed gently and said, "We don't know that yet, Tommy. The trees have just stopped blooming."

I wasn't having any of that. I said, "No, look. This blossom has a little apricot in it. And look, here and here and here, these have them too. There are lots of apricots." Pete bent down to look more carefully at the spent blooms. He saw that I was right. Many of them did have small but well-defined apricots in their centers.

I remember the stunned look on Pete's face. He just stood there for a moment and blinked. After he had recovered, Pete said to me, "You know Tommy, you're right. There will be *lots* of apricots this year." Pete turned to the other orchardist and said, "I know men who have grown fruit their whole lives who don't have the knowledge of this little child."

The young apricot trees are long gone. They were replaced with multi-million-dollar homes. The other participants in my moment with the trees are dead too. But Lita spent the rest of her life telling people about my brilliant moment among the apricot trees. She told the story just as I told you, without exaggeration or embellishment.

The larger truth in the story went well beyond the cuteness of its telling. By the age of three, I understood plants better than most nonprofessionals. I was an ace fruit-tree identifier. Beyond that, I knew how plants grew and what they needed. Most importantly, I had learned that plants will speak to us—if we take the time to listen.

What I accomplished with the young apricots is not without historical precedence. It is like the genius that was displayed by young Wolfgang Amadeus Mozart. He also had a miraculous revelation when he was quite young. Mozart's family did everything they could to school and train his incredible gift. He ultimately changed music forever. Modern music can be divided into two periods: before and after Mozart.

It was different for me. My revelation to Pete created a small bit of camaraderie for the small group that was gathered in the orchard on that long-ago day. But the lasting importance of what happened with the apricots was truly lost on everyone in my family, excepting me. It wasn't that Lita and her family didn't recognize my horticultural brilliance. They already knew. If they didn't know, I would quickly tell them. I talked about fruit trees all the time.

But my family name is not Mozart. My relatives didn't care what the latest in an infinite string of messy little boys did with his time. They were too busy running their own routines. None of them gave a shit.

Nothing was done to nurture what would ultimately turn out to be a gift of historical proportions. My mind boggles when I think about what I could have done with plants if I had been given a little encouragement.

CHAPTER 21

Water Torture, Part One

WHEN LITA WASN'T WORKING, CLEANING house, cooking, or partying, she liked to be with me. Most of that togetherness occurred at family outings. We didn't venture far from home on our little excursions. Cars were scarce. Gasoline was expensive.

Ruby's home in Mountain View, California, was surrounded by waterways and swimming pools. No one made any attempt to teach me about water safety. I didn't know how to swim. That was kind of a problem for me. The best no-cost entertainment venues were located on creeks, ocean bays, and reservoirs. My family didn't have a lot of disposable income. We spent a lot of time around water.

Lita didn't know how to swim, either. She had a mortal dread of water. She was afraid of drowning.

The young women in the family liked to go to the Stevens Creek Reservoir. The steeply sloping dam face made a perfect place to gossip, sunbathe, and flirt. The place was packed with happy young people.

I loved to go with Lita to the dam but quickly became bored. There was nothing to keep me occupied. I never saw other young children among the throng.

I usually fell asleep. In one instance, that didn't work out well. I changed position in my sleep and rolled down the face of the dam. My body was like a paint roller spinning down a wall. It took me only a second to roll into the water. Most children were quite thin in those days. Thin bodies are denser than ones that contain a higher percentage of body fat. I sank like a stone. I can still recall the green water closing over my open eyes.

A nearby swimmer dove to my rescue. He pulled me up to the dam face. I wasn't submerged for very long. But it was enough for me to aspirate some water. I sputtered, coughed, and cried.

Lita was embarrassed by my teary outburst. She was even more embarrassed by the commotion I caused. She took it as a deliberate slight against her parenting skills.

Lita didn't provide any comfort. She chided me. Lita said, "You were in no danger of drowning. Stop crying. You're just a big baby." From what little I can remember, all present seemed to agree with her.

The hubbub around my near-drowning quickly subsided. Things went back to normal. Lita and her companions resumed their flirty gossip session.

Those assholes didn't realize how quickly or far I sank into the murky water. I was fortunate that my rescuer could see me. The water at the face of Stevens Creek Dam was more than fifty feet deep. I could have rolled all the way down to the bottom of the reservoir.

The story that arose from the day's events became just another chestnut for Lita to pull out of the fire. To her, it was a charming anecdote. Early on, I learned not to dispute the consensus that "you were in no danger, Tommy." To do otherwise would invite universal scorn and ridicule from my family.

The county of Santa Clara didn't agree with my relatives, though. They quickly realized that danger lurked on the steep face of Stevens Creek Dam. Lots of people slipped, fell, or rolled off the thing. The county closed the area. People can't sunbathe there anymore. That move was decried by some in my family. They said, "The county is spoiling our fun."

I developed a fear of water the day I rolled into the reservoir. It was to be my constant companion for the next thirteen years. No one made any effort to familiarize me with water or to provide swimming lessons. Oh no. That would have been too easy.

Besides, swimming lessons would have removed a known source of entertainment. You see, people seldom missed an opportunity to use my fear of water as an instrument of torture.

Almost every time we were around a creek, pool, or lake, someone threatened to give me "cowboy swimming lessons." That means throwing someone's ass into deep water. I was told hundreds of times through the years that I would "sink or swim." If I didn't rise to the bait when someone dropped that line, they would sometimes escalate their "fun." People grabbed me into their arms. They raised me over the water and said, "I'm going to throw you in."

What happened next was all too predictable. I lost my mind. I went into hysterics. I could remember just one thing at those moments: the green water of Stevens Creek Reservoir closing over my eyes.

That was the reaction that my adult companions wanted to see. They were feeding off my terror. It gave them a jolt.

Once they received their desired reaction from me, things calmed down. Someone would scream at me. They'd say in embarrassed tones, "Hush, now. You're causing a ruckus. Stop being a baby." If that tactic didn't work, a swat on my butt would.

I want for my readers to pause for a moment in their reading. Think what it was like for me. These episodes occurred with regularity until I was sixteen. They happened at family outings and picnics. They happened almost every time my family and I were around a swimming pool. Oh, lordy. Why do adults torture children?

CHAPTER 22

Thank You, Edna, Part Two

Edna Liggett became concerned about what was going on in my life. Truth be told, the stories that M. T. told were years out of date. I wasn't living a whorehouse. My life with Ruby and her family was magnificent. I wanted for nothing.

But when I was about three, Edna finally decided she needed to rescue me. She appeared unannounced on Ruby's doorstep. Without preamble, Edna told Ruby she was going to take me back to Kansas. That was typical Germanic bluntness.

Edna had no intention of handing me over to the flawed and variable intentions of M. T. She was going to raise me as her own child.

Ruby went ballistic. She told Edna, "You come back here again and I'll kick your ass up and down that street." Ruby was serious. Edna knew she would have to kill Ruby to get me away from our family. Edna's heroic attempt was unique. It was the only time in my childhood someone tried to help me. It was also the only time I saw Ruby lose her temper.

I dare not imagine how different my life would have been had I been raised by Edna Liggett instead of Lita. The circumstances of my life taught me that it is best not to engage in wishful thinking. That mind-set is the dwelling place of monsters. It is best that we leave them alone, lest they awaken old memories.

CHAPTER 23

Cowboy Number Three

FAMILY LORE INDICATES THAT SOME of Lita's boyfriends were fun, decent men. Somehow, though, she never seemed to stick with a regular ol' American nice guy. Lita wanted to be with a *real* man. She liked cowboys.

Lita and I were living with Ruby's family in a Mountain View, California, home. Tommy made sure that the women of the house kept the place clean. Hearty meals were served at carefully regulated intervals. There was surprisingly little discord. That is a good trick in a place that housed about eleven people. It was heaven on earth for the fatherless child of a teenage mother.

Lita continued to be more of a sister than a mother to me. Ruby was my real mother. I still called her Momma. I called my actual mother Loeta. I remember speaking that name to her in a very formal way. Like I was walking on eggshells. Like I didn't want to set the bitch off.

I didn't know that M. T. existed. No one mentioned the man.

Between 1951 and 1957, M. T. appeared in just two of Lita's photographs. One of them was taken in 1953. The photo shows M. T. holding me in his arms. I have a puzzled look on my face. That look says, *I just want to escape. Rescue me from another strange guy who says he wants to be my daddy.*

During that period, I didn't know that Tommy Tomlinson was taking 100 percent of Lita's pay. Lita still had to beg Tommy for money to buy navy-discounted cigarettes. She said that Tommy always got something out of the deal. The asshole returned a tiny portion of her paycheck and

Lita Liggett, Tom Liggett, and M. T. Liggett. Look at the expression
on my face. I seem to be saying, *Rescue me from another strange guy who
says he wants to be my daddy.* Mountain View, California. 1953.

demanded a bonus. I sometimes hope that there is a hell. I want people like
Tommy Tomlinson to roast there forever.

I was happy as a clam. I couldn't see that I was living in a toxic stew
of familial dysfunctionality. At that point, the recipe was complete, save
for one ingredient. The final, crucial element was added when I was four.
Cowboy number three arrived. His name was William Frank McMillan
Junior.

Frank appeared a few months after the apricots revealed themselves
to me. He didn't start out as the main contender for Lita's affections.
Photographs from that era show him as being just one of the guys. Lita was
still hosting group dates with the men she was currently screwing.

Frank became Lita's main guy in mid-1954. I don't remember anything
about him early on. The faces of Lita's men sped through my field of vision
and were instantly forgotten.

My first photo with Frank McMillan. Lita sequentially took photos of me with her boyfriends in this spot. I seem to be saying, *here's another strange guy who says he wants to be my daddy.* Mountain View, California. September 1953.

My first memories of Frank are very sudden. One day he wasn't in my life. The next day, Frank, Lita, and I went looking for a place to live. I was immediately torn from Ruby's family. With a few brilliant exceptions, plants would be the least of my concerns for the next twenty-three years.

Frank was twenty-four years old when he met Lita. They shared many similarities. Their childhood experiences were mirror images of each other. Both had been pushed into lives of blind adult duty when they were far too young. The root cause for their problems was identical: the lack of a father to support their weakling mother's huge brood of children.

Frank had been a slave to other people's priorities for better than ten years when he came into our lives. He was sick of the duty and responsibility to which he was willingly but unhappily saddled. Frank was sick of farm work, sick of the military, and sick of caring for little kids. He wanted to cut loose and party hard. Lita was the perfect accomplice for Frank's party endeavors.

There was a complicating factor for Lita and Frank's romantic aspirations: MT still refused to give Lita a divorce. She could not marry Frank. But Lita did not allow her intentions to be deterred by legalisms. She became Frank's "shack-up honey."

That kind of behavior is quite common in 2017. It was much rarer in 1954. It wasn't a topic for polite conversation. The women of in my mother's family were a pioneering bunch of trendsetters. My great-grandmother Mary Stewart started the whole thing off on the wrong foot. She did not live with her husband for the better part of a half century. Ruby was on husband number three. Ruby's sister was a de facto prostitute until the day she was killed. Lita was married to one guy but getting ready to shack up with another one.

The seeds of dysfunction those women sowed in their descendants' future romantic aspirations fell on fertile ground. Many of us would repeat the sad behaviors that we learned at our mothers' breasts. Apples don't fall far from the tree.

Lita was raised in a harsh and unforgiving environment. She was forced to take on adult responsibilities far sooner than should have been expected. In Frank McMillan, she found a man of like circumstance.

His father was also named Frank McMillan. Frank Senior was an inveterate alcoholic and womanizer. He kept a fancy porcelain coffee urn on the kitchen table. It was always filled with moonshine whiskey. Frank Senior completed the jest by drinking whiskey from a dainty teacup. When he wanted whiskey, he twisted the urn's silver spigot. The whiskey-bearing coffee urn and teacup were big jokes in the McMillan family.

Frank Senior could drink all night and then work hard the next day. That behavior was an improvement of sorts over my maternal grandfather, Cleve Snow. Frank Senior worked diligently to feed his family. Taught by a master, Frank Junior adopted his father's methods with the gusto of a rapt student. He lived what he was taught for much of his life.

Frank Senior finished his son's lessons in a traditional way: he passed out whiskey with his to-do lists. Frank Junior freely admitted that he was an alcoholic before his twelfth birthday.

Frank Junior's father worked him mercilessly from a very tender age. That was expected from a boy who was the eldest of six children. Central Texas was hit hard by the Great Depression of the 1930s. It was not an easy place to be a sharecropper.

Frank Junior treasured the few moments he could steal from his backbreaking chores. The streams and wild-land forests of Central Texas are a boy's vision of paradise. But Frank Junior's love of wild places sometimes got him into trouble.

Once, Frank Senior indicated that he was going into town for the day. Alcoholic womanizers do that a lot. They need to get their fix and to stoke somebody else's home fires. He told Frank Junior to stick around the home place.

Frank Senior had devised a homemade electric fence to keep cattle from eating a field of young corn. The fence's operating mechanism was not reliable. It was prone to failure. If it stopped working, someone had to restart the thing.

The younger Frank quickly agreed he was up to the task. He settled in to accomplish the duty of the day. It was hot inside of the shed where the electric fence mechanism was located. Frank Junior knew that it would be cooler down on the banks of Knob Creek. The water ran deep and cool there, even in the heat of the day. Frank Junior thought a quick swim would feel good. He decided to run down to the creek "for a few minutes." No harm would be done. He had done the same thing many times before.

Frank Junior had been watching his father's primitive electric fence mechanism for years. It usually worked for days on end without failing. He had a child's confidence that the fence's mechanism would continue functioning while he took a little break. He ran down to the creek.

Frank Junior enjoyed himself in the cool water. He lost track of time. He was gone longer than he had intended. Frank Junior ran home. He found that his father returned from town much earlier than expected. Frank Junior was in deep trouble. It got worse from there. The electric fence mechanism had failed. A large herd of hungry cattle was loose in their landlord's cornfield. Frank Junior could tell that the entire crop was ruined. A year's worth of potential income was lost to both the landlord and Frank Senior. The farmer would never recover the money or time he had spent growing the crop of destroyed corn.

The monetary loss was only part of his family's problem. There were far deeper implications to consider. That kind of event could get a sharecropper kicked off the farm. Homeless, Depression-era sharecroppers were a dime a dozen in Central Texas. A replacement family that *could* keep cattle out of the landlord's corn would not be difficult to find.

Frank Junior had placed the McMillan family's survival at risk. Frank Senior was angry. He was frustrated. He was drunk as a lord. Something had to be done. So Frank Senior used a leather mule harness to beat his errant son. Those straps are *thick*. Several people told me that he almost killed Frank Junior. The boy hobbled through his chores in a semi crippled state for several days thereafter.

That set of events was a crucial component in Frank Junior's life. They created the man he ultimately became. Frank Junior learned that terrible repercussions occur when you don't do your duty. It also reinforced the notion that extreme corporal punishment is a valuable teaching aid. It was a method he subsequently used to a horrifying extent with me.

Frank Junior got a life-changing gift on his thirteenth birthday. The family's Model T Ford truck had no parking brake. Frank Senior placed rocks under the tires when the vehicle was parked. The rudimentary wheel chocks somehow slipped aside. The truck started to roll downhill. Frank Junior's infant twin brothers were lying on a blanket that was directly in the path of the rapidly accelerating truck.

Frank Senior frantically ran after the truck. He caught up with the speeding vehicle, jumped into the seat, and applied the brakes. He managed to stop the truck with inches to spare. One type of disaster was averted, but another was visited upon the McMillan family. The exertion of the chase and a lifetime of strong drink were too much for Frank Senior's body. He suffered a massive heart attack and died on the spot.

Frank Junior's childhood ended when his father's heart stopped beating. There was no welfare safety net for him and his family. Someone had to work, and Frank Junior was the only person who was able. Frank Junior's mother, Gladys McMillan, couldn't. She was made of stronger stuff than my grandmother Ruby. But deep down inside, she was just a cowboy concubine. Gladys had been raised to cook, clean, have sex, and raise babies. It was that latter responsibility that precluded her from getting a job. She had six children to feed and keep clean.

With his father dead, Frank Junior instantly became Frank Senior in all but name. He became the sole means of support for six other people. Frank quit school. He worked any job that was offered. Frank trapped animals for their fur. He took scut jobs few men would accept. It was rough, but Frank somehow managed to provide for his family. He accomplished that task at thirteen. It speaks volumes about his strength and determination.

Frank joined the army on January 2, 1947. He was seventeen years old. Frank told people he joined the army to secure monetary and medical benefits for his mother and siblings. But there was another reason. He needed the structure and discipline that military service provides to young men. I heard muffled hints of youthful indiscretions that threatened to derail Frank's life. He went into the military to avoid going to jail.

Frank eventually transferred into the US Army Air Corps, the predecessor of the US Air Force. Frank hinted that he got into serious trouble while he was stationed on Midway Island. He disobeyed a direct order from a superior officer. Frank believed the order was dangerously wrong. His actions saved a bunch of lives. The army air corps didn't punish him.

Frank was honorably discharged from the army air corps on September 10, 1949. But Frank's discharge certificate reveals that he was something of a bad boy. The notes section of Frank's official enlisted record and report of separation indicates that Frank had to make up seven lost days. He was absent without leave at some point. That is a very bad thing.

After Frank was discharged from the army, he joined the navy. While Frank was in the navy, he went through marine boot camp. That is sometimes required for navy personnel who will be working with marines. It is interesting to note that Frank served or trained in four out of the five branches of the armed services of the United States.

Somewhere along the line, Frank served as a navy drill instructor. Those guys have the well-deserved reputation of being harsh disciplinarians. Frank used his marine-given training skills to the max. He was a standout badass among accomplished bad asses.

Frank was sometimes called upon to assist the shore patrol. He was sent to civilian bars to break up sailor-caused fights. Frank told me that some of them were riots. Frank wouldn't take a pistol or nightstick into a riotous bar. He said, "Someone might take my stick 'n gun away and use 'em on *me*." Frank preferred to use his fists. He got into fights almost every night. People tell me that Frank McMillan never lost a fistfight.

While Frank was in the navy, he went AWOL on at least two occasions. Frank received a summary court-martial on March 24, 1954. He was confined to base for thirty days.

Frank was discharged from the navy in November of 1954. He'd had enough of the military and its rigid structures. Frank was a free man.

Most people seem to think that it would be difficult to have a stepfather who was a marine-trained drill instructor. Yes, I agree. That part *was* bad enough. But there was something worse in the deal. The marines just focused something that was already a part of Frank's inner being. His personality was twisted because he didn't have a childhood. He did his best to make sure that I didn't have one, either.

The six main players in my early life all came from the same harsh, impatient, and unforgiving cowboy culture. That culture developed as a result of living in places and doing jobs that will kill you, either in the long or short term. The kick of a horse or the scalding water of a spilled kettle could instantly kill or maim. The inhaled dust from plowing or the fumes of boiling lye soap could kill you more slowly. Survival in that culture meant working continuously and without complaint. You got it right the first time or else.

This culture of my forbearers was established by fanatics who had a rigid belief in the Christian God. They were taught to blindly believe and to automatically obey. If someone didn't obey, he or she was crushed or expelled from the society. If you did sin, it had best be accomplished in a somewhat acceptable form. You know, activities such as getting drunk, womanizing, or beating your wife and children.

In cowboy culture, nothing was worse than a real or perceived failure of respect or performance by a male child. If either of those things occurred, harsh, instantaneous corporal punishment was expected by all parties. That type of punishment was even more valuable as a teaching aid when it was unexpected. Sometimes those men would "knock you a-winding" (spinning across a room) when you weren't looking. That was done to demonstrate a boy's absolute powerlessness.

Lots of men who were raised in the cowboy culture will read what I have written and think that I am whiner. I have a perfect counter for that: a father's discipline is generally tempered by a modicum of love and respect. Frank had neither of those things for me. I got the discipline but without any form of moderation. It was hell on earth for me.

CHAPTER 24

The Amazing Invisible Perfect Silent Kid

FRANK MCMILLAN KNEW A SECRET about low-budget rental housing: places that wouldn't allow children were in better condition. Those places had the same low rent. That was important to Frank. Monetary considerations aside, there was a real bonus to the no-kids apartments: there were no "snotty-nosed little brats running around, making noise."

Frank applied his knowledge the first time he and Lita looked for an apartment. He didn't look at rentals that allowed children. That restrictive filter allowed Frank to narrow his search.

We drove up to an old gray house on South Twelfth Street in downtown San Jose. Hand in hand, Lita and Frank walked up to the front door of the house. I trailed behind. It made for a pretty picture. Frank rang the doorbell. An older woman who was as faded and gray as the house met us at the door. She was the building's landlord. Our interview with that woman cast the die for all my years with Frank. The landlady brusquely advised Frank that she did *not* rent to children. She glared at me as she spat out those words. She vigorously stated, "Children are noisy." The landlady pointed at me and said, "*He* would disturb my other tenants."

When Frank heard those words, he turned around and locked eyes with me. I couldn't look away from his steely gaze. He had a sardonic grin on his face. Frank began to speak to the landlady. He spoke in a slow, warm, soft Texas drawl. But his eyes never left mine. He said, "Oh, Tommy will be a good boy. Won't you, Tommy? Why, she won't even know you're here, will she, Tommy?" The menace in his voice was coupled with a killing leer. It was a deadly knockout punch to my four-year-old senses. I almost pissed my pants. I was scared. At that moment, I would have willingly agreed to let Frank saw my arms off.

My little brain realized that an adult had just asked me two questions. I was a polite kid. I knew that I was supposed to answer. But I was so scared I could hardly breathe. My throat was constricted. My chest was tight. I couldn't speak a word. But I could see that Frank wouldn't stop glaring until I provided the response he expected. I finally managed to open my mouth and emit a tiny, strangled squeak. I said, "No." Frank then turned around and began to speak with the landlady. I was forgotten for the moment.

That was quite scary to me. But the worst part of that first interaction with Frank was far more devious and cynical. Four people were standing in front of the apartment house door. Everyone heard what Frank said to me. But the other two people had no idea what truly occurred. Frank had publicly threatened me, but no one else got it. In that regard, it was the first of countless such exchanges that would follow in Frank's long reign as lord and master of my life. People in crowded places thought that Frank and I were sharing positive moments. In truth, I was being threatened.

Ever the apt student, Lita adopted Frank's methods for her own. She used them to great effect long after Frank moved on and left us in the dust.

Frank managed to talk the landlady into renting the apartment to our little family. It was the first in a long string of no-children places Frank selected for us.

I wrote "selected" rather than rented because Lita rented the apartment in her name only. She paid the rent. She didn't use any of Frank's money. Lita failed to see that decision for what it was: a harbinger of her future life with Frank.

Just for the record, what was the prize dwelling Frank won that day? It was a decrepit rooming house in a transient neighborhood. It contained ten small one-bedroom apartments. I hesitate to use the word apartments. The individual units did not have bathrooms. About fifteen people shared one toilet and one claw-foot bathtub. The tub contained no shower. The toilet and bathtub were both located in the same room. If someone was taking a long, comfortable bath, no one else got to use the bathroom. There was almost always a line outside of the door.

I became quite adept at holding my urine and feces inside of my aching innards.

Most of the building's tenants were older, single men. Their hostile glares told me that they weren't pleased to have me as their housemate. They were pissed off at the landlady for renting to a family with a kid. The other tenants couldn't say anything to *her*. That old harridan would have kicked them out. They took their frustrations out on *me*. I was a hated presence. Thanks, Lita.

Would you allow a four-year-old child to wander alone down the hall to bathe or use the bathroom in that type of place? Lita did. She said, "Tommy is a good boy. He won't cause any trouble." What about the trouble that a bunch of unknown, older male transients could cause a preschooler, Lita? It's a wonder I am still alive.

For my part, I didn't disappoint Frank or the landlady. I can state with absolute certainty that woman didn't know I existed after our rental interview. I knew what the consequences would be if she complained to Frank.

Our landlady didn't need to worry. I already knew how to be quiet. As soon as I was born, I was immersed in training to be the amazing invisible perfect silent kid.

Ruby had learned to hate the sound of children's voices decades before my arrival. She was not shy about admitting that fact. Ruby would wince when children raised their voices. This was an attribute she passed on to some of her children. Especially Lita.

By the time that Frank came into our lives, I was well schooled in the art of speaking and playing quietly. But his arrival saw me graduate to a new level of silence.

Frank set the tone for all of our possible futures on the very first day we moved in together. Here's how that happened. We had just moved our belongings into the apartment. Frank called me into our living room. Frank and Lita were sitting together on the smelly old couch that was supposed to be my bed.

Frank roughly demanded that I stand at attention in front of him. I remember his corrections to my technique. "Put your feet together! Put your hands to your side! Stop wiggling! Keep your mouth shut!" A few hours before, I had been in my grandmother's house, surrounded by a roiling mass of loving people. Now I was standing at attention in front of a drill instructor.

But that part was not as bad as you might think. An unwanted child will go to any lengths to belong *somewhere.* Any attention that he or she receives is welcome. Even the bad kind of attention is like food to one who is starving. Looking back on that pathetic little scene, I remember how happy I was to have Frank barking at me. I dearly wanted to be his little soldier. I wanted to belong to this wonderful new group with all my soul.

If that seems strange, look closer into the matter. See what kind of boys were sought to join the ranks of the Nazi Brown Shirts and Hitler Youth. Here's a clue: they were fatherless or disenfranchised kids like me. They would have followed Adolph Hitler into hell. Many did.

Frank repeatedly barked corrections to me in his best drill instructor's voice. I eventually met his requirements for standing at attention. He began to deliver his standing orders for the rest of my life. Those of you who have raised children might think these would center on the mundane details of living. You know, when I would go to bed, brush my teeth, and so forth. Not Frank. He had something much more sinister on his mind.

He wasted no time with preliminary concepts. Frank began the main life lesson he wanted me to learn: "I made the money I have myself. Ain't nobody ever given me *nothin'*. When I die, you ain't a-gonna git shit from me. Git out there and make your own damn money."

More than sixty years have passed since Frank McMillan spoke those words to me. But I can still recall them perfectly. Part of that recollection derives from the flawed memory of a four-year-old child. But some of that memory comes from another source: Frank regularly repeated his inheritance speech to me. He always used the same words and intonation. All his recitations on the subject were of like kind. Frank felt indignant about the possibility I might expect to receive an inheritance from him.

Lita just sat there as he angrily barked out his estate plan to me that first time. I clearly remember that she was smiling. She nodded her head in agreement in all the right places. Frank was her hero. Lita believed that he was the male role model I needed to mold my life. Frank must have given her such a royal fucking the night before that she still had stars in her head the next morning. Lita sure as hell didn't find anything strange about the bizarre nature of Frank's obviously scripted declarations. What am I saying? She probably helped him rehearse.

Back to me, though. I was baffled at what Frank said to me. I had absolutely no idea about the existence of death, money, or inheritances. I was puzzled by Frank's declaration. Lecturing a four-year-old kid about inheritances strikes me as being a lot like teaching a pig to sing. All you get out of the deal is a frustrated pig.

When I told Frank that I didn't understand what his words meant, his demeanor changed. His face turned purple with rage. He jumped up from the couch and snatched me up by my clothing. He bent me over his knee and began to beat the high holy hell out of me. All the time, he kept screaming, "Don't you *never* contradict me, boy! *Never!*" That was the first time that I heard the word "contradict." No one had to get a dictionary to define it for me, though. From that moment on, I knew that disagreeing with Frank on the tiniest of details would get me into capital trouble.

Frank beat my ass for the longest time. All the while he was screaming like a banshee. He repeated the same phrases over and again. Frank finally became winded. He was gasping for breath. I suppose that he ran out of adrenaline. Maybe his arm was tired. My ass certainly was.

I hoped Frank was finished with his discipline. But he wasn't. Frank had other plans. He grabbed the front of my shirt and snatched me off the floor. Frank carried me into the bedroom and tossed me under the bed. Then he stormed away and slammed the door.

I started crying and begging for him to let me come out. That set Frank off again. He stormed back into the room, reached under the bed, and snatched me out. He grabbed me by the front of my shirt with his left hand. He repeatedly slapped my face with his right hand. Frank warned me of dire consequences if I made him "come back in here again." Frank then threw me back under the bed. I stifled my tears. I didn't want a third helping of his anger.

I soon became bored with the cramped space under the bed. I began to check out my surroundings. I looked at the dust balls on the floor. I noted the fine details of the metal springs on the bed frame.

I hated being under that bed. But I realized that I would probably be spending a lot of time there. I made it my secret fort, a place of refuge. I was exhausted by the experience of moving away from Ruby and in with Frank. I fell asleep. I began to learn the fine art of creating something good out of a horrific circumstance. Welcome home, Tommy.

That was my introduction to the "inheritance game." It sure seems to be a staple of the cowboy culture. Frank, Lita, and MT have all played it with me. So sad. So sick. So unnecessary.

The sleeping arrangements in the rooming house set the tone for what was to follow for most of the next six years. Frank and Lita always had a separate bedroom with a nice double bed. During our first years as a family, I seldom had a real bed for myself. Some of our rentals came furnished with a couch. In those cases, I was expected to sleep on the wretched things. But for the most part, they were smelly, ratty, and old. I refused to get near them. Looking back, I find it to be inconsistent that Frank and Lita allowed this small act of willful disobedience. Perhaps their reasons for doing so were pragmatic. They sat on the couch in the rooming house. That old wreck smelled bad. It must have made them feel nauseous to sit on the thing. Maybe that couch unearthed a latent bit of ingrained humanity within them. Who knows?

Whatever the case, Frank and Lita allowed me to sleep on the rooming house's floor. That is not as bad as it might sound. Floors are smooth and flat. Cover them with enough stolen navy blankets and they make a perfect bed. Starting with that first rental, I learned that all floors were pretty much the same. They offered consistency. That was crucial in a life that saw little of *that* precious commodity.

CHAPTER 25

Bastard Redheaded Stepchild

Redheaded stepchild: A person who is neglected or unwanted.

Bastard redheaded stepchild: A person who
is especially unwanted and reviled.

—Tom Liggett's personal glossary of terms

RELATIVELY FEW PEOPLE OWNED TELEVISION sets in 1954. They were a new and expensive technology. People had to find other ways to entertain themselves. When Frank wasn't out partying alone or with Lita, he read. He did this both for entertainment and to educate himself. Remember, Frank was forced to quit school when he was just thirteen. He was both inhibited and energized by that fact. Frank didn't want to be just another ignorant redneck. He wouldn't take night classes. That would have cut into his partying. He educated himself via the written word. In Frank's mind, it contained a magical key. The written word unlocked the door to his untapped reservoir of intelligence. Frank read any type of nonfiction he could get. Books, magazines, newspapers, and more. He read them all.

Frank's favorite book was the Christian Bible. He read a chapter from the Bible every night he was home. But those readings weren't quiet devotionals for Frank. He didn't go off into a corner and read to himself. Frank had to make a production of the deal. He needed to set the stage.

Frank's semi nightly Bible-reading sessions had three unvarying elements. The first was the easiest. I was required to sit quietly at Frank's feet while he read the Bible. I've owned dogs. I know the rules of submission. He was high. I was low. I had to crane my neck to follow his reading. He looked down on me while he read.

The second element required nothing from me. It was all Frank. He read the Bible aloud. Truthfully speaking, those sessions were recitations more than they were readings. Frank had a wonderful speaking voice. He used the stentorian tones of an orator when he read from the Bible. Frank loved the sound of his own voice. He was at his happiest when he was filling a room with his alleged wisdom.

But it was the third element of Frank's Bible reading sessions that were the real mind fuck for me. Frank inevitably began and ended his recitations with the same declaration: "These are just stories. There ain't no truth to them. Don't you believe in them."

From my child's perspective, there was something unusual about Frank's behavior. The bulk of my first four years had been spent in a home that was steeped in biblical imprecations. Ruby's mother, Mary Stewart, spent hours each day reading the Bible. That woman quoted scripture every time someone did something she believed was wrong. At my young age, I had no concept of a supreme being. But the strength of Mary's declarations and the invective with which she delivered them left no doubt in my tiny brain: I knew the Bible contained the absolute truth.

In Ruby's home, willow switches had been used to whip my tiny ass. The Bible had been used to whip my brain. This served to build a rock-solid foundation in my mind. I knew there was something out there that was bigger than our family dynamic. I knew that *everything* centered around the Bible.

Frank's baritone voice reinforced the Bible's truth better than my great-grandmother's shrill harping. But he continually told me not to believe the words that I had come to accept as the truth. The twisted Bible readings were deliberate acts. Frank removed my foundational knowledge and replaced it with the sound of his voice. He removed God as the king of my small world. Frank placed himself on the throne. It reinforced the notion that he was the ruler of my possibilities. Meet Frank McMillan, king god of my four-year-old universe.

My drill instructor stepfather used a tried-and-true method for turning civilian boys into military men. That process forcibly removes all familial and social constructs. Those constructs are then replaced with the desired group dynamic. Raw recruits go into the hopper and emerge as soldiers.

Lita quietly sat next to Frank as he delivered his biblical recitations. She nodded her head in agreement in the right places. Lita was not a weak cowboy concubine, but she was doing her best to learn the part.

There was another reason for Lita to go along with Frank's antireligious Bible readings. She was sick of Mary Stewart's pontification. My poor deluded mother didn't have the sense to realize that Frank had replaced one brand of demagoguery with another.

Money and food were in short supply in the first apartment that we shared as a family. But there was no valid reason for us to be in that predicament. Frank was a journeyman carpenter. It was a union job. Frank openly bragged about earning "doctor wages." Lita was making insanely high tips in an upscale restaurant. Where did the money go?

Frank spent it in honky-tonk bars and on other women. He loved the thrill of the chase and strange pussy. Be damned the fact that he had one of the most beautiful young women in the world waiting for him at home.

To his credit, Frank didn't always want to go out alone. He and Lita went out to drink and dance several nights each week. We lived like paupers so that Frank and Lita could go out partying.

Frank's activities were the opening shots in a war that would continue for many years. He believed that money that was spent on rent or food was stolen from his "honky-tonkin'" (partying) fund. Frank deeply resented Lita's efforts to pull money out of his pocket to pay for normal household expenses. He seldom budged from that position, though he would sometimes relent after a days-long series of running battles with Lita.

Not long after we moved into the rooming house, I got my first lesson on dining with Frank and Lita. They carefully explained that dinner would consist of a few saltine crackers and a tiny bite of canned mackerel. I was quite familiar with those foods. I ate them for breakfast and lunch that day. They were hideous in the morning and worse for wear that night. Seeing that shit on my plate for the third meal in a row caused me to lower my guard. I committed a cardinal error: I complained about our slim rations. That made Frank and Lita quite angry. They loudly advised me that my circumstances were better than the ones that they had endured when they were children. That little refrain squelched all potential arguments throughout my childhood. In their minds, it was the ultimate concept that gave them mental justification for anything they did to me.

Frank and Lita's words had the desired effect: I felt guilty for being greedy. Though I didn't realize it at the time, Frank and Lita had performed a double reversal. They got away without feeding me a real dinner. They also managed to get me into an inferior position. I felt guilty because I complained about the speck of third-class food they provided for me. That was another first for our familial dynamic. Frank and Lita messed up, but they made me believe that it was my fault. In my mind, that's kind of like a rapist's excuse for attacking a well-dressed woman. That was a sick thing to pull on a naïve little kid.

I now realize that Frank took a good box lunch with him to work each day. Barring that, he bought sandwiches from the "roach coach" trucks that stopped at construction sites. Frank was also free in admitting that he got a lot of his calories from whiskey. Lita ate whatever she wanted at the fancy restaurant where she worked. They both had nicotine to "take the edge off." But I was stuck with whatever food was in the house. I existed on slim rations, guilt, threats, and solitude for much of my childhood.

Frank and Lita continually argued about money. There never seemed to be enough. Those arguments always ended in the same way: Frank and Lita said that we had money problems because of *me*. Little Tommy

Liggett—that hungry little boy was always the symbol and the cause for Frank and Lita's money problems.

Frank's arguments about money always ended up sounding like sermons. He ranted and preached on the subject. Every sermon needs to have a good punch line. Frank's fiscal punch lines were always directed at me. Frank would point his finger at me and say, "You need to get out there and bring in some money for the household." He said that I needed to stop being such a burden.

Though I didn't realize it at the time, that was quite a load to put on the shoulders of a young child. But I secretly took Frank's words to heart. I accepted his challenge. I decided to find a way to bring something into our house. I quickly found a solution, though it came from an unconventional source.

Like most other children who were raised in California, I had eaten a lot of oranges. Ruby always seemed to have them on her table. But my eating habits changed after Frank came into my life. I asked for oranges but seldom received them. The refusals were always given with the same explanation. Frank and Lita told me that when they were children, they each received a single orange as their Christmas present. Why should I expect them every day? Why was I so greedy?

I quickly learned to accept a simple fact: oranges were rare and precious things. They were beyond the reach of our family's scant resources. But Frank and Lita's oft-repeated assertion about the high value of oranges gave me an idea. I figured out how to follow through on Frank's suggestion that I should bring some money into the family coffers.

There was a stunted orange tree growing in the semi dead lawn out front of the rooming house. I didn't think of eating the fruit. I knew that oranges were valuable things. Oranges were for people who had money (whatever *that* was). But it bothered me to see valuable fruit hanging on the tree. My nascent orchardist's brain told me that no one was eating the fruit. It was going to waste.

I decided to sell the oranges from our front yard tree and give the money to Frank. I wanted to surprise him with the money. Maybe it would make him like me. I kept my plan to myself. I could hardly wait for Frank and Lita to leave for work. As soon as they were gone, I rushed out into the front yard. Working frantically, I picked as many of the oranges as I could reach. The fruit went into a brown paper bag.

I ran down to the corner market. I knew the place well. Lita sent me there to buy cigarettes. I walked through the front door. A middle-aged Mexican man was sitting on a stool behind the cash register. He always seemed to be there when I went to the store. I shoved the bag of oranges onto the counter. I told the clerk that I had some valuable oranges. Would he please buy the fruit? I promised him that I would not buy candy. I wanted to buy food for my family. We had no food. We were hungry.

The clerk looked at the oranges and then looked at me. He shrugged his shoulders and said, "I have plenty of oranges already. I don't need any more. But I will trade with you because you are hungry." The clerk put the oranges aside. He placed a few brown onions into my paper bag.

I excitedly thanked the clerk and walked out of the store. I'll never forget how proud I felt as I ran home that day. I knew that I was making good on Frank's oft-repeated demand that I find a way to bring something into the house. I was contributing something to the family larder.

I rushed back to the empty apartment and waited for Frank and Lita to get home. As soon as they walked through the front door, I was on them. I thrust the bag of onions toward Frank. I said, "Look, look! I picked the oranges on the tree. I traded them for onions to the guy down at the store."

Frank looked at the oranges and then looked at Lita. They both looked kind of dumbfounded. Frank said, "Why would that guy do that? He's kind of a hard-ass."

I said, "I told him that we didn't have any food. He was trying to help."

Oh boy. Frank went from baffled to incandescent in about a millisecond. He reached down and grabbed the front of my shirt. Frank snatched me off the ground. He held me level with his eyes. Frank screamed, "You told that wetback you were hungry? You told that wetback I ain't a-feedin' you?" Frank didn't wait for my answer. The bag of onions revealed the truth in that sentiment.

Frank threw me down on the floor and grabbed me up by my shirt collar. He raised me to a point where the tips of my feet were barely touching the floor. He kicked my ass with his work-booted right foot. Every time he kicked me, I whirled a little to the left. I was frantically scrabbling my feet. I was trying to run from Frank. I was terrified. I was screaming like a banshee. Frank was screaming like a demented Nazi leader. He repeated the same phrase over and again: "Don't you never tell no one outside a this house that you ain't got no food. *Never!*" Each time I completed an arc in my kick-augmented circle, I saw Lita standing over to the side. I tried to catch her eye the first time around. I wanted her to rescue me. That wasn't going to happen. I got a brief look at Lita's face before I was spun around again. That glance revealed that she was smiling. It was as if she were saying, "This is what Tommy needs. It will teach him how to be a man."

Frank soon grew tired of kicking me around the room. There was important work to be done. Frank let me fall roughly to the floor. He then grabbed the front of my shirt in his clinched fist. Frank snatched me toward him and said, "You're a-gonna take them onions back down to the store. You're a-gonna tell that wetback you was a-lyin' about bein' hungry. You're gonna tell him you lie a lot. You're gonna tell him you're a bad little boy."

I hesitated for a moment. I could tell that Frank wanted a response, but I didn't know what to say. I didn't want to tell the store clerk I had told a lie. Hell, I *was* hungry. Frank *wasn't* feeding me. I hadn't eaten a decent meal in days.

Frank took my hesitation for defiance. He slapped me across the face to get my attention. In a slow, soft voice, Frank said, "You're gonna return them onions to the store. Then you're gonna tell that wetback you was a-lyin'. Ain't you, Tommy?"

I nodded. That wasn't enough. Frank yelled, "Did you say something?"

I said, "Yes."

Frank grabbed me by the hand. He pulled me down the building's front steps. He marched me out onto the sidewalk. I was the perfect little recruit who was being frog-marched in a disciplinary formation. Frank had done this shit hundreds of times in the military.

Frank and Lita dragged me down to the corner store. While we were on our way, they made me rehearse a script. They made me practice the exact words I would use in my declaration to the clerk. When we got to the store, I plunked the bag of onions on the counter. I repeated the lines that Frank had Lita made me practice along the way.

Frank and Lita took over from there. They told the clerk, "There is plenty of food to eat in our house." They further elaborated that I "was a wicked little boy who was just trying to get attention." The clerk laughed at my youthful indiscretion. He added, "Those oranges were too dry and sour to sell anyway." When we left the store, everyone was laughing except me.

There was just one true word in what Frank and Lita said to the clerk: attention. Man oh man, did I ever get Frank's attention when we got home! The spanking I received before we went to the store was just a warm-up. I was beaten high and beaten low. I was yanked around, shoved around, and kicked. I was thrown back under Frank and Lita's bed to ponder the error of my ways. I didn't get any supper that night. What a capper that was for a hellish day.

CHAPTER 26

Alamitos Creek

NOT LONG AFTER THE ORANGE incident occurred, we moved away from the rooming house. Frank and Lita grew tired of our landlady's complaints. They were always behind on their rent. A little less partying would have stretched our household's abundant income further down the bill-paying road. But that prudent concept didn't resonate with Frank and Lita. Frank needed to get drunk with the boys down at the bar every day or two. He needed to spend money to attract strange women. Lita needed to be the best-looking girl at the dance hall a few times a week.

Frank looked for ways to increase their income. He heard that people were earning high wages harvesting walnuts in our local groves. Lita thought it sounded like a good idea. They announced that we were going walnut picking.

Nut gathering was a tradition in Frank and Lita's families. It would be like old home week for us.

The reality of the trip wasn't nearly as glamorous as the sales presentation. Frank got Lita and me out of bed at about four in the morning. I was warm in my sleeping pallet on the floor. I didn't want to move. To Frank, I must have looked just like any of the hundreds of raw recruits he had rousted during his days in the military. He knew just how to deal with boys who wanted to stay in bed. Frank grasped the blanket that was underneath my body. He yanked it up and dumped me onto the floor.

Most normal children would erupt into a sea of tears if you gave them that kind of awakening. Not me. Frank had only been in our lives for a few months, but I knew better than to cry too much or too long. Ruby, Frank, and Lita all saw tears as being a sign of weakness. Any child who was raised by those people knew better than to cry too much or too long. To do otherwise would inevitably evoke a favored expression: "Hush, now before I give you something to *really* cry about."

Once I was fully awake, my thoughts became normal. I was hungry. Who knows what I had eaten the day before. When I told Frank and Lita that I was hungry, I received an angry rebuke. They said that we were going to work on Saturday because we needed to buy food. They had a great nail to hammer into the coffin of my hunger. They said that it was *my* fault that there was no food in the house. I had eaten it all.

Do ya begin to see a trend here? Every bad thing that happened in that household was my fault. That was just a variation on Lita's theme that I had ruined her life by being born. Frank added a key change or three to liven things up. Those two assholes were well on their way toward writing a symphony of hurt for me.

It took Frank about ten minutes to get us out of bed and into his yellow Dodge Sedan. It was easy for them. They were stoked. Lita's endless stream of Pall Mall cigarettes gave her a boost. Frank had a plug of chewing tobacco in his mouth. They were both jacked up by cups of strong, black navy coffee.

Frank also got help from another source: he was well fueled on Kessler whiskey. Frank was drunk before five in the morning. He was in pig heaven. Frank knew how to do it right. He drank smooth whiskey. That kind went down easy. It allowed Frank to sip a back-pocket pint all day long. He was redneck to the bone.

Frank and Lita were floating in a chemically induced state of euphoria. I was going on the threat of another beating and the promise that we would eat "later on."

Frank and Lita continually told me they were broke. Taking that fact in consideration, you would have thought they would select a walnut grove that was close to our home in Mountain View, California. We were all surrounded by miles of groves and orchards of every description. Lots of them contained walnut trees. Gasoline was expensive. Lita wanted to stay closer in.

That's not the way Frank played the deal. Frank turned our purported workday into a full-blown expedition. We trolled through Mountain View, Sunnyvale, and Santa Clara. We drove through miles of San Jose. We traveled down Almaden Road for what seemed to be an eternity. The middle sections of that barely paved track were not much improved from the days before cars replaced wagons.

Just as the sun broke above the hilltops, we turned down a side road. We had been in the car for over an hour. I was half asleep but was quickly awakened by what I saw out of the car's windshield. I was stunned. If I live to be a hundred years old, I will never forget the sight. A small creek picked its way around large rocks, pools, and cut banks. Giant sycamore trees that had seen Indians and Spanish conquistadores but never a woodsman's axe stood sentinel over it all.

Some skeptics might assert that it would be impossible for me to remember a faraway spot I first visited when I was just five. The canyon roads and orchard byways of the Santa Clara Valley were a tangled woodland maze. That was not the case. I remember that place and time as if I were there yesterday. From day one, my brain had been nourished by sights of trees and canyon, field and stream. It was well programmed with the code of what existed around this former Eden. That place's location is etched in my brain.

But the beauty of the side road only carried me so far. I was *hungry*. This forced me to commit the ultimate familial indiscretion: I asked Lita and Frank if the "later on" when we were going to eat had finally arrived. This was met with a harsh rebuke from them. In time, I would learn to keep such shocking questions to myself. I was just at the start of my schooling to be a mindless robot.

Frank drove down a long, narrow side road. This unimproved path probably felt the hooves of Cabrillo's horse. Frank pulled the Dodge into a harvest camp. That place was a temporary collection of the bric-a-brac necessary to oversee a large orchard harvest operation. Wooden crates and boxes were strewn around a 1920s-era flatbed truck. The truck had no roof. Someone had cut it off so that it could pass between the rows without harming the trees.

People were milling around a door that had been placed horizontally across two sawhorses. That was the foreman's table. The walnut-picking crew boss was sitting behind the table, doing paperwork. A small boy sat on the chair next to him.

Frank spoke with the crew boss and negotiated their deal for the day. As Frank was speaking, I noticed the other boy was eating a bowl of Kellogg's cornflakes with milk and sugar. I was standing five or six feet away, but I could smell the creamy richness of the milk. I could hear the cornflakes crunching between his teeth. I was salivating like a dog.

The boy was Mexican. He spoke no English. That was no big deal to me. I had been in the fields since I was a few days old. Most of the people I met in those places didn't speak English. As time went on, I became quite adept at playing with children with whom I shared no common language save camaraderie.

The little boy said something in Spanish to the crew boss. The boss then asked Frank if I would like a bowl of cornflakes. Oh boy. Wrong question. Frank and Lita continuously polished the sheen of their reputations. They wanted the world to believe that they were the valiant sacrificers of all to feed Tommy. Any suggestion that they showed up with a hungry child on a workday would have tarnished their self-congratulatory images.

Frank glared down at me with a ten-megawatt-laser look. I knew that expression well. It was the same one he used on me when our first landlady didn't want to rent to a kid. That look said, "If you say *one* word, if you intimate that you want a *bite* of those cornflakes, I *will* murder you later."

I believed every word that Frank's eyes said to me. I looked at the little boy and shook my head no. That wasn't enough for Frank. That cruel son of a bitch had to rub it in. He glared at me and said, "Don't ya know what to say when folks offer you something, boy?"

I squeaked out a strangled "thank you" and then looked away. I was angry. I was humiliated. My stomach was eating itself from the inside out.

A casual observer would have undoubtedly seen something different from that which actually occurred. They would have believed I was a typical always-hungry little boy who was trying to horn in on someone else's breakfast. The crew boss probably saw a great father who was working on his day off to feed his family. Frank was playing a role. He was trying to look like anything but an Okie who'd showed up at a John Steinbeck–type work camp with an unfed child. But that's exactly what he was. The members of our entourage were just a few years late to play bit parts in *The Grapes of Wrath*.

Frank asked the crew boss if I could remain in the harvest camp while he and Lita went out to pick walnuts. He said that I would "get in their way while they tried to work." Frank told the crew boss that I was uncontrollable. I would disrupt the harvesting crew. Frank made me out to be the bad guy.

That was bullshit. I was raised in the fields. I knew my way around those places. I knew not to get in anyone's way. Frank was a selfish son of a bitch. He didn't want me around. But he didn't want to appear as if he was an uncaring father. Blame Tommy. Use the right insinuations and you can make people believe anything about him. The crew boss quickly agreed with Frank. He didn't need disruptions out in the field.

Frank put on his stern father hat. He told me to sit "over there." He pointed to the chair on the other side of the makeshift table. Frank said, "Don't you get up out of that chair until I come back." He ended that conversation with a stern warning. "Don't you try to slip off on me, boy. I'm a-gonna be checkin' on you." The look on Frank's face told me he was serious. I believed every word he said. You would have needed a three-foot crowbar to pry my skinny ass out of that chair.

Frank and Lita wandered off alone into the walnut trees. They were holding hands and swinging their picking buckets. Once they were out of sight, I began to focus on my new surroundings. The box of Kellogg's cornflakes was still on the table. It was right in front of my hungry eyes, about two feet away. I couldn't miss the thing. It was a flash of brightness against the autumn drab of the trees. The cornflakes box was doing its job. Brilliant people had designed it to catch the attention of hungry young boys from all age groups. I vividly recall what the front side of that box looked like. That is because I stared at it from about six in the morning until dusk.

Beyond cereal boxes, my seat offered me a bird's-eye view of an ancient nut-harvesting operation. The table in front of me was the nerve center and breakroom for the place. People came and went all day long. They turned in harvest chits and got paid. Some sat and spoke with one another. The workers seldom spoke to me. I was a patch of blond in a sea of brown faces.

People ate lunch at the table. I tried not to stare at their burritos. They were wonderful concoctions of cold beans, tortillas, and whatever was left over from last night's supper. The workers passed a chunk of onion from person to person. Some of the workers offered me pieces of their meals. I declined their offers. I knew that there would be hell to pay if Frank returned unexpectedly to find me eating food I "begged" from a stranger.

I wasn't sufficiently mature to realize I was in a pickle. Frank and Lita had dumped me into the middle of a primitive work camp. I was alone with strangers. I hadn't eaten a bite since the previous day. It was cold in the shaded camp, but I had no hat, no jacket, no food, no water, and no toys. No provision had been made for me to use the bathroom. That's one hell of a lot of "no's" for one five-year-old boy to deal with. But deal with them I did! I grew a backbone on that long-gone autumn day. I know that I acquired more self-discipline. Especially as it applies to food.

Through it all, the Kellogg's cornflake box sat in front of me. I stared at it endlessly. I did my best not to think about the pure, raw food it contained. I didn't consider the prospect of reaching into the box and grabbing a handful of flakes. I was more afraid of Frank's wrath than the angry pangs of my churning stomach.

I sought ways to distract myself from the food that was right in front of my face. I began to memorize the front side of the cereal box. I saw the rooster and the fine script lettering. Most of all, I saw the cartoonish rendering of the laughing boy whose visage graced the box. He had buck teeth, red hair, and a goofy-looking expression. The cereal box boy exuded happiness. I thought, *He's really lucky!*

One hour of sitting in front of the cereal box turned into two. At some point, the boy on the cereal box became my friend. I spoke with him. When he failed to answer, I made up his responses and recited them aloud. I took the boys' made-up thoughts and carried them into higher realms of conversation. I was bored.

The cereal box boy told me about his life. He told me about the children he played with. Unlike me, he had *lots* of friends. He was nice.

The boy on the Kellogg's box liked to talk about food. He had lots of food. He told me that he ate fried chicken and biscuits every day. The boy asked me if I knew about biscuits. Had I ever eaten them? I answered, "Oh, yes. Lita used to make biscuits when we lived with Momma. But Lita doesn't make them anymore. We don't have any money for biscuits. I ate all the money."

The cereal box boy finally grew tired of speaking with me. He finished our conversation with a Frank McMillan–type admonition: "You must stop being so greedy, Tommy. You must stop thinking about food all of the time." I knew that the cereal box boy was right; I *was* greedy.

When I lost my cereal box companion, I had to find other diversions. I looked more closely at the tabletop that sat in front of me. It was a door of ancient design, placed sideways. The porcelain knob set was still in place. The paint was peeling away from the paneled surface. I made roads in the door's cracks and peeling paint. These became highways. Escape routes to better places.

Three hours at that table became six and then eight. At some point, even my peeling-paint highways lost their charm. I cast my eyes upward, into the lofty heights of the ancient sycamores that towered over my head. I found that if I sang to the trees, they answered with avian voices. The glorious little creek sang close harmony to my joy. Through it all, my empty stomach grumbled an unwelcome counterpoint. I was hungry, thirsty, and probably needed to take a shit. But at that moment, I was sitting pretty in my chair alongside the wondrous little creek. I was happy.

These were the methods I used to get through that day and innumerable others of like kind that were to follow. I learned that I could imagine my own joy. My sweet dreams could augment the scant portions of happiness I received from other quarters.

Toward nightfall, Frank and Lita returned to the harvest camp. Even though they had been gone all day, they had few chits to cash in. I'm certain that the crew boss looked at Lita and noted her overwhelming attractive power. He had experience in such matters. He knew why two vigorous young people had harvested such a miniscule quantity of walnuts. I'm not being cynical. There is strong historical precedent for such actions on Lita's part. I was the product of an assignation that had occurred in a similar creek-side orchard.

Some folks might say that the crew boss was partially culpable for my predicament. He didn't question why a young child sat alone without food or water all day. He certainly didn't offer me anything beyond a bowl of cornflakes. In that respect, the crew boss was not unique. The history of my childhood is littered with instances wherein well-fed and well-loved people ignored the fact that I was receiving short shrift.

For the rest of the time they were together, Frank and Lita spoke in hallowed terms about the day they picked walnuts. Long after they were divorced, Lita would get teary-eyed when she reminisced about the experience. In her telling of the tale, she always mentioned how terribly broke they were. She never failed to mention they worked for an entire day and made next to nothing. Bending over to pick up walnuts is backbreaking work. They just weren't up to the job. But they pressed on nonetheless. Then, Lita delivered the punch line: "It was all for Tommy." When she got around to telling that last part, Lita would always pause. She would allow her audience to savor the gravity of the moment.

I cringed and kept my mouth shut. I was too loyal to rat Lita out for what really happened on that so-called workday. Then there's the other consideration: I knew that I was in for it. A few minutes after that story was told, one or more people would saunter up to me. They'd reproachfully remind me of the sacrifices Lita made for me. Those lectures always ended with a chiding admonition: "You need to be a better son to Lita." Back then, I didn't have a problem with that concept. The horrors I lived each day were my normal. I believed everything that was said to me was true. I was certain I was the sole cause of all our family's problems.

Seeking to redress my inadequacies, I strived ever more earnestly to become something positive to Frank and Lita and then to Lita alone. That was a thing I never truly accomplished with either one of them. For Frank and Lita, love, food, and shelter were conditional and revocable things.

For Lita, it all derived from a simple concept: I never stopped being the semester child who ruined her life by being born. She made certain that main issue stood as an insurmountable divide between us. I tried but failed to cross that hurdle until the day she died.

The place where Frank and Lita picked walnuts is now part of an extensive hiking-trail network. It is bordered by homes whose value is rated in multiple millions of dollars. The children of Apple, eBay, and Google executives live there. Throughout the daylight hours, the trail is clogged with walkers, equestrians, and cyclists. To see Alamitos Creek and a thousand places like it become Silicon Valley has, at times, driven me to the brink of madness. To me, it will always remain the place where I was deliberately starved and parched in the middle of overwhelming beauty.

Some might find it curious that I found happiness in the pain and deprivation of a horrible childhood. I have a ready counter to that: the life that MT, Lita, and Frank visited upon me was one vast painful moment. The wait between happy times was sometimes quite long. Their incidence was rare. They were here and then gone. I learned to find happiness and food wherever I could. Harsh experience taught me a crucial lesson: I never knew when the next opportunity to sate myself might roll along. Or not.

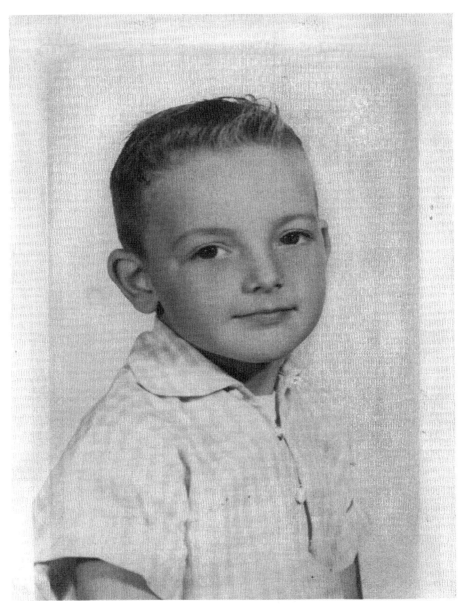

Tom Liggett at age five. What kind of monster could starve, parch, slap, hit, kick, isolate, intimidate, and brainwash this face? The Frank McMillan kind. Mountain View, California. 1955.

Time Flies

WE ONLY LIVED IN THE ratty old rooming house with the orange tree for a few months. It was time enough for Frank and Lita to teach me the first lessons of my new life. The basic template for all our possible futures was now complete. The required pieces are now in place. I can begin to tell you the rest of my story. In this aspect, the portion of this book you have already read serves the same function as *The Hobbit*. While it stands alone as a great book, it is little more than a primer for *The Lord of the Rings*. It is time to begin the main tale.

Frank, Lita, and I moved into a duplex in Mountain View, California. Once again, Lita put up the money and signed the rental agreement.

Our new apartment was a small, separate portion of a much larger house. The house was occupied by our landlords, Rose and Russell Mercer.

Mr. Mercer was the former mayor of Castro City, California. If you look for that town on a map, you won't find it. Castro City was annexed by Mountain View.

Mrs. Mercer had been a nurse in the Spanish-American War. She made the best apple pie I have ever eaten. Lita used Mrs. Mercer's recipe for the rest of her life. My mother would frequently sit in when someone didn't show up for Mrs. Mercer's weekly canasta games. Those women were in their seventies, eighties, and nineties. They found my twenty-two-year-old mother to be enchanting. Everybody loved Lita.

Lita loved me too, though she sometimes had a strange way of showing it. She made a big deal of running around the house in her panties and bra.

Lita brushed it off; she pretended that it was not a big deal. But there was a darker side to her exhibitionism. When Frank wasn't home, Lita insisted that I sleep with her. I vividly recall the first time I noted she was naked under the sheets. The sight of her pubic hair and breasts gave me a tiny erection. Lita was entirely pleased at my reaction. She laughed it off as being normal.

After Lita saw she had gotten a "rise" out of me, she made a special point of showing me her pubic hair whenever we slept together. I went back to sleeping alone. But the memory of my mother's naked body lingered in my mind. It inflamed and repulsed me in equal parts. Welcome to the messed-up world of sex, Tommy.

While we lived in the Mercers' apartment, Frank grew weary of hearing me address my mother as Loeta. He demanded that I start calling her Mom. That affectionate moniker ran contrary to all that I knew as truth. I grew up calling Ruby Momma. In my mind, she was more of a maternal figure than Lita. Ruby never told me that I ruined anybody's life by being born. When I was with my grandmother, she reliably fed me three times each day. I knew where I stood with those two women. You can't bullshit a child, folks. They see and speak the truth, most of the time.

I refused to call my mother anything other than Loeta. Frank saw this as being willfully disobedient. He reacted in a predictable fashion: he beat hell out of me. By that time, I had more than a year of Frank's beatings under my belt and in my mind. My tiny ass had grown less sensitive to his regular ministrations. What am I saying? My backside was *numb* from his beatings.

My lack of reaction to Frank's corporal punishment caused him to change his tactics. He said that I wasn't going to eat until I started calling Lita Mom. It turned into a real battle of wills. The growling in my skinny stomach finally overrode what my heart knew to be the truth. But I wasn't willing to fully prostitute myself to feed my body. Instead of calling Lita Mom, I called her Mother. I think that Frank and Lita realized they had reached a brick wall in terms of my resolve. An impasse of names was reached. I called Lita Mother for the rest of her life. This gave her one more set of reasons to resent rather than love her only child.

When we moved into the Mercers' apartment, Frank and Lita had been a couple for a little over a year. By that time, we had lived in at least two other places. None of those places rented to families with children. Despite their hesitance to rent to someone with a child, the Mercers were quite nice to me. That was unique among the many "no kids" apartments that Frank and Lita rented. But I had already learned my lesson; when we lived in such places, one or more of the other residents would resent my presence.

Mrs. Mercer had old rose plants growing in her garden. I remember tearing the young buds apart to see the unfolded layers of petals that they contained. The fragrance of those immature rose buds was incredible. It remains in my nose to this day.

Across the street was a farm that was a relic of the nineteenth century. The family grew vegetables for market on a small patch of land. I remember the young farmer teaching me how to drink from an irrigation furrow without getting mud in my mouth.

Living in the Mercers' apartment truly was heaven on earth for me. It was a great house in a bucolic neighborhood. Friends and family lived all around us. I could have lived there forever. But, as you have already read, my preferences did not matter to Frank, Lita, or anyone else.

CHAPTER 28

Pint-Sized Hero

LITA WAS SICK. NOBODY COULD figure out what was wrong. Physicians eventually discovered that she had an overactive thyroid gland. Lita had surgery to correct that problem in December of 1955.

Lita was in the hospital for several weeks. I missed her grievously. County Hospital in San Jose didn't allow children to visit Lita's ward. That was a problem for me. I watched other people go inside the hospital to visit Lita. I sat in the car with one adult or another. The visitors returned with reports on Lita's condition. I didn't like that. I knew that Lita was close by. I wanted to see her too. I guess I was pretty insistent on seeing Lita. Ruby knew I wasn't going to shut up.

Ruby went inside of the hospital and talked to Lita. She asked her doctor if she could step out on the second-floor veranda. I would remain in the car and speak to her through the window. The doctor said, "Yes, but only for a few minutes. You are quite weak."

Ruby ran back downstairs to set up the visit while I was impatiently waiting in the car.

The doors opened. Lita emerged from the hospital. But she was not alone. The doctor and an orderly were supporting her. Their arms were locked inside of hers. I almost didn't recognize her. She was thin and frail. Lita had a massive bandage around her throat. She stepped to the railing and gave me a weak smile and a wave. I could tell she was in pain.

I burst into tears, then began to wail. When the doctor saw my reaction, he led Lita back inside. He didn't want her to get upset.

That's when the shit hit the fan. My fifty-three-month-old brain thought they were taking Lita inside to hurt her some more. I believed the doctors were going to kill her.

I couldn't understand why no one was rushing in to help Lita. I believed that my family was going to sit in the car while the doctors hurt her.

I decided to rescue my mother. I made a leap for the car's open window. I damn near made it too. Ruby caught me by my legs at the last moment. She dragged me back in the car.

What happened next was entirely uncharacteristic for me. I was an energetic but well-behaved child. I began to fight Ruby. I was going to go over, under, or through her to get to Lita. I had to help her.

Ruby was stunned. She had never seen me act that way. It took her a moment to regroup. But when she did, she immediately wrapped me up in her arms. That old woman had dealt with *lots* of energetic little boys.

I wasn't going anywhere. But that didn't stop my rescue attempts. I began to scream. If I live to be a hundred years old, I'll never forget what I said: "I'm gonna kill the doctors. I'm gonna kill 'em all!" In case they didn't get the gist of my message, I repeated that phrase a few more times.

Now, I've got to tell you, *that* got Ruby's attention. She gave me a good, strong spanking, right then and there. Ruby chased that with her usual admonition: "Hush up, now. You're makin' a spectacle of yourself." She was genuinely embarrassed by my outburst.

In due course, I calmed down. Everybody in the car was frazzled. Still and all, my actions that day were judged as being notable. Heroic even. In a bloodthirsty cowboy/Indian sort of way.

A few weeks later, one of Lita's old lovers tracked her down. Glen H. sent Lita some letters. They didn't contain the usual hearts-and-flowers stuff. She received that type of drivel from the guys who thought they had Lita all locked up. Glen's letters were kind of subdued in their tone. But you could tell the guy was *really* carrying a torch for Lita.

But Glen's letters revealed something unique. He really liked children. He really liked me. Glen referenced my behavior at the hospital in both of his letters from this period.

The first reference was a doozy. Glen wrote, "Has Tommy killed the doctors yet. Better not until they get you back on your feet."

Wow! That line surprised me. My performance apparently gained some notoriety.

Glen's next reference to me was quite touching: "I'll bet Tommy is getting to be quite a boy by now. So he really sticks up for his mama ha. Well he should, he the man of the house now isn't he. He always was sweet and generous wasn't he, any way the way I remember him he was."

How do you think I felt when I read those words, folks? If you have gotten this far in the book, you have read about Frank's antipathy and brutality toward me.

Why did Lita stick with Frank and not Glen H.? Because Glen was not cowboy enough for her. Oh, Lita. You discarded a good man.

CHAPTER 29

Voices from the Past

LITA WAS TOO SICK TO work. She went on county assistance. Welfare. She needed to pay the rent and buy food.

Lita had spent much of the previous five years bouncing in and out of Ruby's house. Every time Lita got into a jam, she moved back home. That was all right with me. I ate every day when I lived with Ruby. No one in her home ever beat hell out of me.

But Lita couldn't move in with Ruby. The navy had transferred Tommy Tomlinson. Ruby and her minor children went along. That was Lita's excuse, anyway. The reality was much simpler: Lita couldn't move Frank into Ruby's house. For the first time in her life, Lita was forced to make it on her own.

Lita also had another problem: M. T. was trying to gain sole custody of me. He hired private detectives to dig up unfavorable information about Lita. M. T. knew it was difficult for a man to gain custody in a California court. That operation was being driven by Edna Liggett. She wanted to raise me. Wilbur Liggett probably gave money for the private detectives and legal expenses. Too bad they didn't succeed.

Lita said, "People were going all over town, asking questions about me. There were guys sneaking around our apartment. Peeking through the windows."

Lita was trying to keep a low profile. Play the good girl. The particulars of that charade put a crimp in Frank and Lita's relationship. You see, Frank didn't want to live in California. He wanted to be in Texas with his family.

Lita reluctantly went along with Frank's idea. She said she would move to Texas. But she couldn't leave California until the divorce was final. Residency requirements were quite strict in those days. Lita's divorce from M. T. was supposed to be final in July of 1955. Lita and Frank wanted to visit or move to Texas immediately thereafter.

Frank started and quit several jobs in rapid succession. He expected each one to be the key to his big break. But he quickly found reason to believe each job would not deliver his desired good fortune. He was underemployed. Frank brought very little money to the apartment that Lita rented.

Yes, that's right. Lita rented another apartment in her name only. That's two in a row, in case you're keeping score. A year into their shack-up lifestyle, Lita still didn't trust Frank. She needed a secure place to live.

Lita didn't own a car. She had grown accustomed to being chauffeured around by other people. That method worked until Frank's old car died. Lita and Frank obtained a loan to buy a six-year-old Dodge sedan. They also borrowed money from a bank for living expenses. The monthly payments were pretty steep.

Frank's apparent lack of earning potential was getting on Lita's nerves. She said, "I was sick of seeing his sorry ass sitting around the house. I wanted him to go out and get a fuckin' job."

Frank showed Lita how he dealt with argumentative women: he stormed off to his favorite tavern. Frank drank away the small amount of money he still possessed. Some of you might see that course of action as being self-defeating. Not Frank. He was able to get drunk. He got to bitch about Lita to his barstool cronies. Most of all, he got to show Lita who was the boss.

Well, that behavior didn't get him far with my mother. She didn't take much shit from men during that stage of her life. She told Frank to "get your ass on down the road."

That was all right with Frank. He told Lita, "I was planning on going to Texas in July, anyway. I'll just leave a few months early."

Lita said, "Ride on, cowboy."

On February 24, 1955, Frank packed the car and drove away from our apartment. That was a natural thing for a cowboy to do. Ride into the sunset. Well, from a geographical standpoint, the last statement is not quite accurate. As viewed from California, Texas is more in the direction of sunrise. But it's close enough to suit a cowboy metaphor. Frank was riding away from his problems.

Frank quickly rethought the circumstances of his rapid departure. He saw the error of trying to out bluff Lita. He tried to make amends. That's a tough thing to do when you are traveling half a continent away from the object of your affections.

Frank's attempts to soothe Lita's anger took a common route for that era. He wrote postcards and letters. In typical fashion, Lita kept all of Frank's missives. She stored them in her romantic archives. They became part of ever-expanding ream of letters she continually received from her previous schmucks.

Each of Frank's letters contains many interesting kernels of knowledge. Some are Frank's thoughts. Frank also quotes Lita and mentions what she said and wrote to him. I don't have Lita's letters to Frank, but his letters provide me insight about her words.

Lita should have studied that set of letters more closely. They revealed all there was to know about Frank the man. It would have saved Lita and me decades of grief.

The next few pages of this book contain snippets of Frank's letters. I quoted him verbatim. I used his words. His grammar and diction. You might find it a little difficult to follow. Why? Frank wrote in contemporary cowboy dialect. Truth be told, he was on the high end of speakers of that language. Most of Frank's contemporaries would have believed that his letters to Lita were high toned. I ask that you have patience and push through to the meaning of Frank's sentences. They reveal much about Frank and Lita. They will offer you a brief view of a vanishing culture. In some cases, I will translate Frank's words into a more useful form of English.

Frank sent three postcards to Lita between California and Texas. They speak of bad snowstorms and near wrecks. Frank drove like a madman when he went to Texas. He spent far too much money for a car jack in "some little desert town in Arizona." Frank knew that the lack of a jack could kill desert travelers.

Between February 28 and April 2, 1955, Frank sent Lita ten letters and one telegram. They are pure Frank McMillan. They read like the script of an implausible redneck soap opera. Please follow along with me as I skim through some brief highlights of Frank's letters. I'm certain that you will find them to be quite enlightening.

The first letter was written on February 28, 1955. It is pure fluff. It's not as bad as MT's 1951 bullshit letters, but it's close. Frank mentions that he is horny. He talks a lot about his family.

There is just one memorable section in this letter. Frank wrote, "Mother was disappointed because you didn't come baby. That's first thing she said was where's Lita? Why didn't you bring her. And the twins and Don [Frank's siblings] said why didn't you bring that little boy? Turn around and go right back and get him. They already figured what for him to do. There is a pretty little ole red horse they have & they figure they could have Tommy riding him in no time."

Frank went on to mention all of the wonderful people and animals who were waiting to play with me in Texas. Doesn't that sound sweet and nice? Wasn't it special? But there is a flaw in the premise of Frank's letter: all of those people, all of the animals, were in Texas. Lita and I were in California, living on short rations and duress. Talk is cheap, Frank.

The next letter was written on March 7 and 8. It was very interesting. For starters, Lita never opened the envelope. It was still sealed when I opened it in April of 2017. Lita didn't want to hear what Frank had to say. Too bad. The true man was revealed in that letter.

Frank wrote, "I haven't been doing much of anything in the nine days I've been here."

Why? He drove ninety miles to visit his sister. He was also visiting other members of his family.

The letter gets more interesting from that point. Frank wrote, "Jim came over and we went clear back over around Lampassas to an all night fox hunt and just got in [on Tuesday afternoon!]. We had some bad luck—one of the old dogs and two of the pups killed a goat so that just means we'll have to kill the dogs. One of the dogs is worth $50 too. But that's the way it goes."

Most of my readers won't find anything remarkable about Frank's description of the purported hunt. But my bullshit meter went past the redline when I read about the dead goat. Why? Because I know a lot about Texas, cowboys, and the greater McMillan clan. Here's my point: the dog pack was owned by Frank's brother, Jim McMillan. Jim was not with his dogs when they killed the goat. How do I know that? Because he would have immediately called them off if he saw them acting aggressively.

Why wasn't Jim Mc Millan watching his dogs? Jim and Frank released the pack. They watched the hounds bay off into the night. The men then changed into their cowboy finery and went out for a night of drink and debauchery. They returned the next morning to retrieve the dogs. They were met by an irate rancher who told Jim McMillan that his dogs had killed a goat.

Lita should have read Frank's letter. It provided a detailed blueprint for Frank's later activities in Texas.

But Frank also wrote other interesting things in the March 7 letter. He wrote, "Hon, if you come down here be sure to get everything straight before you leave. Have your business mail come to Mom's house c/o her. Then should someone come looking for you she can tell them to go to hell. You can have your personal mail come to wherever you live."

Those lines suggest that Lita was being harassed by M. T.'s private detectives. They were trying to rake up some useful dirt for the ongoing child-custody case. Lita was scared. She was sick. She was a single mother living alone in a semirural area. It got worse from there: Lita had to contend with scary private investigators. Oh, Lita. You sure got yourself into a pickle.

Frank's next letter was written on March 12. Lita never opened that one, either. Frank starts the letter in a forceful manner, "Dear Loeta, I thought I'd drop a little line and see if maybe some of you have died or maybe you broke your arm."

That snarky line indicates that Lita wasn't answering Frank's letters. A few lines Later on, Frank indicated he had applied for a job at a dam-construction project.

Frank's next letter was a real doozy. It reveals Lita's true side. It was written on March 18, 1955. Frank wrote, "Dearest Baby. Sure was good to hear your voice on the telephone last night sweetheart. It left a warm glow inside me. But after reading your letter last night well it kinda gives me a 'blue' feeling again. You could just as well have not mentioned The Pueblo Club baby you know that's one place I object of you going. I don't guess there would be any use in me asking you not to go there especially since Jimmy plays these sex. From the tone you sounded like you couldn't wait till July if you had to. Which you don't."

Wow! Lita sent had Frank a "Dear John" letter. She kissed him off. She told Frank that she was partying at a notorious local bar. That place was a well-known hot spot for hookers.

There is some precedence for Lita's actions and Frank's complaint. Remember, MT complained to his brother that Lita was frequenting a similar type of establishment in 1951.

Frank's letter adds another bit of spice to our story: Lita told Frank she couldn't wait for him to return in July. She wanted to have sex *now*. Lita was screwing other men. But that wasn't enough for Lita. She chased her letter with a phone call. Twist the knife, Lita. Thus was your savage nature revealed.

Lita wasn't working at a regular job during that period. Welfare didn't pay much. Was she selling her ass to keep the lights on? I'm not sure. I believe that Lita was just horny. It had been three whole weeks since Frank left for Texas. She needed to have someone tell her she was pretty. She needed to dance. She needed to get fucked. That type of behavior was pure Lita. She might have seen it as being a win-win proposition. She could get paid and laid all in one step.

Frank apparently wasn't fazed by Lita's declarations. He pressed on with his letter. Frank wrote, "I love you with all my heart—if I had the car fixed and the money to come both I'd sure do it but I don't have."

Frank's car died. He was stuck in Texas. He lived far out in the country with his family. He had no way to look for a job or go to work.

Frank then hit Lita with the letter's real punch line: "If you could borrow a hundred or so I'd sure come as soon as I could."

Wow, wow, triple wow! Frank had been in Texas for three weeks when he wrote the letter in question. He was spending his time visiting relatives and going on all-night fox hunts.

Well, guess what, folks? Most of the Texas fox hunts I ever heard mentioned involved female human foxes, not the four-legged kind. But Lita hadn't been around Texans long enough to possess that morsel of arcane knowledge.

Frank had the guts to ask Lita to borrow the equivalent of an average American's weekly wage so that she could send it to him. Lita was a single mom on welfare. She was sick, broke, and bereft, but Frank wasn't ashamed to stick his hand into her pocket. Great guy, eh?

Frank's behavior begs a couple of questions. Where did he think Lita was going to get the money? Did he really believe that she would find a ready lender? Or did Frank know that Lita would get the money from her "friends" down at the Pueblo Club? Did Frank believe it was OK for Lita to fuck other men, as long as he received the lion's share of the proceeds? Ah, Frank. You were as feckless as Lita. She got pimped by her own stepfather. It looks as if you might have pimped her too. I wonder if other men did the same thing to lovable, luscious Lita.

A few lines farther into the March 18 letter, Frank masked his greedy motives with a smarmy sentiment: "And let me take care of you and Tommy from then on."

That was the payoff line for the greedy bastard. Frank knew that was what Lita wanted to hear. Make Lita believe his bullshit now by committing to take care of me later. That turned out to be an effective stratagem for Frank. Lita believed she needed a man to care for me. Once again, little Tommy Liggett was wielded as the instrument that ruined Lita's life.

Frank's March 18 missive gets better from here. Frank tells about the big country music show he attended. He bragged about hanging around with a famous music star.

Frank mentions that he quit his job. He wrote, "Me and the rattlesnakes didn't see eye to eye."

Frank told Lita that he was making me a "nigger Shooter out of Texas Oak." Just for the record, he meant a slingshot with a hand-carved wooden handle. I included that quote for good reason: to demonstrate how easily the word nigger flowed out of Frank's mind. That concept will hold great relevance in the latter portions of this book.

The March 21, 1955, letter was very interesting. Frank was still trying to get Lita to come to Texas. It was bullshit of the deepest kind. Nothing had changed with Lita's divorce. She couldn't leave California. Frank knew that. But that didn't stop Frank from weaving a fantasy for Lita. Frank wrote, "You could work where Mother works. I'm just talking, you don't have any income really, cause we could make it anyway. So if you want to that would do away with that Public Welfare."

That paragraph was a revelation to me. Lita spoke harshly of her own mother for having gone on the dole. It embarrassed hell out of Lita when she was a child. People in those days really looked down on those who received welfare. My mother never gave me a hint that she had been on welfare.

Frank wrote a great letter to Lita on March 27, 1955. He'd found a job working at a sheet metal fabrication company. That letter contained a very revealing line:

"Me & Jim was intending starting on my car this weekend but didn't because it was to cold & now I ain't got no money."

Let me translate that line from cowboy dialect into plain English: Frank had the money to repair his car at some point during the weekend. When he wrote the letter on Wednesday, the car had not been repaired, and he was broke. Where did the money go? Frank went out partying with his brothers. He drank and fucked the money away.

Frank blithely sailed into this statement: "I'm ready to get Calif gone. If you could get hold of enough money, to come back here & enough to have some work done on the car too."

That statement was pure bullshit. Frank didn't want Lita to come to Texas. He wanted her to send him a bunch of money. How do I know that? Frank knew things were coming to a head with Lita's divorce. She couldn't leave California. That would have given MT a slam-dunk win with his child-custody suit.

Lita was sick, unemployed, and on welfare. She was supporting me all by herself. She was paying the rent and the payments for the two loans Frank foisted on her. How was Lita supposed to come up with the money? More importantly, why was Frank suggesting that Lita *could* come up with the money? From my distant and biased perspective, it appears that Lita had a hidden income stream.

But Frank wasn't done. He hammered Lita some more later on in the letter: "But honey baby the first money you get I wish you would make that bank payment down at Campbell—if you don't elect to come here well if you get hold of the money what you can—I need a hundred but I can use what ever you send."

Frank chased each of the two entreaties for money that were contained in that letter with romantic words. Straight hearts and flowers. He told Lita how much he loved her. He told Lita how much he missed her. Frank sounded like MT in the bullshit-passing department.

But Frank also included a very telling and sinister line in his letter: "So Tutor [Tom Liggett] is getting spoiled. Well I reckon I'll have to start over on him again. Tell him he better be good or I will get him. Don't scare him too much tho. Ha————"

I can damn well guarantee that Lita scared me "too much." She told me what was going to happen "when Frank gets back." Frank was in Texas, but the memories of his brutality and neglect were fresh in my mind. I was scared shitless about Frank's impending return to my life.

Frank wrote two more letters to Lita (March 28 and 30, 1955). They are thinly disguised sales pitches. Frank still wanted Lita to send him a hundred bucks. He needed the money to repair his car. He said that once that happened, he would come home to California.

But he also revealed an important point in the last letter: he was going to delay his return to California. Why? An old navy buddy was passing through Central Texas. Frank wanted to spend the weekend with him. Frank wanted to have a days-long carousing session. With Lita's money.

But there is a curious footnote about Frank's anticipated visitor: he was one of Lita's former lovers. He was the guy Frank replaced in Lita's revolving pantheon of lovers.

My mother truly must have kept an incredible secret between her legs. It allowed her to beguile and hold men. Lita was a force of nature.

Frank finished off his final letter in a curious fashion. Lita had apparently told Frank that she had been ill. She also indicated that she wanted to go swimming. Now, that's a very curious statement, because Lita never learned how to swim. She apparently intimated that she wanted a swimming partner.

Frank responded succinctly to Lita's cock-teasing threat: "I don't want my gal going swimming with no other people."

Frank also told Lita, "But you better get someone to take you to the Hiwayan [Hawaiian] Gardens 'cause itl [it'll] likely be a good while before I can take you." Hawaiian Gardens was a high-toned night club. It offered marvelous food and live music.

That was it for Frank's letters. Taken as a whole, they are quite a set. Frank's words were mind blowing. But you must look at the statistics behind the words to see the real Frank McMillan.

Frank asked Lita to send him a big chunk of money at least nine times. He told her to make loan payments seven times. He made at least six references to hunting trips and parties. He asked Lita to come to Texas seven times. He told Lita he was horny at least four times. He used overblown romantic words more than a hundred times.

Frank had at least two jobs during March of 1955. He took one job fraudulently. The boss didn't want a short-term employee; he wanted to teach someone. Frank told the boss he was there for the long haul, but that was a lie. Frank just needed a week's pay for car repair and travel expenses. He quit that job on the first payday. That says much about Frank.

Frank also made numerous references to Lita dating other men. He acknowledged her right to go out with other men at least twice in these letters. He also indicated he did not approve. The message from that aspect of Frank's letters is very telling. Lita was telling Frank that she was interviewing candidates. Looking for a possible replacement. Frank knew that it usually didn't take Lita very long to find another boyfriend. He had been gone six weeks. The clock was ticking in regard to his romantic aspirations for Lita.

Frank sent one last missive to Lita during his six-week stay in Texas. It was a telegram. The message was short and simple:

April 2, 1955

BABY. DON'T COME. WIRE MONEY. WILL LEAVE IMMEDI-ATELY LOVE=FRANK=

If you're keeping score, you will note that was the tenth time in less than six weeks Frank begged Lita for money. The man was relentless.

Frank's last missive from his early 1955 Texas trip. Lita was recovering
from major surgery. She was broke and on welfare. She was trying
to keep with the payments on the two loans Frank contracted,
yet he continually begged her to send money. What a guy.

Strangers in a Strange Land

FRANK MCMILLAN ARRIVED BACK IN California during the first week of April 1955. He was bone tired from the trip. He slept for almost twenty-four hours on Lita's bed.

Lita must have had some fairly vigorous words with Frank. When he came back from Texas, he was a partially changed man. He still liked to drink and carouse whenever he could. There was no change there. But Lita somehow forced an important reality into Frank's conscious-ness: he was going to work forty hours a week, *every* week. That wasn't negotiable.

Frank didn't have a problem with that. He wanted to keep Lita happy. He burned through a few more jobs in rapid succession, but he made sure he always had a job.

In July 1955, Frank's mother and three brothers came to Mountain View, California. Frank wanted them to move to the Promised Land: the Santa Clara Valley. Frank's family was curious about that place. They wanted to see if they would like to live in California. The answer to *that* question was an emphatic no. They were loath to be away from the bucolic bottomlands of the Little River in Texas. Frank's family had lived in that area since the early 1800s.

In California, Frank's family lived in a dumpy apartment that was located about a hundred feet away from a huge fruit cannery. Lordy, those places stank. They also created a cacophony of sounds that could be heard from miles away. It was a far cry from a place that looked as if it had never suffered from the white man's boots or axes.

After a few weeks in California, Frank's family returned to Texas. Frank, Lita, and I followed them in another car. In Lita's eyes, it was a vacation. It was a chance for her to meet the rest of Frank's large family. Little did she realize that it was just an overture to the symphony that would play and echo for the rest of her life.

We went to Texas and had a great time. I rode a horse. She was a large but gentle former racehorse named Sugar. I was thrilled and frightened in equal parts. When Frank's brother Jimmy sat me up on the horse's bare back, I broke into tears. I was afraid of the huge beast that was moving between my legs. But Jimmy McMillan wasn't having any of *that* nonsense. He quietly whispered in my ear, "You gotta be the boss with these things. You ride the horse or it'll ride you." That important piece of cowboy knowledge stayed with me over the course of my life. It applies to many things beyond equine matters. Thank you, Jimmy.

Tom Liggett, age five, up on a retired racehorse name Sugar.
This photo was taken thirty seconds after my first riding lesson.
Note the look of joy on my face. Moffat, Texas. 1955.

I was five when Jimmy put me up on that wonderful old horse. In Frank's family, that was considered late for kids of either gender to straddle a horse for the first time. The implied sentiment seemed to be that I was a city kid who was playing catch-up ball. That reputation followed me for the rest of my time with the McMillan clan.

After a few days, Frank, Lita, and I returned to California. Frank began to tell Lita how much happier we would be if we lived in Texas. But Lita wasn't having any of that. She knew that she had a great life in California.

Tom Liggett and Frank McMillan. A drill instructor training his little brown recruit. Getting in the car during our second breakneck trip between California and Texas. Lost Hills, California. 1955.

But Pandora's box had been opened. Frank got a taste of the good life during in his six-week stay in Texas. He discovered two things on that excursion. The first discovery was biological. Frank's younger brothers were now men. He wanted to do manly things with them. Hunt, fish, ride horses, get drunk, and fuck as many women as was humanly possible.

Frank's second discovery was psychological. He discovered that he was a lot like his relatives. He would never be happy living anywhere but Bell County, Texas.

Frank stayed in California until December of 1955. He then returned to Texas. That trip was a flawed redo of the trip he made earlier in the year. He couldn't get a good-paying job. He was sick of hunting foxes. Most of all, he missed Lita. She still refused to move to Texas. He returned to California in early 1956.

Frank made three trips back and forth to Texas within an eleven-month period. He was living the life of a roving cowboy. That works if you are a lone roving cowboy. But it didn't work for Lita. She was tired of being broke and alone. Lita gave Frank an ultimatum: "Stay here in California with me—or get gone."

Frank reluctantly agreed to stay in California. Lita believed he would do it. Frank's latter behavior indicates that he must have had his fingers crossed when he made that promise.

But Frank also extracted a promise from Lita. He said, "You can't be having other men a-writin' you if you're serious about me." Frank' suspicions were correct. At least three of Lita's ex-lovers were keeping her in their dreams and chasing her with their letters. All of them were sexy, romantic missives. They were filled with references like, "We sure had a good time—especially at night." That man underlined the words "at night" with three bold strokes.

I'm certain that Lita did her best to hide the letters. But Frank sometimes brought in the mail. He had to see the envelopes. What am I saying? At least two of Lita's ex-lovers were also writing to Frank. They probably compared notes.

Frank knew that Lita was writing to her former paramours. She liked the attention. She was playing them as side bets. Keeping her options open.

But Frank was colder of nature and more calculating than any of Lita's former lovers. He knew that given enough time, one or more of those characters would eventually land on Lita's doorstep. Maybe while he was in Texas. The ex-lover might catch Lita in a weak moment. Like when she hadn't gotten fucked or told she was pretty for a few days.

Frank's experience with Lita taught him how that worked. Someone would eventually replace him in Lita's revolving tournament of lovers. But Frank didn't want to be the lead man in Lita's pack of men. He wanted to be her *only* man.

The cards, letters, and photographs of Lita's former lovers ceased to accumulate in her romantic archives during this period. That was a new thing for Lita. She had spent the previous ten years adding and subtracting male fish from her stringer.

Some folks might think that Lita would have trouble being adored by just one man. I have a ready counter to that: she soon discovered that Frank McMillan was more man than one woman could handle.

This Ain't Thomas the Tank Engine!

Thomas the Tank Engine is a popular character in the *Thomas & Friends* television show. The series is about a fictional railroad.

—Tom Liggett's personal glossary of terms

In July 1956, Frank abruptly decided to move, again. I had just turned six. Frank, Lita, and I had been a trio for almost two years. Lita never gave me an exact reason why we moved out of the Mercers' wonderful apartment. I always assumed that it came down to Frank's nomadic nature. He possessed the cowboy's traditional willingness to abandon a good place that was known in favor of a new one that was not. The book-writing process forced me to find another conclusion. Read on and see if you agree with me.

The rental that followed the Mercers' apartment was something to behold. It was on Hobson Street in San Jose, California. To their credit, they allowed kids there. Meth labs and aardvarks would probably have been welcome in that fleabag too. Anyone was welcome as long as they showed up with rent money.

Just for the record, Lita came up with the money for this rental too. That's three in a row, folks. The girl was consistent. So was Frank.

Ruby's husband, Tommy Tomlinson, was transferred by the navy. The woman I knew as Momma was now hundreds of miles away. Her three minor children were with her. They were like siblings to me.

The older aunts who were like mini mothers to me were married and gone. When they appeared at odd intervals, they partied with Frank and Lita. A visit with one of my married aunts was typically a ten-second affair for me. Lita would tell me, "Say hello to your aunt Margaret, Tommy. We're going out. Be a good boy. Go to bed." I said hello to my aunt and shuffled off to bed. The adults left for a night of partying. I was totally alone in the house.

We didn't live in one place long enough for me to make any lasting friends. At that age, I had absolutely no concept that MT existed. Save for the indifferent attentions of Frank and Lita, I was alone in the world.

The life we led at our previous apartments was just a rehearsal. Hobson Street was the premier for a string of performances that would continue for the rest of my childhood. All the skills I acquired in my apprenticeship to become the amazing silent perfect kid were honed by discipline and practice.

The most useful of those skills taught me how to be alone. Frank and Lita had been leaving me alone for more than two years. Frequent applications of the same treatment brought my youthful solitude to a new level. It was normal for me to wake up in an empty apartment. I scrounged a remedial breakfast, got myself ready, and walked to school. I returned home to the same empty place.

Frank and Lita had things that they had to do. There was work to do, alcohol to drink, errands to run, and parties to attend. Any way you slice it, most of their activities did not involve me.

I can't remember Frank and Lita ever making any big pronouncements about leaving me alone. They got ready and walked out of the door. The most I ever got was, "We're going out. Be a good boy. Go to bed." No explanation was given about their destination. No time was given for their return. That was it; fait accompli.

When we moved to Hobson Street, I learned how to feed, entertain, and protect myself. I did the latter by running from trouble. That was an act that saved my skin many a time in the next thirteen years. Some might call that a coward's solution. I call it the way of a small frog in a large pond.

Hobson Street is the oldest in San Jose, California. That fine city was founded down at the other end of the street. Our old neighborhood was razed in the 1970s. Someone figured out that a plane from the newly expanded airport might crash there. Not much remains of Hobson Street today. There is a single block of commercial buildings that terminates in an ill-used section of parkland.

Hobson Street was a vastly different place in 1956. It was at the edge of a vast, tangled neighborhood that was filled with buildings of every description. Since it was the first street in town, some of the buildings were quite old. Down at our end of Hobson Street, the neighborhood just faded away. I remember seeing more empty lots there than in other places around town. Each of them possessed the relics of a glorious past. Here would be a strange set of concrete foundations. There would be a wide staircase that led up to nowhere. Tall weeds and scraggly trees grew everywhere.

I was particularly vigorous for a six-year-old boy. Fields, orchards, and creek beds were the setting for my young life. I was used to exploring tangled places and finding my way safely back. That old neighborhood was the perfect playground for a child of the orchards. When we moved to Hobson Street, empty, overgrown lots became my kingdom. Streets and alleys became my personal highways. Stray cats and semi tame pigeons became my subjects. I was a six-year-old king with an empire of one.

Echoes of past experiences shared my day. I noted the dying, un watered remains of someone's lawn in the empty lot next door. It contained the same flowering plants that had infested the Mercers' lawns. Their fragrant blooms attracted the same butterflies. Those pale, dying stands of vegetation were a cynical reminder of the lush gardens at our previous apartment.

In those days, one of the largest railroad yards in the western United States was in downtown San Jose. A rail yard is like an interchange where several major highways come together. Trains use rail yards to pick up and drop off cars. Engines, cars, and equipment were repaired in San Jose's rail yard. It was a busy place.

Our shabby little duplex had the fine distinction of being the closest legal residence to the railyard. I say legal residence because we were surrounded by the various small units of a monstrous hobo camp.

Many of my younger readers might not know anything about hoboes or hobo camps. The hard days after World War I drew ever-larger numbers of rootless men to a full- or part-time life of riding the rails. That means hitching rides illegally on railroad freight cars. Those men (plus more than a few women and children) were called hoboes. Wherever large numbers of trains either stopped or were maintained, hobo camps, or "jungles," sprang up. Hoboes used them as places to rest, gather resources, and plan their next move.

Hobo camps have existed since the dawn of railroads. In some ways, they are like the homeless encampments that are prevalent today. But hobo jungles were much cleaner, safer, and better organized and governed than any homeless camp I have seen.

Neither Lita nor Frank seemed to give any thought to the possibility that I was spending vast quantities of time alone on the streets of San Jose. They were oblivious that I shared the sidewalks with transients and people of suspect character. But strange people didn't bother me. I had years of experience in the fine art of avoiding them.

There were lots of normal, workaday people in that neighborhood too. But I didn't get to meet very many of them. There was no opportunity. Frank and Lita made it clear that I could not speak with other people. They emphasized one stricture in particular: I could *never* play with other children at their homes. Part of that rule arose from a halfhearted attempt to keep me safe. But the truth was far more cynical: Frank and Lita didn't want other people to discover that I was left alone most of the time.

I suppose there are noisier places to live than our Hobson Street apartment. Somewhere in India or China, people must live around foundries or suchlike that have higher continuous background noise levels than we experienced in 1956. But that's all relative. A regional rail yard is or was one of the loudest places on earth.

Freight cars got moved around in that old yard. They went to and from trains. They went to and from customers. They were repaired. Some of them were parked.

The engines that move rail cars and parts of trains around a rail yard are called switchers. The crew of a switcher received an order to move a car from point A to point B. The switcher would travel to the waiting car. The cars were attached to the locomotive by crashing them together. The switcher pulled away with the attached freight car or cars. That process created hellishly large amounts of noise. The switchers were constantly accelerating and braking. As the switcher accelerated, its huge diesel engine would change in timbre from a low throb to a frantic chugging. Brakes and wheels shrieked. Bells rang. Couplers crashed. Freight cars rattled and shook. Horns blew. Men shouted and swore.

But the noise was just a part of the problems from that rail yard. It took a lot of fuel to power those first-generation, high-torque diesel engines. Each time the engineer hit the throttle, the primitive engines belched clouds of smoke that went up, down, and everywhere. The individual particles of soot were huge. They drifted on the breeze and settled onto the ground like malevolent black snowflakes.

I suppose that one locomotive working in a yard would be bad enough. But that place was crawling with them. Small, large, diesel, steam, switchers, mainline, work, and two-man cars, or "putt-putts." All types of railroad locomotives were there.

Before air and truck freight became more prevalent, trains carried America on their backs. The San Jose rail yard operated twenty-four hours a day, seven days a week. The bustling industrial might of America knew no nights or days in a 1956 rail yard. My play area was inches away from the nearest track. My bedroom window was fewer than fifty feet away. The noises and smells that emanated from that rail yard were like Dante's description of the lowest level of hell. Lordy, but the shitholes Frank and Lita were willing to rent.

It didn't have to be that way. Frank and Lita both earned high wages. MT was finally living up to his familial obligations. He was forced to respond to Lita's years-old request for a divorce. Of greater import, MT was sending Lita a fat child support check each month.

But I derived little benefit from most of the money that came into our household. A huge portion of their income disappeared into Frank's nightly parties. Two or three nights a week, Lita went along. That took even more money. So they had to live cheap.

CHAPTER 32

Lita Got Pregnicated

LITA'S LONG-AWAITED DIVORCE FROM MT was final on September 5, 1956. She was a free woman. Temporarily, at least. Frank finally gave Lita a good reason to get married again: she was pregnant. They were married on October 18, 1956.

Lita was happy with that outcome. She had successfully replaced MT with another handsome cowboy. She wanted another child. Frank's child. In her mind, it was a two-for-one deal.

I was six years old. I didn't understand any of the chatter that was going on around our little trio. It was all wrapped around two words: pregnant and divorce. I was confused. The words got mixed up in my mind. I began to tell people, "Lita got pregnicated."

People laughed at my youthful mix-up. For a time. That ended when Lita suffered a miscarriage. Lita and Frank were crushed. A baby would have completed their happiness.

They masked their sadness with jokes and parties. Frank said, "Well this means we'll just have to try a little harder." Until then, they were stuck with me.

CHAPTER 33

Here's Your Happy Meal

THE INCIDENT WITH THE ORANGES was the opening shot in Frank and Lita's war on food. Uncounted skirmishes were fought before they laid full siege to my digestive tract.

When they were home, Frank and Lita didn't spend a lot of time thinking about food. They each continued to eat at least one good meal elsewhere more days than not. Lita was the prettiest waitress in the restaurant where she worked. You *know* that she was eating well. They both had nicotine in various forms to give them a boost. Frank said that large doses of alcohol kept him going.

I wasn't so lucky. I ate whatever Frank and Lita left in the kitchen cabinet, and it was empty most of the time. It was never full. My breakfast usually consisted of a piece of dry toast or maybe a bowl of cold cereal. I sometimes ate the cereal straight and dry, without milk or sugar. Lita and Frank didn't go to the store very often. They didn't want to "waste milk by letting it go sour." So they bought less milk. Which is why I had dry cereal for breakfast. Which is why I had a sour mouth most of the time. Dry cornflakes tear your mouth like razor blades.

When school was in session, I usually ate at the cafeteria. They cooked great food in those long-gone places. On some days, a cafeteria lunch was the only decent meal I received. I will always be thankful for those wonderful meals and the hands that prepared them.

But I paid for those meals with my skin. Frank resented the lunch money that Lita left on the kitchen counter each morning. He knew those coins came out of his whiskey-and-soda fund. It gave him another reason to resent me.

Lita was adamant that I *must* eat lunch in the school cafeteria every day. It was a psychological thing for her. When Lita was young, she watched other kids eat good meals while she stood on the side. Cafeteria meals were Lita's way of making things better for me.

Cafeteria meals also gave Lita bragging rights. Most of the other mothers in our group were sending their kids to school with half-stale peanut-butter sandwiches. Lita loved to brag that *her* child ate in the cafeteria every day! It was a wow moment for everyone. My cafeteria lunches were a propaganda tool for Lita; they indicated that she was taking good care of me.

Lunch money for Tommy evaporated in times of extreme financial hardship, though. You know, after Frank and Lita had partied the money away and the rent was three weeks past due. Landlords were more stringent with their eviction techniques in those days. If you got seriously behind on your rent, they would throw your belongings out onto the front lawn. Some landlords would kick you out and *keep* your things. By hook, crook, or empty kitchen cabinet, Lita made sure that the rent wasn't *too* late.

Food was tough to come by when school was out. There were no summer lunch programs back then. The dry cornflake breakfast entrée sometimes became lunch's grand repast. But don't feel too sorry about my restricted diet, folks. I was happy to have food in my stomach. Considering my history with Frank McMillan, that was an improvement of sorts.

But Lita didn't like me to eat cornflakes for lunch. Those things were expensive. She could not afford to have me eat them twice each day. She found other foods for me during the summer or in hard times. Summer/hard-time lunches invariably consisted of whatever strange sandwich Lita could put together. Any type of bread, roll, biscuit, muffin, or pastry got filled with whatever semi protein base material that was on hand.

My all-time number-one horror sandwich was a real humdinger. I remember it well because I ate it every day for about two weeks. Lita bought a full pan of cinnamon raisin pastry at a day-old bread store. In those relaxed times, "day-old" generally meant "week-old." That shit was fossilized before Lita brought it through our front door. The pastry was heavy on artificial cinnamon and white bread but light on the raisins. The pastry was about three inches thick. It was cut into three-inch cubes. The individual pieces looked like dirty white baseballs. But wait, folks, there's more. It was covered with a quarter-inch-thick coating of viscous, semi crystalized sugar.

When I first ate the pastry, I thought that it was all right but not great. The topping was gross. I refused to eat that stuff. My pastry experience went downhill from there. I quickly got to the point where I straight up refused to eat that shit. Frank didn't want to eat the pastry, either. Lita covered the vile concoction with waxed paper and shoved it into the empty kitchen cabinet.

God smiles when mortals tell her their plans. A few days later, Lita ran out of bread to make sandwiches. Sadly, there was no money to buy more bread. Frank had left our money down at the local tavern.

Lita rose to the occasion. She was raised by Ruby. My grandmother's motto was "Make do with what ya got." Lita didn't have bread, but she *did* have the almost-full pan of pastry. She made sandwiches with the weeks-old, rock-hard pastry. I don't know how she cut that crap in half. She didn't own a decent knife. She didn't have a cutting board. For all I know, Lita might have sneaked one of Frank's carpenter saws into the kitchen. Perhaps she sawed the pastry in half. I can't think of any other way it could have been done. By hook or by crook, Lita cut the three-inch cubes of pastry into neat halves.

Lita slathered the pastry with an insane quantity of yellow mustard. She hacked off a one-inch slab of Spam. She cut another slab of brown onion. Lita folded waxed paper around the so-called sandwich. She shoved the mass into a used brown-paper bag. The bag was waiting for me on the kitchen counter each morning. That was my lunch. Just that grotesque sandwich.

I would have liked to enjoy a piece of fruit or a side dish with my repast. But if there was no money to buy bread, there damned sure wasn't any for fruit, chips, or cookies. I was frequently advised that Frank and Lita didn't have chips or cookies in their lunches when *they* were growing up. I learned to do without those things too.

Some folks would sneer at my nightmare sandwiches. Many say that they wouldn't eat that kind of wretched fare. Not little Tommy Liggett. I counted myself as being fortunate to get the stuff. I knew that it was all that I would eat for lunch that day. Heck, what am I saying? I knew that I might not get any dinner that evening.

I found ways to chip off small pieces of the weeks-old pastry. I gnawed around the edges of the bigger chunks. I broke them down into smaller ones. I almost gagged as I swallowed bites of the raw Spam. The strong brown onion made my eyes water. I made a mess of the huge portion of mustard that Lita slathered on the pastry. But I ate it *all*. I even licked the last drips of gross sugar topping that were smeared on the paper with the mustard. It was food! I had something to eat! Each meal was a celebration for me. Thanksgiving, Christmas, and Easter dinner rolled up together and slathered with mustard.

Lita knew that she was feeding me shit, but she didn't care. She delivered the lunch bag with a warning: "You can eat it or fuckin' starve." I always ate.

The episode with the oranges was old news by then. It had taught me a lot of lessons. The biggest lesson was the easiest: I could *never* tell anyone outside of our little trio that I was starving. I had been trained to lie when someone asked me if I was hungry. I automatically said no.

I also knew that it wasn't safe to tell Frank or Lita that I was hungry. It was risky behavior. That type of revelation generally got me a verbal or physical hammering. I knew that it went better for me when I kept quiet. I didn't want to acquire a sore ass to accompany my growling stomach.

Still and all, I was an impetuous child. I needed periodic remedial courses on the fine points of my life. This was especially true when it came to eating. My greatest lesson on "food with Frank and Lita" was easy to learn since it was shoved down my throat.

Lesson day dawned like any other. I got up and went to school. After school, I returned to our empty apartment. That was normal. I was ravenous, but there was no food in the house. Not even a tiny snack. That last part wasn't much of a surprise to me.

Frank rolled in through our front door at about seven. He was only two hours late coming home from work. This meant his normal five-till-two "closing party" at the Rock Castle Tavern had been abbreviated. Who knows why? Maybe he ran out of money. Maybe one of his honky-tonk angels rebuffed him. Perhaps Lita was pressing him to spend more time at home. The circumstances of Frank's early return didn't matter. The effect was definite: when Frank came home early and only half drunk, he was always in a nasty mood. His behavior that night didn't deviate from the norm. Frank was *pissed*.

Frank began to bark at Lita and me before he closed the front door. They went at it for a little while. I decided to add my two cents' worth to the discussion. I interjected that I was hungry. It had been about seven hours since I ate lunch. Truth be told, I was whining. I was *starved*.

Lita advised Frank that there was no food in the house. She wanted to go grocery shopping. That really set Frank off. He said, "I done worked hard all day. I ain't a-goin' out." Here's the translation of that last statement: Frank was tired from work and half in the bag. He wanted to sit down in a chair, drink some more whiskey, read the paper, and pass out early. The subplot to his grocery-buying resistance was much more insidious. Frank didn't want to spend "his" bourbon-and-soda money on food.

Frank and Lita got into a battle royal. It quickly degenerated into a drawn-out screaming match. Lita punctuated her sentences by throwing kitchen implements. She rarely missed. Her unerring physical and verbal hits stoked the flames of Frank's anger. It's a wonder the force of his bull-like bellowing didn't blow out the kitchen windows. Both of those people could out escalate a Bengal tiger. There was no way that either one of them was going to allow him or herself to be swayed by the arguments of the other.

Rather than work on the root causes of their mutual grievances, they found a scapegoat for their frustrations: me. As usual, I came out the loser in their argument. My whining and hunger were driving both the requirement for food and the immediate need for its procurement. I became the villain. Remember, in the Bible-driven cowboy culture, there always has to be a bad guy. That gives the righteous the justification they need to pass out retribution.

Frank and Lita stopped screaming at each other. They began to scream at me. This gave them the pause they needed to collect their thoughts. They decided that we needed to go to the store. Buy something for dinner.

It was about eight when we finally left for the Safeway supermarket. They were still pissed at each other, but even more so toward me. I was as cowed as anyone who ever lived. I tried to push myself down into the car's rear seat cushions. I wanted to disappear into the softness of the woolen fabric.

Frank changed the deal while he was driving to the supermarket. He advised Lita that he would *not* be returning to that place anytime soon. She needed to make the most of their current trip. It was quite late when Frank and Lita began their shopping, but they bought enough groceries to last for a week. That took a long time to accomplish.

We got home from the supermarket at around nine fifteen. Frank and Lita were tired and grumpy. I was tired and hungry. I grabbed a banana out of the grocery bag. I ate the luscious fruit in about three bites. It tasted better than any food I have ever eaten. My impetuous gustatory act shattered the grumpy silence that had settled onto our family evening. It was the spark that Frank and Lita needed to explode into rage. Frank began to scream at me. He preached to Lita. He told her that I was "greedy, sinful, and gluttonous" because I'd wolfed down the banana.

Lita loudly proclaimed that she agreed with Frank on the fine points of his diatribe. She added that they "needed to do something to teach me some manners." Lita and Frank locked eyes as she delivered that last point. It took them about a second to come up with the perfect lesson plan.

Frank grabbed me by the shirt and pulled me toward him. He put me in a tight headlock. I could barely breathe. There was no way that I could fight Frank. I weighed about sixty pounds dripping wet. Frank stood five feet ten inches tall. He weighed 180 pounds. He didn't have an extra ounce of body fat on his lean cowboy frame. Frank was made of bone, muscle, gristle, sinew, anger, and ambition. Frank's body had been hardened by a life of hard manual labor. He was in his late twenties. He was an athlete in the prime of his life.

Once Frank had me locked up like a roped calf, Lita stepped in. She ripped a banana from the bunch. She peeled the banana with an actress's flourish. Lita ordered me to open my mouth. I refused. Lita wasn't having any of *that*. She wound her strong little right arm back like she was a base-ball pitcher. She slapped me across the cheek. The pain and surprise of her strike caused me to scream. Lita's slap had achieved its purpose: my mouth was open. She shoved the whole banana into my mouth. I tried to chew and swallow, but I couldn't keep up with Lita's frantic shoving. She pushed the last bit of banana into my mouth with the palm of her hand. It was more of a punch than an effort to get the offending fruit into my mouth. Kind of like an abbreviated coupe de grace. Except that Lita and Frank weren't through. There was no grace in their sick little coup.

Frank and Lita were laughing their heads off. They had enraptured, demonic looks on their faces. They were enjoying what they were doing to me.

Lita peeled more bananas. She shoved them into my mouth at an ever-increasing pace. I couldn't swallow them fast enough to suit Lita. She kept pushing faster and harder. Some of the bananas went down my throat; some fell onto my shirt and then down to the floor. Through it all, I played the obedient child; I held my mouth open to enable Lita's ministrations. My acquiescence enraged her. This wasn't what she wanted to see! The bitch wanted to see me *suffer*.

Lita escalated her tactics. She tried to shove a whole unpeeled banana into my mouth. At long last, I had enough. I clamped my jaws tight. Lita tried to force my jaws open with her hooked thumb, but I think that she was afraid of being bitten. Abandoning that course, Lita sought another: she shoved the pointed, blossom end of the unpeeled banana though my clenched lips. Those soft organs were no match for the hard banana or Lita's harder muscles. My lips were torn asunder. They were quickly shoved away. That left my tightly locked teeth as Lita's final obstacle to my death or subjugation.

The wailing scream that had accompanied her performance went up in pitch and timbre. She screamed, "Open up your mouth, you little fuck! You want to wolf down bananas? You want to be greedy? Open up and eat this banana, you fucking little pig!" That wasn't going to happen. My fight-or-flight response had kicked in. This was primal shit. I was going on instinct. My brain wasn't willing to stand down while my cowed sensibilities allowed Lita to choke me to death. I clenched my jaws tighter.

That behavior enraged Lita even more. She started to pound the end of the banana into my lips and teeth. Still I didn't give in, but the banana did. Nothing was left of that noble fruit but a mangled string of peels. Lita dropped the peel onto the floor. She reached for another banana. They were all gone. She had shoved eight or ten large bananas at or into my mouth.

Lita slapped her arms down to her side. She was worn out. The last of her adrenaline was spent. She slumped her shoulders and stomped out of the kitchen. Her part in the evening's performance was done.

Frank was just getting warmed up, though. He spun me out of the headlock in which I had been held for the last few minutes. I stood there a moment, choking on the remains of the bananas. My breath came in gasps, but I found it hard to breathe. Frank had bruised my throat and chest. The fucker almost squeezed me to death.

Frank didn't give me much time to ponder my aches and pains. He grabbed my shirt and jerked me toward him. He slapped me on the side of my head and said, "Look at the mess you made on this floor. Your mama worked hard all day to feed your sorry ass. Do you think that she wants to look at this mess when she gets up in the mornin'? Do you think that she wants to clean up your shit?" I shook my head. Frank slapped me on the side of the head again. He said, "What? Did you say something? If you I did, I can't hear you."

I said, "No."

Frank slapped me again and said, "No what?"

I said, "No, my mother doesn't want to see my mess in the morning."

Frank said, "I'm goin' to bed. I come back in here tomorrow mornin', this kitchen better be cleaner than it is now." For further emphasis, he added, "Don't be makin' a bunch a noise in here, boy. I'm a light sleeper. You don't want to be wakin' me up."

I said, "Yes, sir" and turned to face my cleanup job. I trudged around the kitchen, picking up pieces of bananas and the kitchen-implements-cum-weapons Lita had launched earlier. I was tired. I was sore. I could barely breathe. My lips were bruised and bloody. Several of my teeth were loose and wiggly. But I had found victory in the day. Despite all that Frank and Lita could do, I had some food in my stomach. That would be good later. I knew that I slept better when my stomach wasn't grumbling.

I cleaned up and went to bed. I don't remember anything special about the next day. It couldn't compare with what had happened the night before.

Many people have told me that I need to forgive Lita for what she did to me with the bananas on that long-ago night. They'll say, "She was just twenty-four years old. People do strange things when they are young."

But Lita's subsequent actions made it impossible for me to forgive her. I'll never forget the last Christmas party I attended with Lita's family. I was fifty-eight. Lita's pièce de résistance for family dinners was her old-fashioned banana pudding. Many of my relatives asked Lita to bring it to their gatherings. I agree; it was a wonderful dish. Lita was a fine cook.

One of my relatives mentioned that I should get some of my mother's banana pudding before it was gone. Lita overheard that comment. She picked up the bowl, looked me in the eye, and said, "Tommy likes bananas, don't you, Tommy?" She then gave a low, evil laugh. Those around us had no idea what had just occurred. They undoubtedly saw it as a quiet moment between a mother and her son. They did not realize that when I looked in my mother's eyes, I was staring into the abyss.

I suppose that an old woman's last slip of a phrase shouldn't be taken too seriously. But my mother had a life script. She repeated those same lines to me at every family gathering, decade in, decade out. In so doing, Lita revealed herself as being profoundly evil. How do you forgive someone who never stopped force-feeding you with their sickness?

CHAPTER 34

We Don't Need No Education

We don't need no education.

—*Roger Waters*

BETWEEN KINDERGARTEN AND THE SECOND grade, I attended six schools in three districts. They were spread across two states.

My first shot at the first grade was unique. Lita had a meeting with my new teacher during the first week of school. My teacher said that every other parent in my class had joined the parent-teacher association (PTA). The teacher indicated that if 100 percent of the parents joined, she would receive special recognition. I don't know if all the families had really joined. But I distinctly remember the teacher telling Lita they had. When Lita didn't seem to get the gist of the thing, the teacher repeated herself.

Lita wasn't an idiot. She knew where the teacher was going. Lita explained that she worked all day. She needed her evenings to do housework, run errands, and recoup.

Lita's response irritated the teacher. She got angry at my mother. The teacher said, "If you don't join the PTA, I won't teach Tommy."

That really set Lita off. She cussed the teacher out and laughed in her face. Lita stormed out of the room. I was standing beside the teacher's desk. I was stunned. I was riveted to the floor. I had no idea what had just happened.

Lita got all the way to the classroom door before she figured out that I wasn't behind her. She turned and screamed, "Get your ass out of there, right now." I hustled out of the room. Lita stomped off at a fast clip. I ran to catch up with her. She would have been impossible to lose, though. Her voice would have led me through the toughest maze. She was raging. She was screaming at the top of her lungs. "You fuckin' people don't have *any* idea what it's like for me to raise this little bastard all by myself." She varied the lines of her tirade as she stormed off the schoolyard. But the basic theme of her monologue never varied: Lita didn't have time for this shit.

All the teachers in that school were having parent conferences that afternoon. It was warm outside. The classroom doors were open. Heads started popping out of those doors. Most of the teachers in my school witnessed a portion of Lita's tirade. I was mortified. I never wanted to set foot on that campus again.

Lita raged at me all the way home. I don't remember if she indicated that her outburst was my fault. That wasn't necessary. I believed that every bad thing on earth was my fault. I don't remember anything else about that day. I never seemed to remember much that happened in the hours and days that followed one of Frank and Lita's blowups. I was stunned. I floated through life in a dazed condition.

Lita viewed her interaction with my teacher as being a personal victory. At family gatherings Lita fondly recalled how she "told off Tommy's teacher." My family always thought that it was a funny story. No one ever realized that the real punch line was on me.

My teacher made good on her promise. Early the next day, she moved my desk to the far end of the room. I was separated from the other students by at least ten feet. That was step one in my teacher's carefully orchestrated program of nonteaching.

Step two was demonstrated the first time I put my hand up to ask a question. The teacher ignored me. She pretended I wasn't there.

Step three was even better: the teacher didn't speak to me in a normal voice. In fact, she rarely spoke to me. When she did speak, her words were sparse, loud, and focused. The teacher rebuked, scolded, criticized, and humiliated me. Any attention she gave to me was negative.

Things were better when the teacher ignored me altogether. I sat at my desk and stared into space. My training as the amazing invisible perfect silent kid served me well during my time in that woman's classroom. I was unfazed by my teacher's abuse and neglect. I ate those two commodities in my cornflakes without milk almost every morning.

I spent most of the school year sitting alone and quiet at an empty desk. I remained separate from the other children. My teacher didn't teach me *anything*. I can't remember a single thing I learned in that woman's class-room. I certainly didn't learn to read.

I knew how to understand a few numbers, but I knew nothing useful about arithmetic. My scanty mathematical knowledge was flawed. You see, I'd learned to count from the Mexican kids in the apricot-drying sheds. Most of the numbers I did know were in Spanish, not English.

In the annals of my childhood horrors, the time I spent living on Hobson Street stands out in singular fashion. It was a milestone. Frank and Lita shifted their brutality and neglect into high gear when we lived on Hobson Street. That apartment's kitchen was the scene of the great banana-shoving incident. We were living on Hobson Street when Lita pissed off my teacher. And it was there that I had my first offer of a sexual favor (more on that a few pages on).

I received my first kitten while we lived on Hobson Street. One day Frank came in drunk and roared up the driveway in his car. He ran over the kitten. I witnessed the whole thing. I saw that poor kitten's intestines squirt out of its mouth. I went into hysterics. That set Frank off. Frank screamed at me, "This is all your fault. If you hadn't gotten that cat, this wouldn't have happened. You ain't no good at takin' care of them fleabags. You don't deserve no more. You ain't gettin' no more."

From the moment of my birth, I had been told by Lita that every bad thing that happened was my fault. I believed that I had caused the kitten's death. Every time I replayed the tapes of my kitten's death in my mind, the same thoughts kept coming back: *You caused the death of your kitty. You don't deserve to have another one.*

The process of writing this book changed me as a person. It opened my eyes about many things. I finally understood the underlying reason for the rapid escalation of abuse and neglect I experienced while we were living on Hobson Street.

That reason was quite simple: it was the first time that Frank and Lita weren't being watched by others. That was how Frank had arranged things. He didn't want anyone to examine the fine points of his life. He wanted to be left alone.

That was why Frank was so eager to leave the magnificent apartment we rented from the Mercer family. It wasn't cowboy restlessness that drove him away from that place. The Mercers and their vast group of friends took keen interest in the activities of the young family that plopped down in their midst. Frank wanted his home life to be out of the sight of anyone who knew him more than casually.

The ancient Roman poet Juvenal wrote, "Who will watch the watchmen?" Ruby had been the lioness who stood guard at the door of my life. But she was living far away. She would not return for several years.

There wasn't anyone in my life who cared enough to notice that a little boy was being starved, beaten, and left totally alone.

There is a sad footnote to my Hobson Street experience. I was six years old. I didn't really grasp the concept that Lita was my mother. I had absolutely no idea M. T. existed. I didn't have a dad. I had Frank. Dads were things that other little boys enjoyed.

When I was seven, M. T. knocked on our front door. He appeared completely unannounced. It was as if he'd dropped out of the clear blue sky. He was in San Jose for one day only. I don't remember much about that day except that M. T. gave me a bicycle. He bought the much-repaired thing from a sailor at Moffett Field Naval Air Station. M. T. made a big deal of showing me how to ride the bike down the middle of Hobson Street. It was great. Frank and Lita stood on the sidewalk. They cheered as M. T. coached me. M. T. was holding onto the bicycle's seat and handlebars, and then he wasn't. I was riding a two-wheeler all by myself! Frank, Lita, and M. T. cheered even louder. "You're doing it, Tommy." I was on top of the world.

Then the frame of the bicycle broke into pieces. The bike was junk. I spilled onto the pavement. I was tangled in a mass of frame pieces, wheels, and drive chain. I hit the ground hard. I erupted in tears. Neither Frank nor M. T. was having any of that shit. One or both said, "Buck up there, cowboy. Men don't cry." They were embarrassed by my behavior.

They lifted me out of the bicycle wreck and dusted off my pants. M. T. was sad because the bicycle had failed. He said, "Don't worry, Tommy. I'll bring you a brand-new bicycle real soon." M. T.'s promise dried my tears. I was elated. I would get to see my dad again. I would also get a new bicycle. That would allow me to explore the farthest reaches of Hobson Street. Yippee!

M. T. was with me for just a few hours that day. He showered me with love, affection, and gifts. He made me feel like I was the most important thing in the world. That was the first and only time anyone had done that type of thing for me. Then M. T. vanished. He was there and gone. He left me with a stone in my heart. A few hours before, I was blissfully unaware that I had a dad. Now I missed not having one. Heartbreak, heartbreak, childhood be thy name.

M. T.'s visit carried me through the next few weeks. I told everyone I met, "I have a dad! He's coming back to see me! He's going to bring me a new bike!" People got tired of hearing me say that shit. I was like a one-note flute. I said the same thing over and again.

Well, folks, it pains me to admit that the promised bicycle never materialized. Neither did the return visit from MT. I didn't see that asshole for another seven years. I would have been better off if he had left me alone.

Fast-forward a half century. I emptied Lita's house after she died. I found a pair of high-quality photographs that were taken during M. T.'s single visit with me. They look like they were taken by a professional photographer. I had absolutely no idea that the photographs existed before I found them buried in Lita's belongings.

The photos are of M. T. and me. We are both wearing brand-new Levi's 501 jeans. The pictures depict a handsome M. T. and a cute me doing beguiling things.

Anyone who saw those damned photographs would think that I had a great dad. But it was all smoke and mirrors. The photos were as posed as the rest of my life. I was a stage prop. I was the tool of callous and uncaring people.

Tom Liggett with MT. I was seven years old. Isn't this a perfectly framed photograph? Don't we make a pretty pair? It was all smoke and mirrors. Three hours before this shot was taken, I didn't know M. T. existed. He filled me with a child's dreams of family and new bicycles. None of that happened. I didn't see M. T. for another seven years. Thanks, dude. Stevens Creek Dam. July 1957.

CHAPTER 35

Sexualization 101

A FAMILY OF FOUR PEOPLE lived across the street from our Hobson Street duplex. There was a daddy who worked outside of the home. There was a mommy who worked inside of the home. They had two boys; one was about six, the other was about four.

We lived on Hobson Street for about a year. Those boys were the closest thing I had to friends. I didn't get to visit with those boys very frequently. Frank and Lita didn't want me to be around anyone when they weren't at home. They knew that other people would ask, "Where are your mommy and daddy? Why did they leave you all alone?" Frank and Lita knew I would spill the beans. They didn't want other people to realize how much time I spent alone.

The man across the street bought his older son a new BB gun. The father asked me if I would like to go with them to shoot the gun. I obtained parental permission to go along.

We drove down Gish Road to Coyote Creek. The father parked the car on the side of the road. We walked along the creek bank. The father loaded the BB gun. He showed his son how to shoot. The boy was soon hitting his targets. The father beamed with joy. He said, "Isn't my son a fine marksman?"

I provided the obligatory, "Oh yes, sir, he's really something." We got in the car and drove home. Neither member of the father-son duo offered to let me shoot the gun. I was just there to provide an audience to their familiarity. I was a prop, just like with Frank and Lita.

That type of strange scenario was played out countless times with other fathers. They took me along on outings so that I could bear witness to their familial devotion. It was like taking a starving man to a banquet but not allowing him to eat. To hell with those who denied a fatherless boy the crumbs from their tables.

Frank, Lita, and I sometimes had dinner with the family across the street. Those events were always held at their house. I don't think that any of those people ever set foot in our apartment. That aspect of their supposed friendship is very telling.

I remember one evening we spent with the neighbors across the street. We ate dinner. The adults sat at the kitchen table, chatting. I went off to play with the two brothers. I soon discovered that I needed to urinate. I excused myself from the brothers and went into the bathroom. It felt good to empty my bladder. The two brothers abruptly walked into the bathroom. They crowded next to me by the toilet. They began to urinate. Try to picture three young boys simultaneously pissing into the same toilet. There's your *real* Norman Rockwell moment.

The younger brother looked at me and said, "Let me suck your dick." The older sibling instantly chimed in, offering to help. I was stunned. All I saw was the urine streaming out of my penis. I didn't want anybody to put *that* nasty thing into their mouth. I was embarrassed. I zipped my fly and walked away.

Though I didn't mention that incident to anyone else, it represented something of a milestone: it was the first time that someone offered to have sex with me. I was still years away from knowing what the word sex meant. But words and actions are two different things.

Actions in the sexual arena are derived from the fact that there is something compelling about human genitalia. We spend our whole lives in a futile quest to cover, uncover, touch, and not touch our own and other people's "naughty bits." It's as if we all have magnets in our crotches and iron in our brains.

Those brothers' attempts to get me to engage in sex play were followed by others of like kind. When I was six or seven, two family members masturbated in front of me. I didn't participate in that episode either. I found the whole spectacle to be revolting. Especially the finish.

I didn't know it at the time, but such actions were apparently commonplace in my mother's family. Long before I was born, older family members were sexualizing the younger ones. Lita was quite proud of the fact. She said, "Everybody was doing it. I did it with my cousin." It was a family tradition.

I'm certain that's what must have happened with the two brothers who offered me fellatio. The younger one initiated the play, but the older one was undoubtedly the real aggressor.

It is not good for children to become sexualized. An engorged penis contains an awesome power, even if it is aged in the single digits. Few young boys have the sense to deal with that kind of two-edged sword.

When I was seven, I began to make comparisons between my three sexual experiences. I found my mother's pussy-displaying behavior to be embarrassing. My relatives' masturbatory displays were disgusting. But the offer from the two brothers was vaguely intriguing. No, I'm not saying that I wanted to play with the brothers in an intimate way. But their actions planted a seed within me. I learned that people enjoy playing with each other's private parts. I was still years from acting on such thoughts. Nonetheless, the seed of premature sexualization took root in my psyche and began to grow. Thus were fired the opening salvos in my great war on human sexuality.

CHAPTER 36

Water Torture, Part Two

TOMMY TOMLINSON, RUBY, AND HER minor children were living at China Lake Naval Air Station during this stage of my story. Lita missed Ruby and the children. She wanted to visit them. She asked Frank to drive her to China Lake, but he refused. Frank was willing to drive to Texas at a moment's notice, but he was unwilling to regularly take Lita to see her mother in Southern California.

Lita decided to take a Greyhound bus. I went along for the ride. The bus stopped in Mojave, California. Ruby and Tommy Tomlinson picked us up at the station. We rode back to China Lake in Tommy Tomlinson's new Chevrolet sedan.

It was a very interesting visit. I hadn't seen the person I called Momma for several months. I reconnected with everyone in her family. We had lots of fun outings—and one that was not so fun.

China Lake Naval Air Station is located on the edge of the great Mojave Desert. It gets hotter than hell in that place. The base swimming pool is a big attraction to navy personnel and their families. Tommy Tomlinson wasted no time showing Lita and me the huge pool. He explained that we would go there the next day. He looked at me and said, "Doesn't that sound like fun? "I don't remember exactly how I responded, but I do recall how I felt: scared.

I didn't have to come up with an answer for Tommy Tomlinson about the upcoming pool visit—he already knew. He used that knowledge to torment me until we actually went to that place. Over and again, he'd say, "We're going swimming. I'm gonna teach you how to swim." He never failed to laugh as he delivered the last line.

When pool day finally came around, I was truly scared. My mind was wrapped as tight as rubber band.

We got to the pool, but I refused to go near the water. I didn't want Tommy Tomlinson to make good on his promise to throw me in the pool. All the other kids jumped right into the pool. They kidded, teased, and begged me to come in the water.

I shook my head with an emphatic no. I chewed my fingernails down to the quick. But I knew that sooner or later, Tommy Tomlinson was going to make good on his promise. For a while, it looked like that wouldn't happen. After a few cans of Falstaff beer, though, Tommy Tomlinson finally figured it was torture time. He snuck up behind me and snatched me up. One moment I was standing on the ground. The next moment, Tommy Tomlinson was holding me up in the air and walking toward the deep end of the pool. He stepped right to the edge and held me over the water. The smell of the chlorine and the sight of the blue water beneath my feet scared me so badly, I almost shit my pants. I was screaming like a banshee. Tommy Tomlinson added to my fear by providing a running commentary on the salient points of the sink-or-swim water-training method.

Every eye in the pool area was turned toward me and Tommy Tomlinson. Some of the drunken sailors offered him tips on his technique. No one came to my aid.

After what seemed to be an eternity, Tommy Tomlinson stepped away from the pool. He lowered me down to chest level. Ruby came running over with a camera. She said, "Tommy, I'm going to take a picture of you. I'm going to send it to you. I want you to see how bad you look when you raise such a ruckus."

Ruby made good on her promise. She took a well-framed photograph. I have included that photo in this book. Note the condescending look on Tommy Tomlinson's face. He was mocking me. But the real tragedy in that photograph is revealed in my face. Look at my mouth. It is pulled into a grim rictus. See the cringing fear in my eyes. I was half out of my mind from fear of drowning.

But that sick little photo has more to reveal. My arms and legs are wrapped tightly around Tommy Tomlinson's torso. I had him locked up in a child-sized death grip. I was clinging to my abuser (just as I always did). I knew my abusers were all that stood between me and the deep blue sea.

Tommy Tomlinson and Tom Liggett. Note how I am clinging to his torso. I knew my abusers were all that stood between me and the deep blue sea. Base swimming pool, China Lake Naval Air Station. 1957.

CHAPTER 37

Tumbleweeds

LITA QUIT HER JOB AT the fancy restaurant. The manager pissed her off. Lita was sick of waiting on other people; she had been doing that for over twenty years.

Lita needed to find another job. She looked at the want ads in our local newspaper. She saw an ad that piqued her interest. The manager of a local Sprouse-Reitz five-and-dime store was looking for an assistant manager. Lita quickly dialed the phone number that accompanied the ad. A pleasant young man answered the phone. He and Lita had a nice conversation. He said, "You've got the job. Can you start right now?" Lita said yes. She drove from our Hobson Street duplex to the corner of Hamilton and Meridian.

Lita parked the car in front of the Sprouse-Reitz store. She walked in the door. A young man was standing by the cash register. Lita identified herself as being the woman who answered the ad. He said, "I'm the store manager. I'm going on my honeymoon. I'll see you in two weeks. Here are the keys. Here is the cash envelope. Hold onto the daily receipts until I get back." The nice young man turned around and walked out the door. Lita said that the whole conversation was less than a minute long.

Lita stood in the middle of the store. She had the keys in one hand and an envelope full of cash in the other. She knew nothing about retail. She knew nothing about the store's stock. Lita said, "I needed to learn quick."

The trusting young man returned two weeks later. The cash drawer was balanced to the penny. The shelves were stocked and faced. The floors were clean. The glass on the front door was sparkling clean. Lita had successfully completed her probationary period. She was the full-time assistant manager of a five-and-dime store.

Lita loved the job. She was making good money. The manager was seldom there. He let her run the store. She did it all—checking, ordering, stocking, cleaning. Lita loved the customers. Most of them were wealthy mavens from the Willow Glen neighborhood. The customers loved Lita too.

The Sprouse-Reitz store occupied three-quarters of a long, low building. The last quarter of the building housed a restaurant where Lita would sometimes grab a cup of coffee or a bite to eat. The restaurant was owned by a small-time businessman named Doc. Doc and Lita became friends. Doc had something to do with the gasoline station that was across Meridian Avenue from the dime store / restaurant building. He said that the gas station was looking for a night manager.

Doc wondered if Frank would like to work at the gas station. Lita thought that Frank would. He was sick of pounding nails. He was sick of manual labor. He had been doing it since he could walk.

Frank quit the carpenter's union. He took the job at the gas station. It made for a cozy arrangement with Lita. They only had one car. Frank and Lita thought that working in the same place would simplify their lives. It took me to a lower level of hell.

When Frank and Lita worked their old jobs, I was alone most of the time. That was bad, but it had its perks. No one was yelled at me when I was alone. I also got to do what I wanted. I built forts in abandoned foundations and stairways. I made boats out of cast-off bits of lumber. I looked at plants in abandoned lots. I petted every stray cat that allowed my approach.

Frank's stints at the Rock Castle Tavern were hit-and-miss affairs. Sometimes he was home at night. Lita could tolerate that kind of abusive balance. But the gas station job upset that balance. He was at the gas station five or six nights each week. He was at the tavern on the others. Lita didn't want to be away from her man *every* night.

Lita found a ready solution to that problem. She would "visit" Frank at the gas station. These weren't like the fifteen-minute visits she paid me while she was working at the bakery. Lita went to the gas station almost every night. She stayed until closing. Lita said that they were the best times of her life. Frank was at work. She had a captive audience. He wasn't drunk. Lita told my aunts that they went into the bathroom and "got frisky." Frank kept the bathroom clean.

But there was a fly in the ointment of her happiness: me. Lita began to feel guilty that she was leaving me alone. She believed that I needed more companionship. Lita took me to the gas station each night that Frank was working. How late were we there? Until Frank sold his quota of gasoline and could shut off the lights. Not before. Frank sometimes met his quota at ten in the evening. It was sometimes three in the morning when he locked the gas station doors.

What was that like for me? Oh, I can tell you in fine detail. Those memories were burned into my brain by frequent repetition. Frank worked at that gas station for months. Here's how a typical evening at the gas station went for me: Lita parked the car on the side of the gas station lot. She walked directly over to Frank. If he was with a customer, she would just wave and then walk on. If he was alone, she would give him a kiss. Frank would give me a gruff greeting. "Men don't get affectionate with each other" was an oft-heard Frank motto.

My first familial gas station visit set the tone for all that followed. Frank showed Lita the gas station office. It was a stark metal cube that was fronted by glass on two sides. A doorway led into the service bay. The rear wall was blank. Aside from a few corporate posters, the place was barren. The furniture completed the office's jail-like ambience. It consisted of a green metal desk and a couple of matching chairs. All were painted in US Army olive-drab green. It was military surplus furniture.

Frank waved his arm around the office and said, "There ain't much to see. I don't spend no time in here anyway. I'm supposed to be outside, a-helpin' customers." That was the end of Lita's tour.

Next came mine. Frank said, "I can't have no brats runnin' around this place. I don't want you a-pesterin' my customers. If you get hurt, I might lose my job." He then said, "Sit your ass in that chair. Don't move unless I tell you to. You got that?"

I quickly said, "Yes, sir." By that time, I knew full well that Frank didn't accept nods from me.

I sat in the hard metal army chair several nights a week. I had no toys and nothing to occupy my mind. If I wanted to use the bathroom, I had to get Frank's or Lita's attention. I couldn't leave my seat to ask about *anything*. Frank would have taken that as willful disobedience on my part. I sat quietly in the chair. Frank and Lita were always ready to unleash the full weight of their wrath upon me. I knew that it was best to remain invisible.

Most nights, there was no food. Dinner for me on such nights usually consisted of a promise that I would eat "later on." That faint hope was always paired with the imprecation, "If you don't stop your whining, I'll give you something to *really* cry about."

I sat and sat. At some point, I fell asleep. Frank brusquely woke me up. He said, "Come on, Tommy. Ya can't lay there all night. I gotta get me some sleep." I staggered out of my chair, entered the car, and fell asleep again. Frank roused me when we got home.

I didn't sleep very well in the metal chair. The car ride offered a few minutes' more rest. A couple of hours in my own bed and it was time to get up for school. I dragged myself through the ensuing days. I was beat. I tried to sleep at my school desk. But the neglectful teacher wasn't having any of *that*. No one slept in *her* classroom! My overriding sleepiness gave her another weapon.

Lita added boredom and sleep deprivation to the semi starvation that she regularly served me. I was sleepwalking through life. I was in a waking nightmare.

Every succeeding night at the gas station was like the first, with one notable exception. Just a few months before, the block behind the gas station had been covered with fruit trees. Now it was being developed as a shopping center. Brand-new blacktop had replaced the trees. The paving equipment was parked on the perimeter of the lot.

I was awakened from my fitful slumber by the sound of a loud engine. Someone was driving the pavement-rolling machine around the parking lot. They were doing laps around other pieces of equipment.

This was exciting stuff! I forgot that I was never supposed to part ways with the metal chair. I ran to the rear of the gas station. I wanted to see what was going on. The parking lot was dark. I couldn't see much, but my ears told me the story well enough. In the distance, I heard childish laughter and the put-putting of the pavement roller's small gasoline engine. Over it all, I heard Frank screaming, "You kids get offa that machine. You might hurt somebody."

I soon caught a glimpse of Frank. He was chasing the kids who were driving the machine. When the children saw that a screaming wild man was catching up with them, they abandoned their vehicle. They threw catcalls and jeers at Frank as they retreated into the darkness.

I was laughing my ass off. I thought that it was the funniest thing I had ever seen. Those kids were having *fun!*

Frank walked over to where I was standing. He was angry. He was shaking. He was muttering about something the kids had said to him. Frank walked up to me and said, "What are you doing out here? Why aren't you sitting in the chair?"

I told him, "I heard the noise. I wanted to see what was going on."

Frank said, "I'll bet you thought them kids was pretty cute. I bet you thought that was fun. Didn't you?"

I was full of fun and excitement. I was energized. I failed to grasp the danger of the moment. I said, "Oh yes! I would *love* to ride the little putt-putt machine." Oh boy, Tommy, you really stepped in the shit with *that* comment.

Frank grabbed me by the shirt. He slapped my face and then spun me around. Frank kicked my sorry little ass all the way around the building and into the office. He slapped, hit, and kicked me some more. Frank picked me up and threw me into the chair. He tossed me like a basketball. Frank walked over to me and said, "You move your ass out of that chair again, I *will* kill you. Do you understand?"

Oh, I understood plenty well enough. I was beaten, battered, and bruised. I felt like I had fallen off a cliff. I determined that I would *never* leave that chair unless I was ordered to do so.

Someone in the gas station company saw that Frank was doing a good job running their station. They gave Frank a promotion: he became part owner of a gas station franchise in Gilroy, California. Frank was ecstatic. He said, "This is my big break!"

But there was a catch to the deal. The previous franchisee had abruptly abandoned the gas station. The gasoline company needed someone to run their station *now*. Frank jumped at the deal. We quickly moved to Gilroy.

Frank and Lita didn't think about the effect our quick move had on me. The school year was almost over. Just three more weeks remained. No one cared that I was torn away from the few friends I had made during our short time on Hobson Street. Truth be told, neither one of those considerations bothered me very much. I didn't mind moving away from the Hobson Street hellhole. I certainly didn't mind escaping from the teacher who didn't teach me. Two bad things were removed from my life.

Frank and Lita performed an uncharacteristic act in Gilroy: they rented a nice house. It was on a quiet, well-kept street. Huge elm trees provided both shade and ambience. I had my own bedroom. I even had a bed. The large backyard contained a small orchard. I can still name the varieties of fruit trees that grew there.

A big family lived across the street. They had a couple of kids who were my age. An old blind uncle lived with the family. He played children's games with us. It was paradise for me.

I liked my new teacher. She was clueless about what to do with one such as me. I vividly remember the sole parent-teacher conference that Lita attended. My new teacher asked Lita, "How can it be that Tommy knows absolutely *nothing*?" The teacher elaborated on the subject. She said,

"Tommy doesn't know his letters. He doesn't know his numbers. He doesn't know *anything*."

You might think my teacher's hardball question would have given Lita pause. It did not. Lita instantly chirped, "Tommy was born two months prematurely. He has always been behind everyone else."

Lita never failed to pull that chestnut out of the fire when she needed an excuse for my perceived indiscretions and shortcomings. But there was a problem: that wasn't an accurate fact. It was a carefully crafted lie. I was almost full term when I was born.

Lita told people I was born prematurely for a simple reason: she didn't want them to know that I was conceived before she was married. Later on, Lita told people I was immature to provide cover. A plausible excuse for my unexplainable failures. It gave her an out.

But Lita conveniently failed to mention our frequent moves houses or the negligent behavior of my previous first grade teacher. Lita sure as hell failed to mention that I was regularly staying up until past midnight.

For some inexplicable reason, my new teacher promoted me to the second grade. She must have naïvely assumed that I would be attending that same school the next year. She must have thought that a known second-grade teacher at her school would give me the help I needed to catch up with my peers. Oh, sweet lady, you didn't know how Frank lived his life, did you? That naïve little teacher set the stage for one of the biggest humiliations of my life.

Meanwhile, things were moving along on in terms of my sexualization. By this time, I was well used to the sight of Lita's naked body. She knew that I was embarrassed by her behavior. This only seemed to cement her resolve to parade around in various stages of undress.

You might think that this would have put me off on women, but it didn't. I put her behavior into my old mental trick bag. It resided there with the other instructions and advances that came my way. I encapsulated the infection before it did too much harm to my psyche.

During our short tenancy in Gilroy, my sexual barometer received a small uptick from an unexpected source. A married couple dropped by to visit with Frank and Lita. They brought their daughter with them. She was about my age. I had not previously met any of those folks.

The adults wanted to talk. I wanted to show someone the small backyard orchard. As usual, the adults weren't interested. The daughter perked up when I mentioned the fruit trees. That was great news to me.

The little girl and I wandered out back. As soon as we got into the orchard, the little girl revealed that she wasn't interested in fruit trees, either. I wasn't surprised. Excepting Lita, nobody I knew showed much enthusiasm for fruit trees. I was used to folks saying, "Uh-huh" and acting vaguely bored whenever I started going on about the wonders and vagaries of fruit trees.

It turned out that the little girl didn't want to see anything outside. She wanted to get out of the house so that she could urinate. First chance she got, she lifted her dress, squatted down, and took a long, luxurious piss. She never stopped talking during that process. In fact, she looked me right in the eye. The little girl seemed to be amused by my discomfiture. She grinned like a monkey. She asked, "Would you like to look at my pussy?"

I nodded and walked over to her. I got down on my hands and knees and looked up at her vulva. That was an easy thing to accomplish because the girl wasn't wearing panties.

This was different than the times Lita had forced me to look at her privates. Lita was my mother. Despite all that she could do to the contrary, I knew that it was wrong for me to get a charge out of looking between her legs. There was another consideration: Lita was hairy. I couldn't really detect many of the fine details of her vulva.

None of those constraints applied to my newfound friend. The girl was my age. She was *quite* eager to show me her genitals. It was thrilling. It made my little penis throb. Just as I was taking a better look at the girl's plumbing, she decided to reveal the punch line to her joke: she squatted down farther and produced an adult-sized turd.

The look of surprise and dismay on my face made the little girl break out into uncontrollable laughter. At about that time, we heard the adults coming out of the house. She quickly pulled down her dress and stood up. We must have had guilty looks on our faces because someone asked us what we were doing. The little girl and I smiled at each other and said, "Nothing."

Frank noticed the seconds-old turd lying on the ground. He laughed and said, "Musta been a dog come through here."

I was Lita's only child. The terms of that singleness isolated me from a large part of the realm of secret knowledge that exists between siblings. The astounding quantity of time I spent alone cemented that ignorance. I wonder, is it common for other children to experience the same type of precocious sexual fumblings I experienced? I'm certain that such behaviors are more prevalent in some families than in others. At six, I was well acquainted with the fact that it was prevalent in *mine*.

Things with Frank's new gasoline station venture didn't work out well. He had to work more hours and later at night. This meant longer hours and more missed dinners for me. I don't remember much about the Gilroy gas station office or chair. They shared too much in common with their San Jose counterparts. One jail is like another, as seen from the inside.

Frank started driving a taxi cab. He came and went at all hours. After a couple of months, he decided to abandon the Gilroy gas station venture.

Lita was working as a waitress in a local restaurant. We were living off her tips. All accounts indicate that she made a bundle at every restaurant. Who wouldn't want to be served by the prettiest woman they ever saw? Besides, everybody liked Lita.

The stress of Frank's business failure made him want to move again. But there was a problem. None of our moves brought Frank any closer to the place he *really* wanted to live: Texas.

Lita didn't want to move to Texas. She had lived in places that had similar climates. She didn't like them. Lita preferred the San Francisco Bay Area's mild climate to the heat and cold of Texas. She also didn't appreciate the astounding quantity of insect life in Texas. Lita enjoyed going to the mountains and the beach. Most of all, she didn't want to leave the various elements of Ruby's large family.

Frank and Lita began to argue incessantly. It looked as if they might split up. Frank said that he was moving to Texas with or without her. In the face of his ultimatum, Lita acquiesced and said that she would move to Texas. She didn't want to accumulate a second divorce before her twenty-fifth birthday.

You might think that Lita's acquiescence would bring some peace to our family. It didn't work out that way. Frank and Lita fought day and night. Lita told everyone in her circle that she was not happy with the prospect of moving to Texas. She told Frank a hundred times a day that she was not happy. But she would go. She would "take one for the team."

There were no surprises in my mother's behavior. Like most all favors that Lita granted in life, she exacted a definite and exorbitant price from the recipient.

CHAPTER 38

Riding into the Sunrise

DURING THE EARLY YEARS OF their marriage, Frank and Lita traveled light. Part of that came from the mechanics of their lives; they were young. They hadn't acquired many possessions.

The larger part of that concept derived from Frank's cowboy viewpoint. He regularly said, "I don't want to own anything I can't throw in a car and git gone in thirty minutes." Replace the word car with saddlebag and you will reveal the kernel of his viewpoint. Frank behaved like a nineteenth-century American cowboy who was riding between ranches.

Moving from house to house is tough. Moving across a continent adds a level of difficulty. Using a car and trailer as the sole conveyance of people and household goods takes the difficulty off the scale. This forced hard choices on us. We couldn't take a lot of stuff with us to our new landing spot.

I was almost seven when we lived in Gilroy. Frank had been in my life for about thirty-three months. In that time, we had lived in at least five dwellings. I had made at least four moves with Frank. All of them began the same way. Frank stormed into our house. He tossed a cardboard box in my direction. He would then say, "Put your things in that box, we're moving to [our mystery destination] right now."

The moving boxes that Frank threw at me were always small. The first time I saw one, I questioned Frank. I told him my things would not fit in the box. I did not want to leave most of my possessions behind.

My childish declaration elicited the recitation of one of his most-loved judgmental sayings: "You're in love with them things. Being in love with things is a sin. You're greedy. You're gonna burn in hell for it."

Sometimes, Frank would grab his ancient Bible and read an assortment of verses. On moving day, those verses seemed to center on human greed. The frequent applications of Frank's biblical whip always ended the same way: sinners (like me) would burn in hell forever.

When Frank said those things to me, I believed them to be the absolute truth. At such times, I felt a double whammy of emotion. I felt bad about losing some pitiful items. I also felt evil for wanting to take them with me. In Frank's eyes, the abandonment of my few belongings was justified. Each move became an object lesson in morality for Tommy.

I always seemed to get the short end of the moving stick. Toys and garden things are much more expendable than household appliances. I left the most stuff behind at our old dwellings.

Frank came into our lives in 1954. I am very glad that we were not living in 1854. I would have been stuffing things into saddlebags. Those contrivances are smaller than the tiniest automobile trunk. But there is a larger truth: Frank would have been happier if he owned just what would fit into a pair of saddlebags.

Frank's cowboy proclivity for precipitous moves left little time for planning. That first move to Texas was no different. Frank and Lita spent a tense twenty-four hours getting ready to go. They turned off the household utilities. They sorted through our belongings (most of them went as gifts). They cleaned the house. Last of all, they packed the car and small U-Haul trailer.

That was a lot of work to accomplish in twenty-four hours. Most people would expect a lot of chaos. Not our family. Frank ran our moves like military operations. But there was a price to be paid for their efficiency: Frank and Lita worked through the night so that they could leave the next day. When they were packed and ready to move, they hadn't slept for at least thirty-six hours.

In similar fashion, the preparations for our move to Texas were finally complete. No blood had been shed. The tired couple took a nap and tore off a piece of ass. They needed clear heads for the long drive ahead.

A few hours later, Frank roused us. We got into the car. Frank was worn out when he got behind the wheel. He had a heck of a drive ahead of him. Frank had to drive half the length and all the breadth of California. He had to drive down and across Arizona and New Mexico. He had to drive halfway across the huge state of Texas. Most of that passage went through the desert. That's a whole lot of driving for anyone to make. Especially a tired man.

High summer was approaching. Automobile air conditioning was a rare and expensive technology in those days. It was a luxury that few people we knew could afford. Most folks barreled down the desert roads with the windows open. Every redneck and black man I ever knew called it "four-seventy" air conditioning. That means four windows open at seventy miles per hour.

There were no interstate highways between California and Texas in 1957. Our trip would be 1,650 miles. Most of it was on two-lane roads. Those old highways went through every one-horse town in the universe. Frank would drive like a maniac for a few miles and then crawl through a dried-up little town at fifteen to twenty-five miles per hour.

Regular travelers through those parts knew that small roadside municipalities derived much of their income from traffic citations. God help you if you gave a backwoods constable some lip. He'd knock your ass into the middle of next week and *then* hand you the ticket. You sure didn't want him to wake up the local justice of the peace in the off hours. Hard experience demonstrated that it was always best for an outsider to drive slowly through wayside towns.

Those pre freeway roads followed routes laid down by Indians and white pioneers. They were built in places that met the needs of people, horses, mules, and oxen, not cars and trucks. The roads stuck to rivers, streams, and lakes where thirsty livestock could drink.

Draft animals tire easily if they are forced to climb and descend steep grades. But until recently, there was no practical way to cut easier routes through mountains and hills. For these reasons, the highways from California to Texas wound around hills instead of through them. There were thousands of small grades and descents to test overheated engines, primitive brakes, and tired drivers.

Those narrow roads provided the only routes for cars and truck across the United States. The traffic was horrendous. Heavy trucks carried a lot of freight. In those days, heavy trucks had very little power and horrible brakes. If truck drivers went down long grades at anything much above a crawl, they would lose their brakes. Imagine an out-of-control, sixty-thousand-pound truck screaming downgrade toward you.

Cars that were doing seventy miles per hour shared two-lane roads with trucks that were creeping along at ten. Everyone was in a hurry to get across the desert wastes. Tired car drivers continually passed lumbering trucks. Drivers jumped out into the oncoming traffic lane at the earliest possible moment. That risky behavior caused an incredible number of head-on collisions. The highways between California and Texas were littered with overheated vehicles and wrecked hulks.

We had traveled via the same route two years earlier, when we escorted Frank's family back to their home in Texas. That had been a somewhat relaxing trip. We slept in motels and ate in restaurants.

Our first cross-country move with Frank was an entirely different creature. It set the tone for all our future Texas trips. As soon as we got into the car, Frank made it clear that he was going to get us to Texas as quickly as possible. He added a new phrase to my vocabulary of cowboy terms that day. He said that we were going to drive straight through. Driving a car or riding a horse straight through means that you only stop to take a piss and to check and fuel the conveyance. Nothing else happens along the way. No sightseeing, no rest stops, no motels, no restaurants. Most of all, there was no whining from assorted wives and children. Or else.

We started our trip with a loaf of bread, two pounds of unsliced bologna, some brown onions, and a full tank of gas. At regular intervals, the car was topped off with gas. Likewise, we were topped off with inch-thick slabs of bologna and onion. More bologna was bought as needed. We had no ice chest to prevent larger quantities of sandwich meat from spoiling in the desert heat.

Any complaints pertaining to the quality or quantity of the food were met with Old Testament quotations and imprecations. Frank usually ended his food sermons with the same thought: "You're lucky to git what you got."

I was born and raised in cowboy culture. I knew lots of people who regularly drove between California and points east. They knew all the routes. They knew the time it took to traverse each of them. They knew which routes were best during various seasons. Most of the men in that group made special efforts to equal or better a previous record for completing the trip. Frank was no different. He drove like a madman between California and Texas.

Frank was driving horses and mules before he was ten years old. Not long after, he was driving cars and trucks. That was about the same time he became an alcoholic. Driving horses, mules, cars, or trucks while he was impaired was not a big thing for Frank McMillan. Most of the males he knew were doing the same thing. Long practice and excellent motor skills made Frank an adept, if not safe, drunk driver.

Frank saw our trips to Texas as manly adventures. He was taking on the elements, just like countless generations of his forefathers. Frank viewed bourbon whiskey as a reward for his heroic driving. Disregarding contrary scientific evidence, he also believed that alcohol was a stimulant.

Every few minutes, Frank reached under the seat, picked up a bottle, and took a swig. He bought whiskey in pints. They were easier to conceal, carry, and use.

The roads were terrible on that trip. The car and trailer were overloaded. Frank was tired *and* loaded. That combination created some horrific moments.

I remember one of them as if it were yesterday. We were barreling down a remote West Texas highway. We had just driven through the curiously named town of Mule Shoe. That place's claim to fame is the statue of a mule that graces its central portion. I like mules, so that's OK with me.

We were at the beginning of day three of our little sojourn. It was about two in the morning. Lita was slumped against the glass of the passenger-side window, asleep. I was sitting in the center position of the front seat, beside Frank. I had been moved there so that I could talk to Frank. I was supposed to keep him awake. That was unique. The son of a bitch usually didn't want to be near me.

Frank reached under the seat to grab a whiskey bottle. He discovered that it was empty. Frank had no problem with that; he was prepared. Frank reached for one of his under seat spares. But the bottle was slippery. It repeatedly squirted out of his grasp. The bottle finally slipped away from Frank's probing hand. This frustrated Frank. He wanted a drink, *now*. It would have been logical for Frank to pull over, stop the car, and retrieve the bottle. That's not the way that he wanted to accomplish the bottle-retrieving operation. Frank told me, "Grab the wheel. I'm a-gonna git me a bottle." He then added, "It's just like grabbin' a trout that's a sleepin' under a rock. Ya gotta slip up on 'em with both hands." Frank laughed; he thought that last line was pretty funny.

I told Frank that I had never steered a car. I could barely see over the top of the dashboard. I didn't know what to do. Frank countered, "Stop being such a titty baby and just steer the car." Frank did not leave room for more argument. He took his hands off the steering wheel. I grabbed the wheel with both hands and held on for dear life.

Frank looked down. He was using both hands to fumble around under the seat. The bottle-retrieving operation seemed to go on forever. Frank wasn't in much of a hurry. That asshole was enjoying my discomfort. Twist the knife, Frank.

At first, the highway ran straight, but I could see there was a curve in the distance. I begged Frank to slow down. That really pissed him off. Frank hit the gas pedal. His 1953 Dodge Red Ram had a powerful 331-cubic-inch Hemi engine. The overloaded car roared like a lion and accelerated like a scared cat. He backed off the throttle. The car quickly lost speed.

Frank continued to fish around under the seat for the errant whiskey bottle. He was bent over the steering wheel and had both of his arms between his legs. The bottle slid farther under the seat.

His elbows were bumping into his knees. This made his control over the car's throttle jerky and erratic. He would hit the gas pedal and then release it altogether. This caused the car to dramatically speed up and slow down.

We were rapidly approaching the curve. I began to scream. I could see that the car was going to run off the road. Frank needed to take corrective action, *now.*

Frank finally located the whiskey bottle. The curve was upon us! He grabbed the wheel and hit the brakes, then the gas pedal. The car and trailer skidded across the traffic lanes. But Frank kept us on the road. Disaster was averted.

Frank was *pissed.* He said, "Little titty baby can't even steer a car. You almost wrecked us." He was invigorated by my failure. He raged at me as we raced through the night. The adrenaline rush kept him awake. Frank's driving technique improved.

Through it all, Lita slept like a baby. Just as she always did.

Frank McMillan, drunk and pissed off on moving day. Frank expected me to steer this overloaded rig from the middle seat. I don't know why we didn't crash. Gilroy, California. 1957.

CHAPTER 39

Welcome Back to the Nineteenth Century

FRANK McMILLAN MADE GOOD ON his promise to drive straight through. We made it from Gilroy, California, to Temple, Texas, in less than three days. Frank drove every inch of the way. He didn't stop for one minute of sleep. You'd expect Frank to be tired as he approached our destination. That wasn't the case. The third travel day was in Texas. Frank was home. The closer we got to our destination, the more he perked up. He was looking forward to seeing his family. He was *really* looking forward to being in Texas for the long haul. He hadn't lived in that much-beloved place for almost ten years.

Frank's family was excited about his return. To them, he was Junior, the beloved eldest son who'd sacrificed his childhood to support the family. When Frank left Texas to join the army, he was a boy. Ten years later he was a man. His family wanted to become better acquainted with the man.

Frank called his sister when we were a few miles from Temple. She gathered up the McMillan siblings and their children. They were waiting at Janita's house. Now, you might not recognize it as such, but Janita is a name. That moniker was inadvertently hung on Frank's sister. That woman's name was supposed to be Juanita, but the country doctor who filled out the birth certificate didn't know how to spell it. He left out the *u*, and thus was born the name Janita.

That kind of thing seems to have been prevalent in the older West. Remember, my mother was supposed to be named Lolita. It's sad to note that in the 1930s, two country doctors didn't know how to spell common Latin American names. Texas was a part of Latin America for a long time before it was anglicized. But the white man has never been shy about dipping into the well of cultural ignorance.

There is one more revelatory aspect to Janita's name. Remember, my grandmother, Ruby intended to change Lita's name (Loeta Bernice Snow) to her intended name, Lolita Fay Snow. Ruby never "got around to doin' that." Those were the same words that Gladys McMillan used about Janita. Both of those women were cowboy concubines to the bone.

Back to our arrival in Texas. Frank pulled into Janita's driveway and quickly hit the brakes. About twenty members of his family swarmed our car. To me, they looked like a litter of puppies. They were all squirming up, trying to kiss our faces.

I had met most of Frank's relatives. But that was two years in the past, when I was five. The memories were few and weak. I knew that I was among strangers. I felt pretty shy. Scared even. But my child brain knew that these people were a lot like the people in Ruby's family. I thought, *it might be OK*.

I could tell that Lita felt the same way. She was the new girl in town. Lita and I were strangers for about one second. The vast McMillan clan enveloped us in their love.

The adults went into the house for cool beverages. I stayed outside with the other children. It was about ninety degrees in the midday sun. The other children soon went inside to have a cool drink. Texas yards were old hat to them. The other kids hadn't spent the last three days cooped up in a speeding car that was piloted by a drunk. I wanted to be outside.

I was in paradise. Janita's small house was surrounded by wild land and lawn. It was a riot of green. Everything was lush and vibrant. This was a change from the deserts I had so recently traversed.

I was an explorer kid. I had been wandering alone in wild places since I could walk. There was much for me to see. Oh boy, I had a *lot* to learn about Texas. I wandered off the edge of Janita's park-sized front lawn. I saw an anthill. Now, we've all seen lots of anthills. You probably think that one looks pretty much like the other. But my six-year-old eyes had never seen an anthill like *this* one. The thing must have been ten feet wide and three feet high. The barren crest looked like Mount Vesuvius. I thought, *Wow! Ants! I like ants! I play with them in the garden!*

I ran over to the anthill. The surface on the mound was smooth. It looked as if it was made for sitting. I plopped my skinny butt in front of the opening that dominated the top of the mound. I began an intense study of ant behavior. I wanted to watch the little suckers as they went about their normal activities, just as I had countless times back in California.

But I soon discovered I wasn't in California. I was sitting on top of a red harvester ant colony. A *huge* one. Those ants weren't happy about my intrusion. Hundreds of them swarmed out of the ground. The outliers of the group took a few seconds to get to the top of my chest. They were the trailblazers. Hundreds of their companions quickly joined in the foray. My torso and arms were instantly covered with ants. They tucked their little ant asses and stung me. I tried to brush them off, but that didn't work too well. Most of the ants were on my chest. They were embedded in the weave of my T-shirt. The ants wouldn't budge. They were stinging me like crazy. Each ant didn't have much of a sting, but they packed a mighty punch when they stung in aggregate.

I didn't understand what was happening. I thought that the little bastards were going to cut me up into pieces and carry me down into the hole. I began to scream. I ran into the house, wailing like a baby. I burst into the quiet of an afternoon-tea-drinking party. About twenty sets of eyeballs swiveled in my direction as I screamed through the front door. Welcome to the McMillan family, Tommy.

Most of the gathered adults were amused at my behavior. Frank was mortified. He took me outside and picked the ants from my T-shirt. He said, "You better straighten yourself out, boy. Stop bein' such a titty baby."

The other children were less tolerant of my indiscretion. They were embarrassed for me. Even two-year-old kids in Texas knew better than to sit on a red-ant hill.

I suffered no lasting damage to my body. But the tone of my future life in Texas had been set. I would be a part of the McMillan family for the next thirteen years. No matter how hard I tried, I was always the new kid. I was always behind the other children.

At first, our Texas move seemed to be a good idea. It took me and my mother to a happier place. Frank's vast family loved my mother. Everybody loved Lita. The McMillans took Lita and me into the bosom of their family. Frank's siblings treated me like I was one of their children. I spent the first four years as an integral part of a similar family.

When Lita moved in with Frank, I was ripped away from her family, except as a sometimes visitor. But there was no "sometimes" to what Lita and I experienced with Frank's family. We were immersed daily in their love and discipline.

Frank and Lita rented a dilapidated duplex in Temple. It did little to dispel Lita's low expectations about the apartments that Frank selected. Lita hated bugs. She didn't want to move to Texas because of them. That place is insect heaven. God must have punished Lita with our new duplex. It was one of the all-time great bug hotels of the known universe.

We moved our belongings into the duplex. Frank, Lita, and I then went to dinner at Janita's house. We returned home late at night. It was pitch dark inside of the duplex. Frank walked into the kitchen. He turned on the overhead light. When we'd left the kitchen earlier in the day, the walls and counters had been light colored. Now they were *black*. The walls behind the sink and the kitchen counter were completely covered with German roaches. I'm not exaggerating—every square inch of the kitchen's walls and counters was painted black with scurrying roaches. Lita screamed. I gaped. But Frank just stood there. He was a native Texan. Such sights were apparently old hat to him.

In a few seconds, the roaches vanished into cracks and cabinets. But they had left their calling cards behind. Roach shit and nymph cases littered the counter top. *Thousands* of nymph cases. Frank and Lita flew into action. They used washcloths to sweep the roach detritus into the trash.

Lita wept. She was brokenhearted. She knew that our food would be prepared on the counter top. Welcome to Texas, Lita.

A normal person would have told our landlord to bring in an exterminator. Not Frank. He said, "Can't do nothin' about this. No matter what they do on this side, they'll just come back over from the other apartment." That was it. There was no more discussion on the matter. Frank gave no voice to the notion that the landlord could also spray the apartment on the other side of the wall.

We lived in that shithole duplex for just over a year. We were treated to a roach extravaganza each time we turned on the kitchen light. There never seemed to be a bottom limit for the shitholes Frank and Lita were willing to inhabit.

Frank was part of a huge family. They were spread in and around Temple, Texas. Their forbearers had been among the first Anglos to settle there. Almost all of them were cordial and loving in their mutual relations.

There was one great exception, however. Frank's sister Janita was married to a man named Lynn Hayes. He was universally disliked by the McMillan brothers, though Lynn behaved as if he was superior to everyone else. Truth be told, he was a real, all-purpose asshole.

Janita and Lynn had two children. The youngest was a boy. He was about two when we got to Texas in 1957. His name doesn't matter, since he plays no substantive part in my narrative. Just one aspect of that little boy stands out as being important: he was the apple of his daddy's eye. As such, he could do no wrong. Lynn and Janita also had a daughter named Nita. She was about ten when we moved to Texas. Lynn Hayes was *not* pleased that his firstborn child was a girl. He demonstrated his dissatisfaction in every possible way. He berated Nita for a multitude of real and perceived faults.

I thought that Nita was a wonderful person. We became fast friends. The foundation of our partnership stood on a simple concept: we were both unwanted children. We were the pariahs of our immediate families.

Nita quickly told me about her most prized possession, a portable radio. She'd received it as a present. Portable radios were quite rare and expensive in 1957. I told Nita that I wanted to see it. She leaned in and said, "OK. It'll be our little secret." Nita and I sneaked into her parents' bedroom. She opened the closet door. Her radio was stored on the highest shelf. She pointed to the radio and said, "Isn't it beautiful?" I agreed that it was. I had never seen such a small radio.

Nita closed the closet door. She rushed me out of her parents' bedroom. She said, "I don't want to get caught in here. I'm not supposed to look at my radio."

Nita provided me with the details of that circumstance. Not long after Nita had received the radio, she'd committed an error. She'd done something her father perceived to be wrong. He took the radio away from her and said it would be returned after a specific period. It didn't work out that way. He quickly discovered more faults that needed to be corrected. Each time Nita did something wrong, her father would say, "Well, that will be another two months that you don't get your radio." The radio detention period became a living thing. It never stopped growing. I never saw Nita touch her pathetic little radio.

When she and I were alone, Nita spoke of the fun she and I would have with her radio when she got it back. She always ended those fantasies with the same one-liner: "I just need to stop being such a bad girl." Her self-denigrating words were virtually identical to the ones I used.

Ah, Nita. Sweet, perfect Nita. The deck was stacked against us, girl. We chased parental love and acceptance, and our parents created ever-higher obstacles to block our paths. Neither of us ever reached the summit of parental acceptance. A pox on those who suffer little children with lives of quiet desperation.

The McMillan family saw what was going on with Nita and her father, but no one stepped in to help. What could they do? Lynn Hayes was an asshole. Good people stood by while he did horrible things.

Knives cut both ways, folks. If people in your circle do bad things to others, they will eventually get around to you.

Frank's mother, Gladys ("Granny Mac"), lived in a mid-nineteenth-century house out in the country. In her youth, it had been the home of the man who employed her family. Granny Mac endlessly mentioned that she was living in "the boss's house." She was quite proud of that feat. Granny Mac told me that the home had been built in the years before the American Civil War. That old house allowed a dangerously rudimentary electrical installation as its only concession to the modern world.

The McMillan boys and their mother. Front row, left to right: Gary McMillan, Donald McMillan, Larry McMillan. Back row, left to right: Frank McMillan, Gladys McMillan, Jimmy McMillan. Back porch of Gladys's house. Reed's Lake, Texas. 1958.

Granny was proud that her house had what she called "running water." That kind of water is delivered in a pressurized pipe. Yes, Gladys McMillan's rented house *did* technically have running water. It came from a rusty pipe that poked up outside of her back door. There was no faucet. Granny Mac had to turn on the pump. She closed the circuit by twisting two cotton-insulated wires together.

The experience of years has allowed me to look at that situation from a different perspective. Granny Mac was raised in a world of hauled water. People spent their days toting water buckets. That was hard work. Granny Mac risked electrocution every time she needed water for her home. But in her mind, that was better than hauling the stuff.

Granny Mac was especially proud of her kerosene cook stove. It advertised its presence to anyone who walked into the house. A jet fuel reek permeated everything. The smell was all right with Granny Mac. She didn't have to stoke wood or clean ashes. She had spent enough time doing that when she was younger.

But Granny Mac didn't take a pass on using wood as fuel. She washed the family's laundry in a gigantic, round-bottom, cast-iron kettle. It was a relic of the nineteenth century. The kettle had a mouth that was almost two feet wide. It weighed well over a hundred pounds when it was empty.

Granny Mac filled the kettle with buckets of water. She then placed firewood and kindling underneath. She added soap and dirty clothes to the boiling water and then stirred the simmering clothes with a long stick. She used the same stick to transfer the clothes from the kettle to a large tub. That was the rinse cycle. Granny Mac then reused the water in the kettle to boil another load of clothes. She added more water and soap as needed.

If she had lots of clothes to wash, Granny Mac would have to change the kettle water. I was always amazed at how that process was accomplished. Granny Mac needed to move the kettle off the fire before she dumped the water. The splashing water might extinguish the fire.

Granny used two long, thick sticks to maneuver the heavy kettle off the fire. That was a delicate and exceedingly dangerous operation. She looked like an ace pilot with control sticks in her hands. That woman was *good*.

Granny Mac washed laundry for three grown men and herself. She also washed for whatever grandchild was staying with her at the time. She washed all the household linens. That's a lot of washing. It took a lot of wood to boil the water for the laundry kettle. But she was in luck; virgin hardwood forest stretched for miles behind her house. It was firewood on the hoof. Frank's younger brothers used axes and ancient whipsaws to fell dead trees.

Most people who cut firewood process the tree where it falls. They load the stove-length pieces in a truck and then drive them home. The McMillan boys didn't have a truck. One of them had a nice car, but he damned sure wasn't going to ruin his backset with chunks of firewood! He fucked on that hallowed space on Saturday night. Women don't like to get splinters up their asses. So the McMillan brothers found an innovative way to avoid putting firewood in their car.

A disused private road ran behind Granny Mac's house. It trailed down into the river bottomlands. The McMillan brothers looked for dead trees that were close to the road. They felled them in ways that pointed the thick portion of the tree toward the road. Then the brothers used a chain to connect the tree to the car and dragged the tree up the road to Granny Mac's house.

I remember my first experience with the McMillan foresters. I was playing in Granny Mac's backyard when I noticed some activity on the private road. That was unusual. It was usually deserted. The forest seemed to be moving up the road. No, it wasn't the whole forest, just one tree. In a few seconds, I noted that a green car was dragging a large tree toward Granny Mac's house. Frank's brother Donald was at the wheel. I just stood there, stuck in my tracks. I was amazed. Donald was laughing his ass off. He was enjoying the look on my city-boy face. He called out to me as he passed, "Don't ya git run over by my tree, boy." Ever the joker. Donald McMillan was a wonderful man.

Donald stopped about seventy-five feet from Granny Mac's back door. The tree was in its final resting place. It didn't remain in the yard for very long. Granny needed wood, *now*. I heard her say, "If ya'll want clean shirts come Saturday night, ya better fetch me some firewood right quick-like." Now, Granny Mac rarely used the phrase "right quick-like." When she did, it meant, "Move your ass immediately."

Donald McMillan and Tom Liggett. Texas was heaven for
men, dogs, and little boys. Reed's Lake, Texas. 1958.

Granny Mac's backyard was littered with tree parts, wood chips, loosely
stacked piles of wood, ashes, washing machines, and Texas-sized piles of
cow shit.

I once used a cow turd to scandalize the greater McMillan family. An
overachiever steer dropped an incredible pile about ten feet from Granny
Mac's back door. It was a high plateau of green. That sucker was three feet
wide. The cow was really eating well. My over worked brain saw opportunity where others found annoyance. I gathered a long stick from the wood-
pile. I tied a rag to the stick to make a rudimentary flag and then stuck my
flag into the plateau turd. In my mind, the flag was a tribute to the cows,
who were the mascots of that place. They had the run of Granny Mac's
backyard.

The cows stared at me through the bedroom windows. They didn't
seem to mind sharing their time with me. I didn't mind, either. I was sleeping in a small outpost that was located on the frontier of a bovine world.

Cows were normal parts of Granny Mac's backyard. Washing machines weren't, but a half dozen of the things were scattered around the yard. You wouldn't expect that in a place where clothes were boiled in a pot. Those washers had a story to tell.

Granny Mac's house didn't have air conditioning. You opened the window and prayed for a breeze or that the temperature would drop below a hundred degrees. It was hard to sleep.

Frank's brother Larry wanted a fan to help him sleep, but he didn't have the money to buy one. Then he discovered that wringer-type washers have a fan blade on their drive motors. They move a fair amount of air.

Larry looked for discarded washing machines and brought them home. He removed the drive motors and attached an electrical cord to them. If the motor worked, he set it on the windowsill. Voilà, Larry had a fan. He was quite pleased with himself. He began to leave his fan on any time he was home.

The washing-machine motors were quite old when Larry repurposed them. They were not designed for continuous operation. They burned out at a fast clip. But that was not a problem for Larry. He would just find another junk washing machine. Hard times drive redneck ingenuity, folks.

The front room of Granny Mac's house did yeoman duty. It was the hub of the McMillan family's existence. Granny Mac listened to the radio in that space. I caught the tail end of the great American radio era in Granny Mac's living room. I always came in from the woods on Saturday morning because I wanted to hear *The Lone Ranger*. I soon realized that show was better on the radio than it was on television. I got to create my own images. I could lie on the floor to draw pictures on castoff scraps of paper. I have always been a multitasker.

One wall of the front room was filled with a large fireplace. It provided the only heat in Granny Mac's house. The fireplace was made of bricks and rough Central Texas stone. My young eyes thought that it was large enough to contain a small car. But that fireplace wasn't large enough. It couldn't keep up with the chill when a blue norther swept down from Canada. The hundred-year-old hardwood planks in Granny Mac's house were strong but cracked. Cold air found little resistance as it flowed through the rooms.

Granny Mac's front room was dominated by a long table. It was the family's all-purpose meeting place. The McMillan brothers played poker on Granny Mac's table. They didn't gamble; they *played*. They enjoyed the camaraderie. I can remember the banter that went on between the brothers. A stranger would believe they were arguing. They weren't. The brothers would say things like, "Goddamn it, Hoss, are you going to play that card or sit there scratching your ass all night?" Another would say, "Be careful how you chunk [throw] that card at me. You hit with me with that sumbitch, ya better make it chocolate, because I'm gonna make you eat it."

Frank had four wonderful brothers. They treated me with kindness and compassion and made life wonderful for me when I was in Texas.

CHAPTER 40

Chef Lita

LITA TAUGHT THE MCMILLAN CLAN many lessons. The first of these was served on Granny Mac's table.

Modern, city-dwelling people call their evening meal dinner. That name has changed in its meaning. In 1950s Texas, the daily progression of meals was breakfast, dinner, and supper.

Sunday dinner was the big McMillan family event of the week. Most of the siblings gathered at Granny Mac's house for that seminal meal. McMillan Sunday dinners were rigid in their progression and substance. It was like communion in church. In some general sense, I suppose that Sunday dinner *was* the McMillan family's church.

The women and girls spent all morning preparing deep-fried chicken, corn bread, mashed potatoes, and gravy. If it was in season, corn on the cob was also served. Dessert was generally a fresh-baked pie or chocolate cake.

After Sunday dinner was prepared, the men and boys sat at Granny Mac's table. The women and girls served dinner to the males, but the females did not sit down. The women and girls did not eat dinner at that time. They stood in the kitchen, watching the males eat. The given excuse for that demeaning behavior was simple: Granny Mac's table wasn't large enough to accommodate the entire clan. Love and good manners should have dictated that the entire family sit together during Sunday dinner. Other families made it work. Lita's did.

But the McMillan females did not eat Sunday dinner until after the men and boys had eaten their fill and left the table. That generally took over an hour. The women and girls would get whatever remained. I remember the leavings being picked over and cold. The females in the McMillan family ate chicken wings and bony backs saturated with cold, congealed grease. It was symbolic of contemporary female servitude.

For the males of the family, Sunday dinner was grand social event. It was a veritable feast. The McMillan males ate mountains of food. It wouldn't fit on the table at one time. As soon as a serving dish was emptied, a man or boy would shout for more. They did not say please or thank you. The males yelled out their food orders. They said, "We need some more mashed taters in here." They expressed no gratitude for the food and drink that were served.

But some of the males had plenty to say. The men shouted jibes to the passing women. They said, "It looks like your ass is getting a little bigger there, sis." Or, "What did you do to your hair?" Or, "Do you buy that perfume by the gallon at a dime store?" Those quips and others of like kind were met with universal male laughter. The other men and boys elaborated on what was being said about their wives, sisters, and mothers.

Lita found that kind of behavior tough to swallow. She couldn't believe that she was seeing a hardworking mother act as a servant for her six-year-old son. She couldn't believe that women were made to eat males' table scraps. It made her blood boil. But she didn't want to cause a stink. She was trying to fit in with this new family. So she kept her silence.

An insignificant thing finally brought Lita to her break point: iced tea. That beverage was a seminal part of the Texas culture I experienced. The McMillan family iced tea recipe was unlike any I have seen. The women dropped a large handful of Lipton tea bags in a cooking pot without removing the strings and tags from the tea bags. Cold water was added, and the pot was brought up to a low, rolling boil. It was then brought down to a high simmer and boiled some more.

Granny Mac cooked her tea for about half an hour. The resultant liquid was dull black with brown undertones and had a nasty-looking rainbow sheen on the surface. The base tea stock looked like thinned-down asphalt roof sealer. And that was just the start. The tea needed to be sweetened before it was consumed. Granny Mac liked *lots* of sugar in her tea. She turned the stuff into syrup. The sweet tea McDonald's serves is a pale echo of the old-time McMillan family iced tea I drank in Texas.

The McMillans preferred to drink their iced tea (or "ass tay" as it was pronounced in the local dialect) in tall, wide glasses with lots of ice. That would keep you going on a hot Texas afternoon. Heck, Granny Mac's iced tea could probably have revived a corpse.

Massive quantities of that lethal brew were served to everyone in the family. I saw local women put it into baby bottles. Modern people believe that sugar makes children hyper. They should have seen how children in the McMillan family reacted after they had about a quart of Texas iced tea in them. These are soft times.

But let's get back to what happened at a specific McMillan Sunday dinner. The men and boys were sitting around the table. The women and girls were standing in the kitchen, awaiting orders. The men called out for whatever dish was needed.

But it was different when the males wanted a refill on their iced tea. They didn't shout out for tea; they raised their glasses and rattled the ice. They didn't say a word or make eye contact with the female servers. They didn't need to. A female would instantly scurry over with a pitcher and refill the raised glass. If more ice was needed, she would run to the kitchen to get it. The females wordlessly accomplished their serving tasks.

Lita endured this type of behavior for about two weeks, playing her expected role as submissive wife. But things changed during her third McMillan family dinner. Frank's brother Larry raised his tea glass and automatically rattled the ice. He had undoubtedly done the same thing hundreds of times in the past. But Larry made a new mistake: he made eye contact with Lita. Lita was dumbfounded. An adolescent was treating her like a servant!

Lita held Larry's gaze. He stared back. Their eyes locked for what seemed to be an eternity. Lita broke the impasse. She said, "Get up off your lazy fuckin' ass and pour your own fuckin' tea." But that little declaration wasn't strong enough for Lita. She added a white Southerner's ultimate coda: "I ain't your fuckin' nigger."

I don't remember Lita's exact words after that opening jab, but she didn't shut up. She elaborated on her initial theme. Lita stood there and aired her mind.

The gathered multitude was silent. No one in the room had any doubt about the meaning of Lita's words. But nobody mustered up the guts to challenge her. The strength of Lita's long declaration left no doubt about one particular aspect: she was willing to push the discussion into dangerous, uncharted territory.

The day was saved for the cause of male pride and feminine subservience when another McMillan female quickly refilled the offending glass. But the die was cast. Lita had made her point. She didn't care how the other females behaved. She was *not* going to be any man's servant.

Sunday dinner ran its regular course that day. But things were kind of subdued afterward. The McMillans were stunned. I was quiet. I knew Frank and Lita. I knew the final act of the day's show would be worse. In that regard, I was not disappointed.

Lita was cordial as she bade farewell to the McMillan family. Hugs were given by the females. The males shook hands. Men don't hug men.

Things changed for our little trio once we got into the car. Lita was off-stage. She didn't have to play for an audience. She began to hammer Frank before he drove out of the driveway. She screamed, "I ain't goin' to be *any* goddamned man's nigger." Frank was full of dinner and whiskey. He felt humiliated by Lita's behavior. It was a repudiation of the status quo. Frank was *pissed*. He met Lita's anger head on and returned it with rage. I'm surprised that their joint screaming didn't explode the car windows.

Those fools yelled at each other for a long time. They defended the righteousness of their individual causes. Mr. Immovable Object, meet Mrs. Irresistible Force. Frank and Lita eventually found a grudging detent. They came to an impasse. They were worn out.

I was quietly weeping in the back seat. I realized the inevitability of what would occur next. I knew what happened when Frank and Lita could make no progress in their conjoined arguments. They turned their anger on me. I was not disappointed in my prediction. Lita initiated the attack. She turned around, locked eyes with me, and said, "I *will* fuckin' kill you if you *ever* try to pull that shit on *me*."

Lita knew that was a rhetorical statement. So did I. There was no reason on God's green earth for me to do such a thing. Lita punished me because I was alive. She hated me because I was breathing. Why would I add fuel to the fire?

I played my cowed child role. I blubbered, "I didn't do anything. I'll get my own tea. I promise."

My response reignited Frank's anger. He screamed, "Stop being such a fuckin' titty baby. Stop crying." The back seat of Frank's Dodge should have contained a boy-sized hole. I tried to force myself down through it innumerable times.

Our Sunday dinners with the Mc Millans continued, with one notable change: no one expected Lita to play slave for the males of the family. But the second-class eating arrangements of the fair sex continued. Who knows what was said or done to the other females when they were behind closed doors. I don't want to know the answer to *that* question.

It didn't take Lita very long to figure out that she couldn't change the cowed behavior of the McMillan women. Eons of inertia were working against her. But Lita wasn't comfortable with the dietary arrangements. My mother would *not* eat cold chicken with clammy mashed potatoes and con-gealed gravy every Sunday for the rest of her life. That was the first crack in the façade of our new life in Texas. Life wasn't as perfect as Lita had thought. It was a rude awakening for my mother.

For Lita, things ran deeper than rattled glasses and congealed gravy. Yes, my mother had won the day when she refused Larry McMillan's demand for a refill. But she didn't go away easy, even when she had won a fight. Lita was never a gracious winner. Two hundred years ago, she would have stood over her vanquished enemies with their steaming testicles in her clenched fist.

Lita was did not rest on her laurels as a trendsetter. She pressed on with her education of the McMillan clan. My readers should remember something at this point: Lita's best lessons to me always involved food.

Lita knew that deck was stacked against her. Women in Texas didn't have much power. Lita had to use the limited power that she was given. And she was powerful in the kitchen.

As these events were unfolding, Lita was just twenty-four. But she already had better than twenty years of stove-front experience. Lita was well on her way to being the third-best home cook I have ever seen.

Lita made a sweet suggestion to the other McMillan women. She said, "You already work too hard in your own kitchens all week long. Why not let me take over the cooking next Sunday dinner?" Lita conveniently failed to mention an important fact: she was the only woman in the group who was working outside of the home. When my mother wanted to be coy, butter wouldn't melt in her mouth.

No one wanted to argue with Lita. They had seen her temper. People agreed that she would prepare the following week's Sunday dinner.

Lita's first offering as chef du jour was spaghetti with red sauce and garlic bread. Most of my readers probably believe that is plain and unobjectionable fare. Sadly, you are wrong. Most of you don't fully comprehend the depths of cultural isolation that enveloped the McMillan brand of cowboy in 1957.

It took Lita all week to accumulate the ingredients for her spaghetti feed. Italian food wasn't common in Central Texas. She baked the French bread from scratch. She worked hard all morning. Granny Mac's kerosene stove was a reliable tool. Lita had everything ready to go at noon. The girl knew how to feed people on time.

Lita carried out the first dish to the men. Here was the long-awaited spaghetti with red sauce. She was proud as a peacock. She knew that her red sauce was the *best*.

Lita placed the bowl of spaghetti in the middle of Granny Mac's table. She stood back and waited for a response from the assembled males. That didn't happen. Granny Mac's front room was as silent as a tomb. You could have heard the proverbial pin drop.

The McMillan males stared at the bowl of spaghetti. They were giving it quizzical looks. They began to shoot furtive glances at each other. Their eyes said, "What the hell do I do with this stuff?"

The initial moment of silence stretched into a pregnant pause. No one wanted to irritate Lita. That group saw humor as a balm for the ills that life visited upon them. They always seemed to find a snappy comeback, no matter how dire the circumstances. So finally, one of the McMillan brothers opened his mouth and let fly. He said, "Lita, that looks just like a bowl of worms. Why are you feeding us worms?" I'm certain that the speaker expected to mask his culinary confusion with a typical round of laughs from his brothers. But none of the other men uttered a peep. His comment stood out like a fart in church.

Now, you all know that I am Lita's son. Because of that fact, I have spent my entire life in and around kitchens. I have become somewhat accustomed to varied criticism of my offerings. That is the cost of doing business when you are a cook. Even with me, though, such complaints are best kept on the polite side. Cooks, by their very nature, tend to be sensitive people. "Don't mess with the cook" is the refrain two restaurant managers were forced to learn the hard way from yours truly.

In that regard, Lita was no different than me—but with one notable exception: her cooking skills were linked to a viciously short temper. I saw the feral look that flashed across Lita's face after the McMillan brother made his "worms" comment. I wanted to dive under the table. I thought to myself, *Aw, shit, Tommy. That boy has truly gone and stepped in it now.*

Lita must have gotten laid the night before, because she showed remarkable restraint in her response to the young cowboy's oafish remark. Her response was brief and quiet. She pulled one of her favorite culinary chestnuts out of the fire. Lita said, "Eat it or fuckin' starve." She chased that bit of advice with a wolfish grin. Lita locked eyes with the young man. She did not back down. I have known few sane men who could hold Lita's angry glare for as long as *he* did. If he didn't piss his pants, I don't know why.

Everyone in the room was holding their breath. They knew that Lita had worked hard on the spaghetti. Even those of short acquaintance knew that Lita placed great importance on receiving just praise for her labors. Everyone knew that what happened next would make the difference between a happy Sunday dinner and high holy hell on earth. Every person in the room had seen Lita's temper erupt for reasons that were more trivial than a young man's ignorant comment. The young man chose discretion over valor. He reached for the bowl of spaghetti. He filled his plate with a politely significant portion and passed the bowl to the next person. The males resumed a subdued form of normal conversation.

They mixed a fair amount of curiosity with their trepidation. You could tell what they were thinking: *How will this strange new dish taste?* The hungry cowboys dove into Lita's meal. You could tell that none of them had ever eaten spaghetti. The noodles fell off their forks and onto their plates, shirts, and laps. The game changed when they finally got some of the spaghetti into their mouths. Two minutes before, they were acting like Lita truly *was* trying to make them to eat long red worms. Now they were shoveling Lita's marvelous creation into their mouths. The day was saved for all; the crowd cheered Lita.

Lita had a marvelous way of saying "You're welcome." She brought out her *other* dish. In her hands, she had a cookie sheet full of garlic bread. Lita made *fine* garlic bread. She proudly placed the bread in the center of the table and stood back. Eager hands snatched the bread and prepared to eat. But that process was short circuited. One of Frank's brothers asked, "What's that smell?" His question arose from another fine point of cultural ignorance: none of the McMillans had ever smelled garlic in its pure, unadulterated form. Lordy, but if that didn't set Lita off. She took that naïve cowboy's culinary inexperience as a personal affront. She ran back into the kitchen, sobbing.

I don't really remember what happened next. I know that the males eventually ate her garlic bread with the same gusto as the spaghetti. One of them later told me, "That garlic bread took some getting used to. It's kind of like eating pussy; it's great, once you get past the smell."

Lita's first experiences with the McMillans' Sunday dinners were not good. But in the end, they were one of the things that made the family know and love her. Lessons were learned all the way around. Lita finally understood that the McMillan family hadn't been exposed to the wide range of foods that were available in the San Francisco Bay Area. She began to cut them a little slack. She learned how to take their initial reactions to her culinary offerings as naïveté, not rejection.

To their credit, Frank's brothers learned to keep their mouths shut until they had tasted what Lita set before them.

CHAPTER 41

Wild Boy

I SPENT A LOT OF time with my grandmother Ruby before she moved away from the San Francisco Bay Area. I constantly begged Lita to let me "spend the night with Momma." Frank and Lita readily complied with my requests. They didn't want to see my sorry ass any more than was absolutely necessary. There were times during which I all but lived with Ruby and her family. I loved the arrangement. Then Ruby was gone, and I was alone.

It wasn't much of a leap for me to transpose my visiting behavior onto Granny Mac. She didn't treat me any differently than she did her own grandchildren. Thus began a new status quo: I begged to go and stay with Granny Mac on weekends and school vacations. Granny Mac cheerfully complied. We liked each other's company.

Before we moved to Texas, I was alone and hungry much of the time. I had been a feral boy who spent his days wandering through debris-filled empty lots. I avoided human contact on the streets. Most of the people I encountered didn't know me or were derelicts.

Another world waited for me outside of Granny Mac's back door. I wandered through a cornucopia of wilderness. I seldom had company on my woodland perambulations. In a technical sense, I was still alone. But I was in a more exciting place. There were other pluses too. I knew that Granny Mac had a warm dinner and a smile waiting for me back at the house.

I had people of all ages vying to be with me. They wanted to teach me interesting things. The horrific drive to Texas turned out to be the magic carpet ride to a wonderful life.

The McMillans were from the same social class as Lita—poor white trash. Both families arose from the Scots-Irish culture. Those people herded cattle and horses for many thousands of years. Our ancestors fled English depredation at about the same time. Thus was seeded cowboy culture on a new continent.

German immigrants to North America were industrious. Most of them weren't boisterous. When it was time to bear arms in common cause, the German settlers were glad to have the Scots-Irish around. But when the wars were over, the staid Germans liked to see our kind get down the road. Why? When the Scots-Irish weren't provided with big wars, they created smaller ones everywhere they went.

Few sane men picked fights with the men in Frank's family. The McMillan kin would knock your ass out before you even got started.

My mother's family derived from the lowest form of white trash. Some of my relatives were shiftless or incorrigible. Frank's family was of another kind. They stayed in one place for well over a hundred years. This marked them as being well up in the redneck pecking order. The McMillans were white trash, but they were locally respected white trash.

Frank's family accepted me 'n Lita. That was a big deal. It was like being an English commoner who was elevated into the minor gentry. Being on the inside of the redneck gentry allowed me certain advantages. I saw the inner workings of a culture that was subsequently destroyed by modern sensibilities. Many of the things I experienced in Texas were unchanged artifacts from millennia gone by. It was a heck of an introduction to cowboy life.

The McMillans picked pecans in the fall. They shot squirrels at will. They saw no wrong in killing squirrels out of season—the local woodlands were full of the things. But Frank's family were good custodians of the land. I was warned, "Don't you never shoot up in a squirrel's nest, boy. Might have babies up in there. They won't never fall down out of the nest. It would be a terrible waste of squirrel."

At least one member of Frank's family had a catfish trap or two sunk in the river. Those traps were illegal. You had to hide them well and watch out for the game warden. The local warden used a boat in his search for poachers. His outboard motor had no muffler. You could hear the warden's boat from a mile away. That gave poachers lots of time to melt into the forest. My child brain thought that was a cozy situation.

But some things didn't change for us in Texas. Frank continued to read the Bible to me whenever he could. He began and ended those sessions with the same tired declarations: "These are just stories. There ain't no truth to them. Don't you believe in them."

But there was a problem: I *did* believe the stories. How could I not? The Bible stories he read were compelling. Their truth seemed to be unassailable. Much of my belief came from the eloquence of Frank's delivery. He was quite a showman. The words of the prophets added weight to Frank's oratorical talents. Countless other charlatans also found great success with that ruse.

But I had outside help to bolster my belief in the Christian God. Central Texas was a hotbed of religious fervor. Jesus was on the radio. Jesus was on television. Jesus was on highway billboards all over that land. His name was on the lips of a high percentage of the people I met in Texas. Lots of those people chided me because I wasn't attending church. Many of their declarations were not gentle. They usually ended with a scary punch line: "You're gonna burn in hail [as hell was pronounced in the local dialect] if'n yew don't git right with Gawd."

I took their pronouncements as being the gospel truth. Frank had been with us for about three years. Every time I did something wrong, he told me I was going to burn in hell.

My readers might find that last part to be a little ironic. I beg your indulgence. I was just seven years old. My undeveloped brain didn't catch the natural contradiction in Frank's words.

Someone in my orbit began to hammer me because I wasn't going to church. I don't remember who. It is truly not important almost sixty years on. I remember the salient point, though: I received continual offers to attend the local hard-shell (fundamentalist) Baptist church.

I wanted to go to church. My requests were disregarded by Frank and Lita. I began to pester Frank. He finally acquiesced to my demands. Frank said, "You can go, but you ain't a-gonna like it."

I gave in to other people's incessant imprecations. I went to church. In those times, "going to church" was a multipart, day-long operation. It began with Sunday school. I was quickly separated from the known attentions of the person who'd coerced me into my religious journey and left in the company of total strangers. That was quite unsettling to me. But it was a good move by the church staff. It is the key component of an age-old indoctrination process. Take away that which is known and replace it with something new. Separate and conquer.

I was led into a small room that was furnished with a semicircle of chairs. A group of children was sitting quietly. I don't remember if it was a mixed-gender group. I only recall seeing boys. They sat stiffly in their chairs. They were perfect little soldiers. What am I saying? They were quieter than any group of soldiers I have seen in a classroom setting. That should have been the tip-off. I should have seen what was coming, though I didn't have the sense to realize it at the time.

Our instructor walked into the classroom. My first impression wasn't good. She didn't seem to be the warm and engaging sort. She began the class with a long-winded prayer. Her monologue was boring. It wasn't interesting like Frank's Bible reading. The opening prayer seemed to go on *forever*.

Our teacher finally got down to the lesson of the day. It was about Israelite bondage in Egypt. The word Egypt brought me out of a prayer-induced, semi catatonic state. I knew something about Egypt! The night before, we'd seen a movie called *The Egyptian*. I jumped out of my chair and said, "I know all about that! I saw a movie about the Egyptians last night."

I suppose I was trying to impress the teacher with my advanced knowledge of the ancient world. I hoped that my declaration would be an icebreaker. But the teacher gave me a deep-freeze glare and said, "Movies are sinful. We don't condone going to movies here." That statement took me by surprise. Everyone I knew liked movies.

I looked around the classroom. I was expecting to find support from the other boys. But my classmates were staring down at their hands. No one made eye contact with me. The other boys looked like they were scared shitless. I was confused. Why wasn't I getting any encouragement from them? I sat down, shut my mouth, and folded my hands.

The teacher was angered but unfazed by my revelation. She pressed on with her lesson. A few minutes later, she began to speak about the pyramids. I don't know why she did that. The Bible doesn't have a whole lot to say about pyramids. Maybe it was an attempt by the teacher to include something in her sermon that young boys might find to be remotely interesting.

The pyramid topic brought me out of my funk. I thought that I knew all about pyramids. Just a few hours before, I'd watched a movie that was about pyramid construction techniques. I leapt up out of my chair and began to tell everybody in the room about what I had seen.

Our teacher had probably taught Sunday school for thirty years. There was a good chance that she had never been interrupted by one of her young charges. This strange-talking boy from California did it twice in just a few minutes. Worse yet, I had injected doctrinal heresy into her sermon. Our teacher exploded. She went into a blind rage. The teacher screamed, "Movies are sinful. You're going to burn in hell. You're going to burn in hell, hell, hell."

Whew. *That* outburst got my attention. Once more, I looked around the classroom for a shred of support from my fellow indoctrinates. Not a chance. They were inspecting their manicures more intently than ever. Most of those poor souls had been attending that church since they were born. Their last bit of free thought had been whipped into submission years before.

I finally understood the base concept for that morning's class. No, I didn't quite grasp the full scope of their sect's religious doctrine. But I did understand what happened when folks screamed at me. I did not want to risk an escalation by our teacher. I shut up for the duration of the class.

Sunday school finally ended. I met up with the person who'd taken me to church. She led me into the sanctuary. The service contained nothing that was memorable to me. It was all fire and brimstone. I didn't find any of the love that the Christian God reputedly offers.

Small towns have arcane systems of communication. Information seems to travel faster than light. The story of my Sunday school experience preceded my return home. Everyone in the family knew about the little boy who repeatedly spoke heresy in church. Frank was delighted. He repeated the story for as long as I knew him.

I didn't return to the hard-shell Baptist church. I experienced enough screaming during the week. Why volunteer for more on Sunday morning?

CHAPTER 42

Dope the Kid

I GREW TEETH. SHORTLY THEREAFTER, they began to cause me problems. When I was six, I got a major abscess. My jaw was very swollen. People said that it looked like I had the mumps. An oral surgeon removed several of my juvenile molars. The removal part was the key to the dental care program that Lita and Frank applied to me. They waited until I was half dead with a mouth infection and then pulled my teeth.

Things got better on the dental treatment front after we moved to Texas. Frank's sister Janita was a nurse. She found ways to get me better medical care. She convinced Frank and Lita to fix my teeth before they rotted. Thank you for caring, Janita.

My teeth were in horrible condition. I spent a lot of time in a dentist's chair. My dentist wasn't gentle. He was always in a hurry, and he caused me a fair amount of pain. I began to lose my patience. So did the dentist. He gave Lita a box of prescription tranquilizer tablets and told her to give me a tablet a half hour before each appointment. I would be more compliant in the treatment chair.

When my dentist handed Lita the tranquilizer tablets, he made a false presumption. He believed he was dealing with someone who cared for the welfare of her child. You know, a mother who would administer the pills as directed.

The dentist didn't realize that Lita treated her job as a religion. Shiftwork was her holy communion. Her religion demanded that she *never* leave work early. Lita viewed any absence from work as heresy. She didn't want blots on her magnificent work record. Then there was the other part: Lita didn't want to remove money from her budget. Frank always needed money to spend at dance halls.

My dentist's office hours were nine to five. Lita worked from seven to five. She was forced to leave work early when she took me to the dentist. She hated to do that, so she left work later than she should. Lita ran late when she picked me up for my appointments. She was always pissed off. The dentist's order to dope me up added a new dimension to her anger.

On a particular dentist day, Lita picked me up at school and advised me that we were late. She was angry. As she pulled away from the curb, she shoved a tranquilizer tablet in my direction. It was about the size of a dime, but much thicker. I held the tablet in the palm of my hand. It looked *huge*. I didn't know what to do with the thing.

Lita took my hesitation as a defiant act. She screamed, "Swallow that son of a bitch!" I asked Lita if she had any water. She screamed louder, "No, just swallow the fucker!" I put the huge disk into my mouth. I tried to swallow it whole, as directed. My throat closed shut. I gagged and spit the tablet into my hand. That *really* set Lita off. She was screaming at the top of her lungs. I don't remember the exact words of her diatribe, but every sentence ended with the phrase "Take the fucking pill!"

I hunkered down in my seat. I was afraid that I would choke on the tablet. Lita finally calmed down a little. She said, "Just chew the pill and swallow it." Seeing no other course, I put the tablet in my mouth and chewed.

Damn, that thing was bitter! It tasted horrible. I dry-chewed the last pill chunks just as we pulled into the parking lot at the dentist's office. We were very late. Lita had cut her minimum-time-off-from-work formula a little too tight.

Lita was pissed, and she advised me that it was my fault. She said, "If your damned teeth weren't so bad, I wouldn't have had to take time off from work. If you weren't such a fuckin' baby, you would have swallowed that pill. If you weren't such a fuckin' baby, you wouldn't even have *needed* that pill." I believed her. Years of training had taught me that I was an evil child. Everything was always my fault. I shouldered the blame by apologizing for being such a baby.

Lita railed at me all the way from the car to the dentist's front door. My nerves were jangled from being yelled at. I was afraid of being in the dentist's chair again. The chemical taste of the tranquilizer tablet remained strong in my mouth. I was a mess.

We swept through the office door. Lita instantly softened her demeanor and put a big smile on her face. The unhappy dentist was standing in the lobby. He got right to the point. "You gave him that pill a half hour ago, right?"

Lita simpered, "Yes, sir, I did." It took a pure Southern belle to deliver *that* little performance. Fifteen seconds before, she had been a raging banshee. Now she was as cool as a cucumber.

The dentist wasted no time on pleasantries. He was rough with his Novocain shots, and he didn't wait until they had taken effect. He operated with mechanical efficiency. The dentist was fueled by a tight schedule, and he wasn't going to make the next kid wait because of me. It was hell on earth.

The tranquilizer kicked in just as the dentist completed his labors. I was zonked. I didn't want to leave the chair. I wanted to take a nap. But there was no time for that. The next kid was waiting. The dentist grabbed my arm and yanked me out of the chair. Lita helped me to stagger out of the room. She made a good show of half dragging/half carrying me to the car. She undoubtedly looked like the embodiment of a perfect mother.

Lita took me from the dentist to Janita's house. The tranquilizer was still working. I was loaded. We had dinner with Janita's family. The conversation that night hinged on my visit to the dentist. The adults all seemed to believe that I was a big baby.

Frank allowed everyone at the dinner table to take their potshots at my psyche. When they were done, *he* chimed in. Frank said that he once had a tooth filled without any Novocain. That got everyone's attention.

Frank said, "It hurt. I don't want to do that again." Everyone at the table saluted Frank's toughness in the dentist's chair and turned their comments on me. The assembled guests at Janita's table compared Frank's heroism to my weakness.

That's the way it went with the cowboy culture in which I was raised. Cut with the knife of comparison. That tool is most effective when we are compared with those who are as gods to us. No matter how high we strive, we can never be their equals.

Every old-line cowboy family seemed to have a godlike man as its patriarch. In varying degrees, they were all men like Frank. They replaced the Christian God with the force of their personalities and the sound of their voices.

CHAPTER 43

The Lost Prototype

GRANNY MAC'S HOUSE STOOD ABOVE the inaccurately named Little River. Whoever supplied that moniker must have viewed the river during a period of extreme drought. At such times, it is reduced to a trickle of water that is ten or twenty feet wide. But for most of its history, the Little River has been anything but a trickle.

The Little River drains almost eight thousand square miles. Rainfall amounts of over an inch per hour are not unusual in Central Texas. Major rainstorms sometimes last for long periods. When that happens, the streams that supply the Little River become mighty rivers. The Little River transforms itself into a wide, ravening monster. But in the 1950s, dams were built on tributary streams. The Little River finally lived down to its name.

A few miles downstream from the confluence of the Leon and Lampassas Rivers, the newly created river flows through a low place that is called the Little River Valley. For uncounted eons, the Little River overflowed its banks frequently enough to create small lakes. When the river diminished, the lakes remained for indefinite periods.

In 1834, various members of the Reed family received land grants in the Little River Valley area. The seasonal lake was given a name: Reed's Lake. In 1834, John Burnett Reed built a cabin of pecan logs on the lakeshore. Current historical sources are dismissive of Reed's Lake. Some of them call it a buffalo wallow. But the people in Frank's extended family didn't see it that way. Most of the time, Reed's Lake was a decent-sized body of water. Other years, it would be completely dry.

I trust McMillan family accounts more than I do historical archives. Their senses were finely tuned to the status of Reed's Lake and the Little River. Members of Frank's extended family farmed the lake bottom when it was dry. They caught fish when the lake was full. They trapped fur-bearing animals on its lush banks. Everyone picked up pecans in the fall. The Little River Valley was the McMillan family grocery store.

The main road through Central Texas crossed the Little River at Reed's Lake. The aptly named town of Reed's Lake grew on the riverbank. The town contained a fair-sized cotton gin. But that didn't last too long. Floods along the Little River were common. The town and the cotton gin were washed away. Most of its residents never returned.

Frank McMillan's aunt Ona ("Ownie") was married to a man named Jerry Silver. In life, his actions mimicked the Pa Kettle character in the 1950s movie series. Jerry was a lazy, drunken womanizer. I grew up hearing stories about Jerry's various flaws, foibles, and failed enterprises. Most of the stories centered on his heroic efforts to avoid work. Jerry put more effort into *not* working than others did at work. He was a rotten apple in my opinion.

Jerry Silvers knew someone who owned three parcels along the river in Reed's Lake. He ascertained that the neighbor wasn't paying property taxes on the parcels. There was a story that went along with that failure, but I have forgotten the details. Perhaps no one wanted to give me the straight scoop on the deal. "Need to know" isn't confined to top-secret military operations. Truth be told, I never wanted to know what went on with Frank's extended family.

Jerry discovered a quirk in Texas law. If you paid the taxes on someone else's land for a given period, you would become the legal owner. Jerry Silvers paid the property taxes on the three parcels in Reed's Lake and eventually won legal ownership on the parcels.

Those fields have marvelous soil. One of them was locally known as the Jack Patch. Whatever you planted there would "jump up out of the ground like a jackrabbit."

Jerry found a way to maximize production from the Jack Patch: irrigation. He pumped water from the Little River for use on his field. By contemporary Bell County, Texas, standards, it was a radical concept. Jerry grew incredible crops on his irrigated land for a year or two. He then quit farming. Jerry was famous for coming up with excellent ideas that he never carried to fruition.

When I arrived on the scene a few decades later, a rusty pipe was the only evidence of Jerry's irrigation enterprise. The Jack Patch had become a cow pasture.

I remember my first exposure to the Little River bottomland. It bordered on the miraculous. One of the McMillan brothers said that he wanted to go to "the river." The question in some people's minds might have been, which river? Central Texas is crosshatched with an assortment of streams. But to the McMillan clan, there was only one place that was qualified as *the river*: The Little River. They specifically meant Reed's Lake.

My first visit to the Little River was typical of most that would follow. The McMillan brothers loaded a bunch of men and boys into a car. I can't remember a time when females were asked to come along for a visit to the river. This was an exclusive, boys-only club. The ostensible reason for this was simple: the McMillan brothers wanted to go skinny-dipping. But the brothers didn't actually swim there very often. They just said they were going skinny-dipping to exclude females from their trips to the river.

The actual reason for the male-only nature of McMillan outings was quite simple: the brothers could speak openly when they were in the company of males. The boys would not repeat what they heard while they were with the men. But the girls were more bonded to the women. They could be counted on to listen for and repeat certain code phrases they heard while they were with the men.

I had never been to the Little River. The day was just an outing for me. There was also an extenuating circumstance: I was sick. I had a high fever. I didn't notice the fever because it was so darned hot. Later that night, I was seen by a physician.

We drove south out of Temple on the main road. The driver turned right onto a secondary road. We drove down one of Texas's well-maintained gravel roads. The driver turned down a smaller road. He stopped at a gate. We had arrived at our destination. My first impression of the place wasn't good. The road was ugly. The gate was uglier. We were surrounded by an expansive mesquite scrub. Everything in sight was covered with a thick white layer of road dust.

All the color in the surrounding landscape was muted by the dust. The glaring Texas sun made it hard to look at *anything*. It was about 105 degrees outside and significantly hotter in the crowded car. I didn't give two shits where we were going, just so I got away from the press of bodies.

One of Frank's brothers got out of the car and opened the gate. He remained standing there until the car had passed, and then he relocked the gate and got back into the car. We drove on. Then something wonderful happened. It was as if the gate were a magical portal into the past. The well-maintained gravel road narrowed and became a two-rut wagon track.

It was cooler in this new place. We were in the shade. The harsh Texas sunlight lost its battle of subjugation to a jungle of plant life. Insanely green grasses covered the ground. Shrubs and flowers of middling height were scattered here and there. But it was the trees that dominated the scene. They were mixed hardwoods, large and lush. Their canopy provided respite from the relentless Texas sun.

The wagon road quickly became a barely visible mud trail. We stopped near an inconspicuous cow shed. Someone told me it was the cabin that James Burnett Reed had built in 1834. Frank's brother Donald was born in that cabin. The McMillans explained that it was the oldest Anglo house in Texas. I must admit that the fine details of history didn't matter to me. I was gaping at the wild, reckless beauty of the place.

We got out of the car and proceeded on foot. As we walked, the mixed hardwood forest gave way to an endless bottomland glade of pecan trees. I had never been close to a pecan grove. I remember thinking they looked like California black walnuts. Their sour stink reminded me of creek sides back home.

A large turtle was lumbering down the road. Someone told me that it was called a terrapin. I called that lumbering old beast wonderful.

The ever-diminishing dirt road and the foundational remains of old buildings were the only signs that the hand of man had touched this place. I turned around to look at the natural beauty from a different perspective. I was startled by what I saw. A massive apparition was standing above the trees. A wrought-iron suspension bridge was in the middle the wooded cow pasture. No one had told me the bridge was there. The McMillans wanted to surprise the newcomer. They were rewarded by my awestruck expression. I tried to run across the bridge but was pulled back by calloused hands and warning voices. Frank said, "That ol' bridge is damned near ready to fall in the river, boy. Don't you git too close to 'er."

We walked over to the bridge. I took a closer look. Sure enough, many of the deck timbers were split, broken, or missing. Frank took me by the hand. He walked me out onto the bridge. We stopped midway across. A series of gaping holes rent the deck in front of our feet. We looked down through the openings in the roadway. They looked like windows. The Little River showed its lazy brown progress far below. *National Geographic* never shot their scenes *this* perfectly.

I don't remember being afraid of the rotten old bridge deck. I was completely entranced. It was all like a dream. The family, the bridge, the river, and those glorious old trees. All that my young heart yearned for was centered in the middle of the bridge. It was as if I had died and gone to heaven.

Frank turned around and led me toward the shore. My eyes followed the low-slung iron suspension cables as they made their sloping upward progress. But it was the bridge towers that made the greatest statement. They stood defiantly among the surrounding trees. They didn't look much different than when they'd been raised almost a hundred years before. The rusted towers made a bold statement. They told the trees that they were not ready to die.

The Reed's Lake Bridge was the epicenter of high holy regard for the wild McMillan clan. This was where they learned to swim when they were babies. The McMillan brothers used the bridge as a diving platform. Their mother had been driven to town via the bridge when she was pregnant with that brood.

Modern folks pay little heed to the accomplishments of those who came before them. Everything must be new to be relevant. That is sad. The works of the old ones have much to say if we take the time to listen. The forgotten bridge at Reed's Lake was a pioneering marvel of technology. That structure and a few others of like kind were the first cable-type iron suspension bridges. They were prototypes for one of the greatest engineering accomplishments of the nineteenth century: the Brooklyn Bridge. The Texas suspension bridges were the mid-nineteenth-century equivalent of jumbo jets and smartphones. Suspension bridges allowed mankind to safely cross previously unbridgeable chasms and waterways.

The Reed's Lake Bridge was built on the site of an ancient Indian ford. It was the best place for miles around to cross the Little River. For that reason, it was a key point on a major Indian trail. The Indians were not stupid. They knew the best and easiest ways to travel from here to there.

White men used Indian trails as the roadbeds for their highways. Highways are useless if weary travelers are stopped by flooded rivers and high water. The suspension bridges of Central Texas allowed for safer travel between Gulf Coast shipping ports and points north. The barely visible mud track through the cow pasture had once been the equivalent of a freeway. Traffic for miles around was channeled over the Reed's Lake Bridge. It was a boon to local businesses. Travelers need supplies, services, and places to stay.

The roads that spun off the Reed's Lake Bridge wound like a tangled ball of twine all the way from Temple to Houston. A shorter route was eventually built. In the twinkling of an eye, heavily traveled highways became disused back roads. Small local communities withered in the baking dust.

Some of the roads remain key access points for residents and ranchers. Others passed through private lands. They went to and from nowhere. Some "nowhere roads" were transferred to private owners. They became lost in the sands of time. That's how it went with the Reed's Lake Bridge and its connecting roads. When the bridge was condemned, the road was transferred to private ownership. The busiest highway in Central Texas became a cow trail.

Take note, you who strive for new things. The works of man are ephemeral.

CHAPTER 44

Academy, Texas

I WAS HAPPY WITH MY new life in Texas. My joy derived from one aspect: I had been accepted into the bosom of an old-line Texas family. Everyone was relaxed around me. This was especially true of the men and boys. The McMillan males knew I was a greenhorn. They also knew that when I got thrown, I always got back on the horse. The McMillans also noted that I was a willing and tireless worker. That was important in a culture where everyone was expected to help.

The men and boys of Frank's extended family spoke to me as they did to their own relatives. They said things in my presence that would not have been admitted to an outsider. The McMillans sometimes told me stories I didn't want to hear. Most of them detailed sexual liaisons and business deals gone wrong. For the most part, it was unmemorable stuff. I didn't want to hear gossip. I wanted to go to the river.

But some of the stories I heard from the extended McMillan clan were real doozies. I have *no* trouble remembering them! They will stick with me until I die. I'm going to share just one of those stories with you. It will explain much about the culture that created Frank McMillan.

The town of Little River Academy is about eight miles south of Temple. Little River and Academy were once separate towns. They merged into one town with an improbably long name in 1980. The politics of that eventuality must have been quite interesting.

Academy was named for the historic school that was once located there. We sometimes passed through Academy when we traveled south of Temple. A curious thing sometimes occurred when we drove through Academy. I can't tell you when it first happened. It must have been when I was five. The memory has always been deep inside of my consciousness. I can state with absolute certainty it happened each time I went to Texas. It last occurred when I was nineteen. This thing would happen only when the men and boys were alone in a vehicle. It never occurred when a woman or girl was present.

As we approached Academy, it would get quiet in the vehicle. Then one of the men would break the silence and say, "There ain't no niggers in Academy. We drug one to death in nineteen-twenty-something." (I don't recall the exact date.) I heard that two-sentence story countless times over the years. Its impact on my immature brain didn't diminish with subsequent telling. It felt as if a bomb exploded in in my head. The story burned itself into my memory.

There were several telling aspects about the narrative. The use of the word "we" is very revealing. It establishes the concept that the murder was a collective act. It was condoned by some of the people who lived in Academy at the time. Then there's the second part. The word "we" implies an ownership of the murder that spans human generations. Most of the people who told or heard the story were too young to have participated in the actual event. The use of "we" by someone who didn't participate in a murder is a declaration. It says, "I support the gruesome murder of a black man."

The fact that this story was repeated so often revealed something cynical and dangerous: the horrifically painful murder of a black man decades before was still a proud part of local and familial cultures. It emphasized the belief that their community was pure white a half century later solely because they collectively dragged a black man to death.

The final aspect of the story is equally revealing. In fourteen years of hearing that story, I never heard anyone contradict it. The telling always ended in the same way: the men and boys would nod their heads in agreement. Those little signs of acknowledgment would inevitably be accompanied by a low chuckle or two.

I have lived for sixty-six years. A lot of racism has passed through my field of vision. Not all of it was in Texas. I saw racism in California. Lita's family called Mexicans spics.

But there was a flip side to racism in California: we were generally the only white family in the fields with Mexicans. We got more racism than we gave. We were called gringos and *gabachos*. Those are not gentle terms when they are hurled as epithets.

Mexicans wouldn't steal a basket of green beans from another Mexican. But they damned sure would steal ours. We needed the money as much as the Mexicans did. They didn't care, though. They viewed us as easy white targets. My family didn't whine, complain, or fight the small payback we received from them. Lita just left someone behind to guard the damned beans when she went to take a piss.

The racism I saw in California was not overtly vicious, though it was undoubtedly limiting in many ways. This was especially true for Mexicans. But my childhood ears never heard of a white man lynching a Mexican in modern-era California.

The racism I was introduced to in Texas during the 1950s and 1960s was breathtaking in its scope and overwhelming in its magnitude. It permeated every social stratum, from dirt poor to very rich. Racism controlled every measurable aspect of Texas life. It looked a lot like the vestiges of the caste system in India. I can't discern much difference between low-caste Indians of today and the people of color who lived in Texas in 1956.

Racism in the American South was not a fixed or monolithic thing. It operated on a locally recognized sliding scale. Everybody of every race knew their exact place. Small children knew the rules. It was in their mother's milk and cultural DNA. This is precisely what you would expect from a culture that had several hundred years to fine-tune its hatred.

Most of the time, the white people I knew looked at people of African ancestry with condescension. Blacks were viewed as buffoons or immature semi human beings. There was a practical side to that outlook: blacks were necessary to do the kinds of scut work that no white man would stoop to. But it didn't take much for white condescension to turn violent. There was a whole range of precipitating causes that could initiate white-on-black violence.

Sometimes it was done just for fun. "Nigger knocking" was a valued part of Texas lore and tradition. That pastime was not a specific type of violence. It encompassed a whole range of activities. The most dangerous of these seemed to occur at night. It was an unspoken reality that no one wanted to get sent to jail for "merely" beating up a black person.

One of the most popular of these apparently required a truck, a long carboard tube, and at least two white participants. Those "brave souls" would drive down quiet country roads looking for black men walking alone on the shoulder. If the target was judged to be suitable, the person or persons in the back of the truck would extend the cardboard tube beyond the side of the truck. The object of this "game" was to hit the black man in the back of the head and knock him to the ground.

By all accounts, they would then break out in paroxysms of laughter as they drove on into the night. I never heard anyone express concern for the person who was allegedly laid out on the side of the road.

That kind of dangerous behavior was too violent for one of the more "enlightened" idiots I met in Texas. He told me that he preferred to fill a portable insect sprayer with ketchup, urine, and strained human shit. He apparently had an accomplice drive by a black church that was letting out after service. He said that he sprayed as many of the finely dressed parishioners as he could before his accomplice sped away. The man said that he yelled insults at the parishioners until they were out of sight.

When I was in Texas, I heard numerous second- and thirdhand stories about nigger knocking. No one I knew admitted they had done such a thing (except for the asshole with the shit sprayer). I don't know how many of the stories were true. Some of them must have been invented by local yahoos. They liked to shock the soft Californian with details of hitherto unknown activities.

When I was in California, I heard very little about white brutality and unfairness toward people of color. Black people were called Negroes. But when I went to Texas, I was exposed to a vast assortment of racist activities. Black people were treated like idiot children. They were universally reviled as niggers. The contrast between my two worlds was crazy making.

Most of the time, black people in Texas were ignored when they "knew their place." This was the famous benign neglect that made Jim Crow laws function for the better part of a hundred years.

It was an entirely different situation for Mexicans in Texas. Anglo hatred for Latinos went to a much higher level than it did with blacks. Almost every white person I knew in Texas spoke as if the "massacre" at the Alamo had happened just last week. I knew a *lot* of white Texans who hated Mexicans with a blood passion.

I never heard tell of the Mexican equivalent to nigger knocking. Anglos offered a far worse fate for Latinos in Texas: Mexicans were marginalized. They were pushed to the periphery of Texas society. They were invisible. They were given the worst jobs and housing. Yes, it's true: there *were* people in Texas whom Anglos hated more than blacks.

Except for Mexican women, of course. I was seven the first time I heard the phrase "brown on the outside, pink on the inside." I didn't know what the words meant. But I *could* see that whoever was talking seemed to have a rapturous look on his face. Lots of Anglo men in Texas have thought that Mexican women have fine pussies.

Your author is no exception. Experience has taught me that Mexican women frequently reciprocate in these types of interracial attractions. To my simple mind, that sounds like an easy solution to a lot of problems. Ending racism, one half-breed baby at a time.

The last few chapters detail my primary education about white-trash Texas society. I was exposed to a lot of information in a very short time. It was a lot for a young child to absorb.

But my new life was better than the one I had endured in California. When I was in Texas, I was seldom alone. Frank's brothers treated me like a prince. I got along well with the McMillan children. I had horses to ride, okra to pick, and Granny Mac. Frank's mother was a real peach. I stayed at her ramshackle house as much as I could.

In California, I was the king of back alleys, abandoned lots, and stray cats. In Texas, I was the emperor of pecan groves, flowing creeks, and wild chickens. Life was wonderful—until my entrance into the second grade.

CHAPTER 45

Attack of the Redheaded Bitch

Bitch: A term that has lost much of its meaning because of overuse. An apt descriptor for a particularly contentious woman.

—*TOM LIGGETT'S PERSONAL GLOSSARY OF TERMS*

THE ELEMENTARY SCHOOLS IN TEXAS are vastly superior to those in California. That was especially true in 1956. Children who matriculated from a California first grade into a Texas second grade were likely to have it rough. They would find that they were behind most of their peers in Texas classrooms.

The kids who sat down next to me on the first day of second grade in Texas really knew their stuff. They knew how to read. They could do basic arithmetic.

Things were different for me. I knew very few numbers and no math. I knew a few letters and could print my name. But I had absolutely no knowledge of reading, history, culture, or art. I knew very little about anything.

It didn't take more than a few hours for my new teacher to become aware of my sorry condition. A kind person might have seen that I was hopelessly behind my peers. He or she would have found a way to gently ease me back into the first grade.

This was not the case for the teacher I drew. She took my lack of knowledge as a character flaw. Look at it from her standpoint: someone who knew as little as I did *had* to be lazy, right? I have often wondered if her overall opinion arose from the harsh side of cowboy culture. Who knows? In that time and place, it was entirely possible.

The real deal breaker between me and my new teacher came in the manner in which she chose to advise me of my sloth: she screamed at the top of her lungs. This was quite a departure from the teacher who refused to teach me. That woman at least had the grace to ignore me when I ignored her.

During the first week of school, my new teacher asked Frank and Lita to attend an emergency conference. She told them that I knew nothing. They feigned complete ignorance about my condition. Lita offered her typical insistence that all my problems arose solely as a consequence of being born two months prematurely.

That bit of sap had been good enough to fool the naïve little teacher in Gilroy, California. But it didn't fly with my new one in Texas. My new teacher told Frank and Lita that I needed help with my schoolwork. They agreed I would receive help every day.

In the hallway after the meeting, Frank told Lita that my problems in school derived solely from one sector: my new teacher was a "redheaded bitch with a temper." Lita agreed. She said, "I never met a redhead who wasn't a bitch." Frank and Lita didn't say anything about getting me the academic help I desperately needed. I didn't get help with my homework that night.

Early the next day, my teacher grew exasperated with me. She belittled me with a loud message: "You are lazy. You know nothing. I am going to send you down to the baby first graders." The other students erupted in laughter. Some of the other students catcalled and said things like, "Baby, baby, baby. Tommy's gonna be a baby first grader. Baby, baby Tommy."

That little scene set me over the edge. I'd spent most of the previous school year on the receiving end of another teacher's rage. Now I told myself, "There will be no more days like this." I decided I would set the teacher straight about some things. Tell her what was going on. I stood up from my desk to address her. But I didn't know exactly what to say. Lacking words of my own, I used those of Frank and Lita. I parroted what they had said to each other after the parent-teacher meeting. I looked the teacher in the face and said, "Your problem is that you are a redheaded bitch with a temper."

I meant no malice with what I said. It's basic stuff. Kids repeat what they hear. Look at it from my perspective: I was a powerless young boy. I was being punished because I'd received poor teaching the year before. I was being tormented by a cruel bully. My grandmother Ruby used to tell me, "Tommy, you can make even a good dog bite." Yes, I told my teacher off. It was the only thing I could do to defend myself. Yes, I called my teacher a bitch. She clearly lived down to the word.

My words apparently struck a nerve within my teacher. The redhead had finally reached her limit. Her voice went up a couple of octaves. Her scream became a wail. The teacher flew down the aisle. She snatched me up. She held me up in the air and shook me like a rag doll. The teacher looked at the other students and triumphantly announced, "I'm taking this baby down to be with the other baby first graders." It was grand theater. My classmates erupted with hoots and cheers. They sounded like a bunch of hyenas charging in for the kill.

My teacher dropped me to the ground and then picked me up. She wrapped her arms around me and pulled me out of the classroom. She half carried/half dragged me down the hallway. All the while, she was loudly testifying about the latent stupidity of Tommy Liggett. She slammed open the door to the first-grade classroom and dragged me in by my shirt collar. She threw me into an empty desk. The teacher finished off the performance with a grand recitation. She loudly celebrated the fine details of my failure to all who were in the classroom.

What do you think of that, folks? That was potent stuff for a six-year-old boy to swallow. Believe it or not, my day got worse from there. The school contacted Lita at her jobsite. Lita had to come in for another urgent meeting. That made two consecutive days that she was forced to take time off from work because of me. My mother was already angry when she walked into the school. She got very angry when someone told her what I said to the teacher.

But someone at the meeting got to the real kernel of the problem: Tommy doesn't know anything. How could that problem be rectified? My new teacher knew the answer: parental help with homework. Lita agreed that was a perfect solution. She would have agreed to anything if it meant that she could escape from the meeting.

Lita managed to keep her composure while she was with my new teacher. She was stone faced. Things changed once we left the school grounds. Lita was boiling mad. All the anger she had accumulated over the last two days erupted from her mouth. Lita said, "I had to take off work two fuckin' days in a row because of *you*. We're barely makin' it already, you little fuckin' shit." That was just the warmup. Lita launched right into her main griev-ance. She said, "I am *so* ashamed of you. We ain't got no stupid people on *our* side of the family. You musta got that from your dad's side. You are just plain stupid."

Oh, mother, my mother; I believed every word you said. At that moment, I knew I was the stupidest boy that ever lived.

We had dinner with Janita's family that night. It was a marathon of sermonizing and glares by the gathered adults. It was like the public denun-ciations that happened in the early days of Communist China. The adults took turns chastising me. Their words didn't bother me very much, though. I knew that I had far worse coming when Frank got me alone.

We arrived back home about nine. It was a school night. Frank was tired and half drunk. He began the festivities with threats. He used his best drill instructor's voice. Frank announced that I would have to try harder. His sermon offered no hint of the circumstances that had delivered me to this academic juncture.

Frank quickly moved on to his main grudge. Lita had told my new teacher that someone would help me with my homework. That someone was Frank. Even though it was late in the evening, he decided to help me with my homework. Frank was drunk, tired, and grumpy. I was brain-dead. It was well past the time that a young child should be in bed. I had been pummeled continually for the last twelve hours.

Frank tried to teach me both reading and arithmetic in quick time. I didn't immediately grasp what he was teaching. That pissed him off. Frank began screaming. He said, "You are lazy and stupid. You ain't never gonna do well. You ain't never gonna be nothin'."

Frank reinforced his words with the toe of his right boot. He used that stout-clad implement to kick me into bed. Then he turned off the lights and left the room.

I clearly remember my feelings as I stretched out in bed. I tried not to think about what had happened since I got out of bed that morning. One phrase kept jumping into my mind: "You are lazy and stupid." It was the only lesson that I retained from that unique day. But it was one that I learned well. It was repeated endlessly through my mind in a loop: "You are stupid, stupid and lazy. You are lazy, lazy and stupid." In my mind, I became stupid and lazy Tommy.

The teacher that gave me my second shot at the first grade was wonderful. I learned a lot in her classroom. She found a way to rehabilitate my image at school. Speech and dramatic arts are important parts of the curriculum in Texas schools. The big production of the year at my school was the Christmas show. You would expect that in a Jesus-oriented culture.

The Christmas show for that year had a circus theme. Circuses need to have a ringmaster, and someone decided that it should me. Think of the irony of that. The school allowed a teacher to abuse and devastate me. Then the same school gave me the only big part in that year's production.

Frank's aunt Ownie, an incomparable seamstress, made a ringmaster's costume for me. I wore it to introduce the acts in the Christmas production. I had my own act too; I sang a ridiculous little ice-skating song. It was in the wrong key, but I sang like an angel. I stood alone on the stage. I filled the auditorium with my voice.

The audience was enraptured, with one notable exception: Frank. He was sitting dead center in the audience. He focused his menacing glare on me as I introduced each act. His face grew tight when I sang my little song. I felt joy as I crooned my way through the song. But each note that left my mouth was replaced with sadness. I knew that I was in big trouble with Frank.

My prediction quickly turned into reality. When Frank got me alone that night, he really let me have it. Frank bent down to my level. He grabbed the front of my ringmaster's costume in his claw like hand and pulled me roughly toward him. Frank paused for a moment. He locked eyes with me in a hateful stare. I could smell the rotten whiskey on his breath. Then Frank used his best dramatic whisper to tell me, "I wasn't real pleased to see you up there prissin' like a faggot, boy."

I had heard the word faggot often enough in my life. It usually came into play when Frank and his brothers were speaking about their uncle Arthur. I knew it was a bad word, but I had no idea what it meant. I had no doubt about the meaning of "prissin'." That meant using mincing female mannerisms.

Once Frank was satisfied that I understood his primary thought, he pressed on. He said, "I don't never wanna see you doin' that shit again. Got it?" Oh baby, I read Frank loud and clear. He didn't want to see me sing and dance onstage.

Frank's timing was perfect. He sucked the joy out of my first victorious moment in years. He also added more words to my arsenal of self-hatred and doubt. I was now a lazy, stupid boy who minced around like a faggot, whatever that was. Those words added to the set of knives that followed and cut me for the rest of my childhood—and beyond.

CHAPTER 46

George Jones

FRANK'S LAST POSTING IN THE navy was at Moffett Field Naval Air Station in Sunnyvale, California. He made several friends during his time at that base. Two of those people were musicians of great talent. One of them, Bill Fuqua, was the most talented musician I have ever met. But Bill squandered his musical genius. He was content to drink all night and sleep all day. In between, he played the guitar and sang songs.

The other, less talented musician that Frank knew was named George Jones. Yes, George Jones the country music star. George wasn't famous when he and Frank knew each other at Moffett Field. He was just another marine who wanted to be discharged.

Frank said that when George got drunk with his friends, he would sing a song that he wrote. Frank used to recite the words from that song to me. I have forgotten most of the words, but they went something like, "I'm gonna build me a big ol' wall around Moffett Field." That song was never published, but Frank said he recognized the tune in one of George's top hits.

In the years after he was discharged from the marines, George kept in touch with Frank. One of those contacts was a real doozy. George sent word that he would be passing through Temple as part of a big-name country music show that was on a national tour. The master of ceremonies was a famous country music star—I think it was Ernest Tubb. George sent Frank tickets for the show and told Frank to come to the dressing room before the performance.

When we got to the auditorium, Frank told the usher that George Jones was expecting us. The usher told us to follow along. The dressing rooms at the Temple civic auditorium were located under the stage. As we passed through the stage door, the usher advised us to keep our voices low. He said, "Sound carries up through the stage floor. The audience will hear every word that you say." We were quiet as church mice.

The usher led us down a hallway. But it wasn't quiet. We heard the raucous noise of a drunk who was attempting to sing. The drunken song was quite humorous. I snickered and resisted the urge to laugh. Frank shushed me, but I could see that he was smiling too.

As we walked farther down the hall, the drunk's singing grew in volume. The usher stopped in front of a closed door. This was the fount of the drunken noise. The usher knocked and the singing abruptly stopped. A voice bellowed, "Come in." The singing instantly resumed. Frank pushed me in through the door. I was in front of our little group.

I discovered I was standing about six feet from the open door of a small bathroom. George Jones was the sitting on the toilet, accompanying himself on the guitar. His glittery stage pants were bunched around his ankles. His white ass shined in the light.

George's face lit up when he saw Frank standing in the doorway. It drove the singer into a higher state of merriment. George burst into another musical bout and sang a humorous musical greeting for us. Everyone in our little group laughed, even the poker-faced usher. There was much to smile about; George was doing a particularly good job with *this* song.

Things could have gone on for a while like this. It was great fun. But our reverie was interrupted. Someone shoved his way into the crowded dressing room. It was the show's master of ceremonies. Here was the Man himself (again, I think it was Ernest Tubb). Frank gaped at the intruder with reverence.

The Man was not happy. In fact, he was madder than a wet hen. He wasted no time on social niceties. He launched right into his main grievance. He said, "Now goddamn it, George, I know that you like to hear the sound of your own voice. But your singing is drowning out the people who are trying to perform onstage. The audience can hear you better than they can hear the people who are singing out front. Stop it." The Man didn't say another word. He spun on his heels and stormed out of the dressing room.

I suppose the Man had good reason to be angry. He had to pause a big show to quiet his top star. George complied with the Man's request. But I noted something odd in George's demeanor: he wore a sheepish expression. It was the look of an errant schoolboy who got caught doing something wrong. It was the same look that Frank got when he was trying to cover his tracks.

We didn't stay in George's dressing room for very long. He had to get ready to go onstage. The usher led us out of the dressing room, and we took our seats out in the auditorium.

I got to hear a lot of famous old-line country musicians that night. I heard Little Johnny Roventini shout out his famous "Call for Phillip Morris" line. But the act that George Jones performed on the toilet was the best of all.

CHAPTER 47

The Drinking Buddy

WHILE FRANK RECONNECTED WITH A lot of old friends in Central Texas, he seemed to enjoy the company of one man more than the others. I cannot remember that person's name, but he was Frank's drinking buddy. Frank's buddy had two children. One was three or four years old. The other child was a boy about my age. That boy became the closest thing to a male friend I had during the time we lived in Texas.

Frank's drinking buddy was a hard-ass. He treated his son like he was a recruit in marine boot camp. The drinking buddy continually threatened to "use the belt" on his son.

Just for the record, "the belt" was a Sam Browne army belt. They are wide and thick and have a huge metal buckle. Sam Browne belts were eventually removed from the US Army uniform. Too many soldiers knew them for what they were: whip-chain weapons with a sharp mace on the end. One soldier in a bar could clear a fifteen-foot circle by swinging the things. Sailors and marines hated Sam Browne belts.

I didn't see much in the son's behavior that warranted such draconian threats. Among the boys I knew, he was the best of the bunch. Every sentence my friend spoke to an adult included the phrase "yes, sir" or "no, ma'am." He wouldn't look an adult in the eye, either. The drinking buddy's son always seemed to be staring at his shoes.

At the time, I didn't note my friend's behavior as being unusual. Half the boys I knew in Texas behaved like perfect little robots. The other half were spoiled princes. There didn't seem to be much middle ground between the two.

My friend didn't mention anything that suggested that his father was particularly abusive. A high percentage of the boys I knew in Texas were scared shitless of their fathers. That was our normal.

We got together for after-dinner dessert with Frank's drinking buddy every couple of weeks. Those events were always held at the buddy's house, never held at our roach-infested duplex. That aspect is very telling.

One evening after dinner, Frank announced that we had received an invitation to go to the drinking buddy's house. He indicated that the buddy's wife had made a chocolate cake. That woman was apparently known for the quality of her cakes. That sounded great to me. I loved chocolate cake.

Before we left for the buddy's house, I noticed Frank and Lita acting strangely. They were milling around by the front door and seemed hesitant to leave. I could tell that something was going on. I thought, *are they gonna drop me off at someone else's house again?*

Frank noted my consternation and said, "Your little friend don't know how to mind his daddy. His daddy needs to take the belt to him ev'ry day. But your friend don't never seem to learn his lessons. His daddy has to spank him harder and harder." Frank paused. I could tell he didn't know what to say next. His demeanor revealed that a difficult thought was stalled on the tip of his tongue.

Frank's uneven delivery of the current message was scaring me. I didn't know where this was going. No matter what, I knew that the rest of the story wasn't going to be good.

Frank broke the ice. He said, "The other night, your little friend disobeyed his daddy one time too many. His daddy hit him with the belt, but your friend didn't get the message. So his daddy turned the belt around and swung the buckle." Frank paused again to let the last sentence float and hang.

I was quickly becoming more frightened. Frank had my complete attention.

Once more, Frank broke the silence. He said, "That boy got hit in the eye with a belt buckle. It put the boy's eye out."

I didn't know what to do. Was I expected to say something? Frank apparently didn't know what to say, either. He had a concerned look on his face.

Frank finally revealed the reason for his stilted revelation. He said, "When we get there, I don't want you to be a starin' at your little friend's face. I don't want you to be a-askin' him a whole lot a questions."

Now I got it. Frank was providing me with a script. He was adding new players to our sick little charade. That wasn't difficult for me. I had been playing this game for more than four years.

It was uncharacteristically quiet in the car as we drove to the drinking buddy's house. A cloud hung over the upcoming visit.

We went into the buddy's house. The daddy, mommy, and two children were all lined up in a row inside of the front door. Everyone was perfectly cleaned and combed. Every shoe was polished.

Frank and his buddy gave each other a hearty handshake, and Lita and the wife gave each other cheerful hugs. I shook hands with the younger child. Then I turned to face my friend. Everybody was watching me to see how I would react. I was dreading the moment. I hadn't really looked in my friend's direction.

I looked at his face and saw a changed landscape. His eye was covered with an ugly, stained bandage. A droplet of dark fluid was oozing down his cheek. That was bad, but it was the rest of his features that revealed the real tragedy. I knew my friend as being a bright and playful boy. He was perfect in all ways. That boy was gone. He was dead. The person who now stood in his place was a shadow of his former self. He was sad. He was downcast. He was a zombie.

I just stood there, holding my friend in a never-ending handshake. Neither I nor the other boy said a single word. We just stared at each other's faces. My two eyes and his sole remainder were locked in a death grip. Our eyes were trying to say things our voices were not allowed to. We were trying to communicate, but we had no words. Just one message got through: our three eyes shared the same brand of sadness.

Frank finally broke the moment. He put his hand on my shoulder and shoved me toward the kitchen.

The host showed us to our seats around the kitchen table. Everybody sat, except for the host's wife. She was scurrying around, getting ready to serve coffee and cake.

In due course, the famous chocolate cake arrived. The wife placed it in the center of the table with a flourish. Everyone around the table cheered. It was a beauty. The wife had done her job. Cake and coffee were served. The children got milk.

I suppose the cake was pretty tasty, but I don't remember. I was in a shell. I was numb. Everyone was speaking around me, but I didn't hear their voices. I couldn't look my friend in the face. Had I done that, I would have started crying. I knew that almost anything I said would be wrong. I just played my role. I was a robot in sleep mode.

The evening progressed quickly. It was a work night, and everybody had to get up early the next day. Lita helped the wife with the dishes. We donned our coats, shook hands, and walked out the door. That was it. A good time was had by all. It was just another shitty day in paradise.

I was still numb as we got in the car. I didn't know what to do. But I knew that sooner or later, Frank would find inspiration in the events of the evening. In that regard, I was not long disappointed. Frank broke the silence in the car. He eyes were looking at the windshield, but his words were directed at me. He said, "It's too bad 'bout that boy's eye. I don't never think it's right to beat someone with a belt buckle. His daddy shoulda stuck to usin' the belt." Wow! That statement blew my mind. Frank was being sympathetic to the one-eyed boy. The lie in *that* sentiment was quickly revealed. Frank turned in his seat and locked eyes with me. He said, "Still and all, what happened here should be a warnin' to other little boys." He broke into a huge grin, chuckled to himself, and turned back to the front of the car.

Oh boy, Frank. I read your message loud and clear. You took me to your drinking buddy's house so I could see what had happened to my only friend. You wanted me to know there was no limit to the brutality you were willing to visit upon me.

CHAPTER 48

Fun and Games in Central Texas

THE MAIN AXIOM ABOUT LIFE in Texas in the 1800s indicates that "Texas was heaven for men and dogs but hell for women and horses." By the time I arrived in Texas, automobiles had reduced wear and tear on the local horse stock. But men and dogs continued to behave pretty much as they had in the nineteenth century.

Neither of those groups realized that the door was closing on their old ways. A few years down the line, people found ways to restrain the testicles of men and remove them from their dogs. I sincerely wish that I could have been in Texas when feminism blossomed. It must have been a sight to behold.

The Old West never quite faded away for Frank and his brothers. Once or twice a week, they went coon hunting. In the Central Texas dialect, coon means raccoon.

Frank's brother Jimmy was a bona fide hunter. He always had a large pack of hounds, and they were quite effective at hunting game. Jimmy McMillan was the last real Texas cowboy I knew.

But the kind of hunting that Frank did with Jimmy was different. The McMillan brothers loaded Jimmy's hounds into a truck and drove to Reed's Lake. The dogs were released and went howling off into the night. The McMillan brothers then donned their hidden caches of cowboy finery. They left Reed's Lake and the dogs behind and went to enjoy an old-time Texas Saturday night.

The loss of cultures isn't generally born of catastrophes but the shedding of small details. Few contemporary Americans grasp the appeal of the old-time Saturday night. I think that the last gasp of that tradition was embodied in the 1981 song "Working for the Weekend." For the generations that came after that song, every night seems to be Saturday. The effect of that seminal party night was diluted and lost.

In old Texas, most people worked from sunup to sundown. This was especially true during the growing season. There never seemed to be enough hours in the day. People were tired when they got home at night. Many of them wanted to get drunk, eat, and stagger into bed.

Saturday was different. When people got out of bed in the morning, they knew that better things awaited later. That sentiment kept them going through the day. They looked forward to fun times. After they had taken a bath.

Countrified Texans of old didn't bathe as often as modern Americans. There were a lot of reasons for this. There was no running water in most country houses. Forget about the domestic water heater; they didn't have that either. When people wanted to bathe, they had to draw the water from a well or stream. The water had to be heated on an old-fashioned stove. That was a lot of work.

Most people didn't own a bathtub. Bathing was done in all-purpose galvanized steel washtubs.

People had large families in those days. It was not possible to draw, heat, and pour bath water for hordes of kids every night. Remember, those country women worked as hard as the men. But the women generally worked longer hours.

Farm women bathed their children in shifts. They began after noon on Saturday. They wanted the children to be clean when the men came home.

Old-time women didn't heat any more water than was necessary, and they used the same dirty water to bathe several children. The last child used cold, dirty water. It was full of the rough general-purpose soap that had been sequentially added by the other children. It was *nasty*.

I'm glad that I lived with Granny Mac out in the country. It gave me a small taste of old time Texas life—and the bathing habits that went along with the deal. My experience with country bathing techniques taught me that the worst part came at the end. People didn't rinse the soap from their bodies as we do now. They *wiped* away the soap with a washcloth. Most of the soap remained on the skin. The soap residue made my skin itch like crazy. I can only imagine what it must have been like for my ancestors. Those folks were using rough homemade lye soap. It must have eaten them alive all week.

Much of what I witness in modern life is incomprehensible to me. I see advertisements that tout gentle detergents for delicate skin. Today's all-purpose prima donnas wouldn't be able to handle an old-time cowboy bath. Every stage of the process would be repugnant to them.

In the country, most people didn't bathe for hygienic considerations. They just wanted to wash the stink off their bodies. Folks were preparing themselves for Saturday night dances and Sunday church.

It is very difficult to travel long distances with draft animals. That is especially true if you are transporting a large family. Because of that aspect, every small crossroads community had its own gathering place. There were Masonic lodges, church halls, and specific-purpose buildings.

Each community hall catered to its preferred type of music. Some featured polka bands. Most favored country music. The bands were top-notch. There were lots of musicians in the cowboy culture of old. Many people grew up in places that were short on entertainment. You either made your own or became very bored.

Most of the patrons in cowboy dance halls were drunk. This led to lots of merriment and lots of fights. Remember, a high percentage of cowboys were descended from the fighting Scots-Irish. Dance hall owners knew that fights meant broken furniture and lost revenue. Everyone knew to take it outside. "Outside" meant the rough, gravel-covered parking lots. Most people wouldn't bring a fancy car to a Texas Saturday night dance. They knew that two or more enraged, drunken cowboys might be rolling around on the hood. No one wanted to get their paint scuffed during someone else's fight.

The McMillan boys were a force of nature when they got into fistfights. Frank McMillan always claimed that he didn't like to fight, but he got into a lot of fights. His bouts lasted just long enough for him to punch his opponent one time. Then it was lights out for the other guy.

Frank's cousin Bill White was the best fighter in the family. He was the US Navy all-fleet boxing champion. In case you don't know, that was a very big deal. Bill White was known all over the South as "the man who had one-punch fights."

The extended McMillan clan was Scots-Irish to the *bone*. Those boys should have worn kilts when they went to dances.

Drinking and fighting were an interesting sideline for the McMillan brothers, but their main object was women. In that regard, they were not disappointed; *lots* of women went to Saturday night dances. Young and old, rich and poor, thin and heavy, married, engaged, and single. Every conceivable type of white woman was in attendance. Those women shared one commonality: they were there to dance with cowboys. Most of the time, the women furnished their own cowboys. If not, lots of willing applicants were in attendance.

I can recall no details of the McMillan brothers' sexual exploits. They made scant mention of such things around me. "Little pitchers have big ears" was an oft-quoted old saw that pertained to all children, especially me. Lita was my mother, while four years into our lives together, Frank was little more than a brutal, drunken stranger to me. He knew I would tell Lita if I saw him with another woman.

When we moved to Texas, Frank quickly settled himself into a thriving McMillan family construct. Many of the married members of Frank's extended family acted as if they were single. At least one of them, Lynn Hayes, had a well-known affair of long standing. He treated the other woman as if she were a simultaneous wife.

Frank's twin brothers were not yet married. They did all that they could to cut a wide swath through the local female populace. I suppose that added incentive to Frank's infidelities. Show the new generation how it's done.

Back in California, Frank had been stuck with the honky-tonk angels who frequented the bars in his circle. A steady diet of anything gets stale. This is especially true when she has been eaten by countless other men before you.

The taverns in California were close to home. Frank was always on the lookout for a surprise visit from Lita. That kept his extramarital adventures on a somewhat manageable scale.

Those factors did not apply in Texas. Dance halls were scattered far and wide across the landscape. Frank knew that Lita would not show up at a barely known, gravel-road dance hall thirty or forty miles from home.

The geographical immensity of the McMillan family partying construct lulled Frank into carelessness. It never occurred to him that Lita might catch him with another woman while he was in Texas. That never happened to any other man he knew. Frank McMillan cast himself adrift on a sea of whiskey and women.

Frank had another reason to believe that Lita would never catch him with another woman: local tradition. Many of the Texas women of that era had very little power. That forced them into cowlick submission. They were cowboy concubines.

Local history validated the principal concept of the philandering game: it didn't matter if a cowboy concubine discovered that her husband was cheating. There was little she could do to change the situation. Most of the women I knew in Texas had little education, no salable job skills, and a house full of minor children to feed. It would have been fiscal suicide for her to rock the boat.

When I lived in Texas, I saw a seemingly endless parade of wives blissfully ignore the reality that their husbands had something extra going on the side. Maybe the women were secretly happy that their husbands were expending their sexual energy between other legs. Remember, that was before the advent of the birth control pill. If a wife got nailed by a horny cowboy every night, she would have been pregnant all the time. Even the most devoted wife has her limits.

Frank was playing cards with a deck that was stacked in favor of the men. But he unwittingly put a wild card into play when he brought Lita to Texas. She wasn't like anyone else in the local herd of Texas women. She was not born in the confines of their pen.

Lita had a sharp, incisive mind. She also had keen eyes and a sharp nose. Those attributes were the joker that trumped Frank's king.

Have you ever been around someone who hunted wild game with hounds and horses? If the answer to that question is yes, you probably noted a fine detail: hunters smell like mud, sweat, shit, dog, horse, and whatever animal they kill.

Frank returned from his weekly coon hunts smelling like cheap perfume and unwashed sex. You would think that the boy would have taken careful precautions to avoid detection. Not Frank. Frank was overcome by an anesthetic of his own creation. He totally forgot himself. Frank blissfully returned home early each Sunday morning, took off his clothes, and crawled into bed with Lita. If she was too sleepy to note the smell of other women on Frank at that moment, she couldn't fail to miss it later. Lita washed his underwear and fine cowboy shirts. All is revealed in the laundry basket.

Before we left California, Frank and Lita had been fighting incessantly. Those fights were temporarily suspended when we got to Texas. Frank and Lita were happy. But when Frank started tomcatting around, their battles began anew. Lita told him, "I'm gonna pack up my shit an' get on back to California if you don't straighten up and fly right."

Frank denied messing around with other women. He promised Lita he would behave. That was bullshit. There was no way that Frank was going to stop having fun with his brothers. He became a little more cautious with his prowling, but he still went out with his brothers on Saturday night.

Lita and Frank argued every day. But it brought no change in his philandering behavior. So Lita tried another tack. She spoke with the other

McMillan wives about their husbands' unfaithful predilections. The other wives told Lita that she was wrong. There had to be innocent reasons why the boys came home smelling more like cosmetics counters than sweaty hunters.

Lita didn't give up that easily. She forged ahead with her reasoning with the other wives. When pressed, they inevitably played their ultimate card: even if the boys *did* go out "dancing" on Saturday night, they always came home on Sunday morning.

Lita grudgingly went along with this line of reasoning for a few weeks, but she quickly realized that it would not supply her with a solution to her problem. It galled her to know that Frank was out screwing other women while she sat at home with me.

That last point reveals the crux of the problem. Lita's anger derived as much from being excluded from Frank's fun as it did from jealousy. She sure as hell didn't want to spend any quality time with me. Especially on Saturday night.

Great battles are seldom fought as set pieces. Blind chance and circumstance usually bring opponents to the clash. That's how Frank and Lita's greatest battle was staged.

It was a stormy Saturday night. Frank announced that he was going coon hunting. Lita was pretty naïve about masculine activities, but she knew that *nobody* hunts raccoons in the middle of a days-long Texas thunderstorm. But she didn't voice any suspicions or objections about Frank's hunting trip. She was cool as a clam.

When Frank went out at night, he usually took the one car that he and Lita owned. That little twist served its unspoken purpose: Lita would be stranded at home. There was no way that she could look for Frank. That's a good plan for a philanderer.

But on the pivotal night, Frank didn't drive their car. His rationale was simple: Lita wouldn't drive in stormy weather. Oh, lordy. Frank really underestimated his woman *that* night. Harsh experience taught me that once Lita set her mind on doing something, she damned well found a way to get it done. Frank was about to learn that lesson the hard way.

Lita displayed a calm demeanor as Frank walked out the door to go hunting. She kissed him sweetly on the cheek. That sweetness quickly proved to be a ruse. A few minutes later, Lita grabbed her purse, and we got into the car. She was already pissed when Frank left, but she quickly talked herself into a higher form of rage. She yelled at me, the windshield, and the blowing rain on the road. I'm certain that even the hidden stars up in the clouded skies got the gist of Lita's diatribe.

She told me that she was going to put an end to Frank's shenanigans once and for all. I did my level best to hunker down and disappear into the seat cushions. I didn't know where this was all going, but I didn't want for Lita's anger at Frank to transpose itself to me.

Lita wasn't off on a blind search for Frank; Texas is a big state. Lita had a plan. She revealed the pure genius of the thing to me as she drove down the road.

Lita knew that many of the dance halls Frank attended were located far out on gravel roads. She didn't think that the McMillan brothers would risk a long journey on rain-swamped secondary byways. Lita guessed that the boys would stay on the paved roads close to Temple. She knew of only one dance hall that met that set of specifications. "Those bastards are at Jerry's Place," she told me. Ah, Lita, you missed your calling, girl. This is the rare stuff of which great generals are made.

A less devious person would have driven straight out to Jerry's Place. That type of straightforward confrontation wasn't harsh enough for Lita's Indian sensibilities. She wanted witnesses to her coup.

Lita drove around Temple, trying to get other McMillan women to ride along as partners in her scheme. Most of the women were too cowed to participate in what they viewed as being a foreign and dangerous act.

Lita did manage to get Frank's sister Velma and her three young daughters in the car. I suppose that Velma went along with us because she was on the outs with her husband. Misery loves company. Hell, maybe she was bored and wanted to see Lita in action.

There was no equivocation about how *I* felt that night: I saw a glimmer of hope. I prayed that Lita would get me away from Frank's brutality and neglect.

Battles are sometimes won when the weather benefits one side over another. I have heard many old-timers say, "Air conditioning made it possible for Yankees to live in Texas." I lived in Texas before common folks had air conditioning. I *know* that adage is true. Heroic measures were called upon to make life in those times passable, if not comfortable.

Frank's uncle Jerry Silvers owned the aptly named Jerry's Place tavern. It was a rough-hewn drinking hole that offered few amenities. Jerry Silvers didn't have the money to install and operate an air-conditioning system, so he placed swing-up garage doors along the front of the building. When the doors were open, the interior of the tavern was bathed with outside air. In operative terms, this meant that the inside of Jerry's Place was only about 105 degrees.

When Lita drove up, she saw an open parking space in front of the roll-up doors. The windshield offered a bird's-eye view of what was going on inside.

Jerry's Place was packed. Every square inch of floor space was filled with drunken cowboys and women. Fortune smiled on Lita yet again. Frank was on the very edge of the roiling mass, dancing with another woman. He was facing away from the parking strip. The headlights of Lita's car illuminated Frank. He looked like he was onstage.

Lita's worst fears had been proven. A normal woman would have lost her mind. But there wasn't much about Lita that could be called normal. She didn't break out in hysterics; Lita went into full-on Indian mode. She got out of the car and carefully closed the door. Lita slowly crept in Frank's direction. She was stalking him.

Frank had no idea what was going on. He danced in rapturous oblivion. I watched his hips sway with the music.

The view through the window was reminiscent of the movies I saw at the drive-in theater. The scene was perfectly staged. It was like when the bad guy sneaked up on the good guy. But this was different; the roles had been reversed. I hoped that the good girl would win this time.

Lita walked up behind Frank and tapped him on the shoulder. Frank was slow to react to her touch. Guys tapped each other on the shoulder at dances to signal they wanted to cut in. Lita tapped Frank on the shoulder again. He turned to see who was trying to cut in on his dance. Expecting to see another tall man, Frank didn't lower his eyes enough to note Lita's five-foot-tall body. He finally looked down. The expression on Frank's face changed from bliss to horror as he beheld the enraged apparition that was standing behind him.

Lita didn't hesitate once she had Frank's attention. She wasted no time on pointless words and declarations. Lita launched a massive roundhouse punch to Frank's jaw. She put every ounce of her hundred-and-twenty-pound, work-hardened body into her clenched fist. That punch rocked Frank to the soles of his Justin boots. It spun him around. He was stunned. Frank paused for one tenth of a second.

That gave Lita time to launch her main attack: she jumped onto Frank's back and wrapped her legs tightly around his waist. Then she wrapped her left arm around his neck in a death grip. That monkey-like hold allowed Lita a full range of motion with her lethal right fist. Damn! That woman had the fastest, hardest little fists that anyone ever experienced. Lita landed about ten punches in two seconds. Then she suspended that behavior and attempted to pull Frank's hair.

Compared to punching, that might sound relatively harmless. I refute *that* sentiment! Lita was known far and wide as being a master hair puller. I'd seen her strip most of the hair out of a woman's head in just a few seconds.

Frank later told me he thanked God at that moment that he had recently cut his hair short for the summer. That saved him a lot of damage. Lita couldn't get a good grip on his hair. Otherwise she would have been pulling out chunks of bleeding scalp along with Frank's hair.

Jerry's Place went from dance hall to pandemonium. The patrons in that dive were accustomed to seeing fights between men. Fights between women were less common. But no one had ever seen a woman beat a man so thoroughly. The other cowboys must have really been stunned to note that the beaten man was a local pugilistic powerhouse. These considerations caused the other men to hold back. The crowd left a polite space between themselves and the embattled couple. They didn't know what to do.

Lita upped the ante, leaving no doubt about her intentions. She screamed out variations of the same line over and again: "I'm going to kill you, you fuckin' bastard!"

That statement was a tipping point for the bystanders. They knew that if Lita was given enough time, she would kill Frank. A man rushed in. He tried to pull Lita off Frank's back. She viciously lashed out with her foot. He drew back, wounded. Another man tried the same thing but met a similar result. There was a momentary lull in bystander response. It was apparent that no one wanted to meet Lita in single combat.

The crowd finally figured out there is safety in numbers, they all rushed in. Five strong cowboys did their best to get Lita off Frank's back, but they couldn't do much to lessen Lita's efforts to kill Frank with her bare hands. Men would rush in and then draw back, wounded by Lita's slashing fists and feet. It looked like a catfight. It was a rolling blur of activity.

The sound of the fight was horrific. A choir of male voices sang an angry chorus. Lita's screams cut through the noise with a high descant. I heard that damned fight in stereo—everyone inside of the car was screaming too.

When the men rushed in to grab Lita, it became too much for me. I lost my mind. I thought the crowd was hurting Lita. I wanted to rescue her. I grabbed the door handle and began to get out of the car. Frank's sister didn't want me to join the fight. She reached over the back seat and wrapped her arms around my neck. Velma was stronger than she looked. I was doing everything I could to escape her clutches and screaming my head off. Poor Velma. God bless you, woman.

The crowd finally managed to pull Lita off Frank's back. She landed on her feet and sprang into a crouch. Lita spun around and faced the crowd. She acted as if she was going to attack them all. Some of the bystanders bore wounds that had been inflicted by Lita. They didn't want more. The bystanders backed off, leaving a polite space between themselves and the warrior couple.

Frank was bent over at the waist. He was gasping for breath. Lita had almost succeeded in her quest to choke the life out of Frank. He couldn't speak.

That was all right with Lita; she had plenty to say for the two of them. She was not subtle in the words that she used to tell Frank they were done. She finished her declaration with a closing statement: "The bitch you were dancing with can have you."

I seriously doubt the unknown woman in question wanted anything more to do with Frank. She melted back into the crowd. The other woman probably knew other married men she could fuck. She didn't want to worry about a crazy wife who might turn on *her* next time around.

Lita screamed something at Frank, the crowd, and the McMillan brothers. She turned away from Jerry's Place and began to walk back to the car. The crowd parted like the Red Sea for Moses. They didn't want anything more to do with Lita's various lethal body parts.

My mother began to cry before she got to the car. Someone who didn't know Lita might think that her tears derived from the pain of Frank's betrayal. I knew otherwise. The tears she cried that night came from the deep well of her anger. Wise people sought cover when Lita began to cry. Uncounted generations of men in my family have learned similar lessons from their women.

The weather was clear when Lita attacked Frank, but another line of storms came through just as she got back in the car. It was a monumental downpour, even by Texas standards. The rain was coming down at better than an inch an hour. Poor Lita; she didn't like to drive in the rain. A less determined woman would have pulled over to wait for the storm to pass. Not Lita. She wanted to get herself away from Frank as quickly as possible.

The pounding rain brought visibility down to zero. We couldn't see the ram's head ornament on the hood of the car. That didn't stop Lita. She knew that the two-lane road had a centerline. Lita opened the car door and drove to the left until she could see the centerline through the open door. She kept her eye on the line for almost eight miles and drove back to Temple at about five miles per hour.

It took us a long time to get back home. I fell asleep in the car. I woke into a dazed stupor when Lita half carried/half dragged me into the house. We were soaked with rain.

Lita was still pissed. She told me angrily, "Get in the bed." I never made it that far because Frank walked through the front door. He looked like a contrite puppy who has soiled the floor. I was surprised to see him. I thought the son of a bitch was gone. Ah, I was so gullible.

Lita saw Frank's entrance in another way: it reminded her that she had failed in her homicidal intentions. Frank was still breathing. Lita immediately cast about for ways to remedy that failure. She grabbed the old bent-barreled shotgun that Frank had inherited from his grandfather. Frank didn't react when Lita armed herself. He just stood there. He knew that she didn't know how to operate or fire the shotgun. He also figured that Lita didn't know where he kept his shotgun shells.

Frank later told me that he kept his distance for another reason: he feared the gun's power as a club more than a firearm. He knew Lita better than anyone. When she figured out that she couldn't fire the shotgun, she would use it like a baseball bat. Frank knew it was safer for him to remain outside the radius of her swing.

Lita held the shotgun in one hand, and with the other she opened a drawer in Frank's dresser, rummaging for shotgun shells. All she found was a handful of .22-caliber cartridges. She got a delighted look on her face when she found the bullets. Lita believed that she had completed her arsenal.

Frank still didn't react to Lita's augmented state of armed readiness. He just stood there. Frank was quite surprised when Lita figured out how to break open the action of the shotgun. His expression became more focused.

Lita slid a tiny .22-caliber cartridge into the almost three-quarter-inch-wide breech of the shotgun. The .22 slid down the barrel and plopped on the floor. That enraged Lita even more. She ramped up her anti-Frank invective. Lita slid another bullet into the shotgun breach. It followed its predecessor to the floor. She shoved bullet after bullet into the shotgun. There seemed to be no limit to her screaming. She kept getting louder and louder.

Lita turned back to Frank's dresser and opened another drawer. Frank's eyes lit up like a Roman candle. Lita had discovered his hidden cache of shotgun shells. That stirred him from his inactivity.

Frank stepped toward Lita. As expected, she swung the shotgun at Frank's head. Frank was ready for *that* move. He ducked and grabbed the shotgun from her hands.

I saw a look of resignation cross my mother's face. She slumped her shoulders. Adrenaline couldn't carry Lita forever. She wisely saw that there was no way she could fight against Frank's superior physical advantage.

But Lita wasn't done. She added a finale to the night's disgusting performance. She grabbed Frank's Stetson hat off his head, threw it to the floor, and stomped it into an unrecognizable mass. Unhappy with that level of destruction, she grabbed a pair of scissors and methodically cut the hat into small pieces.

Why would Lita do such a thing? Because she correctly saw Stetson hats as being the ultimate symbol of Texas masculinity. Lita knew it was the uniform of men like Frank. It was the prime lure he used to catch women.

Lita threw the scissors at Frank and told him to get out.

I watched Frank and Lita's fight from my hallway/bedroom. Frank had to pass by me on his way to the front door. I was surprised by what I saw. His face bore the contrite expression of a schoolboy who had just been spanked for stealing cookies. Frank was crying like a little girl. He looked at me and whined, "Your mama is kicking me out."

I didn't say a word. I was afraid that Frank would redirect his sorrow into anger. But there was another aspect to my silence: I didn't want to reveal that I was delighted. I wanted to watch Fran McMillan's back as it passed through the front door.

After Frank was gone, Lita broke into tears. I tried to console her, but she didn't want my help. Lita gave me a hard shove and pushed me away. She walked into the bedroom and slammed the door.

I stood outside of her bedroom door for a few seconds. I was stunned. I had seen things that were not suitable for young eyes. But the uncaring bitch made no attempt to soothe me. As usual, it was all about Lita, all about Frank. My mother offered me no scraps from her orgy of emotion.

Weariness overrode any feelings I had. I wandered back to my bed. I was finally alone. I was happy that Frank and Lita hadn't turned their anger on me.

The morning sunshine woke me up a few hours later. The house was quiet. I really needed to pee. The bathroom was on the other side of Frank and Lita's bedroom. I was still half asleep as I staggered through the bedroom. Midway through, I was startled awake.

Frank and Lita were screwing like monkeys. They noted my presence but didn't cease their mutual ministrations. They leered at me.

I didn't go to the bathroom. I turned around and walked back to my sleeping space. I forgot about my full bladder. Bigger problems were on the horizon for me. The night before, I'd watched Frank walk out the door. I was delighted. I believed that I had been liberated from Frank's abuse. My sense of liberation was destroyed by the rapturous grins I saw on Frank and Lita's faces.

A few hours later, we went over to Janita's house for Sunday breakfast. No one said anything about what had happened in the previous sixteen hours. *The Stepford Wives* had nothing on me and Lita that morning. We crammed any emotion, any psychic damage that Frank had caused, into the furthest recesses of our memory.

It took many years for scientists to figure out that semen has a calming effect on females. Lita certainly was calm on that fine Sunday morning.

I felt lucky because I ate breakfast and spent time with people.

Frank suffered no lasting repercussions for his bad behavior. "The band played on" is the refrain from an old song. It also describes life with our little trio. Lita continued to work like a dog to support Frank's womanizing.

I stayed off their radar as much as I could. Frank's favored axiom was "Children are best seen and not heard." I voluntarily carried that thought a step further. I knew that things went better for me when I was not seen, either.

Thank God for Granny Mac and the escape that her nineteenth-century paradise offered to me.

CHAPTER 49

Riding Back into the Sunset

NOT LONG AFTER THE TAWDRY events at Jerry's Place, Frank announced he was moving back to California. He never gave a reason for that change of heart. The decision was pure Frank. Lita and I were happy in Texas. We didn't want to move.

Lita was forced to rationalize another of Frank's irrational behaviors. She had to find some good in the deal. Lita said, "I will get to spend more time with my family." That sentence belied the abiding truth of our new life in Texas: Frank's family treated Lita and me better than our own blood relatives back in California did.

Yes, I was happy in Texas. But deep inside, I didn't really care where we lived. Why? Because I knew that Frank didn't want to live in one place for very long. It was better for me not to become attached to one locality. In my mind, Frank's decision to move back to California was just another statistic in the long line of his blitzkrieg relocations.

Moving day in Texas began in similar fashion to its six California predecessors. Frank tossed a small cardboard box at me and said brusquely, "Put your things in that box." Four years earlier, I had balked when I saw the small container. I didn't want to leave the bulk of my belongings behind. But I didn't think that way anymore. I came to view preparing for fast moves with scant baggage as an autonomic response. You know, kind of like breathing. Most of the time, you do it without thinking.

We made another breakneck trip to California. I won't share the details of that trip with you. There was nothing memorable in its progress. It was just like the previous trips and the ones that followed.

I felt like a child-sized ping-pong ball. Balls don't mention their transit over the net. Back and forth, back and forth they go. Their journey is a brief respite. They know they will get smacked again when they get to the other side.

While we were living in Texas, the navy had transferred Tommy Tomlinson back to Sunnyvale, California. Lita's mother and three younger siblings were waiting for us when we returned. It was a marvelous homecoming.

Frank and Lita got right into the business of finding a place to live. Frank called that activity "house hunting." The rental housing business of today is quite different from what it was in 1958. Modern landlords want a detailed application and credit check. That requires time and planning for would-be renters. Back then, people who sought rental housing looked in the classified section of the newspaper and made a few telephone calls. They looked at apartments and met with landlords. If the terms were mutually agreeable, a handshake and exchange of cash sealed the deal. The landlord handed you the keys, and you had housing.

Frank and Lita always found rental housing during the first day or two of their search. For them, house hunting was a simple process. Their list of requirements was quite short: they wanted the least expensive place that they could find. They also didn't want to live in a building that allowed children.

Modern parents agonize about finding homes in areas that have the best schools. They compete to find homes that are close to parks. They avoid busy streets. Frank gave no thought to *my* needs. For him, it was all about money. He remained firm with his great monetary conviction: money spent on rent and food was stolen from his party fund.

Frank saw Tommy Liggett as the symbol and cause of his penury. He viewed my needs as personal slights, especially when those needs required money.

These are the reasons why we lived in poor, run-down neighborhoods. But there was a trick in that concept. Frank and Lita didn't realize how bad those neighborhoods truly were. I never saw either one of them go any farther than a next-door neighbor's house. Lita never walked me to school. That was too bad. One walk down those mean streets would have scared her witless. Much in life comes down to a question of perspective and usage.

Our first post-Texas house was no exception to what Frank and Lita usually rented. It was in a typically rough neighborhood—no surprise there. But that house *did* come with a unique attribute: it was only available to rent for a month. That was a revolutionary concept in 1958. An enterprising schoolteacher wanted to make some ready cash from her home while she was on a long vacation.

Most people would find living in three different homes in five weeks to be a daunting prospect. Not Frank and Lita. They saw their monthlong stay as an interlude. It gave them the time to find an apartment in a less expensive area. Frank and Lita succeeded beyond their wildest dreams with *that* goal!

The people who built San Jose sited their homes on the streets that radiate off both sides of Santa Clara Street. Those neighborhoods were solidly middle and upper class in their composition. They remained so for the better part of a hundred years. Homes that were built over a century-wide span lined the streets. Stately Victorian mansions sat side by side with 1950s "cracker box" houses.

By the mid-1950s, downtown San Jose neighborhoods were in transition. It wasn't an overt dynamic. The differences weren't readily discernible to casual passersby. Most of the grand old homes were well kept. It took closer inspection to note what was happening to downtown San Jose neighborhoods.

Poor people of all races were moving in. Mexicans began to see downtown San Jose an attractive and affordable place to live. It was an escape from the poorer and rougher areas on San Jose's East Side. That change was not lost on the white population in downtown San Jose. Successful Anglos were moving away. They wanted to live in the new subdivisions that were spreading out from Central San Jose like cancer. White flight was in full force.

The percentage of owner-occupied homes in downtown San Jose diminished. The percentage of rentals increased. You might think that would cause a housing glut. It didn't. Lots of new people were moving to the Santa Clara Valley. They wanted to cash in on the burgeoning job market. Competition for rentals was keen. This was especially true for the least expensive rentals. Like the ones Frank and Lita were seeking.

Frank and Lita looked at just two prospective rentals during that bout of house hunting. They refused to walk through the door at the first house. The manager said that a former tenant had been murdered there. That gave Frank and Lita the shivers.

Frank made some more telephone calls. He then drove to meet a landlord at 123 North Tenth Street, San Jose. It was a well-maintained, one-bedroom duplex that was about sixty years old. The rent was quite reasonable. Frank liked that.

Why was the rent so low, Frank? Because the front door of the duplex was about fifteen feet from one of the busiest thoroughfares in San Jose. Tenth Street is four lanes wide. It is noisy and dangerous. Living there was akin to camping on a freeway shoulder. Residents at 123 North Tenth Street risked death and dismemberment every time they backed a car out of the driveway.

Congratulations, Frank and Lita; you succeeded in your quest to find another flawed place for us to live.

But wait, there's more! Frank and Lita talked their way into another no-children apartment building. I remember how *that* came about. Their spiel to the prospective landlord was perfect. They made their usual promises. Frank tossed out his old reliable lines. He finished with the best one: "No one will even know that Tommy is here, will they, Tommy?" He even finished that trite little speech with his trademark glare. Oh, yawn. That asshole was getting downright repetitive.

I was four years old when Frank told our first landlord that Tommy Liggett was invisible. I was inexperienced then. I was scared and intimidated. I bought into his silent-kid bullshit. While we lived in that place, I spent most of my time behind closed doors, alone.

I was a different person when we moved into the Tenth Street duplex. I wasn't an intimidated preschooler. I was a rambunctious eight-year-old boy. I had spent the past year playing in the lush bottomlands of the Little River. Now Frank and Lita assumed they could lock me in another box. Bad move, Lita; I was too much like you to go down easily.

An elderly woman lived in the other half of our duplex. She had been there for more than thirty years. I was the first child to move in next door. She was horrified that a young boy was living in "her" building. Our new neighbor hated me with a blood passion, and she spared no effort in hiding that fact from anyone. Every time we crossed paths, she found some way to harshly belittle me.

Our new neighbor didn't realize that such behavior was old hat to little Tommy Liggett. People had been screaming at me since I was born. I just added her to the list of people who regularly screamed at me. I ignored the old witch. The neighbor soon discovered that she couldn't get a rise out of me. This raised her anger to a higher level. She ramped up her invective. Nothing worked. I remained cool as a cucumber.

How did I maintain my composure? Was I some sort of Buddhist monk? No, I was scared shitless. I knew if I said a single word back to our neighbor, she would complain. Frank would beat high holy hell out of me. Given the choice, I'd take an old woman's invective over Frank's well-placed kicks to my ass any day.

Frank's position didn't derive from the concept that I should respect my elders. Nor was he trying to save me any further grief. He hated our neighbor. As usual, he was only looking out for himself. Frank knew that if I gave our neighbor a bona fide reason to complain, we would get kicked out of the duplex. I became one more person's punching bag.

Frank had good reason to stay in our latest apartment: it was just three streets over from the Rock Castle tavern. He could get blind drunk and have a short drive home. Living in the Tenth Street duplex reduced Frank's risk for a drunk-driving arrest.

A racy ashtray from a rough bar. Lots of roughnecks and loose women hung out at the Rock Castle. Frank McMillan could have bought a bunch of houses with the money he left in that place.

I tried to fly under my neighbor's radar. But I always seemed to cause problems for her. One of those problems was real. I liked living in our new apartment. It had a large backyard. The property had two nineteenth-century barns sited around its edges. I explored and reexplored those barns. They were full of artifacts from a bygone age. Wooden barrels and crates. Strange iron tools. Wheels for nineteenth-century vehicles. That was the perfect playground for Tommy the feral boy. I wanted to explore.

There was a large open space between the barns and the duplex. It was covered with gravel and dirt. I have always loved to play in the dirt. At that age, I loved to dig holes. These made foundations and basements for my architecture, tunnels for my sand mines. I built Spanish missions and medieval forts.

In no time at all, my holes and cities covered the backyard. One day a friend of our terrible neighbor stepped in one of the holes and broke her ankle. I felt horrible about that accident. The woman who'd injured herself was always sweet and nice to me.

The landlord told Frank that I could only dig holes around the backyard perimeter. I filled in the holes that were in the middle of the backyard and withdrew the frontiers of my cities to the edges of the property.

The incident of the broken ankle caused our neighbor to hate me more fervently. I am surprised that we didn't get evicted because of the injury. Maybe our neighbor was as mean to the landlord as she was to me. Something had to give.

Help sometimes arrives from unexpected quarters. My teacher at Horace Mann School was wonderful. I learned a lot in her class. The teacher encouraged her students to bring in curious objects for show-and-tell time. Most of those items were mundane. Children in those days found loveliness in common things.

But the show-and-tell items weren't all commonplace. I'll never forget one item in particular. It was quite unique. I was half asleep at my desk during a show-and-tell session that seemed to go on *forever*. Some girl was droning on about her new hair barrettes until the teacher finally convinced her to sit down. The class exhaled a mutual sigh of relief. The teacher allowed one more child to show what he brought. A little boy stepped in front of the class, holding a large paper bag. Without preamble, he reached into the bag and pulled out a four-foot-long dead gopher snake. It was the largest example of its kind I had ever seen. The boy explained how his family had killed the snake. I instantly woke up. As soon as I saw the snake, I received inspiration. It was as if the clouds parted and choirs of angels descended. They shared the knowledge of a grand idea with me. I came up with a plan.

During recess, I wasted no time in acting out my designs. I sought out the boy, who was surrounded by a crowd. I waited until the other boys drifted away and then told him that I wanted his dead snake. He played coy. The boy asked, "What do you have to trade?" Well, two can play coy. I had a pocketful of marbles. I hated the things. I was a lousy player. I only had them because every boy was supposed to have a pocketful of marbles. The boy took the marbles and handed me the bag that contained the snake. He smirked, believing he'd gotten the best end of the deal. He obviously didn't know me. That snake was destined for better things than a silly-assed game of marbles.

The rest of the school day seemed to stretch on forever. When the last bell rang, I bolted out of the classroom door and ran home as quickly as I could. I slowed down as I approached the front of our duplex. No one was around. I thought, *the coast is clear.*

The doors to the duplex's two apartments were side by side and separated by less than three feet. I crept onto the front porch and wrapped the dead gopher snake into a coil. The head was in the center, resting on the outside coils and facing the neighbor's front door. I stood back for a moment to admire my handiwork. I knew that I had created a perfect rattlesnake mimic.

I knocked on our neighbor's door and then ducked inside of our apartment, leaving the door open a crack. I wanted to see what happened.

The neighbor opened her door. I watched her eyes go from side to side and then down. Her eyes locked onto my mock rattlesnake. The neighbor let out a scream that must have been heard two blocks away. She slammed her door hard enough to rattle the windows. I leapt through our door, grabbed the snake, and went back inside. I laughed my ass off. Don't mess with Indian kids, mean neighbor ladies!

I savored my fun for a moment and sat back to await my punishment. I knew that I was in trouble with Frank. I possessed no doubt about the probable outcome of my little snake show: I was going to receive a royal ass-whipping. I'd known that before I coiled the snake. My eight-year-old brain saw that as the cost of doing business. But I knew that a sore ass was a small price to pay for the grand payback I'd visited upon our evil neighbor.

When Frank and Lita came home that night, I told them what I had done. Frank attempted to give me a spanking. But that didn't work out too well. He couldn't spank my ass while he was laughing. Frank made me bury the snake out in the backyard. He said, "Bury it deep. Don't want no dogs a-diggin' it up."

The episode with the snake had an unexpected consequence: our mean neighbor vacated the premises. She was gone in less than twenty-four hours. It was the fastest move I have ever seen. That girl was good. Frank McMillan might have learned something from her.

Things got better for me around the duplex. A kind married couple moved into the other side. They were nice to me. The man was a harmonica expert. He played fun songs just for my ears.

An elderly couple lived in the house next door. Their last name was Reynolds. Mr. Reynolds was the first real friend I ever had. We talked for hours. These sessions consisted mostly of stories about his long life. He told the same stories over and again. I didn't mind. Mr. Reynolds was the first person who spent time with me just because he enjoyed my company.

Mr. Reynolds was an avid gardener. He immediately noted my latent gift for gardening. Mr. Reynolds worked in small ways to help me develop my talents. He had a row of apple trees that were the pride of his garden. They were big and lush. He told me that all the trees produced wonderful fruit, with one exception. He said that tree required more winter chilling than it received from our mild San Jose winters. When Mr. Reynolds saw that I caught the gist of his comment about winter chilling, he pressed on.

He told me all about the winter chilling requirements for various types of fruit trees. I was enraptured.

Mr. Reynold's lesson about apple-tree-chilling requirement might seem to be an insignificant part of my story, but it's not. It made me realize that different varieties within a plant species are unique. They have different cultural requirements. That was a crucial bit of gardening knowledge.

Mr. Reynolds gave me a banana squash seedling and provided me with detailed planting and care instructions. That plant grew well. It engulfed our entire backyard, right up and over the fences. My prowess with that single plant provided yet another amazing-Tommy story for Lita. She placed it in her arsenal of cute things.

Tom Liggett with banana squash. Vines in background. This was my first big crop. Backyard, 123 North Tenth Street, San Jose, California. September 1959.

My understanding of plants took a large leap in the Tenth Street backyard. It arose from an accident of purpose. I was becoming more ambitious with my miniature cities. They now had larger walls and gravel foundations.

But I noticed the cities looked stark. They contained no greenery. Seeking to remedy that defect, I broke off twigs and stuck them in the dirt. They made wonderful trees. In my mind and in the dirt, they made grand avenues and wonderful orchards.

But I also noted that my mock trees soon wilted. That took some of the life out my cities. I cast around for better candidate sticks. I noted a scraggily old jade plant at the rear of the property. Every house in downtown San Jose seemed to have the things growing in their yards. I wasn't entirely enamored of that type of plant, but I thought, *these might make good trees for my cities.*

I stuck some of the jade plants in the dirt around my cities, expecting them to wilt. I thought, *they are so squishy, they have to be delicate.* I was wrong. The jade plants were still vibrant and alive the next day. The next week saw no change; they were beautiful.

I allowed my mock cities to stand for a week or two. But I always tore them down to build something else. I was raised in the Santa Clara Valley. I knew how urban renewal worked. Out with the old, in with the new was the order of the day.

When I pulled out the jade plants that I'd used as mock trees, I made an amazing discovery: the stems had roots! That was a real aha moment in my development as a gardener. I learned how to propagate plants from cuttings.

I used new jade-plant stems for my latest trees. I found stable places for my rooted cuttings. The edge of the backyard was soon covered with a forest of jade plants.

An old Methodist church stood around the corner from our duplex. I like to sit on the church's rear step and listen to the pastor's wife practice the organ. It marked the first time that I fell in love with a specific type of music. It instilled me with a lifelong passion for organ music.

From time to time, I attempted to attend services in the Methodist church. It was a kind and loving place. The pastor's sermons lacked the fire-and-brimstone aspect of the Baptist churches in Texas.

When Frank discovered that I was attending church services, he renewed his anti-Christian belief assault. On the rare nights that he was both home and sober, he continued to read the Bible to me. He employed his tried-and-true tactics. Every Bible reading began and ended with the same, tired phrase: "These are just stories. Don't believe them." But I had a problem: I *did* believe the Bible stories. I continued to attend Sunday morning services at the Methodist church.

Frank quickly determined that words alone couldn't keep me out of the church around the corner. He introduced an all-new strategy: Frank went to church with me. I was delighted! I wouldn't be going to church alone. I quickly discerned the flaw in *that* line of reasoning.

When we entered the church, Frank took a seat in the back pew. He sang the requisite songs with gusto. He even put a few dollars in the collection plate. I caught the glances of the regular parishioners. They liked the look of the tall, lean cowboy who was sitting in their back pew.

All was perfect with Frank, the church, and me until it came time for the pastor to deliver his sermon. Frank was now in his element. Each time the pastor made a point, Frank whispered a contrary opinion into my ear, quoting chapter and verse as he did so. His diction and logic were perfect. The private sermon Frank whispered into my ear that morning was better than the preacher's. But it was twisted: Frank's whole oratorical objective was to demonstrate that everything in the pastor's sermon was a lie.

The real mind fuck in those performances was far more insidious. Everyone who saw Frank whispering in my ear thought, *Wow, look at that devoted father encouraging his son.* Too bad they couldn't see beyond Frank's handsome visage. They would have seen Frank as being the embodiment of Satan, the devil.

One of those sessions made me see the futility of going to church. But my mind was still conflicted about the validity of Christian theology. Human society told me that God is love. Frank told me it was all a lie.

CHAPTER 50

Isolation

I SPENT VAST SEGMENTS OF my childhood living in a free-range version of solitary confinement. It was normal for me to be alone. That was not quite as bad as it might seem. No one screamed at me when I was alone. It was less painful than being in the company of those who viewed me as a complication, not a person.

I was just a few weeks old when Lita worked at the bakery. She left me totally alone for at least five hours at a time while she was at work. That arrangement was not the result of an emergency, nor was it a spur-of-the-moment decision. It was the opening salvo of a carefully executed program of neglect.

I have seen plenty of impoverished mothers who always found babysitters for their children. Not Lita. It all came down to a simple consideration: babysitters cost money that was needed for men, rent, cigarettes, clothes, and parties.

When Lita became a functional adult, she used her extra money to party. When Frank rolled into her life, she began to pay for his fun too, even though he was still bragging about making "doctor wages."

Yet Lita's pay still wasn't always enough. Off we'd all go to the finance company. Frank and Lita borrowed money at usurious rates to pay for day-to-day living expenses.

I hated our visits to the finance company. Lita screamed at Frank all the way there and back. By the time we arrived back home, they were both screaming at me. They were not shy in voicing the opinion that I was the root cause of their fiscal problems. Most of their finance company visits ended the same way: Tommy Liggett received a royal ass-whipping for one contrived reason or another.

They used that bullshit excuse to vent their frustrations on me, even though MT had been sending a fat child-support check to Lita for better than two years. I was a major and reliable profit center for our little household.

But beating my sorry little ass didn't change the dynamic of our family finances. Lita continued to work every minute of overtime she could get. This gave Frank more time and money to spend on his girlfriends. That vicious cycle waxed, waned, and repeated itself for over the course of their relationship.

No one outside of our little trio perceived the truth of the matter. It was veiled by the smoke screen that Lita threw to the world. She portrayed herself as a heroic teenage mother who sacrificed everything for her child. I can't argue with certain elements of that story. My mother's life did change irrevocably when she became pregnant with me. That seminal event forced her into adulthood in a precocious and unprepared state.

But that doesn't excuse most of Lita's behaviors. I am now in a position where I can compare my upbringing to the one I provided to my children. I know what it is like to be a divorced parent. I know what it is like to bring a stepparent into children's lives.

The difference between the care I gave to my children and that which Frank and Lita provided for me is glaring. The book-writing process forced me to examine those differences, and the results of that examination destroyed the illusions I formerly harbored about my own childhood. I narrowed down those conclusions to one concept: Lita didn't put much effort into being a parent.

Yes, Lita portrayed herself as being a hero for providing for me. But everybody must live somewhere, even if they don't have a child. I don't see much of Lita's widely celebrated self-sacrifice in her housing choices. We lived in at least twelve rentals between 1954 and 1960. Just two of them had a second bedroom. In the other rentals, I slept in a hallway or on the living room floor.

That set of statistics proves that Lita repeatedly chose to rent studios or one-bedroom apartments. In a symbolic sense, that detail was very revealing. Lita was telling me and the world that she was going to live as if she did not have a child. I was like the little piece of parsley that sits beside a store-bought sandwich. I was just along for the ride.

When I was eight, Lita stopped waitressing and began doing shift work in manufacturing plants. She sometimes had to work the "swing" or evening shift. Frank and Lita came up with a sound plan to cope with her new work hours. They agreed that I'd walk home from school in the afternoon, just like always. Frank would come home a couple of hours later and prepare dinner. He even volunteered to help me with my schoolwork. He would also see that I got a bath. I would be in bed by nine.

Sadly, it didn't work out that way. Frank saw Lita's late work schedule as an ongoing opportunity. He could "cat around" almost every night. Frank took great care with one detail: he was always home by midnight when Lita arrived home. That was easy. Frank never had it so good! When Lita wasn't around at night, he went totally off of the wagon. In cowboy terms, that means he indulged himself with a full-on orgy of strong drink and women.

Lita was oblivious to the situation. Frank was in pig heaven. Think about what it was like to be me. I came home to an empty house and fell asleep at nine without ever seeing another human being at home. Frank left for work before I got out of bed in the morning, and Lita was asleep in the bedroom. I received strong warnings: "Don't wake up your mother. She works hard to feed you. She needs her rest." I prepared a rudimentary breakfast and went to school.

When I came home the following day after school, the cycle began anew. Taken in aggregate, that set of behaviors had a devastating result. Uncounted weeks passed during which I never had contact with an adult at home, from Sunday night until Saturday morning.

It gets worse from there. If Frank and Lita had "errands to run" on Saturday morning, they would be gone when I awakened. They usually did not return until late in the afternoon.

This meant that I sometimes had people around me at home for no more than about thirty hours per week. When Frank and Lita went out together on Saturday night, that period of face time was reduced even more. Whole weeks went by wherein I saw my family just a few hours. These extended periods of forced solitude began when I was seven and continued on a sporadic basis until I was about seventeen.

Please pause for a moment in your reading. Consider what I have written in the last few paragraphs. Try to imagine what it was like to be a seven-year-old child who regularly spent more than five contiguous days without any human contact at home. It was horrific.

I sought human outlets to ease my loneliness. I tried to make friends with some of the children from my school. But that was tough; most of them lived blocks away from my home.

But a larger impediment prevented me from making after-school friends: social convention. Relatively few American mothers in the late 1950s worked outside of the home. Normal stay-at-home moms saw me as an embarrassing aberration. I represented a wrinkle in the fabric of their well-ordered worlds. This was not a new concept to me. I had first seen it years before on Hobson Street. None of the mothers I met as a young child wanted a dirty, hungry ragamuffin who talked too much hanging around their houses after school.

Aside from our neighbor Mr. Reynolds, I didn't find real friendship while I lived on Tenth Street. That didn't stop me from pressing my cause with other children.

One of my failed friendships got shoved down my throat. It derived from my unfailing efforts to befriend a boy named James Rumpee. James was the son of the pastor of the Methodist church around the corner. Yes, that is the same church I attempted to attend. James was also in my class at school.

I considered James to be my friend. Looking back now, I can see that my feelings were not reciprocated. To James, I was the feral boy who lived around the corner. James and his family considered everything about me to be uncivilized. People sometimes pet stray cats as they pass by. In that measure, James's family tolerated my company. But James's family knew that if they fed me, I would never go away.

My teacher offered another impediment to my friendship with James: she used him as the model for my school performance. She began many phrases with the words "James does this" or "James does that." My teachers failed to discern the differences between James's after-school life and mine.

An incident occurred that finished my friendship with James Rumpee. He and I were taking turns jumping off the roof of the low shed that bordered his backyard. It was dusk. I failed to see the nearly invisible braided steel cable clothesline and caught the clothesline in my mouth. It broke out three of my front teeth and almost snapped my neck. I dropped to the ground, stunned. Then I ran home as quickly as I could. That was my place of security. I screamed at the top of my lungs and spit out bits of broken teeth along the way. I was choking on the clotted gore that filled my mouth.

I ran through the door of our duplex. It was empty. Lita was at work. Frank was out chasing his drunk. I called my grandmother Ruby on the telephone and told her I needed help. A few minutes later, Pastor Rumpee walked through the front door. He spoke to Ruby on the telephone, and she asked him to take me to his house. They didn't want me to be alone. Ruby called Lita at work, and my mother returned home an hour later. Lita got an emergency appointment with a dentist that night.

Lita told the story of my broken teeth for the rest of her life. She never failed to mention the frantic nighttime rush to the dentist. In the eyes of her family, Lita's actions were heroic. She left work to provide medical care for me.

No one thought to ask Lita or Frank any hard questions about the evening's events. A good one would have been, why was an eight-year-old boy left alone at dusk? Another one would have been, did he have his dinner?

But that wasn't the way it went vis-à-vis Lita's family. It was the elephant in the room that no one ever mentioned.

I know that the accident in James's backyard killed the last modicum of friendship he felt toward me. He pulled away. I made several attempts to play in his backyard, but those visits became strained, unusual, and abbreviated. I could tell that James and his family were disgusted by me and mine.

It was easy to see that James's father really liked me. But he saw how I acted and how I lived. He didn't need the complication of having me around his home. The point was made moot when Pastor Rumpee and his family moved to a plush new suburban home in the wealthy Willow Glen neighborhood of San Jose. White flight took the Methodist church out of the inner city. I lost the one child who was my friend. I had absolutely no one to be with after school.

By the time of James's departure, I was well versed in a simple reality: it was not safe for a young boy to be alone out on the street. I was just four years old when I first walked alone on the mean sidewalks of downtown San Jose. Truth be told, I was too naïve at that time to be afraid of what was happening.

My life on Hobson Street taught me to be wary of strangers. It forced me to be aware of who was around me. Because of those experiences, I was comfortable with being alone on the streets of the inner city.

But our Tenth Street neighborhood was different. It was more densely populated than Hobson Street. Many of the people who lived around me were Mexicans. Even if the children from those families spoke English, few of their parents seemed to do so. It's tough to have a conversation or develop a meaningful relationship with someone with whom you share just a handful of words.

In my mind, all those isolating details were moot. I knew that even if I made a few friends, I would soon be forced to move away from them. I was living in solitary confinement.

Writing this book finally made me realize just how much time I spent alone when I was a child. Being alone was my default setting. It is not unusual for abused kids to think that what is happening to them is normal.

People have occasionally told me that I should have complained to someone outside of my family. I should have mentioned that I was being neglected. I tried telling someone that I was hungry or lonely just twice during my childhood. Both of those lapses resulted in draconian reprisals from Frank. I found that it was best to stay busy and to keep quiet.

While it was quite difficult for me to be alone most of the time, I had other more pressing matters to occupy my mind. While we were living in Texas, we ate most of our evening meals with Frank's sister Janita. When we returned to California, that resource was no longer available to me. My old friend hunger moved back into my life. Once they were away from the support and watchfulness of other people, Frank and Lita reverted to the default pattern of neglect they'd established at the Hobson Street rental.

It is difficult for any young child to be alone. Try thinking about what it was like to be a young child who was both alone and hungry. No, I wasn't hungry all the time. When Lita wasn't working nights, she cooked good meals. She was a marvelous cook. We sometimes ate with family members or at restaurants.

But things were different when she worked the evening shift. Frank inevitably went into full-on party mode. I was left to shift for my own meals. I had been preparing my own breakfast for years. That was no problem. But I was used to getting something more substantial at night.

I was no cook. Besides, it's impossible to cook food that you don't have. Frank's partying ate up a huge portion of our family income. Money that should have been spent on food was being spent elsewhere. Poor Lita did her best to work every minute of overtime that she could. But that was barely enough money to keep a roof over our heads.

When times were tough, Lita didn't buy any more food than was absolutely needed. I ate what was in the house. I taught myself how to boil potatoes and make toast. But there was a problem with that menu: there was seldom any bread in the house. The bread we had was reserved for Frank's lunches. That left the potatoes. I ate them pretty much every night. Boiled potatoes, salt, and pepper. That was my dinner. It didn't bother me to eat them day in, day out. They were like manna from heaven for me.

The Irish proved that potatoes and whole milk are a fairly complete and wholesome diet. That race multiplied in their millions by eating such fare. But I didn't always have the milk. Frank and Lita bought groceries as infrequently as possibly. They knew that if they bought too much milk, it would go sour. That would be a waste of their hard-earned money. They bought less milk than was needed.

I can't imagine any modern American mother who would allow her eight-year-old child to light a World War I–era stove with a match and cook a meal on the thing. But I did. I also made sure the kitchen was spotless when I finished. There would be hell to pay if I left a mess for Frank and Lita to clean.

But I was a typical lazy eight-year-old boy. I didn't go through the bother of cooking if I didn't have to. That left the food items that didn't require much preparation. As soon as Frank and Lita hooked up, I learned to be thankful for Kellogg's cornflakes. Put 'em in a bowl with milk, and you've got a meal. When the milk runs out, cornflakes taste just fine dry. But they tear up the roof of your mouth something fierce when you eat them that way. Your mouth will be sore for a week. Early on, I learned to crush them in a bowl with water before I ate them without milk.

I didn't complain about eating Kellogg's cornflakes back then. For breakfast, they were a break from boiled potatoes. They made a right handy dinner when that was all that was available. Many was the evening meal I ate that consisted solely of them. I can't bear to look at boxes of Kellogg's cornflakes in the supermarket now. I ate too many of them when I was a kid.

I feel the same way about Sunshine saltine crackers. Lita always had some lying around because she liked to eat them with Skippy peanut butter. The stale remains of a months-old sleeve of crackers is the finest meal on earth when that's all you have.

I became like a foraging coyote on the prowl. I always started my search in the refrigerator. It was empty most of the time. I moved on to the lower cabinets. When that failed, I would drag a chair to get up onto the kitchen counters. I wanted to look in the higher cabinets. Lita sometimes hid small morsels up there that she didn't want me to find.

Lita's grandmother Mary Stewart was deathly ill. Mary wanted to present Lita with a Christmas gift. That poor old woman didn't have anything much to give. She presented Lita with a U-No candy bar. Lita treasured that small gift for months.

I knew Lita wouldn't eat the U-No Bar. I guessed she'd hidden it somewhere in the kitchen. I looked in every cabinet, every drawer in the kitchen. I eventually found it tucked away on a top shelf.

I'll never forget how I felt when I held the U-No bar in my hand. I was shaking. I was starving, but knew that I couldn't risk eating the whole thing. That would have been obvious to Lita. I chose what I thought was the safer course and pried a few tasty crumbs off the end of the candy bar. Then I carefully replaced the U-No bar on the shelf. Lita didn't seem to notice what I had done. Over the next few weeks, I crumbled off more of the candy bar. This behavior continued undetected and unabated for quite a while. The poor little U-No bar looked as if it had been gnawed by rodents. When Lita finally figured out what I was doing, she broke down in tears. The candy bar was a symbolic last gift from her grandmother. I was horrified when Lita took the remains of that candy bar and threw it into the trash. I remember thinking, *I'm hungry. I could have eaten that.*

Frank heard Lita crying in the kitchen and came in to see what the ruckus was all about. When he was made aware of what had happened, he reached into his repertory of tirades and pulled out one of his favorites. It was all about "little boys who are going to burn in hell because of their greed."

Frank knew all about hell; he sent me there with the whipping he gave me for making Lita cry over a candy bar. Frank made Lita cry with some regularity, but that was all right. God help me if I ever made her shed a single tear.

Speaking of tears, I had one meal that was so good, it *really* made me cry. One of my exhaustive searches turned up nothing in the house but a brown onion. I seized that dry onion and ripped off the outer skin with my fingers. I ate it like an apple. I remember that onion's fumes made my eyes water and nose run. I didn't find out until the next day that strong raw onions can be very caustic. The inside of my mouth was sore for a long time.

I hope there is a hell. I hope the torments in that place match the earthly sins of its residents. I hope Frank and Lita are being subjected to the treatment they visited upon me.

I want them to perpetually search for food under sofa cushions. I want them to seek fuzzy Lifesaver candies and sticks of chewing gum that have fallen out of visitors' pockets. In their personalized hells, I want Frank and Lita to be grateful to discover that kind of hidden treasure. I want their cold hearts to be teased with the vain possibility that it will satisfy their never-ending hunger pains. I did that very thing. And I was overjoyed when I discovered tenth-rate fare.

CHAPTER 51

Cape Fear

HUNGER AND SOLITUDE WEREN'T THE only problems my small brain was forced to process. I had another, less tangible but ever-present companion to accommodate: fear.

It was well known that Mexican street gangs were prevalent in our new neighborhood. They were a dangerous bunch. This was demonstrated to me by a story I heard.

I walked about a half mile to and from Horace Mann School each day. As I passed various streets, other young boys would join me. I generally walked to school with the same core group of children.

One time I missed a day or two of school because we traveled to Earlimart to visit a sick relative. When I returned, I met a member of our core group. He became excited when he saw me. The other boy said, "Tom, Tom, oh man, where were you?" That was a rhetorical question. Without waiting for my response, he launched into the main reason for his excitement: somebody had hit somebody in the head with a lettuce knife (a short machete).

I wasn't expecting that kind of story to be the root of the other boy's excitement. I just stood there with a baffled look on my face. He was undeterred by my inaction and got right to the punch line of the story. The boy said, "The lettuce knife got stuck in the guy's head. He was kicking his feet and shitting his pants as he was dying. Man, it was *soooo* cool. You shoulda seen it."

I was eight or nine years old when I heard that story. I was horrified by the callous manner in which the tale was told. The boy recited it with the same joy a normal child might use to recall a favorite movie or a trip to Disneyland.

The other boy's pleasure in witnessing the murder of another child was alien to my sensibilities. It was a watershed moment in my life. The boy's story introduced me to the inner workings of a culture that celebrates death. It was just the first of many anecdotes of like kind that I would hear for the next fifty-odd years. In that time, I witnessed enough violence from that culture to write a few stories of my own.

My life was changed after I heard the boy's anecdote. I ceased to be the happy-go-lucky kid who spoke with old people, looked at graffiti on the sidewalks, and sought out stray cats in a need of a pat. For the duration of my tenure on Tenth Street, I became a much warier person. Gone were the days in which I wandered the streets just to look around.

This newfound brand of fear increased my isolation. I rushed home from school as quickly as I could. When the sun was shining, I spent my after-school hours tucked away in our backyard. I made forts out of cast-off lumber. The tiny cities I built out of sticks and mud became more elaborate. I grew jade plants in well-ordered rows to mimic the nurseries and grand boulevards I saw in photographs. I reexplored the old carriage barns at the rear of our duplex.

I didn't mind being alone during the day. As soon as darkness fell, I became a different person. I was scared out of my wits. I locked myself inside of the duplex. Truth be told, I was locked inside of my own head.

I tried not to remember the story about the boy who had the lettuce knife stuck in his head. I tried not to think about the strange people I saw on the streets. Most of the time, I was all right. But my fears sometimes got the best of me. I continually checked and rechecked our apartment's doors and windows. I wanted to make sure they were locked and that no one was peering in.

One dark and lonely evening, I thought I heard someone shuffling around outside of out apartment. I thought I heard someone rattling a window. I became obsessed with a singular thought: he or she was going to bury a lettuce knife in my head. I believe that I had a small psychotic break that night.

I called my grandmother Ruby on the telephone. I told her about my fears. By the end of the conversation, we were both crying. In that moment, Ruby was empathetic to my plight. But she soon grew tired of my drama. Ruby told me to "hush up and stop acting like a baby."

Ruby subsequently told Lita and Frank about my tearful call to her. I received a whole spectrum of severe punishments for *that* indiscretion. Remember, everyone in the family was living the fictionalized story of Lita, the great sacrificial lamb.

This incident and others of like kind taught me an important lesson: I could not look to other people for solace and companionship. I learned to seek peace within the confines of my own head. I did this by keeping my brain occupied with thought. When I was not busy, loneliness, hunger, and fear got the most of me. My mind raced off into unwanted directions.

When I was about eight years old, the main savior of my life was revealed to me: I finally learned to read. I required years more than my peers to perfect that skill. That was due in large part to a total lack of parental involvement in my education. Our frequent moves didn't help either.

But when I did start reading, I took to it with a vengeance. The first thing I read was *Superman* comic books. I read and reread them as quickly as I could. Many people in our circle thought that comic books were the work of the devil. They continually harped on Lita, adamant that I should not be reading comic books.

Lita ignored the comic book naysayers. She was delighted I'd finally learned to read. Please don't take Lita's relief as a sign of parental devotion, though. Her real joy derived from another quarter: she could cease to be embarrassed by the distinct possibility I was an idiot child.

Frank was part of the large crowd that didn't want me to read comic books. He thought they were a "frivolous waste of money." Then there was the big objection: Frank didn't have "funny books" when he was a child. Why should I have them? I quickly learned to keep my comic books out of Frank's sight.

More importantly, I learned to limit my collection to ones that had manly topics. I learned *that* painful lesson when I bought a Disney *Cinderella* comic book. Frank said that I was a titty baby for reading such girlish stuff.

Being ever slow on the uptake, I made the mistake of asking Frank to take me to the movie that accompanied the comic book. That request caused hi, to fly into one of the worst rages I experienced at his hands. He slapped and kicked me around the room. He kept screaming, "You're just a little faggot. I'll be goddamned if I take you to see a movie that was made for titty babies, faggots, and little girls."

Lita just stood there nodding as he was kicking me around the room. As usual, she went along with Frank's movie choices and his corporal punishment.

Later in the day, Lita took me aside. She admitted that she had been looking forward to watching the *Cinderella* movie. But she didn't have the resolve to get into a three-hour pitched battle with Frank to push the issue.

I quickly learned to find other reading materials that were somewhat more appealing to Frank's literary tastes. I accomplished that feat through a nearly vanished part of American retail history: the old-fashioned secondhand store. People who shop at today's sanitized thrift stores such as Goodwill have no idea what the secondhand stores of old were like. They weren't called thrift stores then. They were affectionately called junk stores by their patrons. Those places came and went like mushrooms after an autumn rainstorm. One day, we would drive by an empty old building. The next day, a crude hand-lettered sign would appear: "Joe's Treasure Store" or "XYZ Bazaar." Heck, most of them didn't even have signs or names.

The people who frequented junk stores were always on the lookout for new ones. When someone discovered that a new store had opened, they passed this valuable knowledge to other shoppers of like kind.

Lita loved to shop at secondhand stores. There were quite a few reasons for that affinity. Many women like to go shopping. That takes money. Much of our little family's income was used to support Frank's love of whiskey and loose women. There was very little left over to purchase necessities. Lita rarely had the money to shop at stores that sold new things.

But Lita's love of junk stores went beyond monetary considerations. She was raised in a culture that was mobile and impoverished. My grandmother sometimes had trouble obtaining sufficient money to feed her large family. She didn't have the money to buy things that were not absolutely necessary for survival.

Then there was the mobile part of my mother's upbringing. The less you owned, the easier it was to move. Lita was accustomed to leaving things behind. This made her love the new treasures that she found along the way. Most of Lita's new childhood treasures were someone else's castoffs. She learned to find such things at secondhand stores.

Junk stores also gave Lita an activity that she and I could do alone. Frank was quite vocal on the subject, saying, "I wouldn't be caught dead in a junk store." He believed such places were beneath his dignity.

Most of all, Lita sought the sense of unbridled adventure that junk stores brought to her workaday life. You never knew what you would find in the unsorted piles and boxes.

When I was eight, a particularly interesting junk store opened a few blocks away from our Tenth Street duplex. It was in an 1860s-era false-front building that looked like it belonged in a cowboy movie set.

Lita and I walked through the front door of the junk shop and saw the usual piles of old shoes, broken lamps, and bric-a-brac. Lita wandered off to one side, while I looked more closely at the tangled mass of stuff that filled the inside of the building. I noted that the junk store had books. *Lots* of books. They stood in stacks by themselves and rested in overfilled boxes.

Books were something new in my life. I had just learned to read proficiently but had never read a whole book. I walked over to the book stacks.

There were more of them than I imagined. I didn't know where to start. I didn't know what I wanted. It was an overwhelming sensation. I thought I was out of my depth. I remember thinking, *why not go over to the other side of the store to where the toys are kept?*

I took a deep breath and opened the nearest box. I found it was filled with old but not ancient books. They were typical of those I saw in the homes of old people. I suppose they were a random sample of the books that had been popular twenty or thirty years previously.

I looked at every book in the first box but found nothing remotely interesting. I looked through several more boxes and still didn't find anything that I wanted to read. I don't know why I kept digging through the stacks of books. It was as if some inner voice was leading me on.

One title eventually jumped out: *Bomba the Jungle Boy*. I read the first paragraph. The story line instantly took hold of my consciousness. I slammed the book closed and ran to Lita. I begged her to buy it for me. She looked up from the box of junk she was plowing through and said yes. Lita was always more amenable to my requests when Frank wasn't around.

My shopping day was over as soon as Lita said yes. I sat down on a pile of boxes and dove into my new book. It was published in 1926, but the ensuing thirty-two years had done nothing to diminish its power on my unfilled little brain. The story line detailed the adventures of a young boy who wandered alone through the jungles of South America. That connected with me! I wandered through the concrete jungles of downtown San Jose every day. As I read on, I forgot about my frightening, hungry, and lonely world. I became Bomba the Jungle Boy. I shared his problems and adventures.

Bomba the Jungle Boy was the first book without pictures I ever read. It marked a watershed moment in my life. I learned that books could transport me out of my own harsh world and into interesting places.

Frank's response to my book was typical: he thought that the title was sissified. His overly developed "gay-o-meter" was always on high alert. He also advised me that the name Bomba sounded suspiciously ethnic. He said, "I don't want you to be a readin' no damn book that has a nigger as the main character." I assured Frank that the title character was not of African descent. The book became slightly more acceptable to him.

Since Frank failed in two different lines of attack against the novel, he reached for loftier goals. He thought that novels were frivolous and vaguely sinful. He believed that reading should be done solely to illuminate oneself. Frank was a more perfect form of human; he rarely read works of fiction.

But Frank never voiced his real objection to my new book: I derived pleasure from its pages. Remember, Frank was raised by a drunken, tyrannical father who worked him mercilessly. Most of the opportunities Frank Jr. had for recreational reading disappeared when his so-called childhood ended at the age of thirteen. Frank was jealous that I lacked the crushing responsibilities he was saddled with at my age. Any display of childishness or softness on my part was inevitably met with disdain, scorn, or violence by Frank.

Beyond Frank's vague and capricious objections to my choice of reading material lurked another, more ominous reason: he seldom missed an opportunity to threaten the removal of *anything* that brought me joy.

I did not risk any behavior that would cause Frank to change his mind about my book. I did not want him to take it away. I read the damned thing only when I was out of his sight.

Frank's incessant Bible reading had prepared me for such an eventuality. I remembered a passage that said, "Stolen bread is sweet when eaten in secret." My newfound love of reading added joy—and another stressor—to my life.

I spent every moment I could wrapped in the all-encompassing womb of *Bomba the Jungle Boy*. Each page I read took me further away from my bleak, hungry, and lonely existence. It took me just a few days to devour the book. I read the last line, and the fantasy world of Bomba vanished. My own all-too-real life instantly reappeared.

I begged Lita to take me back to the junk shop. I wanted to see if there were any more interesting titles buried in its stacks. She agreed to my request. I think that her acquiescence derived largely from a single detail: as junk stores ran, the new one was particularly well stocked.

We went back to the junk store. I ran through the front door and sought out the owner. I told him how much I loved *Bomba the Jungle Boy* and asked him if he had any more books of like kind. He got a Santa-like twinkle in his eyes and said, "I think I might have some things you might find interesting."

The store's proprietor was a willing coconspirator to my literary adventures. I don't believe he was trying to make a sale. He was feeding off my enthusiasm. We went through every box, every stack of books, every nook and cranny in his junk store.

We found several more titles in the Bomba series. Some were in near-perfect condition. Others were lacking covers. Some had whole sections missing. I didn't care. No rich kid ever loved his new Ferrari as much as I did those damaged books.

That first set of novels opened a magical gateway to my imagination. I used it to expand my horizons and intellect. I can divide my life into two sections: before I discovered *Bomba the Jungle Boy* and after. That little book changed the course of my life.

Over the next few years, junk stores fed my burgeoning imagination with books of all sorts. Some of them would greatly expand my knowledge of sex and gardening.

This was a typical pose for me. I was in the middle of a good book. At that moment, I didn't want to do anything but see how the story ended. In front of Ruby Tomlinson's new Spartan trailer, China Lake Naval Air Station. 1957.

CHAPTER 52

Auntie Mame

Auntie Mame is the title of a 1955 novel by Patrick Dennis.
The novel is a fictionalization of the real-life adventures the
author experienced with his aunt Marion Tanner. In the novel
(and the stage productions and movies that followed), Mame
teaches a young boy about life in a wondrously eccentric way.

—*Tom Liggett's personal glossary of terms*

THERE IS AN OLD SAYING that approximately states, "When the student is
ready, the teacher will appear." I don't know who first came up with that
line, but it was true in my case. When I was seven, a teacher entered my
orbit. He had no equal in my life or in his generation. He added leavening
to the dough of my nascent intelligence.

Every family seems to have at least one member who is different from
the rest of its members. My aunt Betty and I filled that role in Lita's family.
The mood and tenor of any family gathering was altered when either one of
us entered or left the room.

Frank's family of inveterate backwoodsmen produced one of like kind,
but in spades: Arthur McMillan. He excelled in many different areas. His
creativity and wit overwhelm the term genius.

Arthur was born in a rough part of Oklahoma. The sere plains in that
place made the verdant bottomlands of Central Texas look like heaven on

earth. Arthur became an orphan while he was in his early teens. He was thrust into the unwelcoming bosom of a distant relative's home. The Dust Bowl made life hell for those who stayed in Oklahoma. A hungry mouth was not a welcome attribute, especially in a long-term guest. Arthur's foster family worked him like a mule. They made him earn his keep—and then some.

Arthur's unique intelligence and wild inquisitiveness caused problems with his host family. A peculiar boy's questions were not welcome in a culture that required sameness and rigid order to get people through the day. When I recall my problems of like kind, I suspect the actions of Arthur's host family were driven by jealousy.

World War II gave Arthur the lift he needed to escape the confines of his family's version of cowboy culture. He joined the army and quickly rose to the rank of sergeant major. Those of you who don't know much about the old army might not fully recognize the significance of that feat. In rank, sergeant major is below the lowest commissioned officer. But the power of that exalted enlisted grade goes beyond all comprehension. Few officers of any rank dare to tangle with a well-regarded sergeant major. Most people achieve that rank at the end of a long military career. Arthur did it in just a couple of years, when he was still in his early twenties. That speaks highly of his talent, intelligence, drive, and people skills.

After the war, Arthur went to Southern California. He quickly opened two upscale restaurants on Hollywood's fabled Sunset Strip. Arthur's distinctive signature was scrawled on each piece of dinnerware. McMillan's became one of *the* trendy places to dine and to be seen. The cream of Hollywood talent wanted to meet the tall, handsome, and charming Arthur McMillan.

I don't know how Arthur became one of the great chefs of his era. He was entirely self-taught. In basic terms, I suppose that much of his culinary talent was of a similar nature to the instinctual knowledge of fruit trees with which I was gifted. I harbor great sadness that the gulf of years between us prevented me from acquiring more of Arthur's wild and varied culinary knowledge.

When Arthur entered my life, the Sunset Strip restaurants were long gone. So were several other promising careers, including being a world-class singer of classical music. I have heard many renditions of Beethoven's Symphony no. 9. Arthur's was the best. It made the hair stand on the back of my neck.

Arthur didn't like to speak of his past. It made him sad. At most, he would say, "I wanted to free myself so that I could walk along the banks of the Ganges River." Arthur never made it to India. He never went much of anywhere, excepting California and his native Oklahoma. But that didn't stop him from moving ever onward in his mind. I suspect that propensity was drawn from the well of cowboy restlessness he shared with Frank.

The apartments Arthur chose during his tenure in San Francisco said much about his character. A quirk of San Francisco law dictated that residential buildings with more than three stories must have an elevator. Those buildings that had three stories or fewer did not. Most people didn't want to hike up three flights of stairs, so third-floor San Francisco apartments were generally less expensive than others. Ever a tightwad, Arthur always lived in third-floor apartments.

Arthur had a beautiful Steinway rosewood baby grand piano that weighed almost as much as small automobile. He loved regaling his guests with exciting stories about how movers got the piano in and out of his various third-floor apartments. Because he moved frequently, he had a lot of piano-moving stories.

The cowboy culture in which I was raised was rife with sayings and traditions, holdovers from a bygone era. Frank and Arthur McMillan shared a favorite axiom: "Children are best seen and not heard." Arthur knew that Frank taught me in the old cowboy way. I knew how to behave. I could be counted on to sit quietly at a fancy dinner table for hours and keep my mouth shut. Even in 1958, that was a rare trait among children. But it certainly was true of the children *I* knew.

My years of training to be the amazing invisible perfect silent kid paid a wonderful dividend: I got to go with Frank and Lita when they attended

Arthur's fabulous dinner parties. My first serious contact with Arthur was at one of those parties.

At that time, Arthur was a renowned chef. You might expect that the food was the high point of Arthur's parties. Yes, the food *was* good. But it was usually plain fare such as roast chicken with paprika. He usually found a way to startle his guests' citified palates. He would serve traditional foods from Oklahoma. Turnips, for example. But he would dress them in ways that took their flavor to the moon. That was pure Arthur McMillan: keep it simple, but shake up the guests' expectations.

Food was never the star attraction at one of Arthur's parties. Arthur and his guests shone above everything. The best and the brightest of the San Francisco intelligentsia attended those long-gone events. If a famous author, singer, psychic, religious figure, or poet was in town, that person might sit next to you at Arthur's table.

You might expect an eight-year-old boy to feel out of place at that type of party. Not me. I was happy that I was with people. I was delighted to receive a hearty meal. This was during the time when my typical dinner was sometimes a handful of stale crackers or cornflakes with water.

You might also expect that the adults at Arthur's parties would resent my presence. That was not the case. The writers liked me because I loved to read. The singers liked me because I had the voice of an angel. The psychics *loved* me. One famous psychic reportedly said, "That child has the strongest gift of sensitivity I have ever seen." Most of all, the adults at Arthur's parties liked me because I acted like an adult.

But there was another, more important reason why I was welcome at Arthur's parties. My presence at such gatherings added sparkle, hope, and perspective to other guests. You see, Arthur and most of his friends were homosexuals. That isn't a big deal in these liberated times. In 1958, it was a *very* big deal.

Yes, I know San Francisco has always been more understanding of "unusual" behavior than many other American cities. But most of the men in Arthur's circle of friends were raised in an era wherein being queer was dangerous. Homosexuals were beaten, killed, incarcerated, and sent to mental hospitals.

Many of Arthur's friends had taken extended tours of the lower levels of hell because of their homosexual tendencies. This was especially true of those men who had been drafted into the armed services during World War II. Years later, I learned that all the gay people who sat around Arthur's table had their own horror stories. The truth of their hurt was written in the lines on their faces.

Arthur McMillan lived in the midst of a closeted generation of homosexuals. People of that sort enjoyed being around children. Young people provided them with hope that goodness and life would continue after they passed away.

Arthur McMillan lived in the midst of a closeted generation of homosexuals. People of that sort enjoyed being around children. Young people provided them with hope that goodness and life would continue after they passed away. Front row, left to right: Kenneth Hayes, Nita Hayes, Arthur McMillan and Tom Liggett. Back row, left to right: Janita Hayes and Lita McMillan. San Francisco, California. 1959.

Some of my readers are undoubtedly thinking, *Yeah, Tom, Arthur and his friends just wanted to get into your tight little pants.* Nothing could be further from the truth! Neither Arthur nor any of his friends made a pass at me. Until I turned eighteen. That's more than I can say for some of my heterosexual relatives.

Because of Arthur and his friends, I like to think that I was raised in the gay community before there was a visible and popular gay movement.

For my part, Arthur's parties and sleepovers allowed me a view into a world that was completely different from the one in which I was trapped. Arthur knew that this was true because he had been raised in the oppressive confines of the same culture.

On the other hand, Arthur was unaware that I was being subjected to a boot-camp-like regimen of brutality and neglect. He didn't realize that I regularly spent the better part of the week alone in our apartment. He also had no idea that I sometimes existed on a starvation diet.

Aside from giving me a decent meal and some companionship, Arthur's gatherings allowed me to make a huge intellectual leap. This came in large part from Arthur's influence on my reading habits. Here's how that worked: someone would give Arthur a book. He read the book. The salient points of the book were discussed at Arthur's next party.

I sometimes found topics at Arthur's parties interesting. This was especially true if the topic had a sexual reference. I knew very little about sex but was titillated by the subject. Biology marches on, folks.

The books that Frank and Arthur discussed frequently had religious topics. When they discussed *those*, I shut down my ears and brain. Frank continually used religion as a weapon. I got enough of that shit at home. I didn't need it at Arthur's parties.

After Arthur finished reading an interesting book, he would lend it to Frank. When Frank read the book, he left it on a table in our living room. He wanted the books for decorations. Frank was a braggart. He liked to show off his "superior" intellectual prowess to the people who came to visit.

I was chronically short of reading material. Partly that was because I was a speed reader. Since I was usually alone and bored, I burned through books at an incredible rate. Lita didn't have the time or money to take me to junk stores frequently enough to keep up with my voracious literary appetite. She damned sure didn't pull time out from her busy day to take me to the public library.

That left the books Arthur passed on to Frank. I attempted to read those powerful works. Most of the concepts were above my level of comprehension. But I read a large proportion of the words. Most of it was boring stuff, but it beat sitting alone in an empty apartment. This was especially true when the days were short and I couldn't dig in my garden.

Don't get me wrong; I didn't instantly turn into some sort of egghead. I still devoured every comic book and boys adventure novel I could get. But I couldn't acquire enough books of that sort.

Any way you cut it, the result was the same: I was reading the great authors of the day and their predecessors when I was just eight years old.

Let's take a step back for a moment. A year earlier, I couldn't read or do arithmetic. My intellectual turnaround was miraculous. Most parents and family members would have seen my precocious choice of reading material as a cause for celebration. Many of them would find ways to develop that type of latent genius. That was not the case with Frank and Lita or the rest of my extended family. They *all* thought that my voracious reading habits were strange. Some even thought that the wide variety of subject matter that passed through my brain was harmful to my morals.

When she was visiting with other people, Lita loved to introduce the topic of my advanced reading ability. She was quite proud of my accomplishment. But she placed my reading in the same trick box as my early gardening genius: it was just another cute Tommy story. I provided Lita with bragging material. But none of that added any value to my life. Lita, Frank, Arthur, Ruby, and everybody else in my family were too busy chasing their own interests to give a shit about anything I did. They continued to ignore me most of the time.

CHAPTER 53

Foragers

My grandmother Ruby loved mustard greens, but she was too lazy to grow them. She either bought them at the store or received them from wild stocks. She seldom saw mustard greens in the market, so that left wild greens. Since Ruby was also too lazy to pick wild greens, someone else had to accomplish that task. Before I came around, that someone was Lita. Poor Lita was already caring for almost everybody she knew, but she willingly added foraging to her list of chores. Lita didn't mind picking greens for Momma. It gave her the chance to be alone in wild and disused places.

Ruby was mighty particular about her mustard greens. She liked the right kind of greens. They also needed to be in the optimal stage of their life cycle. If Ruby didn't believe the greens were just right, she refused to cook them. This forced Lita to become a sharp-eyed seeker of wild greens.

Lita began to infuse me with her love of wild places and growing things as soon as I was born. I was a quick study. It didn't take me very many years to become the de facto mustard-green seeker of the family. No one ever stated that outright; it just happened. I didn't mind. I was an apt forager of long standing. Wherever I went, I looked for abandoned, neglected, or wild places. I loved the thrill of the hunt. I never knew what I would find. Sometimes I found interesting things to eat.

Ruby's experienced eye forced me to become selective about what I picked. The first time I found a nice stand of mustard plants, I harvested a whole sack full for Ruby. I ran back home as quick as I could, thrust the bag at Ruby, and said, "Here, Momma, I picked these for you."

Ruby opened the bag and took a skeptical peek inside. "Tommy, these greens ain't no good," she said. "They ain't hot enough."

I asked, "What do you mean, Momma?"

She took a leaf from the bag, tore it in half, and put it into her mouth. She offered the other part to me, then made a face as she chewed the leaf. "See? It ain't got no flavor. Folks only eat these when they's a-starvin'."

I tasted the mustard leaf. She was right. It *was* bland.

Ruby took another leaf from the sack and said, "This here mustard's got a light, smooth leaf. There's another kind. It's got a dark-green leaf. It's all rough and spiky. Makes a bigger plant too. Looks like a tree. That's the one you want to eat." I knew the plants she was talking about. I had noted them during my child-sized explorations.

Ruby didn't know the names of the two species of mustards that grew locally, but she did know that one was better than the other. I eventually learned that the greens I'd picked were from white mustard plants. She liked greens that came from less common black mustard plants.

Ruby emptied the bag of greens in the trash and handed it back to me. She said, "Now, you go back to where you picked them other greens. You look a little harder. Maybe in a moist, shaded place. You'll find what you're a-lookin' for."

I was on cloud nine. Ruby had given me an important job. I rushed out of the house and went back to the creek. I made a careful search of the creek bottom and surrounding fields. I only saw the pale green plants of white mustard. I wandered around for the longest time and finally went out of the creek bottom and onto the upper banks. In the distance, I saw the tree-like plants I recognized; here were plants of black mustard. I ran over to the plants. It took me about ten seconds to cram a bunch of them into my bag.

I ran back to Ruby's house. I think she was surprised to see me holding another bag of greens. "Momma," I said, "these greens are plenty hot. I tasted 'em. They burned my mouth."

Momma didn't even bother tasting *these* greens. She looked at them with disgust and said, "Tommy, these are too old. They will be tough. I know there are some young plants out there somewhere. It's the right time of the year. You go back there and find me some younger leaves. I'll cook 'em up for you with turnips."

Oh boy, this was fun! This was an adventure. I ran to another part of the creek. I needed to find the right kind of mustard plants. Most of the new candidates were the undesirable white mustard. Most of the black mustard plants were too advanced into bloom and seed. But I looked hard and eventually found what I was looking for in a shady corner of the creek bottom. Ruby was right. You couldn't fool that old Indian. These leaves were smaller, more tender. But I didn't want to take a chance; I tried one of the leaves. It was easy to chew—and hot as hell. I remember thinking, *Momma will like these.*

My grandmother beamed when she opened the third bag of leaves. She said, "These are just right. Let me show you how to clean 'em up and cook 'em." She did that very thing. Ruby taught me the true best way to cook wild mustard greens.

Ruby's mustard tutorial was an addition to my small arsenal of food-gathering knowledge. Lita founded that repository in my mind before I could speak. Almost everything I cared about revolved around food-producing plants.

Lita had good reason to encourage my interest. She was a magnificent cook, but she didn't always have the best ingredients. This forced her to be aware of the wild or free foods that came her way.

Every spring and fall, Lita and I looked for wild mushrooms. My mother was wise enough to realize they could be a dangerous food source. Wild mushrooms can kill you. Lots of people told Lita that you could eat this wild mushroom or that one, but she always shut them down in midsentence, saying, "I know you are probably right. But I don't trust you—or myself. I'm stickin' with what I know—button mushrooms."

Lita and I usually didn't have time to go on serious mushroom hunts. But sometimes one of us would stumble upon a patch of mushrooms. When that happened, Lita would pick enough for our dinner. Oh, lordy. You have no idea what Lita could do with beef and mushrooms.

Sometimes we went on mushroom treks with friends and relatives. Those outings tended to be more productive. One time, Lita and I filled our claw-foot bathtub to the brim with perfect button mushrooms. Lita and I gave bags of mushrooms to other people. We gave cooked mushrooms to loved ones. Lita sautéed the mushrooms, and I peeled and chopped the garlic. I was seven years old. I was in heaven. I was in the wild land with Lita, and then I was in the kitchen. Life didn't get any better for me.

We gleaned fields for their wondrous leftovers. Green beans and tomatoes were high on our list of desirable fields to "scrap." Onions were at the top of that list. Farmers only picked the best and largest of the onions, leaving half the crop in the field. I remember a time when Lita and I got to a field just as the famer was turning to destroy the last row. We ran in front of the tractor to grab the onions before they were destroyed. We got about fifty pounds of onions. Some of them looked a little strange, but most were perfect.

The cheerful farmer smiled and waved as he roared past us. He was used to seeing such behavior. Chances are that man knew what it was like to be hungry.

Lita and I walked down the side of the field on our way back to the car. I bent and picked up a perfect onion that had been sliced in half by the plow. Lita and I looked at each other. She said, "Someone could have eaten that." I nodded in agreement.

We picked up walnuts along creek beds and roadsides. We knew we were in a race against squirrels. Lita said, "These will make great cookies when it gets cold." Lita's instincts told her to stockpile food against winter need. Too bad she didn't have much to store.

My mother *hated* store-bought jams and jellies. She said, "Store jam is too sweet. It ain't got no flavor." Lita had a ready counter for *that* problem: she *loved* to make preserves and canned whole fruit. But there was a problem with jam making: Lita didn't have a reliable fruit source. She also didn't have the money to buy fruit. More importantly, she didn't have the time to seek out sources of fresh fruit.

My abilities as a feral boy rescued Lita's jam-making aspirations. I wandered high and low, down every street and into every creek bed I could find. I knew the location of every visible fruit-bearing tree, bush, and vine within a mile of the places I traveled. I knew 'em in the winter when they didn't have any leaves. I knew 'em in the spring, when the spent blossoms fell like snowflakes. I knew where to find 'em in the summer, when the fruit was ripe.

Sometimes the fruit-bearing plants I discovered were on public land. That made the issue of ownership moot. We picked what we wanted. Mostly, though, I sought fruiting plants that were on private property. The fruit from such places was generally higher in quality than that which came from wild stocks.

But the fruit that was located on private property belonged to somebody. We couldn't just march in and take it. I knew how to deal with *that* conundrum. I watched plants through their bloom and fruiting stages. As the fruit began to ripen, I watched closer. When the fruit got ripe, I checked to see if it was disappearing from the plants. If no one was harvesting it, I knocked on the front door. I had my spiel down pat. I would say, "Pardon me for bothering you, but I see that you have a [whatever] tree. It doesn't look like anyone is picking the fruit. It will make a stink when it falls on the ground and will draw flies. Would you like me to get rid of the fruit for you?"

Some folks automatically said yes. Skeptical types had another angle. They would ask, "You're not going to sell the fruit, are you?"

I had a ready answer for that too. I would say, "Oh, no, my mother and I are just going to make jam. We will give you a few jars if you let us have the fruit." A tiny fraction of people wanted to sell the fruit. Others said they would use the fruit themselves. I obviously passed on those trees.

Once I had the fruit lined up, I warned Lita. I'd say, "The blackberries down in the creek are gonna get ripe next week." Or I'd remark, "I found a tree of Blenheims [apricots]. We'll need to move real fast on them—they are already a little overripe." Lita seldom failed to react when I issued one of my fruit advisories. She would put almost everything else in her life on hold when she heard of a fruit source.

On picking day, Lita and I headed off with buckets, dishpans, and laundry baskets. Sometimes we borrowed a ladder from a neighbor. My mother and I had great fun harvesting fruit, getting stuck by thorns and stung by insects. We laughed our way through the work. We both knew this was the way it was supposed to be—an Indian mother with her child, accepting nature's bounty.

We always harvested every piece of fruit we could find. Lita's motto was "You never know when you're gonna get more fruit." There was another reason for that too. We both knew that it is very bad to leave unpicked fruit on a tree. The fruit "mummifies" into disease-carrying pustules. Even Indians of a lesser kind know how to be stewards of the land.

Top fruits such as apricots, cherries, and peaches were prized by the home gardeners who grew them. Those folks used what they grew. They were loath to give their bounty to a ragamuffin child.

That left other kinds of fruit, types that people don't commonly utilize for jam making. Cherry plums, for example. Young children were the only people I knew who regularly ate that fruit. Cherry plums have tart skins and mushy, watery pulp. They have very little flavor. They are insipid. They make watery, semi tasteless jam. But that didn't deter me 'n' Lita—we canned what I found.

Sometimes the fruit I found wasn't of the best quality. It was past its prime. People would only let us have fruit after they had taken what they wanted from the tree. We filled buckets with mushy, half-rotten ground-fall plums and apricots. Lita was happy to receive the fruit but unhappy about the quality. She would say, "Tommy, the best jam is made with slightly

Tom Liggett and Ruby Tomlinson. I found a tree of ripe cherry plums in front of an abandoned house. We filled a bathtub with our harvest, and Lita and I canned it all. San Jose, California. 1959.

immature fruit. What we're collecting here is too mushy. Mold will grow in the jam. We're gonna lose some jars."

Being ever resourceful, ever the philosopher, Lita added a thought about our ground-fall fruit. "Last week, these would have been perfect for drying. I'm sorry we don't have a place to do that. It's too bad that most of this wonderful food didn't get eaten. Somewhere, someone's hungry. They would have loved to have it."

Finding, harvesting, and transporting the fruit was the easy part. Putting it into jars was more difficult. Lita and I sometimes ended up with a bathtub full of fruit. That's the best place when you are faced with a shortage of suitable containers.

We occasionally harvested two or three hundred pounds of ripe fruit. That stuff will go from perfect to rotten in less than twenty-four hours. Lita was fanatical; I never saw her waste a single piece of fruit, even when we had a large quantity. There were times we worked for eighteen hours straight to process a mess of fruit.

Each piece had to be inspected, cut, peeled and chopped. From the age of six onward, I was Lita's little fruit processor. She would hand me one of the aged apricot-paring knives she'd stolen from Pete the orchardist years before. She sat me down on a kitchen chair that was surrounded by three more chairs. These were my work tables. A container of unsorted fruit was on the chair to my left. A dishpan for processed fruit sat on the middle chair—this was the mother lode. A dishpan for culls, peels, and pits sat on the chair to my right. A smaller vessel sat in my lap. This was my working pan.

Lita helped me process fruit until there was enough to start a batch of jam. Once she put the sugar and pectin in the kettle, she would call me over and say, "Tommy, come stir the jam." I dragged my chair over to the stove, stood on the chair, and stirred Lita's cheap old enamel pot with a huge wooden spoon. I had to use both hands. Lita would say, "You be careful not to drag that kettle off the fire. It will burn you." Ah, Lita—I had no intention of doing that, girl. The burns I received from splatters of boiling jam made me see the truth in your words. I was careful as I could be.

From the age of six until I was well into my fifties, I stirred thousands of jam batches for Lita. Each of those operations shared two constants. First, Lita always warned me, "Don't let it stick." The second characteristic was more profound: I was in heaven. I loved making jam with Lita. It was just the two of us in whatever overheated, overaged, second-rate kitchen we had at our disposal. We were in our own little world when we were working together.

The circumstances of our life allowed Lita and I to make first-class jam from fourth-class ingredients. We knew that was as good as it was going to get. We were grateful for the scant portions of joy we received. That's the white-trash way.

CHAPTER 54

Family Matters

We live in a world that is defined by human suffering. Hard times force extended families to relocate en masse from one region to another. People who embark upon disaster-initiated moves seldom take very many material things with them. The collective memories and traditions that they bring to a new place are all that remains of their old life. The power of shared history is potent stuff. It can bind an old family together in a new land.

That's how it went with Lita's family. Everyone remembered leaner times in other places. Most of Lita's relatives were doing well in their new Promised Land. This gave them reason to celebrate their newfound prosperity. They did this by visiting. Compared with today's always-connected lifestyle, that sounds like a mundane activity.

Ah, so much has been lost in our race for the new! Visiting as it was done by those living on the Great Plains of North America is a dying art. Little remains of its traditions.

The distances between people in olden times were vast. Getting together was a lot of work, even for those who lived close to each other. When my family left Oklahoma, telephones were rare. Letter writing was expensive, slow, and impersonal. Folks looked for opportunities to get together, transact family business, and talk. Much of this tradition was brought to my family by our Indian ancestors. Indian bands fiercely protected their own territory. They also sought opportunities for trade and camaraderie.

The kind of visiting I witnessed when I was a child was the last vestige of cowboy/Indian culture in my mother's family. It became ingrained as an integral part of our lives. They carried this tradition when they went to California.

The old style of visiting lived on in my family because folks kept it alive through practice. My relatives got together quite frequently. Visiting was casual in its schedule but rigid in its functions. For example, with afternoon visits, you made sure that you left before the host family sat down to dinner. Drop-in visitors did not expect to be fed by their hosts. A contrary expectation was considered the height of bad manners for many members of Lita's family.

The leave-before-dinner rule of visiting also had another effect: it got the women home to cook for their own families.

Lita's family got together several times each month, almost always at a relative's house. They were large gatherings. Parties sometimes had fifteen or twenty attendees. Eight was considered an intimate gathering. It was a wonderfully chaotic mass of food, drink, song, dance, and gossip. For me, such gatherings were an echo of past days when I lived with Ruby. They were yearned-for respites from the crushing solitude I endured most of the time.

Until Frank arrived, my aunts and uncles were like my sisters and brothers. Just a few years later, I watched them bring their own children to family gatherings. Over the years, a high percentage of such gatherings were hosted by my grandmother Ruby and her husband, Tommy Tomlinson. They lived in a small Spartan house trailer with Ruby's three youngest children.

Ruby refused a lowball offer to buy a house in Mountain View, California. She didn't want to be left behind when Tommy was transferred by the navy. She knew that he would take up with other women if she wasn't around to act as watchdog. Tommy was a tall, good-looking sailor. Sailors sometimes live down their reputations. Many of them have a woman in every port. Ruby didn't want to lose her hard-won meal ticket. At her age, she would not be able to snare another.

Frank McMillan, drunk and angry at his birthday party. Lita McMillan is on the right side of the photograph. Kitchen, 123 North Tenth Street, San Jose, California. July 1959.

Frank McMillan, drunk and angry at Big Basin State Park. Johnny Crossland is on the left side of the photograph. 1959.

Trailer living offered Ruby a great deal of stability when Tommy Tomlinson was transferred to another stateside base. Her home and belongings were waiting for her when she got there. But it made for cramped quarters with two adults and three children living in the thing. Three kids slept in a pair of tiny niche-type bunk beds. Crowded conditions were the order of the night. Except for Tommy and Ruby, of course. They enjoyed a full double bed in a private room.

When a dozen of her friends and relatives came to visit, Ruby's house trailer became a crowded place. We were packed together like sardines in a can. It was wonderful. Folks ate and drank. They chatted and gossiped. They played cards. Almost all the adults smoked. By extension, their children did too. The incredibly high incidence of lung cancer in Ruby's children and grandchildren pays terrible homage to that fact.

It was exhilarating for my grandmother to have her children and grandchildren visit. When she thought that the visiting session had run its course, she shooed us out. That was another rule of old-style cowboy visiting: you didn't overstay your welcome.

Lita and her siblings knew that Ruby was the nervous type. Because of this, they had the *real* parties in their homes. Those gatherings tended to be alcohol fueled and longer lasting.

Ruby's children danced the linoleum off the floor. I have never seen such a group of accomplished and enthusiastic dancers in one family. I like to think that the love of dance might have come from my Indian ancestors. Who knows? That is yet another family trait that died with my mother.

Many of Frank's relatives came to live or visit in California. They sometimes joined in with Lita's family at parties. When our extended families got together, they talked about everything, especially their children. That was the hot topic of the day. The baby boom was in full swing. All over the world, people were breeding like flies.

I dreaded public discussions about children. I knew there was a fair chance that my relatives would end up on one of my least-favored questions:

What is the ideal number of children in a family? There was a good deal of disagreement on that issue.

There was only one aspect of that topic that was met with universal approval: *everybody* believed that it was not acceptable to have an only one child. Why? It was common knowledge that only children are *always* spoiled brats. Popular culture added fuel to that myth. Contemporary newspapers, magazines, movies, and television invariably portrayed only children as being overindulged little monsters.

Frank and Lita's huge extended family contained just one only child: me. When folks started a discussion about only children, I knew I would end up under the microscope. I quickly learned the value of leaving the room when topics containing references to only children were brought to the table.

Frank and Lita usually wouldn't allow me to exit gracefully. They rudely shouted at me, "Get back in here! You need to hear this!" The drunken adults would erupt in cheers and jeers when they heard that announcement. My family knew what was coming. It was time for some high theater. Tommy Liggett always played the title role of eternal villain.

Frank and Lita made me stand in the middle of the room. Frank didn't have to tell me to stand at attention. I'd learned that part of the drill four years earlier. I had it down pat.

Frank would begin a scripted presentation about "spoiled brats." He loudly told all present, "I ain't a-gonna raise up no spoiled brats in *my* house!" Frank received more cheers and nods of agreement as he made that seminal point.

But that was just the introduction. Frank quickly shifted into the specific point of his sermon: how he was going to change the terrible Tommy Liggett. Those rants seemed to go on *forever*. But I was patient. I had been here before. I knew that the crowd would grow weary of hearing Frank's tongue wag. Audience disinterest eventually forced him to shut up. The party wandered in a different conversational direction.

But the mood and tenor of such gatherings changed for me. I dreaded what inevitably followed one of Frank's anti–Tommy Liggett diatribes. I knew that assorted loved ones and total strangers would give private lectures to me. These centered on one topic: I was lucky to have Frank McMillan as a father. Everybody loved Frank.

Those private little interludes ended up with people telling me, "You need to treat Frank better. You must try to be a better person." I agreed with my critics. I believed that Frank was the best dad in the world. I believed I was a very bad boy.

But that was the easy part of the evening. I knew that worse was waiting for me later when Frank got me alone.

Our family parties ended with cheers, hugs, and good humor. Things changed as soon as the last guest left or we entered our car. The speech Frank had given at the party was a milder version of his real sentiment. It was just a warm-up. When Frank got me alone, he didn't have to be so nice. He became a maniac. He *really* let me have it. Frank railed at me all the way home. He made sure that I understood his main point: there was no way that he was going to raise a "typical only child."

Frank's twisted diatribes always ended up in the same way: with me blubbering. I begged him to give me another chance. I knew that I was expected to end my plea with the statement that Frank was the best dad ever. It wasn't difficult for me to say any of those things. I agreed with his every point. Every thrust was met with a contrite response from me. I said, "I know that I am a spoiled brat. I know that I am greedy and selfish. I know I am a stupid boy who will never do well."

The soul-baring contrition I offered to Frank would sometimes be enough to soothe his anger. Sometimes it wasn't. He would kick me from the car to the house. When we got inside, Frank tore through my room (if I had one) and my small collection of beloved things. This latter act did not derive from any destructive tendencies on Frank's part. He was looking for a mess. I was a kid. There was a mess. That gave Frank the chance to pull out all the stops and regress into full-on drill instructor mode. He emptied the drawers, bags, and boxes that held my belongings and scattered them around the room.

Frank then offered his pièce de résistance. He screamed, "Look at this mess! Clean it up!" He then kicked and scolded me around the room while I frantically picked up my belongings.

Lita watched Frank's sick performance for a short while. She offered approving nods in all the right places. This was what Lita wanted for me. She was always telling someone, "I'm proud of Frank's influence on Tommy." Thanks, Lita.

CHAPTER 55

1930s Movie Monster

LITA'S FATHER, CLEVE SNOW, BOUNCED in and out of our lives. He was a passing figure, here one day, gone the next.

As you might recall from my earlier description of Cleve, he was a skilled tractor driver who couldn't hold down a job because of his drunkenness. He spent a lot of time in county jail farms, which dried him out. But when he was released, his promises to do better and work harder fell by the wayside as soon as he had enough money in his pocket to get falling-down, pants-pissing, bar-fighting, passing-out drunk.

My readers might be wondering why I chose to include this information about my grandfather. I did it to set up a story. When I was about eight, I finally managed to persuade a schoolmate to come play at my house. That only happened twice while we lived on Tenth Street. In that place and time, most mothers kept their children close to home. Few mothers in those days would allow their children to visit a home where their children would not be under adult supervision. That seriously reduced the possibility that another child would come to my house after school.

I was very excited to have my friend over. No one had ever seen my backyard creations. I wanted someone to join my exploration of the nineteenth-century carriage barns on the property. I desperately wanted someone to see my private world. That fervently desired day had finally arrived. I was taking someone to visit my backyard!

I walked from school to my friend's home. His mother fed us a snack. That was wonderful. My friend and I said good-bye to his mother and walked in the direction of my duplex. We discussed the things we would do once we arrived. My friend was excited. He wanted to see the carriage barns. He liked "cool old stuff."

I didn't notice any of the sights on the way to my apartment. I was lost in our conversation. As we approached the duplex, my companion stopped dead in his tracks. He recoiled and said, "Ooh, there's a hobo on your lawn!"

I followed the other boy's gaze. Bigger than life, there was Cleve. He was passed out in our tiny front yard. He was lying on his side, crumpled in a half-fetal position. I said to my friend, "That's not a hobo. That's my grandfather."

I can't blame my friend for believing that Cleve *was* a hobo. My grandfather wore the universal uniform of the incorrigible street-drunk: soiled, oily jeans and a filthy long-sleeve shirt. His pants and shirt were half unbuttoned and sagged away from his middle section. His hair looked like a ragged, oily mop.

My friend and I were standing about ten feet away from Cleve. That was close enough for us to be overwhelmed by the assortment of smells that were emanating off my grandfather. It was a repulsive mixture of body odor, rotten alcohol, rotten shit, ammonia, and stale vomit.

The sound of our voices roused Cleve from his stupor. He rolled over and attempted to speak. He was too drunk to speak coherently. His words came out as unrecognizable growls and barks.

I was just eight, but I already had years of experience dealing with people who were blind drunk. I knew what was coming next. Seeking to lessen the damage, I kept my silence. My friend lacked my education in drunken behavior. He was visibly shaken. He was trembling like a leaf. I thought my friend was going to shit his pants.

The other boy and I were frozen. Neither one of us truly knew what to do. Then Cleve upped the ante. He was raised in cowboy culture. Men of his era expected boys to speak when they were addressed by their elders. Cleve viewed our failure to respond to his grunts as disrespectful. He got angry.

Cleve turned up the volume of his unintelligible rant. He attempted to stand. Cleve failed in his first attempt. He got angrier. Cleve finally remembered how his legs worked and began to stand. It was a slow, arduous process. Cleve was waving his arms around above his head. He did that both for emphasis and to maintain his balance. Cleve looked like a horror-movie monster who was rising out of the grave. The best old-time horror movie actors were poor imitations of my grandfather that fine afternoon.

When Cleve finally managed to stand somewhat upright, he lurched toward the two of us. He was still yelling, still waving his arms. The foul smell increased as Cleve drew closer. My poor friend finally had enough. You could tell that he was horrified by the stumbling, ranting apparition that was rapidly coming his way. My friend gave me a disgusted look and ran away as fast as he could.

I was just as repulsed as my friend. But I couldn't run away from Cleve. I was home. I had nowhere else to go. Ever the respectful child, I stood there while Cleve yelled at me. After what seemed to be an eternity, I finally got the gist of what my grandfather was trying to say. He accomplished this feat more with pantomime than by the power of his eloquence. Cleve was hungry. Lord knows when he had last eaten.

In due course, I managed to get Cleve into the duplex. As usual, there was very little to eat in the place. I remember finding a lone can of sardines in tomato sauce. Frank bought them to eat when he came home drunk. Frank ate a *lot* of sardines. I found the taste, smell, and texture of the things to be repulsive. I didn't want to eat them even when I was starving. Sardines in tomato sauce were the absolute last food of choice for me. That's why the horrid things were still in the cabinet.

Cleve seized the can of sardines. He was ravenous. He attempted to open the can, but his forays in that direction were met with various fumbles and drops, punctuated at regular intervals by what were clearly swear words.

It's amazing that someone who is too drunk to speak can still cuss. That shows the power of intent and practice, I suppose.

After a great deal of work and even more swearing, Cleve finally managed to half open, half tear most of the cover from the can. In the process, much of the sardine-infused tomato sauce that used to be in the can was now on Cleve, the kitchen counter, and the floor.

The smell of the sardines combined with Cleve's rotten miasma created an almost visible fog of rottenness that surrounded me and my grandfather. It made my eyes water.

I don't remember how that sorry interlude with my grandfather ended. The memory is lost in the countless other drunken interactions I endured. Most of those episodes all ended in the same way: the drunk yelled, hit, or vomited on me. At least Cleve didn't smack me around. That was an improvement over Frank's usual drunken behavior.

Later on, I tried to tell Lita about what had happened with Cleve. She *really* went off on me. She remembered her father from the days when he came home at night with hugs, money, and rock candy. Lita burst into tears and said, "How can you be so disrespectful toward my daddy?" That made me believe that I had done something wrong. I felt guilty because I'd complained about the loss of an after-school visit.

When Frank got home, Lita told him that I caused her to cry. He added another layer of hurt on my day by beating me like a rented mule.

Bad news travels fast. When I got to school the next day, my name seemed to be on every child's lips. Countless sets of young eyes followed me around the playground. When I approached other children, they would stop talking, snicker, and walk away.

The word was out: "That weird alone kid has the scariest, stinkiest grandfather of all time waiting for him at home. Don't go to Tommy Liggett's house." Their behavior added another layer to the onion of my isolation.

CHAPTER 56

Sex as a Disease

I WAS NINE IN 1959. People had been showing me their genitals for more than five years. They did this to instruct, entice, embarrass, tease, or titillate me. Nobody had tried to touch my privates or get me to touch theirs, though. Because of that saving grace, I could brush such things off as minor annoyances.

It was during this period that the men in my family began to speak more freely about sex when I was around. I suppose that's a common occurrence in all families. But it had a little twist in my family: the women also started talking about sex.

In the late 1950s, magazines that featured nude photos of women were becoming more prevalent. Some of the men in my family went out of their way to show me those magazines. If I live to be one hundred years old, I will never forget the first *Playboy* magazine centerfold I saw. The model was wearing a demure top and nothing below. The front of her body was turned away from the camera. She was looking back over her shoulder. That woman sure did have a fine ass. Talk about imprinting. Whew!

I didn't realize that skin magazines and open discussions about sex were new things. They were the guns that fired the opening shots in the wars for sexual freedom that occurred in the 1950s, '60s, and '70s.

I was too naïve to know about sex or cultural revolutions. It was uncharted territory. I saw that some people liked to show off their private parts. I understood that people liked to touch their own private parts and those of others. Beyond that, it was no big deal.

A male relative noticed my interest in nudie photos and gave me a copy of a low-budget skin magazine. I immediately discerned that *Playboy* was superior in every measurable aspect.

The low-budget magazine had inferior paper, photos, and jokes. That last bit was important to me. I loved the raunchy photos of women that were published in men's magazines. But I also liked the stories and jokes. I did not understand most of the sexual concepts at the root of them, but I did recognize one point: they were quite funny. Men's magazines joined comic books and adventure novels on my short list of sought-after reading material.

When my relative gave me the skin magazine, he said, "Don't let your mother find this. If she does find it, don't tell her I gave it to you." That warning reinforced the notion that racy magazines were forbidden fruit.

The man who gave me the magazine thought that Lita would be angry if she found it in my possession. He obviously didn't know my mother very well. She talked about sex all the time. She ran around the house in various stages of undress. She teased and posed for me.

I didn't fear Lita's anger. I just didn't want to feel embarrassed if she found me with a skin magazine. I also didn't want to encourage her flirty behavior toward me. I hid my stash of racy literature from prying eyes.

I spent uncounted hours alone. This gave me the time I needed to ferret out the meaning of the words in the racy magazines that came my way. No, I still didn't understand much about the mechanics of sex. I didn't know how babies were made. But the printed word revealed that sex was a lot of fun—and that it caused a lot of problems.

The late 1950s skin mags I saw offered predictable erotic fare. When they weren't available, I sought out the nudie paintings in our *Encyclopedia Britannica*. Just for the record, the best nudes in the 1958 edition of *Encyclopedia Britannica* are in volume 17, *P to Plant*.

I was aware that when I looked at erotic photos, my penis got very hard. It felt like it was going to explode. I thought that was all there was to the deal. It became a routine: I looked at nudie photos and got hard for a while. That was it. I didn't know enough about human sexuality to know that the best part came at the end. Specifically speaking, I had no concept that orgasms existed. I didn't know that men use erotic photographs for masturbation aids.

Years before, I felt revulsion when I saw the result of my relatives' masturbatory efforts. It didn't occur to me to do the same thing to myself. In my one serious effort to stroke my penis, I tried playing with myself in the bathtub but got soap inside my urethra. It hurt like hell. I didn't try *that* again.

At this point in our story, Frank and Lita began to get more ambitious about their partying. They figured out that they really liked to go up to Reno, Nevada, for hot weekends. Frank and Lita didn't really enjoy gambling, but Reno was just a few hours away. The motel rooms were inexpensive. Better yet, the food and drink were free. Frank could get bombed and not destroy our broken family budget. They both said they went to Reno to get away from me.

Up to this point, Frank and Lita had left me alone when they went partying. That didn't work with the Reno trips. Two or three alone nights in a row was just too much, even by their casual standards of childcare.

Frank had a drinking buddy who was willing to lend a helping hand. He offered to watch me while Frank and Lita went to Reno. The drinking buddy was on his second marriage. He and his new wife created a blended family of four children. One was a baby, and two were a little younger than I was. The oldest was a boy about fourteen or fifteen.

Frank and Lita left me with the drinking buddy's family several times a month. But there was a problem: the host parents went out at night. They left me and the other children under the care of the teenage boy. Bad idea. That kid was a real monster.

At first, things went well with the older boy. During the day, we walked around the streets and creeks, just like normal kids. Too bad he didn't keep things on that level.

One day, the older boy said, "I want to get a model airplane kit and put it together." That sounded like a fun idea. I'd always wanted to put together a plastic model. The other boy and I walked to the local supermarket, where they sold airplane kits.

The boy found an appropriate model kit and the right type of glue. He also grabbed a few bags of pistachio nuts to eat on the way home. That was normal stuff, right? Wrong! Instead of going through the checkout line, the kid walked out the side door of the store. He didn't pay for the nuts, glue, or model kit.

I was flabbergasted. I had never seen anybody shoplift. I had no idea that people did such things.

The other boy was *stoked*, elated. He excitedly told me how he had accomplished the deed. "Timing is everything," he said. "Don't spend too much time loitering inside the store. Folks might get suspicious. Wait until all the clerks are busy, away from the doors. Then you casually walk out."

I was horrified. That little creep was a well-versed shoplifter. Worse yet, he was trying to induct me into his "profession." He was fishing in a rain barrel with *that* sentiment. I didn't get a thrill from his larcenous act. I was revolted. I knew that there were honest ways to obtain money if you applied yourself.

People like the twisted boy have good reason to recruit others. When they do bad things alone, they stand out. They are unique. But when they catch other people doing the same thing, they think, *See, everybody else is just like me. That makes it all right for me to do bad things.*

I now see that the shoplifting incident was the end of my friendship with the other boy. It creeped me out. I tried to tell Frank and Lita that I didn't want to go to his house. They brushed off my objections as being signs of homesickness. Frank said, "Grow up. Ya can't stay home all the time." Frank and Lita found more and more opportunities to dump me off with the other kid and his family.

Look at it from Frank and Lita's perspective. They'd found a perfect way to assuage any guilt they felt about leaving me alone most of the time. My visits with the other boy offered them free babysitting. They could go to Reno more often and have parties that lasted days. It was a win-win situation for them.

Their convoluted logic was pure horseshit, of course. By that time, I had learned the great lesson of my childhood: I was usually better off when I was alone. The progression of time and the other boy's deeds revealed the truth of *that*.

One night, the other boy took me down into the family's basement. There was a lot of old furniture and junk in that dark space. We sat down on a musty old couch off to one side of the basement. Without preamble, the other boy began to molest me. I managed to fight him off before much damage was done.

I don't remember how I finally convinced Frank and Lita that I didn't want any return visits to the twisted boy's house. Maybe they took a closer look at the house and its occupants and saw that it was not a good place for me to be. My visits to the hell house were terminated.

Years later, I heard vague rumors that the twisted boy had committed an unspeakable act. No one would say what it was, but I suspect that it involved sex. I feel sorry for the person or persons on whom he perpetrated his actions. Most of all, I am glad that I got away from him when I did. He was the first adolescent sexual monster I met. I would meet another one a couple of years later.

CHAPTER 57

A Hamburger for Tommy

LITA LOVED TO VISIT PEOPLE who were laid up in the hospital. It was one of her favorite activities. Her grandmother Mary Stewart provided ample opportunities for visiting. Mary spent the last few years of her life in a Hayward, California, hospital. When Lita wasn't working the night shift, she visited Mary every Wednesday afternoon.

On visiting days, I rushed home from school. Lita preferred to leave as early as possible to avoid rush-hour traffic. The distance between our San Jose duplex and Hayward was less than forty miles, but the freeways we take for granted today were not yet in existence. Lita drove all the way on two-lane roads. It sometimes took two hours to get to Hayward.

The hospital that was caring for Mary Stewart didn't allow children to visit, so I had to sit in the car while Lita visited. Lita always gave me the same speech before she went inside: "Don't you leave this car for *any* reason. Don't even open the fuckin' door. Don't you try to slip off on me, either. I'll be watching you." Lita mimicked Frank's intonation when she delivered that last threat. Her angry glare that told me she wasn't playing.

I sat alone in Lita's car for two or three hours on visiting days. It was boring stuff for an energetic young boy, especially before I learned to read. Lita made it worse because she never brought anything to entertain me.

Year after year, summer, winter, spring, and fall, I sat in a car while Lita visited her grandmother. I can't recall any of the individual visits. They all looked the same. I stared at the sky, adjacent cars, and the trees that ringed the parking lot.

I made an intense study of the fabric that covered the seats of Lita's 1948 Plymouth. Almost sixty years have passed since those long-ago days, but I can vividly recall many details of the car seat. I followed the seams in the fabric like they were highways. At their ends, I found adventure. The old seat was worn. The stiches in the seams were broken and stood erect. My bored imagination made them into soldiers standing in lined array. My active brain made battles with adjacent seams of stitch-soldiers.

In due course, Lita came out of the hospital. I had been sitting in the car for at least four hours. I knew that I would be stuck to the seat for the long ride home.

I came to dread our Wednesday visits. I knew that I wouldn't get out of the car for at least five hours. No bathroom breaks, no chance to stretch my tired legs. I sat there like a perfect little soldier.

The time and boredom factors of our Wednesday trips were onerous to me, but they couldn't compete with the main drawback: hunger. I knew that I wouldn't get anything to eat while we were gone. By about six in the evening, I was very hungry. Who knows what kind of meager lunch I might or might not have eaten at noon.

A caring mother would have offered some sort of a snack to tide me over the hours. Not Lita. Frank and Lita didn't believe in afternoon snacks; they ruined the appetite for dinner. Besides, Frank and Lita didn't have between-meal snacks when they were young. Why should I?

I didn't have to tell Lita that I was hungry. That was a given. Sometimes she promised to buy me a hamburger "later on." That hope would keep me going for a little while, but sooner or later, I would tell Lita I was hungry. The result of that little dance was predictable in its outcome. Lita generally allowed me the grace of saying that I was hungry one or two times before she *really* unloaded on me. She used my whining complaints as a springboard to vent her frustration. Lita yelled at me because she couldn't change the circumstances of her life.

It didn't take long for me to figure out how this visiting thing was going to play out. I was going to be hungry on Wednesday night, no matter what. I learned to keep my mouth shut. That wasn't as tough as it might appear. I was an old hand at bearing my hunger in silence. It was better than the alternative. If I pissed Lita off, I would still be hungry, but she would yell at me for half an hour. Lita taught me that it was best to take my hunger straight, without a psychological pummeling on the side.

Lita had four different sets of relatives who lived between Hayward and San Jose. She sometimes dropped by all their houses during our Wednesday trips. Lita must have had some important things that she wanted to say to them, because she was violating the leave-before-dinner rule of old-time visiting. Our relatives didn't seem to mind that violation; some of them happily tore into dinner while we stood and watched.

Some of you might find that a little hard to believe. You couldn't conceive of eating your dinner while hungry relatives stood by, unfed. You folks never met Lita's uncle Jack. That guy was famous for his behavior at restaurants. Jack would take his family into a restaurant and order one meal. He would then eat the meal while his family sat and watched. They ate *nothing*. What a guy.

Lita's uncle Clarence wasn't that way. He always offered us dinner. That evoked a familiar and well-practiced response from Lita. She would get an embarrassed look on her face and say, "Oh, no, we couldn't do that. We were just on our way out to get a bite to eat, weren't we, Tommy?" As Lita spoke, she flashed me a look of veiled malevolence. Her eyes were saying, "You'd better not disagree with me, you little bastard." I know that's exactly what she meant. We rehearsed that little scene before we walked into someone's house. Just for the record, she invariably used the word "bastard" during our rehearsal.

Lita and I made our Wednesday trips for years. In all that time, she bought the promised hamburger just once. Because it was a singular occurrence, I can vividly recall the details. We visited Lita's grandmother in Hayward and then stopped at the homes of two of her uncles. Both families were sitting down to dinner when we arrived. I watched two sets of hungry relatives eat their dinners. I didn't get a bite. As usual, Lita provided me with a stern warning beforehand: "Tell them you're not hungry." I accomplished that feat with the grace of an emotionless robot.

It was quite late when we left the second house. In a rare bit of compassion, Lita said that she was going buy me a hamburger. I was stoked. She was finally going to make good on one of her vague food promises. Woo-hoo!

It was 9:00 p.m. when we finally pulled into the restaurant parking lot. The manager was locking the front door. Lita rushed in and bought a hamburger. She didn't get French fries or a drink, just the plainest, least expensive burger they sold. Heck, what am I saying? Lita was only in the restaurant for a minute or two. She got a leftover burger. Lita got into the car and tossed a bag into my lap. I was starving. That burger smelled *wonderful.*

I quickly opened the bag, grabbed the burger, and pulled off the wrapper. Lita startled me out of my reverie, saying, "Why, you fuckin' little shit. You know that I don't eat in the car. What the fuck do you think you're doing? You wait until we get home to eat that fuckin' burger. You fine with that, or do I throw that son of a bitch out the window?" I quickly rewrapped the burger and stuffed it into the bag. I didn't want to lose my hard-won meal.

Lita drove on through the night. The hamburger sat on my lap, venting its savory aromas to my starved senses. A few minutes later, Lita announced that she was going to stop at her sister's house in Milpitas. She said, "Why not? We have to drive right by their street anyway." I was crushed. The inside of the car was permeated with the smell of my pitiful little hamburger. The aroma caused my empty stomach to churn and ache.

But I was worried about something else: the bag was still sitting on my lap. I could tell that the hamburger was getting cold. I knew that it would not taste good later. I begged Lita to allow me to eat the hamburger before it got cold. That *really* caused her to go off. She unleashed the lode of her accumulated wrath. She said, "There's only one fuckin' burger in this car, and it's yours. But you want to eat that cocksucker right in front of me. You are a greedy little shit. You only think about yourself." On and on she went.

I felt like an ungrateful wretch, but my hunger got the best of me. I abandoned the safe road of silence and asked if I could take the hamburger into my aunt's house and eat it there. This caused Lita to scoff in disbelief and then say, "We only brought one burger. Don't you know how rude it is to eat in front of other people?" As a capper, Lita threw in the punch line of the ages: "You're worse than your uncle Jack."

Great. I hadn't eaten a bite in about nine hours. I had been holding a delicious-smelling hamburger in my lap for half an hour. When I complained, she compared me with the greediest person in the family. Thanks, Lita.

I was a blubbering mess when we pulled up to my aunt's house. Lita was still ranting at me. I was hungry and tired. I knew that it was past my bedtime. I knew that I had go to school the next day. Most of all, I knew that I was a greedy, undeserving little wretch. I knew that I didn't deserve the little hamburger or anything else that Lita provided for me.

I was still crying as we walked up my aunt's front door. Lita warned me not to make a scene or she would tell Frank. That provided ample reason for me to stifle my tears.

When we got inside, I dipped into my trick bag of well-practiced lines and behaviors. I became Tommy, the perfect little robot. Neither Lita nor I made mention that I hadn't had dinner. I sure as hell didn't talk about the wonderful hamburger that was cooling in the car. Somewhere along the line, I fell asleep. Who knows how late it was by then.

I woke up as Lita half carried/half dragged me to the car. Lita was a short woman. I was a good-sized child. Lita's brother-in-law commented, "Ya need to stop babying that boy." My aunt clucked about Lita's wonderful skills as a mother. They turned and walked into the house.

That was wonderful theater. It was pure Lita. When she was with other people, she never missed the opportunity to play the doting mother. Through her actions, she was saying, "Look at the valiant Lita. She's attempting to carry a sleeping child who is her near equal in size." The woman should have been an actress. What am I saying? That woman *was* an actress.

Lita's demeanor changed when she heard my relatives go into the house. She became brusque with her speech and rough with her mannerisms. I was still half asleep when she yanked the car door open and attempted to shove me in. I finally woke up and lost my balance as I fell into the car. I grabbed for the seat to regain my balance, and the bag that contained my hamburger fell out. The bag opened and the hamburger rolled under our feet. I yelled out a warning to Lita, but she mistook my impassioned pleas for caution as defiance.

Lita screamed, "Get your fuckin' ass in the car." She shoved me inside with renewed vigor. I reacted with horror when Lita stepped on my hamburger. Her foot skidded on the greasy paper. The hamburger smeared across the pavement. This caused Lita to slip and fall against the car. It knocked her breath away. Lita's brain shed its last bit of rational thought. She went off into a full-blown Lita rant. She screamed, "Look at what you did! You ruined your hamburger! It's all your fault! Look how you wasted the food I bought for you! Look at how you take care of the things I buy for you!"

Lita's anger renewed her energy. She finally managed to push me all the way into the car. Lita slammed the door and walked around to the driver's side.

Hunger overrode my cowed sensibilities. I thought about the hamburger that was lying on the ground. I opened the door and jumped out of the car. I got down on my knees and used my fingernails to scrape the hamburger remains off the pavement. It was not an easy thing to do. The hamburger looked like a glob of Sheetrock paste smeared on a wall.

I knew I didn't have much time. Lita was screaming like a banshee. I used both hands to scrape the hamburger off the pavement as quickly as I could. As soon as I managed to pry a little chunk loose, I shoved it into my mouth. It was full of dirt, motor oil, pebbles, and God knows what. I didn't mind; no high-end meal had ever tasted any better to me than the first bite of that cold, gritty burger. To my starving brain, it was delicious.

By this point, Lita had lost her mind. She was in full dudgeon, madly revving the old Plymouth's engine. In between bursts of engine noise, she screamed, "Quit fuckin' around and get in the car." When that failed to get my attention, Lita pulled out her ultimate wild card: "I'm going to leave you here."

That last comment snapped me out of my food-driven frenzy. I was afraid that Lita would drive off without me. In my mind, I had abundant cause to fear her words. Frank and Lita had spent the last few years saying, "I'm going to get rid of you." That was their ultimate threat. It was a good one. I was terrified of being kicked out of my family. That prospect evoked more horror than all the beatings, starvation, and mind fucks they imposed upon me.

I had never seen Lita this angry. I remember thinking, *she is finally going to leave me behind and kick me out of her life.* I was scared shitless. I left most of the hamburger on the ground and scrambled back into the car.

Lita was now in her element. She had a captive audience. Lita felt limitless rage about the circumstances of her life, and she spewed it forth on me. From a physiological perspective, that was a beneficial thing to do. Lita had been up for better than eighteen hours. She had worked hard and driven halfway around the San Francisco Bay. She had another thirty minutes of driving before she saw her own front door. Yelling at me gave her an adrenaline surge, the boost she needed to get home. Tommy Liggett, the eight-year-old amphetamine capsule.

Some people might believe that the small portion of the hamburger I ate was made of unpalatable stuff. Others might think that I was disappointed to leave much of my hamburger lying in the street. Not me. My feelings were the same as when Frank and Lita had crammed the bananas down my throat. I was pummeled but sated. Despite all that Lita could do to the contrary, I got some food into my stomach. It was a little gritty from being smeared into the asphalt, but it was food. Once it was in my stomach, neither Frank, Lita, or the birds in the trees could take that away from me.

Somewhere on that long road home, I drifted off into a deep, blissful sleep. Lita's endless rant lost its power over me. For the moment, anyway.

CHAPTER 58

One-Eyed Monster

WHEN I WAS EIGHT, LITA began to realize I was bored. She told people she wanted me to have something to do when I was alone. That was a significant statement on her part. It was the one time in her life she acknowledged I spent a criminally huge amount of time alone.

A normal, caring mother would have found ways to ensure that I received adequate care and companionship. Not Lita. Babysitters were out of the question; they cost money. You might expect someone in Lita's position to ask relatives for childcare assistance, but Frank and Lita didn't want to do that. They weren't willing to expend that much effort. They said, "I'm not going to ferry a goddamned kid around."

The transportation issue provided a ready excuse for Frank and Lita to leave me alone. Their true intentions were evil. Frank and Lita didn't want anybody outside of our little trio to ascertain the true nature of our lifestyle. No one knew that Frank partied several nights a week. No one knew I spent consecutive days and nights alone.

Frank and Lita isolated me so that others would ask fewer questions. They kept me in solitary confinement to enable their lifestyle.

Lita built my jail from the bedrock stones of her indifference. She didn't do anything beyond the bare minimum for me. Lita was not engaged in my school or the local community. She had no idea who was in my class, and she didn't know any of my classmates' mothers. If you used the term "playdate" with Lita, she would have thought you were making a pass. (And she might have said yes.)

I received numerous offers to join the Cub Scouts. Lita wouldn't allow that. She said, "I'm barely makin' it. I don't have money for no fuckin' Cub Scout uniforms." That was bullshit. Cub Scouts grow out of their uniforms. Cast-off uniforms were free for the taking. Lita's problem with the Cub Scouts came from another direction: mothers were expected to help with meetings and so forth. There was no way Lita was going to commit to a regular activity that tied up her free time. That was when she cooked, cleaned house, shopped, visited relatives, and partied.

Frank cast the vetoing ballot on the Cub Scout resolution. He thought their uniforms were sissified. Frank said Cub Scouts were "too cute. Boys ain't supposed to be cute." Anytime he saw Cub Scouts, he said, "They look like a bunch of titty babies a-prissin' around in their little faggot uniforms."

I knew that I wasn't going to find appropriate human companionship, so I tried another tactic. I told Lita I wanted a cat. I loved cats. Anytime I got around cats, I wanted to hold and pet them. Lita agreed to it. She liked cats too.

Lita somehow managed to score a major kitten. It was a purebred seal-point Siamese. They were rare and expensive things in those days. God knows what Lita had to do to get the thing.

Lita named the kitten Ti Wah. I'm not quite sure how she came up with that. Maybe it was the name of a favored restaurant. I didn't care what name Lita gave my kitty. I was enraptured. I played with Tai Wah for hours at a time.

Sadly, I didn't realize that my roughhouse play was amplifying the kitten's aggressive tendencies. In just a couple of weeks, the little animal got downright mean. One of my uncles made the mistake of teasing my kitten, and it viciously attacked him. His arm was deeply lacerated in several places. I was horrified when I saw the blood flowing from the gashes in his arm. When I came home from school the next day, Ti Wah the kitten was nowhere to be found.

Lita told me that Frank had run over the kitten. That was a believable story. Remember, I watched Frank run over my first kitten.

Devastated by the loss of Ti Wah, I retreated inside of myself. I drew morbid drawings. One depicted Ti Wah in the path of Frank's Dodge sedan. Others depicted Gothic tombs with inscriptions of Ti Wah's birth and death dates.

Tom Liggett with Ti Wah the kitten. This cat was my only real friend. I adored him above all things. Tenth Street, San Jose, California. August 1959.

It was all a lie. Frank didn't run over my kitten. Years later, Lita told me that Frank put my kitten and a brick into a potato sack and dropped the sack into a creek. That's how cruel-assed rednecks dealt with unwanted cats in those days. Some undoubtedly still do.

My second attempt to get a cat in my life had failed as miserably as the first. Frank and Lita said that it was all my fault because I'd made the kitten so mean. That was a lesson I learned well. I never played rough with another cat.

I was alone once again. Lita came up a way to make my solitude easier to endure. She watched harried mothers plop their children in front of TV sets. Hyperactive little monsters instantly became somnambulant robots thanks

I was crushed when my kitten disappeared. I had no one to speak with about my problems, so I made drawings. Even then, I knew I was no artist. Still, I put my hopes, dreams, fantasies, and sorrows down on paper.

to television. Lita saw other parents use the new medium as an unpaid baby-sitter. Why not do that herself?

I wanted to have a television set in our duplex. I was just a normal eight-year-old boy. My classmates told me what they watched on TV. It sounded like exciting stuff. I wanted to be like the other kids. At that age, no book quite held the appeal of *The Three Stooges*.

Frank correctly believed that television was an instrument of sloth. This is especially true with children. But much of Frank's anti television viewpoint arose from a simple concept: when children are watching TV, they aren't working. Frank was jealous of any child who could be lazy and have fun. When he was a child, he wasn't allowed much leisure time. Why should anyone else?

But Frank also had a selfish reason why he didn't want television in our duplex: noise. He worked in construction, a very noisy job. When he got home, he wanted absolute quiet. The unspoken mitigating circumstances to that requirement were that when Frank was home, he was either hung over or wanting to get drunk somewhere else. He was taciturn and grumpy.

When Frank was forced to be at home, he sealed himself into a silent womb of books and newspapers. He demanded that our apartment be as silent as a sepulcher. This meant no radio, no kids running through the house, and no TV.

Since we always lived in tiny one-bedroom apartments, I spent a lot of time pretending I was invisible. There was nothing new in that.

Frank knew that a blaring television would destroy his fervently desired silence. He was firm in his assertion: "There ain't a-gonna be no goddamned TV in *my* house."

Most of the time, Lita gave Frank the last word. But she really disagreed with him on the television question. She wanted me to have something to do during the endless hours I spent alone. Lita spoke with friends and family members about getting a television for Tommy.

Frank saw Lita's talk as a defiant act. He was outraged she was continuing to press the issue. Frank governed his life with a core philosophy: "Everywhere a man goes, he is subject to another man's rules—except at home. A man's home is his castle. He is king. Nobody can tell a man what do once he walks through his own front door." Frank saw Lita's continual chatter about television as a threat to his role as king of our household.

Frank enlisted the aid of his uncle Arthur. This was a natural response; Frank developed most of his intellectual concepts under Arthur's tutelage. Arthur believed that children should *never* watch television. Any mention of that subject around Arthur would result in a stentorian recitation of its evils. Arthur said that the human body would change because of television. It would adapt. That preamble set up the great punch line to Arthur's anti-TV recitations: "People who watch television will grow one big ol' eye right in the middle of their foreheads." Frank added that line to his long list of preachy sayings. He used it on me about three thousand times.

But I have a surprise for you, folks: I agree with Arthur and Frank. No, not the one-big-eye part. The TV-is-bad part. Television *is* bad for lots of people, *especially* children. When children watch television (or use mobile devices), they are not doing something important. They are watching, not doing. They are not gardening, hiking, biking, or reading.

I didn't see it that way when I was nine. I knew that television would offer some relief from the relentless, boring grind of my life. I wanted to see moving images of happy people. I knew that they would bring a candle of humanity into my lonely place.

Lita and I were on the same wavelength. She wouldn't stop talking about getting a TV for Tommy. Frank wouldn't stop preaching about the evils of TV. They were intimately aware of each other's position on the issue. Neither possessed negotiating skills that went beyond pleading, pontification, and quick escalation into blind rage. The result was an endless roiling battle. It was fought in smaller skirmishes whenever they were together at home. When Lita and Frank could find no compromise in their arguments, they turned their anger on me.

It appeared as if financial considerations would doom my aspirations for a television set. TV was a new and expensive technology in 1958.

Lita worked every minute of overtime she could get. She used the money to keep a roof over our heads. Lita didn't have any money for a TV set. Frank resented the money he spent on normal household expenses. Lita had to fight him for every penny she received. There was no was way on God's green earth that Frank McMillan was going to take money out of his party fund to buy me a television set. Frank and Lita concluded that it would be financially impossible to buy a TV. They reached an impasse. The fighting stopped. Quiet times returned to our duplex.

I truly regret that Lita and Frank did not remain in a state mutual détente about television. It would have saved me a lot of future grief. But it didn't work out that way. A well-meaning outsider stepped in to break the truce. One of my uncles offered a free television set. Lita and I were ecstatic. She would gain absolution from the sin of solitude she visited upon me, and I would be able to watch *The Three Stooges*, just like the other boys.

Frank was *livid*. He knew that he had lost his months-long battle with Lita. Frank saw her agreement to take the television as her symbolically repudiating his role as lord and master of our home.

Beyond the psychological loss, there was a concrete fact: television would inexorably alter Frank's quiet little world. His weekend hangovers would be altered by a loud, disruptive device.

Frank didn't go down easy, even when he was defeated. The television was scheduled to arrive in two weeks. That gave Frank time to convince Lita she had made an error. Frank's "convincing" took an unusual form: he spent more time at the Rock Castle tavern. When he was home, he screamed at me or Lita. Screaming didn't take him very far with Lita; she could out escalate a Bengal tiger. That left me.

Lita sometimes worked until midnight, which meant Frank had me all to himself each night. That left plenty of time to pay me back for the problems I caused him. He had all the time in the world to scream at me, to slap, spank, and kick me. Best of all, Frank knew that I would stand rigidly at attention while he visited his depredations upon my soul, just like a recruit in an old-style marine boot camp.

Frank knew that he could batter me all he wanted and I wouldn't say anything. Who would believe me even if I did rat him out? Everybody liked Frank.

Frank knew he had an ace in the hole: he knew I had to keep coming back for more. I thought, *If I complain, Frank will hate me more. Where will I go when he kicks me out of the house?* That wasn't an imagined threat. Frank and Lita frequently told me that they were going to kick me out. They elaborated by telling me, "No one else will have you, because you are worthless." I was scared out of my wits.

When Frank's anger and drunkenness increased, I responded in usual fashion: I burrowed under the covers of my solitude. I cherished the time I spent alone. I dove into any book I could find. I dug deeper holes in the backyard dirt.

In due course, the much-promised/much-lamented television set arrived. It wasn't much of a TV, even by the primitive standards of the day. It was quite old and battered, and some of the control knobs were missing. It was the most beautiful machine I had ever seen.

But my moment of victory was quickly dashed by technological reality: our duplex didn't have an external antenna.

Frank was giddy when this threatened to torpedo my aspirations. He laughed and said, "There ain't no way I'm a-gonna buy no damned antenna to put on that roof." He chased that thought with a barb: "If the damned television don't work, then ya can't watch it, can ya?" He finished his rant with a thought for Lita: "I don't want you to buy no rabbit ears, neither. I don't want to look at the goddamned things in my house. Might poke someone in the eye."

Lita was ready for Frank's last-ditch, Hail Mary effort to prevent an operable television set from coming into our apartment. My uncle told her how to make a rudimentary antenna. Lita placed metal clothes hangers on the antenna terminals on the rear of the TV. I watched intently as she added, removed, shifted, and jostled the conglomeration of hangers.

Lita warned me about the hazards of touching coat-hanger antennas. Primitive television sets sometimes sent an electrical charge through their antenna terminals. They would shock hell out of you. Lita's warnings didn't faze me. I was willing to play with a do-it-yourself junior electric chair. Why? It would enable me to watch *The Three Stooges*.

When Lita began her quest to adjust the coat-hanger antenna, the television screen was a mass of static with no picture or sound. In due course, Lita coaxed a fuzzy image onto the TV screen. But the image was rolling up and down. It made you feel nauseous. My uncle instructed Lita to turn an adjustment knob. That made the image roll in the opposite direction. "Shit!" she said.

"Be quiet, Lita," my uncle said. "You'll get it right." She eventually managed to get a stable image on the screen. Lita turned up the volume. We had television in our living room!

Looking back now, all the argument, electric shocks, and fuss didn't deliver much of a tangible result. Our old TV could pick up three local stations with varying degrees of success. Frank didn't care. He upped the ante and hit me with a new one. He said, "It don't matter none if that goddamned TV gets three stations or a hundred and thirty-three. You ain't gonna be a watchin' *none* of 'em. That television will keep you from a-doin' your homework."

Most normal children would have heeded Frank's brutal threats and not have turned on the TV. But I knew that Frank would find some reason to beat me no matter what. What did I have to lose by watching television? Oh boy, Tommy. You had no idea what Frank McMillan was capable of, did you?

I didn't care about Frank's opinions. I spent most of my time in an empty, unheated duplex. Television returned human voices to my life. That old television set was my savior. It was like manna from heaven. *Nothing* that Frank did could equal the thrill and the companionship I got from watching TV.

I rushed home from school each day to watch television. It didn't take me very long to figure out when the best shows were on, although they didn't have to be the best shows. Good shows, bad shows, dance shows, reruns, and news—I watched them all.

Frank correctly predicted that TV would be bad for me. I became what would eventually be called a vidiot. After I watched TV for a few hours, my eyes burned and my brain felt numb. I felt wretched.

My TV-associated physical issues were obvious. But there was also a mental aspect: I felt guilty. I knew that Frank was right about TV. And I wanted to please him. I wanted to be his dutiful little soldier. I couldn't do that if I was regularly disobeying his orders.

I tried to find things to do around the house other than watching TV. My backyard kingdom occupied some of my free time. But that was not an option in winter, when the days were short.

Books continued to be my favorite pastime. But I burned through them much faster than they could be replaced. Even the nudie paintings in the encyclopedia lost their forbidden appeal. I was hopelessly bored. That left me an empty apartment and the television set. I watched the damned thing.

Frank was still bitterly opposed to having TV in his house. For the first time in her four-year relationship with Frank, Lita had defied Frank's authority, solely to please me. That put the blame squarely on my skinny little shoulders. Things got worse for me after the TV arrived. Much worse.

I am a forgiving person. Despite my experience to the contrary, I expect that other people will be like me and try to do the right thing. For that reason, it was easy for me to believe that our family's months-long war would end after the television set arrived. Silly me.

Whether it was turned on or off, the television set was the first thing that Frank saw when he walked through the front door and the last thing he saw when he left.

The television became a satanic icon, one more reason to brood and fester about the injustice of having someone like Tommy Liggett in his house. Frank's anger stayed at a low simmer all the time.

I learned it was the worst kind of folly to allow Frank to catch me watching TV. When that happened, he stepped into his own private pulpit. Frank preached, "Television is evil. It fills little boys' heads with junk. Boys who watch TV will end up with one big ol' eye right in the middle of their foreheads."

Frank should have paid Uncle Arthur royalties for the last quip. He used that sucker almost every day. Like many of the things Frank screamed at me, he always delivered that line the same way. It was like being in a theatrical troupe that performed just one play. I knew Frank's lines better than he did. I am quite thankful I never chose to become his understudy.

I learned to keep the television volume at a low setting. That allowed me to hear Frank's car when it pulled into the driveway and to make a mad dash across the room to turn off the television.

When Frank walked into the room, he saw the TV was off and I had a book in my lap. I could read Frank's expressions pretty well. I could tell he was surprised to discover that the TV was turned off. He was perplexed. He was disappointed.

Frank didn't remain that way for long. He instantly learned to be stealthier in his approach. We played a cat-and-mouse game.

I didn't know when Frank would return home. That put the element of surprise in his favor. Frank was an old-time hunter and trapper. He knew how to sneak up on his prey. He'd park down the street instead of in the driveway, sneak up to the duplex, and quietly unlock the front door. Then he'd slam the door open and catch me by surprise.

I was a young child who sitting alone in an apartment that was located in a terrible neighborhood. There was a good chance that I was hungry. Every time Frank slammed the door open, I almost suffered a heart attack.

It was like the scene in *The Shining* when Jack Nicholson burst through the door and uttered his famous "Here's Johnny" line. But Frank McMillan's mad entrances were much more frightening than any movie. You can walk away from a movie. I couldn't turn off Frank's entrances. They were repeated month after month, year after year.

Frank's drill instructor training made him see the value of taking recruits by surprise. It put them off balance. That tactic worked on me. After the front door slammed open, my consciousness was focused on Frank. At that moment, he *owned* me.

The Christian Bible explains what it will be like for people to stand in front of God after they die. As per that dogma, people will be judged. I don't have to journey to the afterlife to know how that feels. I already know. Every time Frank burst through the front door, I felt naked beneath his judgment.

Frank's grand entrance was just the overture. He quickly got to the main act. It had a slow introduction. Frank stood silently in the doorway. But he was too drunk to stand still. He gently swayed from side to side, smirking, savoring the moment. Frank loved my terrified expression.

Frank milked all he could from his dramatic entrance and then settled into one of his commonly used scripts. Sometimes he would get right into the "one big ol' eye" speech. That one worked best when he caught me watching TV.

But he quickly grew tired of *that* routine. Frank discovered that he derived the most enjoyment when he came home and found the TV turned off. This gave him the opportunity to make the most of his dramatic talent.

Frank remained standing in the open doorway for a few more seconds. He didn't say a word. That was a carefully crafted move. It increased my terror. It also gave him a final moment to savor the drama of his grand entrance.

Frank would finally begin to speak. He used a springtime-soft drawl to ask me an ice-hard question: "Boy, you ain't been a-watchin' that TV, have you?" Frank allowed that query to hang in the silent room for a few seconds. It was a rhetorical question. Frank had built my prison. He knew that there was nothing for me to do except watch TV.

What Frank did next was brilliant. It came from the script he'd begun to write when he came into my life. Those old television sets produced a lot of heat. They stayed warm for hours after they were turned off. The touch of a finger would reveal if they had been operated recently. We both knew that the TV was warm. Frank's brand of perverse cruelty made the confirmation of that fact part of the fun.

It was about eight feet from the front door to the television set. Frank made that small journey a grand promenade. He used exaggerated, cartoonlike movements. Frank mimicked the long, funky steps Basil Rathbone used when he played Sherlock Holmes. Frank paused when he got to the television set and slowly turned to face me. We both knew what came next. He was loving the play. The audience was scared shitless. I had already seen this fucking movie too many times. I knew it had a bad ending.

Kenneth Kirkley goofing off in the foreground. The television from hell is in the background. I'm sorry that device was brought to our duplex. It offered Frank McMillan an excuse to escalate his abuse. Front room, 123 North Tenth Street, San Jose, California. December 24, 1959.

Frank slowly reached his hand out toward the TV. He then slapped his palm on the top of the television set. Even if I had turned it off an hour before, it would still be warm. It took Frank a fraction of a second to detect the television set had been operated recently. That's all the time he needed to change his demeanor. Up to this point, he'd acted like a languorous, swaying drunk. But as soon as his hand came in contact with the television set, he exploded with anger. The quiet words upon his entrance were replaced with invective and threats.

Sometimes Frank just yelled at me. That was plenty when you consider the power of his drill instructor voice. Frank delivered his invective in the guise of a lesson. In his mind, that gave credibility to his abuse. He was like an Old Testament prophet who was calling down heavenly wrath on an accursed group. Frank screamed out sayings old and new, some of his own and some he'd heard from others. He used the same phrases but in different succession. He quoted the Bible and plagiarized his uncle Arthur.

What Frank's words and demeanor said to me was frightening. But they weren't the main thrust of the thing. Frank was a marine-trained athlete who was in the physical prime of his life. There wasn't an ounce of fat on his lean, work-hardened, five-foot-ten frame. As seen through the eyes of a skinny eight-year-old boy, Frank McMillan was a scary son of a bitch.

Most nights, Frank didn't end his performance just with screaming. He didn't believe that I was getting the point. Sterner measures were required to drive his lesson home. Frank went from the television set to where I was standing in about three steps. It happened so quickly, I didn't have time to prepare. Frank grabbed me by my shirt, yanked me up, and spun me around so that my back was to him. The tips of my shoes were barely touching the floor. He kicked my ass with his right foot. It took considerable effort for Frank to hold me off the floor with his outstretched arm, so each time he kicked my ass, my feet contacted the floor. When that happened, I tried to run away, but Frank yanked me back. The force of the blows spun me around to the left. The combination of my running and his kicking whirled us around the room in tight circles. The faster I ran, the faster he lashed out with his foot.

Someone who viewed that little scene in a movie might think that we made for a comical sight. We looked like a couple of vaudeville comics doing a routine. But there was nothing funny about those episodes from my perspective. Each time they occurred, I thought that the last blow to my ass would be the one that kicked me out of the house.

Frank eventually became winded from the effort of kicking me around the room. His screaming diminished into a quieter form of rage. He always ended his performances with another round of preaching. Frank ran through his repertoire of invective one more time. Most of this magnum opus pertained to the evils of TV and the sloth of Tommy. He inevitably ended those homilies with the reminder that I was the basest form of sinner and that I was going to burn in hell. Thanks for the benediction, Frank.

The script of our sick little charade demanded one final scene before the curtain dropped. Our shared history dictated that I must render my abject submission unto Frank. I did it in spades. I always told him that he was right, that I knew that I was evil. I always begged him to give me another chance. I would do better next time. Most of all, I pleaded with Frank not to kick me out of the house.

The sick combination of Frank's drunken exhaustion and my abject pleading generally made him suspend his cruel behavior for the evening. In any case, Frank had gotten his kicks. Until the next time. He'd say brusquely, "Go to bed." The play was over for the night.

CHAPTER 59

Walking the Floor Over You

"Walking the Floor Over You" is the title of a song
that was released by Ernest Tubb in 1941. Generally
regarded as being the first honky-tonk song, it was the
theme music that accompanied legions of cowboys and
roustabouts through laborious days and drunken nights.

—TOM LIGGETT'S PERSONAL GLOSSARY OF TERMS

I PURPOSELY ENDED THE LAST chapter with a paragraph that included the
word "bed." Where I was sleeping during this period is pertinent to our
story.

Up to this point in their relationship, Frank and Lita rented furnished
apartments. But the Tenth Street duplex was unfurnished. This was an all-
new concept for them. They had to buy a few pieces of furniture. Perhaps
they saw that act as symbolic: Frank and Lita were becoming an established
couple. They were moving up.

Frank and Lita bought a double bed for themselves and then announced
that they were going to buy a couch "for Tommy to sleep on." They made
scant mention of the truth, which was that they needed a couch to entertain
their many guests. This was another case wherein they were living as if I
weren't around. They invoked my name to garner the sympathy vote from
their extended families. I didn't see it that way, though. I was ecstatic. I

looked forward to sleeping on something that didn't smell like fifty years of farts and ass sweat.

Frank and Lita bought our new couch at a cut-rate Mexican furniture store over on San Jose's East Side. That long-gone company specialized in selling the least expensive kind of furniture. It was also the lowest quality kind of furniture. And they sold their goods on credit. From what I could see, they were selling credit more than furniture. That was an important selling point for Frank and Lita. They were flat broke. Most of our family's expendable income went into whiskey, parties, and women.

The cut-rate furniture store had a wide selection of credit options but a narrower selection of furniture. Frank and Lita were quite amused that the selection of couches was so slim. Yeah, Frank and Lita, there were *plenty* of humorous aspects about that purchase, *especially* the couch. It was incandescent turquoise. That was the shade du jour among Mexican couch buyers in 1958.

Our new couch was upholstered with what the furniture store claimed to be Naugahyde. Many of my younger readers may have never heard of that product. It was a first-generation synthetic upholstery material marketed as a leather substitute. You could spill Kool-Aid, chocolate milk, or a whole spaghetti dinner on its surface, and a warm moist cloth and patience would remove the mess without a trace. That was one heck of a selling point. Remember, they were selling the stuff to the post–World War II crowd, who needed indestructible furniture for their hordes of children to occupy while they were watching TV.

I had a lot of experience with couches. My eight-year-old eye saw the truth of the matter: Naugahyde was invented as an alternative to the scratchy, stinky, woven sofa coverings I knew so well. You might well think that it would be an improvement over the rental couches of my experience. Sadly, that was not the case.

Fancy names aside, the couch that Frank and Lita bought was covered with slick plastic. The same characteristics that made it impervious to spilled drinks also prevented it from breathing. When someone sat down on that couch, their butt would sweat inside of their clothes. A bare arm placed on the sofa's sides would *really* sweat. It was like being wrapped in a plastic sandwich bag.

That was the tolerable part. Frank and Lita's new couch smelled like a chemical factory. It released vast quantities of polyvinyl chloride, the chemical that produces the vaunted "new-car smell." The odor that emenated from our new couch was more like "dead-cat smell." Our whole apartment reeked. I suspect the cut-rate furniture store was selling faux Naugahyde instead of the real thing. I never saw another couch that felt or smelled like ours.

I tried sleeping on that terrible couch just once. I quickly abandoned *that* course. The plastic smell made me sick to my stomach. It remained on my skin and clothing until the next wash.

I refused to sleep on our new couch. In uncharacteristic fashion, Frank and Lita deferred to my wishes. It probably made them woozy to sit on the thing. Lita didn't care where I slept, as long as it was away from her. Frank liked the Spartan concept of the deal: young boys should sleep on hard ground rather than cushy beds.

There was a comforting routine involved in making my floor bed. I folded a woolen army blanket in half and put it on the floor. Army blankets made a good bottom pad because they were dark and didn't show floor dirt. I placed one of my great-grandmother's quilts on top of the army blanket, a bedsheet over that, and a woolen navy blanket on top. If it was very cold, I added another blanket to the pile. That might sound like a primitive bed, but it was cozy and warm. The wool navy blanket was scratchy where it touched my bare skin, though. A top sheet or pajamas would have made the experience more tolerable, but Frank wouldn't allow them. He thought that pajamas were for titty babies. Men went to bed naked or in their white cotton underwear.

It didn't matter what I thought anyway. Frank was quite clear: he believed that the wool navy blanket would toughen my skin. I knew better than to press *that* argument. Frank and Lita advised me that I had more blankets than they did when they were children. That was their ultimate trump card. They treated me like shit, gave me substandard things, and made me feel guilty when I complained. That was brainwashing in its purest form.

The sleeping pallet is crucial to our story. It is a key prop in the sick play Frank and Lita staged at our Tenth Street duplex.

Not long after we installed the television set, I realized that I couldn't overcome Frank's overwhelming physical advantage. I did what the vanquished always do when they are faced with an overwhelming opposing force: I retreated. But there was no place for me to go other than my sleeping pallet on the floor. I viewed my pallet as a haven. I was following the old sailors' rule of any port in a storm. I believed that if I was in bed before Frank got home, he would leave me alone. What I didn't understand was that Frank enjoyed his nightly ministrations. He was venting his frustrations on me. Frank was using me as a pint-sized punching bag.

I couldn't rationalize Frank's logic at that point in my life. I was too young. But I knew I was sick of the beatings. I also believed that I was being disloyal to Frank by watching TV. That added more guilt to my pile. I quietly submitted to Frank's wishes and stopped watching TV. I thought that would end his horrific attacks. Oh boy, was I wrong about *that*.

Frank didn't see my actions for what they were: a sincere change of heart. Instead he saw them as a change in tactics. When I changed my behavior, Frank shifted his tactics. He added some new things to his repertoire of abuse.

When Frank discovered that I was in bed when he came home, he became very quiet. He entered softly so he wouldn't wake me. Then he turned on the room's big overhead lamp. The blinding light awakened me. As soon as the light went on, Frank began screaming. In about three seconds, I progressed from sound sleep to terrorized wakefulness. I eventually learned that was another military training technique: turn on the lights, startle 'em out of a deep sleep, and start yelling.

You never heard anyone who could scream like Frank. The walls vibrated with his anger. When Frank was certain that I was fully awake and scared out of my wits, he got into the next part of the program. He reached into his repertoire for material. It seldom varied. His midnight rants centered on my television-viewing habits. At this point in our sick little game, it didn't matter if I had watched TV that night. Frank stopped checking to see if the TV was hot. He automatically assumed that it was and proceeded from there. He was wound up. If I truthfully denied watching TV, he would accuse me of lying and become even angrier.

Our initial post television encounters had occurred when I was standing in front of Frank. I changed things up by being in bed when he came home. This caused Frank to add an all-new trick to his repertoire, one that I experienced in one form or another for the next twelve years.

Frank would reach down into my pallet and grab me by the front of my T-shirt. He'd snatch me up like a rag doll, swing me around to his left, and slam my body into the wall. It knocked the breath out of me. I was stunned. Then he'd hold me against the wall and lean toward me, his face just a couple of inches from mine. His breath smelled like rotten whiskey.

If I live to be 129 years old, I will never forget the words that Frank screamed at me. He said, "What are you doin' a-lyin' up there in the bed? Why ain't you out there a-helpin' make some money for the house?" Frank didn't wait for a response. He went into an all-purpose rant. He yelled about my sloth and generally evil nature. He finished with the simple declaration that all his problems arose because I was living in his house.

Frank punctuated these statements at regular intervals by slamming me into the wall. Every slam knocked the breath from my lungs. This wasn't like the semi comic ass-kicking I had been receiving for the previous four years. This was different. This was personal. I thought that Frank was finally going to kill me.

Thankfully, the mechanics of human biology stopped him before he got that far. The surge of adrenaline that had carried Frank this far was eventually exhausted. He slammed me against the wall with less force. His voice lost its bull-like intensity and became something that was almost human in nature.

This gave me the time to recover my breath and my senses. I went into my normal routine. I told Frank that everything he said was true. My goal at those times was to convince him of the validity of his words and the righteousness of his cause. It was easy for me to say those things. I didn't have to pretend. I believed that I was every terrible thing Frank mentioned.

It was what Frank wanted to hear. My pleas never failed to find a hidden kernel of humanity within the depths of his rage. After I'd debased myself enough, Frank got quiet. He looked from side to side and threw me on the floor. He shouted at me one more time for good measure, "This place is a mess. Clean it up. Go to bed."

I dutifully sorted through my scattered bedclothes and remade my pallet. I knew that it had to look neat for Frank. Or else. Then I turned off the light and got into bed.

Sleep generally eluded me on the nights when Frank really beat me up. On one level, I was afraid that Frank would come back into the room for another go-round of fun. But the real cause for my sleeplessness was far more sinister. Despite Frank's continuing efforts to the contrary, I still believed in the Christian God. Let's take that a step further: Frank was just one of many people who regularly told me I was going to hell. Frank and Lita told me thousands of times that that I was a lazy, greedy, evil, ne'er-do-well.

The combination of those two concepts left no doubt in my mind about possible outcomes. I was beyond redemption. I was going to hell. Not after I died, but *now*. I believed that Satan would crash through the floorboards and drag me down to hell. I sometimes got so worked up, I believed that Satan was on his way; he would be here in a few minutes! That scared me out of my wits. My heart was racing. I thought it would explode.

I knew I was doomed, but I spent hours in prayer trying to lessen the damage. I repeated the same prayerful missives over and again. I still remember some of those frantic-little-boy prayers. How pathetic they seem to me now. I whispered, "God, I know that I am a slothful little boy. Please forgive me for watching TV. I know that I am evil. Please forgive me." My prayers were always of like kind. They never contained any hope that I would receive redemption. It was all cut-and-dried stuff: come what may, I was going to hell. Period. Done deal. I recited those prayers over and again. Then I began to ask forgiveness for praying in "vain repetition." The murmur of my prayers eventually lulled me into restless sleep. What a nightmare.

I was in a real pickle. I didn't know what to do. Frank hammered me when I watched TV. He also hammered me when I didn't. Barring other solutions, I continued with my main plan: I didn't watch TV, and I made sure that I was in bed before Frank got home.

That was just what Frank wanted from me. He used my early-to-bed escape routine to his advantage and figured out how to make his nighttime abuse even more frightening. Frank didn't turn on the light when he entered the duplex but crept into the room and silently yanked me out of the bed while I was still asleep, then slammed me against the wall. I was asleep until my back and head hit the hard surface. It was pitch dark in the room. That changed my sense of perception. It was like being in a sensory-deprivation chamber. My world was populated by pain, the smell of rotten alcohol, and Frank's screamed invective. During those episodes, Frank became my entire existence. He owned me.

How did I survive, folks? I honestly don't know. Frank persisted with his nighttime attacks. Not every night, but frequently enough to keep me on guard. When I went to bed, I never knew if Frank would pick this night to visit me or not.

When I was about eight, I began to walk in my sleep. Frank and Lita didn't immediately identify the true nature of my nightly perambulations. They thought I was just an unruly child who liked to wander around the house in the dark. Frank attempted to correct my behavior through liberal applications of his standard remedy—a hard spanking. That method didn't work. My sleepwalking grew worse. It was evident that something was going on.

One night, Frank attempted to awaken me with a series of slaps to the face. He was screaming. The waking process seemed to take a long time. I felt quite groggy. Perhaps something inside of me didn't want to wake up. Maybe the protective part of my subconscious thought things would go better if I remained asleep. Frank wasn't having any of that. He began to shake my shoulders. That made my neck wobble around. I awoke into a dazed stupor.

I discovered I was sitting on the toilet. I had no idea how I'd arrived at that destination. I could only access about 5 percent of my thought processes because I was still mostly asleep. Frank slapped me again to get my attention and screamed, "Look at that!" He pointed at a huge semiliquid pile of shit on the floor next to the toilet. Frank screamed again, "Why did you shit on the floor?"

I was too asleep to respond to Frank's query. I opened my mouth, but I was too groggy to speak. Beyond that, I had no idea from whence the shit had come.

Frank took my failure to respond as a disrespectful act; he *really* slapped me. That one almost knocked my head off. It roused me a little more, but I still wasn't fully awake. Frank yanked me off the toilet and shoved me to my knees. He handed me a folded terry washcloth and said, "Clean up this mess!"

I placed the dry washcloth in the middle of the shit flow. The cloth floated like a crouton in soup. I wiped the cloth around the floor, but that served only to smear the shit into a wider circle.

Frank became enraged. He grabbed the back of my T-shirt, yanked me off the floor, spun me around, and looked me in the face. Frank said, "I'm a-gonna tell your uncle Larry what you did! I'm a-gonna tell him what a titty baby you are!"

I was sufficiently awakened to feel the sting of that remark. I didn't want Larry to find out that I was a titty baby. I really loved Frank's brother. I began to cry. That set Frank off again. He spun me around and kicked me back to my sleeping pallet, yelling at me all the way.

The next morning, Frank asked me why I'd shit on the floor. I didn't have an answer, and I braced myself for the worst. I figured the beating I'd received the night before was just a warmup. But Frank didn't hit me. He turned to Lita and said, "This boy is walking in his sleep."

Most mothers would respond to that revelation with kindness and understanding. Not Lita. She fixed her mouth into a sneer, looked down her nose at me, and said, "MT walked in *his* sleep. You must a gotten that from *his* side. None of *our* people do that." That was all she had to say. Lita deflected any blame that threatened to expose the flaws in her parenting.

Lita was partially correct in her assertion. Sleepwalking *is* a heritable trait. But stress can also trigger the behavior. Frank and Lita refused to consider the stressors in my life that were increasing the frequency and magnitude of the problem.

Frank's sentiments about my sleepwalking weren't as benign as Lita's. He was usually sleeping off a drunk and needed to get up early for work. He didn't appreciate being awakened by anything less than a house fire. Frank was a light sleeper; he could hear me wandering around at night. He would yell at me and swat me on the butt until I staggered back to my sleeping pallet. That was it for the night.

I began to walk in my sleep when Frank and Lita escalated their abusive behavior. It was the third time they had done such a thing. Each of those periods of escalation introduced a new suite of abusive practices for me to endure. Even when other things subsequently improved for me, the new abuses remained as main fixtures in my life.

CHAPTER 60

Rhesus Monkey

LITA WAS OBLIVIOUS TO THE problems I was having with Frank. Bigger issues occupied her time. The expense of Frank's semi nightly parties had brought the family finances to an all-time low. There was not enough money for food, rent, or other household necessities. Lita worked more and more hours to keep a roof over our heads. The extra hours were in the evening, and her nightly absences gave Frank a free hand to do as he pleased.

No one in our extended family grasped what was going on with Frank, Lita, and me. That ignorance was not accidental. It was part of the misinformation campaign engineered by Frank and Lita. It distracted onlookers and prevented them from seeing what was really happening. Everywhere they went, Lita and Frank threw up individually crafted smokescreens of propaganda. Truth be told, Frank and Lita lied to themselves as much as they did the world. The biggest lies are the ones we tell ourselves.

Some of my readers might wonder about the nuts and bolts of such a thing. How did Frank and Lita live one way and convince bystanders that they were living another? It was quite simple. Frank and Lita wrote scripts for themselves and me. The members of our trio rehearsed their parts. We said the right thing at the right time. Frank and Lita rewrote the story line. They directed it away from the real events. In the false script, Lita became the lamb who ritually sacrificed herself each night to support me. Frank was the stand-up guy who'd stepped into our lives to raise someone else's unwanted semi bastard child.

Those two could have made propaganda films for the former Soviet Union. My mind's eye can see how those movies would be framed. The camera zooms in on Frank and Lita as they stand heroically on a hillcrest. The sun shines on their perky faces. They wear beatific smiles and red neckties. Behind them, flags snap in the freshening breeze. The background music swells to a crescendo and fades. The narrator provides a rousing voice-over: "Here are the heroes of the People's Republic of Sacrificing All for Tommy." The camera lingers for a moment on the milk-fed faces of the happy couple.

But the scene is not over. The producers have written a cute ending. A cherubic young boy walks up to Lita and hands her a bouquet of spring wildflowers. She bends over and kisses the boy on the cheek. He blushes. Lita, Frank, and the child smile into the camera. They stare off into the horizon of a bright future. The camera zooms out, the narrator delivers an uplifting punch line, and the theater lights come up. The audience gives Frank and Lita a standing ovation. Our heroes.

But there's a little problem with that little scenario. The Communist party bosses were saving the people's money to buy Dom Perignon champagne and French perfume. Even considering that, a fatherless kid would have been treated better in the former Soviet Union than I was in Frank and Lita's house. In Russia, I would have been given something to eat after the movie shoot.

Lita was doing her best. She didn't spend much money. She cheerfully put all of her paycheck into the family larder. This was intended to provide the cushion they needed to get ahead of their money problems.

For his part, Frank was supposed to do normal, nighttime dad things with me. That's not how it worked out. When Lita worked late, every weeknight became Saturday night. Yee-haw, cowboy! He was at the Rock Castle tavern every night.

Lita didn't seem to mind that Frank got drunk every night. She knew how to cope with drunks. Her family was full of them. Lita's objection came from another quarter: Frank wanted to drink in taverns. She wanted him to drink at home. But Frank wouldn't do it that way. His friends were in the tavern. Frank loved to lean back on his barstool and shout, "A round for the house on me." The whole place would break out in cheers and backslaps for Frank. He felt no guilt as he bought the friendship of barflies with the family's grocery money.

But male camaraderie only carried Frank so far. He had a stronger motivation to be in the taverns instead of at home: the bars contained a ready supply of lonely women. Frank cut a wide swath through the local female population. He seemed to zero in on married women. He believed that they were safe. Married women had something to lose. They would be discreet.

Frank got by with that little routine for quite a few years. But he eventually managed to end up with a steady girlfriend. She ran a small local diner called the Maverick Cafe. Frank used to take me along when he visited his girlfriend there. We always went in the middle of the afternoon, the slack time between lunch and dinner when the place was deserted. I sat out front with a soft drink while Frank and his paramour disappeared. Business was slow in the front of the café, but it was *plenty* hot in the back.

Frank took me along on his café visits because he needed a "beard." I was covering for him. Later on, at family gatherings, Lita would brag, "Frank and Tommy just had a great day together." After this rousing speech, folks inevitably gave me lectures. They said, "You're lucky to have such a good man as your father. You're not his child. He didn't have to take you on as his own. You need to be extra nice to him."

I couldn't tell those folks I'd spent the morning hours sitting alone in a car that was parked in front of a tavern. I also couldn't mention I'd spent the afternoon sitting in a dive restaurant, listening to Frank pork a bimbo in the back. Frank would have beaten me to death if I publicly admitted such things. He knew his lies were safe with me.

Wow! Frank's girlfriend was getting fucked. Frank definitely was. And I was getting fucked in every conceivable way, excepting for the sex part. Ah, but Lita—hardworking, loyal, and honest Lita—was getting the biggest fucking of us all. Through it all, she worked harder and compensated more for Frank's bad behavior.

Deep down inside, Lita knew that she was losing the battle for Frank's heart. He had wandered further and further away from the path of correct intentions. So Lita used her tool of last resort to tie Frank to her: she decided to have a baby. There was nothing new or devious about that trick. That kind of behavior defines the biological objective of our species. If a woman saddles a man with a kid, there is a better chance he will stick around.

Lita knew that Frank sometimes had sex with other women. She acted like such behavior came with the territory. I suppose that brand of resignation comes from being raised around cowboys. But that didn't stop Lita's grumbling. She quipped, "There would be fewer problems in the world if men would keep that thing in their pants."

But that type of sex was just sport. Lita had a bigger worry: she knew that if she didn't have a kid with Frank, some other woman would.

By this stage of our story, Frank and Lita had been trying to produce a child for almost four years. Lita suffered two miscarriages along the way. Still no baby. They were saddened by their lack of progress.

Not me. I shudder to think what the consequences would have been if Lita's childbearing aspirations with Frank had been realized. Things would probably have been better for them as a couple. Frank's subsequent efforts with another woman proved that theory to be true.

I'm not certain that I would have survived the aftereffects of a mutual natal success on Frank and Lita's part, though. Frank wanted a child from his loins to raise in his own image. Once he attained that goal, I would have ceased to be a distracting encumbrance and become a dangerous obstacle. Frank knew what to do with obstacles; he rolled over them.

If Frank had produced a child with Lita, I would have instantly graduated from boot camp to prison camp. I'm not exaggerating. Look at our family dynamic from Frank's perspective. I wasn't his son by any stretch of that term. He knew it. I knew it. Lita ignored it. Frank and I detested each other. It was visceral. There was no equivocation between us on that point.

Frank was disgusted by who I was and how I acted. His antipathy for me oozed out of his every pore. He was never one to be passive about his hatred. Frank told me that he was going to make me "git gone."

When he got really angry, he said, "I'm a-gonna get me a little nigger kid to replace you." That phrase was the capper of all cappers for me. Frank continually reviled people of African derivation. I knew that Frank hated them more than anything else.

That was the ultimate kick in the teeth for me. Frank was saying that he preferred the company of a child he believed to be subhuman. He repeated his "nigger kid replacement" mantra throughout my childhood. The barb never lost its sting with repeated usage.

Do you think that's as low as it got for me? It wasn't. Lita made it worse. She stood by when Frank said that he was going to replace me. Sometimes she nodded along. Thanks, Lita.

I'm going to pause now in order to offer my thanks to the person who really made this story line possible: Myron Thomas Liggett Senior. Good ol' M. T. He abandoned Lita to the vicissitudes of being a beautiful teenaged mother in a harsh world.

I eventually heard about studies that detail what happens to children when their biological fathers move out of the family home. Statistics show that replacement men neglect, hit, molest, and kill other men's children at much higher rates than do biological fathers. Those studies read like a laundry list of the things that were done to me.

From a biological perspective, Frank's actions were entirely justifiable. All living organisms have the same imperative: to pass their DNA to succeeding generations. If an individual organism's DNA is not transferred, it is lost. If a single bacterium fails to reproduce, that's generally not a big thing. They breed in mass. But the stakes are higher with the larger mammals. Unlike bacteria, individual mammals don't breed in the billions per generation. Their offspring are much dearer things. That is why a new top lion kills the cubs of his predecessor. He doesn't know how long he will be around. He wants the lionesses to stop lactating so that they will come into heat as soon as possible. The new top lion wants to put his offspring in the bellies of his harem.

The preceding paragraphs list the reasons I am glad Frank never got his child with Lita. Now let's take a look at why I am glad Lita never got her child with Frank.

Please reflect on the events of this book. Remember what kind of a mother Lita was to me. I'm going to get right to the punch line: Would Lita have stopped working? Would she have stayed home to raise Frank's baby? I don't believe that she would. Remember, Lita got a big charge out of working and making good money. She enjoyed being the best employee at every job. Any way you cut the deck, Lita preferred working wages to being a mother.

That was the vocational side. Let's cut to the human side. Lita didn't want to care for *any* child. I heard her recite the same phrase hundreds of times: "I changed enough fuckin' diapers for Momma's kids before I even left home. I didn't need to change any more." I fail to see how producing a baby with Frank would have been an operable solution to *that* problem.

Speaking of diapers, who do you think would have been doing changes for Frank and Lita's new baby? Lita was an advocate for equal rights and equal work. Meet Tommy, the diaper nurse.

In later years, Lita told me that it would have been a mistake to have another child. She always used the same words when she expressed that sentiment: "I couldn't handle having you. I damned sure couldn't have handled another one." She couched that particular revelation in the form of a joke, but I couldn't miss the hatred in her eyes. I was your punch line, Lita.

My grandmother Ruby was quite forthcoming about her children's fecundity. She regularly said, "Three of my daughters shoulda never had children." You couldn't lie to that wise, if flawed, woman.

Then there was the perennial joker in the deck: Frank was still in his twenties when he and Lita were trying to make a baby. Do you think he would have stopped partying to save money to support one or more new babies? In my mind, that was never a possibility.

The fine points of human biology slammed the door on Frank and Lita's mutual childbearing aspirations. It all came down to blood. When someone says that she has A-positive blood, she is telling you two different things: he has type-A blood, and it is Rh negative. The Rh factor was first discovered in rhesus monkeys, which led to its discovery in humans. To honor that achievement, it was named the Rh factor.

Lita had Rh-negative blood. MT had Rh-positive blood. Lita's body reacted to the baby (me) she was carrying. This reaction was similar to that which occurs when people are transfused with the wrong type of blood. That is a *very* bad thing.

Rh incompatibilities complicate pregnancies. With the first pregnancy, everybody generally gets a pass. There are generally no discernable Rh-related consequences for the baby, and the mother will recover with no outward signs of damage to herself. But inside mom's body, there's a problem. She now has anti-Rh antibodies in her bloodstream. Her body will recognize the next fetus as being incompatible and will fight it. The fetus fights back. The body's reaction to each succeeding pregnancy becomes more severe.

If my mother had actually succeeded in carrying another baby to term, it could have suffered from hemolytic disease of the newborn. That is a nasty disease.

Not long after I was born, Rhogam was developed. That miraculous drug prevents or lessens the negative effects an Rh-negative woman experiences when she conceives a child with an Rh-positive man. But Rhogam must be administered to a woman immediately after she has a miscarriage or gives birth. That was too late to be helpful to Frank, Lita, or the five babies she lost. Yes, folks, five. Lita lost two sets of twins and a single in her heroic quest to get a tie on Frank.

The last set of twins damn near killed Lita. She got style points for *that* one. She had an Rh-compromised pregnancy coupled with an ectopic or tubal pregnancy. My Lord, my Lord, is there ever enough suffering in the lives of women?

The memories of some of the things I have described in this book are like shadows to me. I know the events occurred, but their fine details are lost in the recesses of my mind. But that's not the way it was with Lita's last pregnancy; I recall that event as if it occurred yesterday.

Frank and Lita received an invitation to attend a high-toned Christmas party. I remember them saying they wanted to "really put on the dog" (dress well) for the event.

It didn't matter that our little family's larder was being given a short shrift. Frank and Lita always found money to buy themselves beautiful clothes. Frank got a new suit and polished his dress shoes days in advance. No cowboy boots for this event. He said, "I'm in in San Jose, not fuckin' Dallas."

Lita was in pig heaven. She was going to a party. Lita would socialize. She would dance. Most of all, she would get a lot of attention. Lita had never met any of the other people who would be attending the party, but she knew she would be the prettiest girl in the room. She would have the best body of any woman in the room. She would be the best dancer in the room.

When Lita stalked onto the scene, she was the human embodiment of the hunter goddess Diana. She killed everything in sight. Male or female, it didn't matter. When Lita set her mind to it, she was a walking sex bomb. I offer thanks to the long-forgotten Indian women who passed down this two-edged gift to her granddaughters. Damn! The way that some of the women in my family look. Whew!

No package is complete without its wrapping. Lita needed to buy a new dress. She announced she was going to take me dress shopping. I was usually amenable to going on excursions with Lita. I'd willingly spend six to ten hours in a car every Wednesday so Lita could visit her grandmother. But dress shopping? I thought that was a horrible activity. I'd rather sit in a car for hours.

When Lita shopped for a dress, she went all over downtown San Jose. I don't know why she did that. Maybe it was some kind of a ritual with her. Lita always ended up finding what she wanted at a store that was called the House of Nine. The store took its name from the fact that it only sold women's clothing in size 9.

My readers might be wondering why they would do such a thing. By today's standards, a woman who wears a size 9 dress is believed to be fat as a hog.

Silly people. Size 9 women are muscular. They are lush. They have curves but not bulk. If size 9 women were cars, they would be four-door Audi sedans. That automobile can ride five people and still run away from a Ferrari on a winding racecourse.

When we finally walked into the House of Nine that afternoon, I was tired. For once, Lita was cheerful and patient with my grumbling. She said softly, "Just one more store, Tommy. Then I'll get you something to eat." She knew that I was hungry. One way or the other, food was usually the price I paid for being in Lita's company.

I remember the dress Lita bought. It was magnificent. You wouldn't expect much from a dove-gray wool garment, but that confection was nothing short of incredible. Before we left the store, Lita modeled her new dress for me. Neck to knee, she was covered. The dress did not show much of Lita's magnificent skin, but it revealed the lush Indian body that lurked underneath. It fit her like a second skin. The girl looked *good*.

When we got home, Lita went at her new dress with a needle and thread. Like all good show women, she knew that *any* off-the-rack article of clothing will look better with a few alterations.

Beyond gladiator flicks, Lita had never heard of the goddess Diana. That didn't stop my mother from emulating that deity's hairstyle. Lita put her lush auburn hair into an up do.

Lita worked all day, went shopping, modified a dress, worked wonders on her hair, fed me, and was ready on time. That's a lot of words for one sentence. She was a lot of woman.

Frank was in a hurry to go to the party. But there was one more thing to do. Lita handed me a camera and said, "Take a picture of us, Tommy."

I saw something through the lens of the camera that night. The camera saw it too. At that very moment, Lita was at the pinnacle of her long run of female beauty, and she knew it. The photos I took that night confirm that fact. Lita was radiant. But God finds ways of reminding us humans that our plans are nothing. He or she certainly finds ways to laugh at our mortal designs.

Lita McMillan at the peak of her beauty. The inscription reads, "Frank: Especially Yours. Love—Lita." Circa 1958.

I was relieved when Frank finally shut the door. The happy couple was gone. I was tired.

The school day had been the last before the beginning of the Christmas break. A time of excited kids and Santa Claus in the classrooms. No one did any schoolwork. The food in the cafeteria was particularly tasty. Our teacher hosted an after-lunch party.

Then there was the rush of buying Lita's dress and watching the happy couple get ready. Through it all, I was carried by the tide of Lita's preparty adrenaline. Now they were gone, and I was alone. It was just me and the good ol' semi functional TV. Merry few days before Christmas, Tommy.

I didn't last long watching TV. I turned it off, grabbed my navy blanket, and fell asleep on the floor. I was exhausted.

At some point, the overhead light flashed on. I was startled awake. I thought Frank was about to tear into me again, so I pretended to be asleep. That small deceit sometimes worked as a ruse to suspend or diminish his nighttime attacks.

I wasn't surprised when Frank reached down and grabbed me off of the floor. He said, "Tommy, Tommy, get up. Get up now." I stood there and wobbled in Frank's hands, primed to get slammed into the wall. I thought, *don't tense up. Stay loose. It'll hurt less.*

But it didn't work out that way. For the first time ever, Frank didn't smash me against the wall. That surprised me. When I finally opened my eyes, I saw a man I had never seen before. He wasn't angry; he was scared.

When I woke up enough so that I could stand alone, Frank let go of my T-shirt. He began to dart around the room like a frightened child. I didn't know what was going on. Frank was talking to himself. He was uttering bits and snatches of sentences, babbling like a crazy person.

Frank eventually said that my mother had collapsed on the dance floor. She'd passed out cold due to severe abdominal pain. Frank had rushed her to the hospital rather than calling an ambulance because in those days, ambulances were unreliable things. They might or might not show up.

I don't remember how I reacted to the news. I must have been sad. But's Frank's manic entrance eclipsed any feelings I might have felt. He told me to get dressed. Frank pulled me out of the house and into the car. I didn't wake sufficiently to pull any cohesive thought together.

Frank drove to the hospital. He had left that place less than an hour before, but he somehow found reason for me to be there too. I don't know why he did that. He knew they weren't going to let me see Lita. Children weren't allowed as visitors to most ob-gyn wards in those days. When we got to the hospital ward, a battle-axe nurse stopped us with a stiff arm and outstretched palm and said brusquely, "You can come in, but the kid stays outside." She sounded like a gun moll dissuading riffraff at a speakeasy door.

I knew the drill. Lita was one of the great hospital visitors of all time. By that age, I knew the layout and the visiting hours of every damned hospital in San Jose and beyond. The nurse wordlessly pointed to a row of hard chairs. I went over and sat down while she led Frank through the swinging double doors to see Lita. They disappeared inside.

I was sitting alone in a dark hallway. I knew my mother was very ill. Frank intimated that she was dying. There was no one there to comfort me. Once again, I was stuck and alone. I soon fell into a fitful sleep. I startled awake when the hallway lights were turned on. At some point thereafter, Frank burst through the ward's doors. He walked by me without stopping, looked over his shoulder, and barked, "Come on!"

I don't recall where we went next. Frank drove here and there. Everywhere he stopped, he told people about Lita in low, grave tones.

Frank didn't speak to me at all. He sought company from the paper-sack-clad whiskey bottle he kept under the driver's seat.

We didn't eat anything that day. I was hungry. Frank was chewing tobacco, smoking cigars, and receiving all the calories he needed from whiskey bottles. The man had a full head of steam built up. He didn't need food.

We eventually went back to the hospital. I got a repeat visit with my friend, the chair in the hall. I sat there all by myself for what seemed to be an eternity. Toward evening, my grandmother Ruby and her husband, Tommy Tomlinson, appeared.

After a perfunctory hug with me, Ruby et al. went inside to see Lita. When my grandmother finally emerged from the ward, she was sobbing inconsolably. I had never seen her that distressed. By this point, no one had to paint me a picture about Lita; this was bad. Through it all, the adults didn't seem to notice I was in the room.

More relatives appeared. They stood around in knots, smoking cigarettes and talking. Yes, they were smoking in a hospital hallway. Hell, in those days you could smoke in patients' rooms if oxygen wasn't in use.

Through it all, I sat in a chair with my hands in my lap. I didn't know which end was up. I dared not think about life without Lita. I didn't want to think about life alone with Frank. That part was scarier to me than losing Lita.

In due course, Ruby took me somewhere. She fed me a wonderful dinner and sent me to bed. That was Saturday evening.

Early Monday morning, I was sitting in a parked car out front of the hospital. I watched in horror as Lita wobbled out through the side door. She was leaving the hospital far earlier than would normally be expected. It had been about fifty-five hours since she'd received a medieval-type hysterectomy. The surgeons had opened her belly like they were cleaning a fish.

When the hospital released Lita, she hadn't yet recovered from the harsh anesthetics that were used in those days. Old-type anesthetics always made Lita extremely nauseous, and she had been vomiting continually since her surgery. She hadn't eaten anything since dinner right before she collapsed. When all of Lita's stomach contents had been expelled, she got the dry heaves. Deep, wracking heaves.

Lita's physician did not release her from the hospital. She signed herself out because Frank had convinced her to check out early. That "convincing" came in the guise of a screaming argument. Lita was lying half dead after losing Frank's twin children, and the bastard was yelling at her about money. Once again, Frank's nightly partying had sucked the family coffers dry. They were broke and up to their eyeballs in debt.

Lita went along with Frank's early checkout plan because she knew that they could not afford a larger hospital bill. Her physician was livid, but Frank got in his face and said, "Mind your own business, old man."

These days, patients generally leave the hospital in a wheelchair. Lita walked out. She had a hospital attendant on one side and Frank on the other. The sons of bitches were walking her out like she was a condemned man on his way to the gallows. I will never forget the sight. Lita was unrecognizable from the glorious creature in a gray wool dress I'd seen less than three days before.

My mother looked like she'd stepped out of a Nazi death camp photograph. Lita seemed to be printed in black and white. There was no color in her face. Lita was in a perilous physical condition, and she was psychologically devastated. Any hope she had of binding Frank to her with a child had gone into the medical waste incinerator along with her ovaries and her fetuses.

The warm, cheerful California winter day betrayed the somber mood of our small group. The sun cast light among us but little hope. Lita was alive. We were happy for that, but very little else.

Seeing Lita in such perilous condition shocked me to the core. I just sat in the car seat, stunned. I don't remember much that was said on the way home. That day passed a long time ago.

When we got back to the duplex, Frank put Lita to bed. She needed to rest and get her strength back. Lita had to get back to work in a couple of days. There were bills to pay.

Frank decided that I would stay with someone away from our duplex for a week or so. Lita would make a speedier recovery if I wasn't underfoot. Thank God for Christmas vacation.

A day or two after Lita got out of the hospital, there was a knock on our front door. Frank was at work, and I was staying somewhere else. Lita struggled painfully to get out of bed and answer the knock. My mother was the child of obligation. She was half dead but got up to answer the door for an anonymous person. Perhaps it would have been better for Lita if she hadn't been so duty bound.

When Lita opened the door, she beheld a woman she knew only as being one of the regulars down at the Rock Castle tavern. Had I been there, I would have recognized her as the woman from the Maverick café, Frank's girlfriend. She was holding a newborn baby in her arms.

Frank's girlfriend was a person who preferred action to words. Without preamble, she launched right into the gist of the thing. She said, "This is Frank's baby."

The girlfriend's declaration was gratuitous. It lacked any validity of just cause. Lita was the wronged party in the deal. She was the wife, not the side action who was complaining at her lover's front door. Lita barely knew that woman and had never done anything bad to her.

Considering that Lita was still suffering the aftereffects of being sterilized, I'd say the girlfriend's actions could accurately be described as torture. Maybe Frank's asshole girlfriend knew about Lita's reputation as a fighter and figured she had to get Lita while she was weak. On any other day, Lita would have gladly kicked the girlfriend's ass and any five men who tried to stop her.

Lita was deathly sick. She didn't have the strength to fight the girlfriend on any level. Kick 'em when they're down, eh? Frank's girlfriend was a stonehearted bitch. I wish a pox on her and all her generations until the stars fall down from the sky.

There is a telling aspect to the girlfriend's visit: that woman knew Lita was deathly ill and alone at home. That knowledge could only have been obtained from Frank. His wife was stuck in bed, half dead and sterilized, but he'd met up with his girlfriend. Thanks, dude; you always found ways to make it tougher for Lita.

At the time these events were unfolding, I didn't know about the other woman's visit. Lita didn't tell me about that until I was an adult. But that didn't prevent me from being swept up in the hellish aftermath of the girlfriend's revelation.

Later that afternoon, Lita unexpectedly showed up where I was staying. She was there to take me home.

Anybody who saw Lita that day would have wondered how she was able to walk. My mother was more dead than alive. She should have been in the in the hospital. But she drove a primitive stick-shift car without power steering across half of the greater San Francisco Bay Area to pick me up.

Lita told my caretaker her tale of woe. She also said, "I kicked Frank out. This time I really mean it." Lita and I got into the car and went home.

That night in bed, I held Lita while she tried to sleep. That was impossible. She was in pain. She had no painkillers. Lita's deep, wracking sobs kept me awake too.

Early the next day, Lita dutifully got up and went to her job. She was working at a paper company where they made all kinds of bags and boxes. Lita's job was to pick up stacks of paper and run them through various machines. Each of those stacks was designed to be as heavy as a strong man could lift. Lita was working like a mule just a few days after she came out of surgery.

I remember Lita coming home from work her first day back on the job. She cooked dinner for me. When I sat down to eat, I remarked that there was only one plate of food on the table. Lita told me, "I already ate." Though I didn't know it at the time, that was pure bullshit. There was only enough food in the house to feed one person.

It would have been easier for Lita to leave me at my caretaker's house. It was still Christmas break. I was out of school. But no deal on that. Every time Lita had troubles with Frank, she clung tightly to me. I became Lita's go-to guy. Her little man. I helped her with chores around the house. I held her in bed at night and spoke softly to her during the day. I did all I could to be her cheerleader.

In spite of a bad beginning to the season, Christmas Eve arrived right on schedule. It's amazing the world doesn't stop spinning just because we are blue.

Before Frank and Lita's relationship blew up, I was full of a child's dreams of Christmas. I knew exactly what I wanted, right down to the model number. I was fervently hoping to receive a Tonka fire truck. Those things were tough; they were made of steel. Tonka trucks were also quite expensive.

When Christmas came, there was a big box for me under my uncle's Christmas tree. The tag indicated that it was from Santa. But I recognized the handwriting; it was from Lita. The big moment came. I got to open the box! It was a fire truck—but it was a cheap plastic one, not the Tonka I wanted.

I inadvertently mentioned that I was disappointed in the gift. Lita started weeping. Every eye in the room was on me. What a shit heel I was that night. That experience helped me to mature a little bit. It made me start thinking more like a man, not an eight-year-old child.

When Christmas vacation was over, Lita drove me to school. That was unusual. It only happened a handful of times during my school years. I knew that something was up.

Lita walked me inside of the school building and sought out a cafeteria supervisor. Lita went into an office with the manager and told me to wait in the foyer. They left the door standing open. The sound of their conversation carried to my sharp little ears. I heard Lita tell the cafeteria woman she had just separated from her husband. She said that she was broke now but would be getting paid in a week or two. Lita flat-out begged the cafeteria woman to let me run a tab for my lunches. Lita said, "I will pay you back every cent when I get paid."

What happened next was totally unexpected. The cafeteria woman yelled at my mother. I'll never forget her words. "You are a bad mother! You should be ashamed of yourself!" The cafeteria lady said more, but I stopped paying attention when she began to yell. Hard experience had taught me that it was best to remain invisible when people started to scream.

I heard Lita's vain attempts to reason with the cafeteria woman. My poor mother was crying; she was begging the other woman to advance the cost of my lunches for a very short time. Each of Lita's entreaties was met by another loud imprecation from the cafeteria woman.

That was the last straw for Lita. She rushed out of the cafeteria woman's office and stormed out the door. Lita brushed by me without saying a word. She left me standing in the hallway, crying and alone. Lita left for her job at the paper company. She eventually told me it was the very lowest point of her entire life. It seemed as if the heavens were aligned against her.

I was standing in the foyer. I didn't know what to do. My shoes felt like they were glued to the floor. I was quietly weeping. The cafeteria woman walked out of her office with a triumphant look on her face. The woman was grinning. She had vanquished her foe! She glared down at me and said, "Why are you standing there? Aren't you supposed to be in class?"

I nodded and walked away from the cafeteria office. I went into my classroom and pretended nothing had happened. The other children were bouncing off the walls with post holiday cheer. I hunkered down in my desk and tried to forget the horrible events of the past two weeks. I tried not to remember the sound of Lita's all-night crying sessions. I tried to forget the nasty scene just minutes before in the cafeteria office. Most of all, I tried to forget I hadn't eaten a full meal in days.

For Lita, the hard part of that day had come when the cafeteria lady yelled at her. For me, it came at lunch. Having blindly assumed that the school would allow me to run a tab for my lunches, Lita had not packed me anything to eat that day. What am I saying? There wasn't enough food at home to feed a mouse. Frank had left us high and dry. There wasn't anything to pack for *either* of our lunches.

I didn't know what was going on. I felt like a cork bobbing in a raging torrent. I was just along for the ride. When the lunch bell rang, I blindly followed my classmates down to the cafeteria. We got into the cafeteria line, just like normal. I noted that the cafeteria woman was standing at the head of the line. She perked up when she saw me enter the room. She wore the same triumphant grin I had seen earlier in the day. It was apparent that the she had been lying in wait for me. She strode toward me, clearly on a mission. I knew I was in trouble. She stopped in front of me and she asked loudly, "Where's your lunch money? Your mother hasn't paid for the month of January yet."

I was mortified. The cafeteria grew quiet. The other children started whispering among themselves and pointing at me. I told the cafeteria woman meekly, "I don't have any lunch money."

The cafeteria woman got another triumphant look and said, "Then we can't have you sneak through the line without paying, can we?" But she wasn't done. She added, "You are holding up the line for those children who *do* have their lunch money!" Then she grabbed my hand and yanked me out of the lunch line.

The cafeteria woman dragged me over to the cashier's table where the lunch clerk took the children's lunch money. The cafeteria woman shoved me into the chair next to the clerk and announced, "This boy doesn't have his lunch money. Make sure that you keep an eye on him. Don't let him try to slip through the line without paying."

I can emphatically state that the lunch clerk exercised due diligence in her duties that day. She glared at me all through lunch and kept an extra sharp eye on me, the nine-year-old potential thief of sloppy Joes and vegetarian chili beans.

I became well accustomed to the lunch clerk's glare. It took Lita a week or two to come up with lunch money. Until then, I sat next to the clerk and ate whatever small thing that my mother had managed to pack, if there was anything. Sometimes I didn't eat anything for lunch during those rough times.

That set of experiences and many others of like kind forced me to steel my resolve. It was tough but not impossible. I was a longstanding master in the fine art of not thinking about my ever-present hunger pangs. Drawing from that hard-won strength, I was able to quietly sit at that hostile table, day after day. I breathed in the savory smells that emanated from the kitchen. I watched the other children eat. All the while, I had little or nothing to eat myself.

Believe it or not, my hunger pangs were the easiest part of that horrid experience. It was much more difficult to deal with the other children. In the week or two that I sat next to the clerk, every child who bought a lunch had to pass directly in front me. Many of them did not have the grace to ignore me. Most of the children had a comment, snicker, or disgusted look to pass my way.

Anyone out there who thinks we need not feed little children because they were born to the wrong parents should seek me out. Note the hard look in my eyes. I have starved while those around me ate. This was because my parents ignored their responsibilities. Shame on any of you who try to do that to another child!

I have often wondered why the cafeteria woman went off on Lita that day. Did some of the details about my flawed home life filter back to Horace Mann School? God knows such tidbits did not come from me. I knew better than to do that. Who knows?

The irony of the cafeteria lunch fiasco is that it was preventable. Lita had an in at Horace Mann School—the principal had been her classmate at Campbell High School. Lita could have spoken to her. She was a very nice woman. She would have overridden the cafeteria woman. Lita could have signed a chit for my lunches, and I would have eaten. I would not have suffered countless small humiliations during my period of enforced starvation.

But Lita did not play that advantage. She blindly accepted the cafeteria woman's cruel decision. As usual, Lita was caught up in her own problems. She didn't put much effort into solving mine.

Lita and I somehow managed to muddle through life for the next few weeks. As soon as she got a paycheck, things got better. Lita provided money for school lunches. The written word carries insufficient power for me to fully convey what that meant for me. Those lunches were a moral and physical blessing. Some weeks, they were the only balanced, nutritious meals I ate.

Over the course of their long and tumultuous relationship, Lita periodically kicked Frank out the house. The contrast between the times he was with us and those he was not was glaring, even to a young child. When Lita was away from Frank, the rent got paid on time. I ate good meals at regular intervals. Lita and I saw the type of movies *we* liked, not the Westerns and war movies Frank demanded.

But there was a much more telling lesson to be learned from Frank and Lita's periods of separation. Those all too brief periods demonstrated that Lita's income, though significantly less than Frank's, was enough for us to live comfortably. Sadly, she never grasped the truth that was exposed in those interludes: Frank seldom had money for anything but booze and whores.

In due course, Frank returned home to us. In a passing nod to camaraderie, he allowed me to help him move out of his temporary quarters. I only spent a few minutes in Frank's apartment, but that was enough to leave an indelible memory. Frank was living in the dark, dank basement of a shabby nineteenth-century house. The sight of that rough place reinforced a known fact: Frank was willing to slip ever further down at home so he could spend money on strong drink and loose women.

The defining event of Frank's return was as strange as the one that had precipitated his departure. He somehow convinced Lita that the other woman's baby wasn't his. He swore on whole stacks of Bibles he "hadn't slept with her in a year." That flimsy cover provided Lita with the excuse she needed to reconcile with Frank. For the rest of her life, Lita happily chirped, "There ain't no such thing as a twelve-month baby."

The glue that repaired Humpty Dumpty's shell came from an unusual source. Frank's girlfriend somehow convinced her husband that the baby was his. Who knows what she told him? Perhaps that deluded cuckold liked the way his wife performed inside of the kitchen and out. Or perhaps it was something simpler than that. Maybe he never found out that he was raising Frank's get. DNA testing wasn't around in 1959. Maybe the kid wasn't Frank's.

DNA studies indicate that 10 percent of the children who are born to married American women aren't the product of a union with their husbands. Given my later experience with that equation, I'm honestly surprised the percentage isn't higher.

Seeing another woman holding a baby that was allegedly fathered by Frank knocked Lita for a loop. That betrayal was bad enough to break anyone's heart. But there was more. Lita had to deal with the female aspect. She knew she would never be able produce a child for Frank now. From that point on in their marriage, it was the elephant in the room.

Lita dodged a bullet with that first bastard claimant. Would be she able to dodge the inevitable next one? The handwriting was on the wall. Lita had failed to rope Frank down with a kid. Would some other woman succeed?

CHAPTER 61

The End of the Beginning

FRANK MCMILLAN BEHAVED LIKE AN errant little boy. If someone wasn't watching, he ran off to play. When Frank was a kid, his dad beat the hell out of him when that occurred. But when Lita worked late, there was no one around to watch Frank. He headed to the Rock Castle tavern or some similar place and reveled in his abandon.

But there was always a fly in the soup at Frank's endless bacchanal. In the bars, he was always the most generous, handsome, and witty guy. When he exited the tavern, Frank entered a different reality. Gone were the whores, backslaps, and camaraderie with fellows of like mind. The knowledge that he'd squandered the rent money weighed heavily on Frank. He got into fights with bar women or other men. The combination of those factors created a predictable result: Frank was usually angry when he left the bar.

He festered and stewed as he drove home. Frank knew that as soon as he got there, his problems would be waiting. He knew that it was back to the wife and kid and a few hours of sleep. He knew that tomorrow he would wake up with a hangover. By the time Frank got to his own front door, he was royally pissed off.

Frank couldn't do anything about the wife and the job. He needed them to provide the framework for his partying. Frank couldn't yell at his boss or Lita without paying hell.

But the rules were different as they applied to little Tommy Liggett. Frank could blame, starve, ignore, kick, hit, wall slam, intimidate, and plain old scream at me to his heart's content. No one would ever be the wiser. He knew that I wouldn't complain; I was too loyal, brainwashed, and intimidated.

Whom would I tell, anyway? We moved too frequently for me to accumulate any real friends. My relatives were too busy living their own lives. They were too busy loving Frank and Lita.

Up to this point in my life, M. T. visited me twice. I remembered just one of those visits. I wouldn't see him again until I was fourteen.

My grandmother Ruby was Lita's best friend and biggest cheerleader. I couldn't talk to her about my problems. She would chide me. She would tell me what a great job Lita was doing. Worst of all, she would rat me out to Lita. Woe be the day that Tommy betrayed Lita by saying that things under the umbrella of her care were anything less than peachy.

Even if I had found a sympathetic ear, who would believe what I had to say? Everybody loved Lita. Frank was everybody's bosom buddy and best chum. They were the life of the party everywhere they went.

I had two wonderful grandmothers. They had each offered to raise me. To give me a better life. Lita spurned their offers. She wanted to prove she could do it herself.

Lita had three serious relationships in the early years after she separated from M. T. Two of those men adored me. But she chose the one who did not: Frank McMillan. That reveals much about my place in Lita's world.

I was living in a parallel universe to the people around me. Everywhere I looked, I saw families who treated their children better than Frank and Lita did me. But I was expected to play the perfect child when I was in public. At family gatherings, I had to pretend that Frank was a doting father. At school, I played lazy schoolboy for lack of parental help with my homework. My brain was regularly expected to convince my stomach that it had received dinner last night.

Everywhere I went, I pretended that nothing was wrong. Any other course would have been seen as defiant by the drill instructor who ordered my life.

I knew that people persisted in showing me their sex organs, whether or not I wanted to see them. I knew this was sometimes intriguing and sometimes creepy. Even though I had never experienced an orgasm, I already knew sex had a dark side. Worse yet, I knew that it felt good when someone held my erect penis. I didn't know what that meant. Some people told me such actions were wrong. But I also noted that a lot of people I trusted were doing the same thing. Where was the correct path?

Three family members stayed with us for extended periods while we were living in the Tenth Street duplex. Things got better for me while they were our guests. But when they moved away, things immediately got worse for me at home. Frank and Lita always reverted back to their default position of abuse and neglect. This demonstrated they could turn their insane behaviors on and off to suit an attentive audience. That ability suggests a hidden purpose to their actions.

I was caught in a perfect hell of deceit and deception.

This was my world as we terminated our three-year stay in the Tenth Street duplex. By then Frank and Lita's pattern of abuse and neglect was well established. The full suite of abusive behaviors that defined the remainder of my childhood and beyond were now in place.

My child brain was not sufficiently developed to understand the psychological concept of powerlessness. Yet my immature consciousness fully realized that I really didn't matter very much to Frank, Lita, or M. T.

I was ten years old. Frank had been in my life for almost six of those years. By that age, I was already well schooled in the particulars of what he expected of me. I knew my place in the world he created for me.

I was Frank's ready-made beating boy. I was like the inflatable toy clown young children love to knock over with a punch. Hit them as hard as you like; they will always pop back up for more. And more. And more—until your arm grows tired from the effort.

I knew I wasn't number one in anyone's book. I knew that any care I received came from the debit side of someone's ledger. No one provided me with unconditional love and support.

I knew any attention I brought upon myself might turn out to be negative.

I was regularly advised that any deficiency of money, food, or time was solely because I existed. This was a burden that I willingly assumed; I absolutely believed I was a greedy little boy.

I was pummeled daily with the Christian God but told not to put any faith in him. I spent hours repeating the same child prayers over and again. I begged God not to allow Satan to drag me down into hell but also believed that each and every night was the one Satan would come up through the floorboards to deliver me into eternal torment.

I knew that the schools I attended and the streets I walked were dangerous places. I knew my passport to safely be in those places expired when the sun went down.

I learned to find joy in weed-infested backyards and stray cats. But that joy was tempered with a caveat: I knew better than to fall in love with any one cat or backyard. Sooner than later, I would be forced to leave them behind.

I was just a baby when I learned that when I was alone, it was quiet. When adults reappeared, the screaming began. Frank and Lita's latter behavior toward me was just a continuation of that concept.

I learned to cherish the things I did when I was alone. When I was alone, no one was yelling at me. When I was alone, I thought I was invisible. When you are invisible, no one can hurt you.

I retreated ever more deeply into books and holes in the dirt. In those places, I found and built worlds that took me away from Frank, Lita, and the mean streets of San Jose.

This was the beginning of an era wherein I lived as a ghost. I breezed through pieces of other people's lives but was not a thing of permanence in any of them.

AFTERWORD

THE ORIGINAL VERSION OF *The Pregnant Majorette* was quite different from the book that now stands before you. I began that manuscript with a clear purpose: to tell my version of the founding and horticultural decline of the San Jose Heritage Rose Garden.

The story grew from there. I immediately realized that any book about my gardening adventures would be incomplete without mention of my precocious knowledge of fruit trees. That first kernel of wisdom swept me over ever-higher peaks in the world of horticulture.

When I completed the outline of *The Pregnant Majorette*, though, I discovered the story was too big for one volume. This is how a book about a famous garden became something else. It became a series about Lita, me, my family, a vanishing culture, and the tumultuous times in which we live. There is nothing unusual about that process. What starts out being one thing is sometimes changed into another by the creative process. That was the first version of the manuscript.

When I expanded the first manuscript, I came to a startling revelation: Frank McMillan was a monster. That premise ran contrary to everything my family and I believed about the man. I grew up being told that Frank McMillan was the greatest father figure of all time. Worse yet, I believed the good things that other people said about Frank. I believed that all his problems were my fault.

When I developed the second manuscript, I came to another revelation: Tommy Tomlinson saved my mother's family, but he exacted a terrible price. This was especially true in regard to his interactions with Lita and me.

Those concepts remained as prime elements in the third revision of the manuscript. I put that version through four rounds of very expensive editing. In February of 2017, the manuscript was ready to be published. I just had to hit the send button. I believed that ten years of hard work was complete.

Ah, Tom; God smiles when mortals tell her their plans.

I originally planned to publish this book without any photographs. Let the words carry the story. Then I thought, *Wait a minute, Tom. You inherited more than thirty boxes of photographs and memorabilia. There might be some nice pictures in there. Put 'em in the book. Match the faces with the stories.*

In early April 2017, I began to sort through Lita's photographs and errata. I quickly made a sickening discovery: much of what my mother told me about her life from 1948 to 1956 was a lie. That was a huge surprise. It also caused a lot of problems for me. Why? Because I based the first three versions of this book on Lita's flawed portrayal of the truth.

Lita's memorabilia brought me to the biggest revelation I gained from this book. I always knew that M. T. Liggett was a piece of shit. But Lita's actions, words and photographs revealed she was too.

Everyone in our extended group of friends and family said Lita sacrificed her youth to raise me. That was pure bullshit. Lita didn't sacrifice much on my account. My mother lived as though she didn't have a child. She used me as a prop to make herself look good. She used me as a child-support profit center. She used me as her personal slave. She used me as a friend when she had no others. She repeatedly tried to use me as a lover. She used me as a whipping boy when she needed an outlet for her frustrations.

I have made some damning accusations in *The Pregnant Majorette*. Some of those accusations arose from what I personally experienced. It was easy for me to remember those things, even if they happened while I was very young. Why? Because Lita and Frank repeated the same abuses over and again. They continually reminded me of their past acts by repeating the same words and phrases. Frank and Lita were proud of what they did and said. They wanted to relive the lessons they taught me.

I repeated Frank and Lita's words in the early versions of this book. When I edited that text, I came to another startling conclusion: I discovered I had written *their* version of the events. The one that was crammed into my brain with brute force and frequent repetition. I thought, *Wait a minute, Tom. That's not what really happened.* I went back through the manuscript and wrote Tom's version of the events. The truth.

I have a casual acquaintance who is a psychiatrist. Stories of abuse are her stock-in-trade. When she learned about the premise of this book, she asked me a simple question: "What if they don't believe you?" That got me to thinking. The more I thought, the more frightened I became. People want to be believed. I am no different. Then I thought again, *I know what I experienced. I know I wrote the truth about everything that happened.* Those stories had to remain.

That leaves the stories I heard second, third, or fourth hand. Those were told to me over and again by people I trusted. I left a few of them intact in the book.

I know I am shaking the tree of old memories with this book and the ones that hopefully will follow. When you do that kind of thing, there is a very good chance things from the past will be shaken loose. Some of those things might be good. Some might be bad. I'm ready for that too. I'm sixty-six years old. I'm tired of hiding in the dark. I'm sick of behaving like a frightened child. And I write this with specific intent and purpose: dealing with living people of blood relation and past acquaintance who are no longer a part of my life.

I have known many people. For one reason or another, almost all of them have fallen away from my sight. Some of them fell away because of my faults. Other people left as a result of collateral damage from our tumultuous times. I excised others because they continually indulged themselves in behaviors I found to be unacceptable.

Here's the punch line to all of this: I don't really care if you were good, bad, or indifferent to me way back then. The no-shows are all the same to me now. I harbor no rancor for any of you. But since you weren't there for me with good intent in the long haul, I have no place for you in my life, now or in the future. Please don't contact me.

—Tom Liggett

June 22, 2017